ROOTS OF RESISTANCE

ROOTS OF RESISTANCE

A STORY OF GENDER, RACE, AND LABOR

ON THE NORTH COAST OF HONDURAS

Suyapa G. Portillo Villeda

University of Texas Press Austin

Requests for permission to reproduce material from this work should be sent to:
Permissions
    University of Texas Press
    P.O. Box 7819
    Austin, TX 78713–7819
    utpress.utexas.edu/rp-form

♾ The paper used in this book meets the minimum requirements of ANSI/NISO
Z39.48–1992 (R1997) (Permanence of Paper).

Library of Congress Cataloging-in-Publication Data

Names: Portillo Villeda, Suyapa G., author.
Title: Roots of resistance : a story of gender, race, and labor on the North Coast of
Honduras / Suyapa G. Portillo Villeda.
Description: First edition. | Austin : University of Texas Press, 2021. | Includes bibli-
ographical references and index.
Identifiers: LCCN 2020008826 (print) | LCCN 2020008827 (ebook)
    ISBN 978-1-4773-2219-2 (paperback)
    ISBN 978-1-4773-2220-8 (library ebook)
    ISBN 978-1-4773-2221-5 (non-library ebook)
Subjects: LCSH: General Strike, Honduras, 1954. | Strikes and lockouts—Banana
trade—Honduras—History—20th century. | Labor movement—Honduras—History.
| Women in the labor movement—Honduras—History. | Banana trade—Hondu-
ras—History—20th century.
Classification: LCC HD5336.B232 1954 P67 2021 (print) | LCC HD5336.B232
1954 (ebook) | DDC 331.892/84772097283109045—dc23
LC record available at https://lccn.loc.gov/2020008826
LC ebook record available at https://lccn.loc.gov/2020008827

doi:10.7560/322185

To young Hondurans and Central Americans, wherever they may live, so that they may know their history.

CONTENTS

Photographs appear following page *164*

ABBREVIATIONS AND ACRONYMS

ADPJ/CEDIJ Archivo del Poder Judicial/Centro Electrónico de Documentación e Información de Justicia; Electronic Center for Legal Documentation and Information

APMP Archivo Privado del Dr. Mario Posas

CCO Comité Coordinador Obrero; Worker Coordinating Committee

CLO Comité de Lucha Obrera; Worker Struggle Committee (a worker committee of the Communist Party)

COCA Confederación Obrera Centroamericana; Central American Workers Confederation (linked to the Confederación Obrera Panamericana)

CTAL Confederación de Trabajadores de América Latina; Latin American Confederation of Workers

FNRP Frente Nacional de Resistencia Popular; National Popular Resistance Front

FOH Federación Obrera Hondureña; Federation of Honduran Workers

FSH Federación Sindical Hondureña; Federation of Honduran Unions

KCLMD Kheel Center for Labor-Management Documentation and Archives, M. P. Catherwood Library, Cornell University

ORIT Organización Regional Interamericana de Trabajadores; Inter-American Regional Workers Organization

PDRH Partido Democrático Revolucionario Hondureño; Honduran Democratic Revolutionary Party

SITRATERCO Sindicato de Trabajadores de la Tela Railroad Company; Tela Railroad Company Workers Union

SUTRASFCO Sindicato de Trabajadores de la Standard Fruit Company; Standard Fruit Company Workers Union

UFCo United Fruit Company

USNA United Sates National Archives, College Park, MD

GLOSSARY

aguardiente: alcohol, commonly a homemade liquor like "moonshine"

auxiliar(es): auxiliary or volunteer police

ayudanta: cook's helper or assistant, usually, but not always, related in some way to the patrona

bananera: banana company

barracón/barracones: worker housing provided by banana companies; the name originates from slave quarters in the colonial period in Cuba

burra: small meal consisting of a tortilla, fried meat, and rice

cabos de comisariato: commissary corporal; company patrol; local paid police

campeño/a: term used as a self-designation by banana workers who lived and worked in the banana labor camps

campesino/a: farm worker in Honduras

campos bananeros (or campo): banana labor and housing camps

capitán/capitanes de finca: captain(s) or supervisor(s), boss(es) in the finca; sometimes also called jefe(s)

caudillo: landowner, strong man; charismatic leader

comandante: police commander

comedor/comedores: eating establishment(s) of a patrona

comensales: clients of the patrona, ate daily and paid monthly

compañerismo: camaraderie, solidarity among workers

contratista [de corte]: contractor (for cutting) who led a work team to cut bananas in the fields

cortero: banana company work position in the fincas referring to the worker who cuts the banana stems; usually a contractor who led a team of 4–10 workers

Costa Abajo: the western north coast of Honduras

Costa Arriba: the eastern north coast of Honduras

cuadrilla: ditch-digging team

cuidar gente; cuidar hombres: an expression patronas use to describe the work of making food or washing clothes for workers

cuque: male cook helper in the kitchen, many times he was a young Black man, but not always

cususa: also spelled cuzusa, homemade alcohol, like moonshine; illegal in Honduras and the banana regions

empleado de confianza: trusted company employee; sometimes called a trabajador de confianza

enmenes: derived from "M&S," the Materials and Supply Department
of the banana operations

finca bananera: banana plantations; often shortened to finca

free labor: concept promoted by the ORIT in the United States to
denote a noncommunist agenda within or about unions or other
labor organizing

gringo: slang term used to refer to North Americans in Latin America

indio(s)/india(s): term used in the north-coast banana region to mean
born in Honduras but not necessarily of Indigenous descent;
could also be used as a derogatory term against people born in
the region

juntero: banana company worker who gathered the banana stems once
cut by the cortero and brought them out (usually on their backs)
to the mulero and mule team for loading

lempira: an Indigenous national hero; the name of Honduran
currency

liberal reform period: the period of social and political efforts to
develop greater prosperity in Honduras by modernizing the
state, separating church and state, promoting national education,
reforming agriculture to benefit foreign investment, and investing
(or seeking investment) in projects or initiatives in the national
interest—often larger-scale, nationwide endeavors to benefit the
populace directly or indirectly. The goal of these efforts may be
referred to as liberal reforms, liberal dreams, or the liberal project.
They often excluded Indigenous peoples, Afro-descendants, and
women.

mandador: overseer, supervisor

mestizaje: the racial, social, and political project of creating
homogeneity through a claim to an indo-Hispanic past of racial
mixture in postindependence Honduras, which excludes Black
and Indigenous peoples from the national project

mestizo/a: a racial construct and identity to which people ascribe that
originated with the Spanish colonial caste system, which sought
to categorize people of mixed race, often classified as those of
Spanish and Indigenous descent. In twentieth-century Honduras
the term is still used as a racial construct claiming Spanish
heritage, and whiteness, in racial mixture. The concept harkens
back to a mythical indo-Hispanic past and is often manipulated
by state projects and has been used to distance the national racial
identity from a Black and Indigenous presence.

mulero: banana company worker who received the banana stems

from the juntero and packed them onto the mule team; the mulero's primary responsibilities were loading mules, leading them to the train, and caring for them

mutual aid society: association established to benefit the welfare of those in need; could be dedicated to a particular affinity group

padrinazgo: patronage

patrona: a woman who worked in the campos as a cook, operated an eating establishment, and was paid by workers monthly.

poquiteros: local landowners, small-scale producers of bananas making up a domestic banana planter class; most were considered part of the local elite in the early twentieth century

testimonio: A narrative told in first person by a narrator who is also the protagonist or witness to the event.

yardero: yard worker who did all kinds of menial work in the houses of the trusted employees and for the company

[la] Zona: the name commonly used to refer to the area where the American Company and workers lived; also called the American Zone or Zona Americana

PREFACE

Los Hondureños deben ver la salida de esta crisis desde
adentro y no buscar soluciones afuera.

FATHER ISMAEL MORENO, SJ[1]

When I began this project, the 1954 banana strike in Honduras stood out as perhaps the single most significant event that had influenced the lives of everyday Hondurans and the course of Honduran history in the twentieth century. From my first visit to the north coast of Honduras, every instinct in me as a former labor organizer and a scholar told me that somewhere in the stories of the strike lay answers about how movements are built, how workers achieve change and affect a national project, and how a nation can confront an empire. I was determined to uncover stories of unsung and unheralded yet important working-class actors, including (or especially) women, who led and organized a national movement and thus successfully challenged US corporate greed and complicit Honduran domestic elites. In 2006, when many of my interviews with former strike participants were conducted, and during the early years of my research, the aspirations for a democratic future for Latin America were still felt across the continent, including in Honduras, with the election of José Manuel Zelaya Rosales to the presidency. Barack Obama's ascendancy in 2008 cast a sheen of optimism over what might be possible among Latinx communities. Against this backdrop, I was excited to contribute to the historiography of how a national labor movement of Honduran workers coalesced from the bottom up in defiance of foreign capital domination and a pliant state.

Then, on June 28, 2009, Honduras experienced the first Latin American coup d'état of the twenty-first century—a violent removal of the democratically elected President Zelaya by the right wing with the support of the US State Department. The 2009 coup rocked Honduras profoundly, and the effects of those ruptures continue today. The entire country has been living successive indignities and injustices born of the coup: three fraudulent elections in 2010, 2013, and 2017 (all endorsed by the United States);[2] a break with the constitution and all rule of law; endemic corruption at all levels of government; violence in civil society (none more heinous than the crimes against the transgender community); Indigenous land theft by foreign corporations; and sale of the country's resources under the banner "Honduras Open for Business." On top of these, the United States' election of Donald Trump and his racist administration's assaults on immigrants and the Latinx community (and all communities of color) have had devastating consequences for Honduras and its people, many of whom are migrating north in caravans as I write because Honduras after the 2009 coup is uninhabitable.

Now, over a decade later, virtually nothing happens in Honduras that does not somehow bear a mark or scar from the 2009 coup. The same is and has been true on the north coast, for the banana worker communities, the organization leaders, and the historical actors I interviewed and worked with during the production of this book and during my political engagement during this period as a Honduran. Indeed, the coup altered the path of my work and created in me a greater sense of urgency for this book.

There is much more to be said and written about the coup, its direct and indirect causes, its consequences, and its prolonged aftermath. This book, however, is not my addition to the growing body of literature on that subject. Rather, I hope this book provides some context for the current conditions in Honduras and traces some vital and lasting connections and inspirations between the 1954 strike and the social justice movements in Honduras today. The 2009 coup, in spite of the terrible things it wrought (or perhaps because of them), has created the conditions for the building of a new national resistance in Honduras[3] with the potential to bring lasting change to the nation, particularly to those most harmed by neoliberal projects: Afrodescendants, Indigenous people, working-class women, and LGBTTI people. Just as awful things have continued since the coup, so too has a resistance continued to build—as Hondurans seek justice and the right to self-determination.

The coup inspired a resistance movement never seen before in Honduras that would lead to the breakup of the bipartisan system of party rule that had lasted for 100 years and the creation of the Frente Nacional de Resistencia Popular (FNRP; National Popular Resistance Front) and a new political party, Libertad y Refundación (LIBRE; Liberty and Refoundation). More importantly, it reignited a wide social movement in the country. The election of Trump and his executive orders around immigration, including the cancellation of TPS/DACA and restrictions on asylum rules, have had a devastating impact on all Central Americans seeking refuge in the United States, particularly Hondurans.

The effects of the events—the coup and the pile-on after—on

Honduran nationals, dual citizens, and the immigrant 1.5 generation have been profound: emboldening a resolve to resist and act in opposition to the coup and in protest of US collusion against democracy, and at the same time setting the stage for a battle against past traumas of survival and strife in the 1980s and under previous periods of dictatorship and authoritarian regimes. For years scholars from the Central American diaspora in the United States have been watching from the sidelines as stories and narratives crafted about us and our countries, some sympathetic with one group or another. It is only recently that a discipline of Central American Studies has begun to emerge, as scholars of Central American descent or origin are entering the academy in sufficient numbers to take part in the construction of that history-making platform. The lack of publications—beyond the 1980s Civil Wars—on Central America is a construction of the same solidarity movement that aimed to save us from US interventionist politics then.

At this current juncture in the country's history, the referential markers of past struggles and past capitalist practices in Honduras are changing, with globalization and a world order in flux. Ten years after the coup d'état that destroyed Honduran rule of law and its economy and generated a massive exodus to the United States, Mexico, and Spain, as well as the largest Resistance movement in the country since the 1954 strike, it seems urgent to tell from a fresh perspective the story about what Honduran workers achieved more than 50 years ago as a project of Honduran resistance and despite repression and exile—to get the story right about how everyday Hondurans won against dominant corporate and foreign interests.

The strike and the history of Central America has been told countless times through a Western gaze, mostly focused on the entrepreneurs and adventurers who developed industries and fortunes in Honduras or on the US government interventions as documented by US agents. This project centers the narrative on Honduran voices and experiences. For me, telling this story by, for, and about Hondurans reclaims a tale of Honduran people's organizing success for Honduras—ever important as the postcoup resistance struggles to tell its truth about the coup in the face of multiple relentless global efforts to "move on" and "get past it" so that the business-as-usual of US dominance in the region can reset itself and continue. The strike and the lived experiences of workers who organized and won it remind us that there was a Honduran national working-class project before bananeras and before US intervention. It has endured since at least 1954 and sees its progeny in the resistance of 2009 through today.

My own positionality has informed this project. Various facets of my identity intersect at different times in my scholarly work, teaching, and community engagement. I am a Honduran immigrant, from the former tobacco-growing region of Copán in the western part of the country (now impacted by globalization and facing continued displacement and migration), close to the border with both Guatemala and El Salvador. The reasons for my displacement from Honduras are hard to pinpoint; they are many, including the politics of US national security in the 1980s and of *el enemigo interno* (internal enemy) in Honduras and the Central American region, which led to the persecution and exile of my brother, and the intragenerational gender violence that led to the separation of my parents during a tumultuous political conflict and low-intensity military warfare in the borderlands near Copán. Perhaps it was also the need for my mother, a woman who valued education but only formally made it to the sixth grade, to seek a better job and opportunities to remake herself and give us, her three children (I am the youngest and the only girl), a better future. I also claim Los Angeles as my home; I am the result of the Central American exodus in the 1980s, first arriving as a child in Pico Union, then moving to Echo Park, and eventually settling in Highland Park. My own migration story is similar to those of other Central Americans who came in the 1980s. These migrations, largely understudied, reflect so many thousands of us Central Americans in Los Angeles, where we constitute the largest population of Central Americans outside of Central America.

I come to this project as a US-trained academic, but with a nuanced bicultural understanding of Honduran culture and politics, which led to many opportunities as an insider, and other moments of exclusion as an outsider, in both Honduras and here in the United States. I have a bruising understanding of what repatriation looks like in light of US cultural and political domination in the region and also of the oft-repeated critique by Honduran leftist and academic circles of the immigrant as the *pequeño imperialista* (the small imperialist), the poor and uneducated. As a woman, a feminist, and an out queer fem,[4] I have also confronted countless feminist dilemmas in fieldwork, and in the traditionally white, male academy. I faced distinct challenges conducting research in Honduras, where I would see all of my political identities collide, and understand in the flesh how multiple feminisms exist and coincide in complex forms. There was complexity in every interaction that had to do with gender, race, and sexuality at almost every turn.

I want to highlight my in-betweenness, my positionality at the interstices, within the borderlands of Honduras, Central America, and the United States, and within multiple physical and metaphoric borders in my gender identity and gender expression. As a Honduran immigrant woman and a Central American–American,[5] in my research I had insight and access as a passing Honduran: I did not stick out, I rode the buses with working people, I got invited into inner circles, and I was quick on the uptake. In so many other ways, I was always on the outside. It was hard to know what brought me in and what kept me out: my Honduran or immigrant identities, my sexuality, my gender, my political beliefs, my position as researcher who would ultimately write a book, my affiliations in the country, being an unmarried woman of a certain age and without children, not wearing a wedding band, my light skin, my Spanish accent—a little Honduran, a little northeast Los Angeles, a little international? I blended in and stuck out, not as a gringa, or the daughter of elites whose kids study in the United States, or as a retornada, the unfortunate deported immigrant, but as something else for which we are still finding names: the working-class immigrant from the 1980s, wanting to return from the Central American diaspora and participate in the history-making in one's own country.

It was hard to know why I was accepted in one space or rejected in another. For example, my light skin in Honduras brought me some privilege, but my Honduran immigrant status and my queerness closed many doors among movement leftists, white academics, the NGO-led solidarity movement, and the elite that dominated most of Honduras. Some of these foreclosures were painful when they came from supposed allies, from Hondurans or from white women solidarity activists, and when they came from Hondurans on the left. But this was the terrain I traversed to find the working classes, the union members, to get invited to their family living rooms, their homes and dances, their rallies and protests, to tell the stories they agreed to share with me of their lives, their hopes and dreams. Workers were eager to talk and share their stories, to remember with me. Despite the layers of oppression and contradiction, exclusion and rejection, at its base (and to workers, it often seemed), I was (simply) a Honduran telling a story of other Hondurans. It is this essence that became all-important to me and centered me, as the coup encroached on all of Honduran existence, and both the horrors and the resistance continued. I saw the importance of my contribution as a Honduran telling a Honduran story—especially at a time when the United States, with a complicit Honduran elite, has ignored Honduran voices, subverted the will of the Honduran people, and promoted a false narrative of Honduran realities for over a decade. And so I embarked on what I thought was a traditional historical project looking at political parties and revolutionary actors only to discover a far more incredible and profound resistance in the everyday life and existence of workers on the north coast, both past and present. I also came to see that the voicing of this history in itself offers a form of resistance, which I am excited to take part in.

Honduras experienced yet another earth-shaking injustice in 2016 when Berta Cáceres, Indigenous leader, an indomitable feminist, unapologetically leftist, was assassinated. On March 2, 2016, Berta Cáceres of the Consejo Cívico de Organizaciones Populares e Indígenas de Honduras (COPINH; Council of Popular and Indigenous Organizations in Honduras) was gunned down in her home by killers protecting a hydroelectric development project by the DESA Corporation (Desarollos Energeticos, S.A.) that sought to exploit the Gualcarque River in La Esperanza, Intibucá, her ancestral lands. Four years later the corrupt Honduran government has not prosecuted the intellectual killers or brought the DESA Corporation under investigation. Her murder challenged all Hondurans to see the urgency of organizing, or challenging power and patriarchy, to defend Indigenous sovereignty. Berta's life, too brief, taught us the importance of telling the past in order to protect our future.

This book was born of this aspiration, with determination and persistence, though interrupted often by direct participation in the building of a resistance movement with Hondurans and other Central Americans, Indigenous peoples, and brown and Black bodies across borders; by the contradictions of solidarity work with US citizens and white Americans, products of first-world privilege; by complicated dynamics of past and present, the dead and the living; and by memory and history itself, obstinate in showing up each and every time to demand its place.

Banana workers continue to demand better wages, better working conditions, social welfare, and a halt to the intimidation, murder, and disappearances that have characterized the banana companies' relationship to Honduras and continue to this day. This book is a conversation starter, meant to highlight the interstices of race, gender, and class and to examine them from a Honduran perspective. I encourage younger Honduran generations and the Central American diaspora to continue to write their histories.

ACKNOWLEDGMENTS

I first learned about the 1954 strike from Mario Argueta's *La Gran Huelga Bananera: 69 Días que Estremecieron a Honduras*. In 1999, I found the book tucked away in a corner of the research library at UCLA where I was participating in a community scholars program designed to bring together local organizers and graduate students to collaborate in support of community-based organizing efforts in Los Angeles. At the time, I was organizing at an immigrants' rights group with immigrant workers from Central America and Mexico. Reading Argueta's book awoke in me an important, abiding, and life-changing interest in understanding Honduran worker history, particularly that of women workers; it planted the seed that became this book.

Writing this book has been a long process, so I am deeply grateful to the University of Texas Press editorial team: Kerry Webb, for finding value in this project, for her leadership and support; Robert S. Kimzey, for his steady guidance and stewardship; Alex Ramos, for his rigorous and sensitive review; and Andrew Hnatow, for offering ready assistance and communication every step of the way.

My research and writing were stalled by very chaotic political events that gripped all Hondurans, such as the coup d'état of 2009 and the continuous violence it sowed; the stolen elections in 2013 and 2017; an unprecedented exodus from Honduras in caravans of thousands of migrating youth, women, and trans folk; unabated government corruption and high-profile narco-trafficking scandals; and now, the COVID-19 pandemic. Throughout these moments I had the enduring collaboration and solidarity of people, both in Honduras and in the United States, who wanted this story to be told, and I am grateful to each of them. My work to build solidarity for Honduras during the 2009 coup d'état gave me the most profound insight into a newly emerging Honduras: a country in resistance. I am thankful to the new generations of Honduran movement leaders who engaged with me in long and passionate debates about history and politics whenever time and the struggle allowed, and all while helping to consolidate a resistance movement. Our engagement has enriched this book.

I want to acknowledge most of all the Honduran women who gave me sustenance. I cannot overstate my appreciation of each of the patronas for sharing their kitchens, recipes, and life stories. In particular, the time I spent with Doña Olimpia Figueroa while cooking was revelatory for this project, and I am especially grateful to her and her family. I thank Indyra Mendoza of Red Lésbica CATTRACHAS, who gave her friendship, support, and solidarity so generously at every stage of this project, including sharing her personal archives, photos, art, and reflections on the life of her great grandfather, Zoroastro Montes de Oca. The CATTRACHAS team also provided community and warmth, a place to belong and be proud of being a Honduran and a queer. I am grateful to Iris Munguía and Gloria Garcia and the teams at FESTAGRO and SITRATERCO in La Lima, Cortes, for the work they allowed me to share in, for the many days and nights of travel and arduous work, and who, along with Evangelina Argueta, Nohemy Salinas Yanes at the Central General de Trabajadores de Honduras in Choloma, Cortés, Yadira Minero at the Centro de Derechos de la Mujer in San Pedro Sula, Cortes, and Zoila Lagos, opened many doors and taught me about being a woman in the labor movement and making oneself heard and seen. Laughter, meals, protests, delegations, and travel between Honduras and Los Angeles, have bonded us as *compañeras* who work hard and fight for justice even harder. I am constantly in awe of the work of Miriam Miranda in OFRANEH and her determination for justice. I appreciate our days spent together in Los Angeles and in various Garifuna communities, which have profoundly informed my intellectual work. In Tegucigalpa, I am grateful to María Eugenia Ramos; Lety Elvir Lazo; Melissa Cardoza; Anarella Vélez; La Colectiva de Historiadoras Feministas; Las Necias; Viena Ávila, director of Asociación Féminista Trans; and Rihanna Ferrera, director of Cozumel Trans; for their critical work, their poetry, imagination, and all of the *jalones* [rides] they gave me deep into an indelibly compromised Honduras. I am especially grateful to Rita Santa Maria and Dunia Perez for their friendship and caring, and all the women they connected me with in El Progreso and San Pedro Sula. Dunia Montoya was a great host who keeps history and memory alive. I thank Bertita and Olivia Zuniga Cáceres and their siblings for sharing their lives so we may know their mother, and their ongoing struggle to keep alight an important flame in the history of Honduras. Lastly, I honor Berta Cáceres, wherever her spirit may be, for building and imagining a new Honduras that confronts its own legacies of racism and patriarchy. All women and gender non-conforming folks in Honduras are indebted to her for showing us that "it is our duty to struggle" [*a nosostras lo que nos toca es luchar*].

In La Lima, Cortés, I am especially thankful to Chico Portillo,

Daniel Madrid Guevara, José Amerto Lagos, Jose Sanchez, and the retired banana finca workers. They all opened their homes to me, shared their lives, contacts, organizational resources, and abundant support and *animo* in ways I could never adequately recount. I am indebted to Luther Castillo Harry for his solidarity, and for trusting and welcoming me and many students to Ciriboya, Colón. I am also grateful to Father Ismael Moreno, director of Radio Progreso/ERIC, and his entire team, who literally provided a desk, *baleadas*, music, friendship, and opened a door to understanding the reality of contemporary Honduras. I thank historian Marvin Barahona who first introduced me to "el Eric" many years ago when I was still a graduate student, and for always being attentive to my questions when I asked. I also thank Don Tomas Erazo Peña in San Pedro Sula, and Agapito and Sylvia Robleda at the CUTH, for candid chats, access to their lives and their memories of 1954. Gerardo Torres Zelaya was keen to help me understand the new generation, and along with Gilberto Rios and Los Necios, showed me another Honduras as we built solidarity across borders as well as time zones after the 2009 coup. Conversations with Nahil Zeron on sexuality and history were illuminating. Billy Lagos and the Colectivo Unidad Color Rosa in San Pedro Sula, Cortés, offered a home for me and the many others who need to belong. I also appreciate the generosity of Carlos Amaya who gave me a complete collection of Ramón Amaya Amador's works to donate to a library in the United States.

The communities of scholars in Honduras and in the United States have been incredible sponsors of my intellectual work and this process. Professor Mario Posas kindly helped me navigate the UNAH and shared his own private archive that helped me to understand the labor and union movements. Dr. Rodolfo Pastor Fasquelle helped open the doors to government archives during his tenure as Minister of Culture before the 2009 coup. Dr. Darío Euraque's intellectual work, advice and feedback over the years have provided an important roadmap to understanding the Honduran archives. I have equally deep appreciation for the UNAH history department, particularly Professor Omar Turcios; Professor Melida Velasquez, who at the time was director of the Archivo Nacional de la Nación; Professor Yesenia Martinez; Professor Ingris Soriano; and Professor Edgar Soriano Ortiz, all training a new generation of emerging historians. I owe my gratitude to Dilcia M. Valle, director of the Archivo del Poder Judicial, and the entire staff in San Pedro Sula and La Ceiba, for graciously putting up with my daily visits and often sharing lunches with me while I consulted the archives. Teresita Campos de Pastor, director of the Museum of Anthropology and History in San Pedro Sula, introduced me to a great library where I often visited to consult and enjoy a *cafecito* during hot afternoons.

Back in the United States, I have had the unwavering support of Chicano/a Latino/a Transnational Studies at Pitzer College and the Intercollegiate Department of Chicano/a Latino/a Studies at the Claremont Colleges, particularly Miguel Tinker Salas, a mentor since my undergraduate years, who believed in me and provided constant feedback and encouragement throughout this manuscript's journey. I am grateful to Gilda Ochoa for encouraging me to always trust my own voice and for her unwavering feminist solidarity. Chicana/o Latina/o Studies colleagues Rita Alcala, Maria Soldatenko, Tomas Summers-Sandoval, Guadalupe Bacio, José Calderon, and Martha Gonzalez provided support and nurturing. Colleagues who provided advice and unwavering support also include Brinda Sarathy, Todd Honma, and Piya Chatterjee, with whom I engaged in long hours of conversation and dialogue about everything—politics, research and writing, the archives—and with whom I share community, joy, solidarity, and sisterhood. April Mayes, Susana Chavez Silverman, Claudia Arteaga, Barbara Junisbai, Juanita Aristizábal, Ethel Jorge, and Paula Gutierrez, all read and provided important feedback, shared wisdom, safe spaces, and happy moments as I finalized this project. Other members of the academic community at Pitzer College have fed and nurtured me. Nigel Boyle, a mentor since my undergraduate years, both as Dean of Faculty and IGLAS program director, was an early believer in me and this project, and funded many research trips with student researchers. I also thank the Women of Color Faculty group for their camaraderie.

Mentors and peers who elevated my thinking, provided safe space, and brought joy and inspiration in various forms, include Isabela Quintana, Munia Bhaumik, Pedro Di Pietro, Karma Chavez, Christopher Loperena, Macarena Gomez Barris, Gabriela Freid Amilivia, John Soluri, Chris Zepeda Millan, Alfonso Gonzalez, Veronica Terriquez, Breny Mendoza, and particularly, Sergio Chavez, who taught me so much during our days at Cornell University. I also thank Claudia Cáceres and Víctor López for their talent and artistic interpretations.

I am very grateful to Mary Roldan, Ray Craib, Derek Chang, Maria Cristina Garcia, Mary Beth Norton, Rachel Weil, Debra Castillo, Michael Jones-Correa, Lourdes Benería and Maria Cook for seeing the value of this story when I was at Cornell, and for allowing me to tell it.

Research and travel was made possible by a Fulbright Scholar

Fellowship (2018); generous funding from research awards at Pitzer College and IGLAS (2012–2018); as well as the Consortium for Faculty Diversity Program, Pomona College (2008–2010); the Fulbright-Hays Doctoral Dissertation Research Abroad Fellowship (2006); and the Ford Predoctoral Fellowship (2005).

I am proud to be a part of the emerging field of Central American Studies in the United States, which is creating space for innovative new voices and a great new body of trans-isthmian diasporic literature. I can't wait to see what will come next from these peer-mentors: Victoria Gonzales Rivera, Ana Patricia Rodriguez, Alicia Estrada, Leisy Abrego, Steven Osuna, Yajaira Padilla, Linda Alvarez, Maya Chinchilla, Sonia Ticas, Arely Zimmerman, Oriel Siu, Kency Cornejo, and Enrique Ochoa, who became a mentor and coeditor—I am deeply grateful for all he offers. Numerous graduate and undergraduate students brought their formidable work ethic and creativity in contributing to my work: Jennifer Cárcamo, Carlos Rivas, Priscilla Cobián Pérez, Sona Patel, Javier López Casertano, Karen Kandamby, Kevin Kandamby, Ashley Dávila, Clara Fuget, Cristian Padilla Romero, Adriana Cerón, Laila Álvarez, and Alex Brown-Whalen. I thank them all for their inquisitiveness and passion in our study of Central America.

I could not have finished this project without the support and encouragement from so many friends and activists. I cannot adequately acknowledge each of their contributions here, but I want to thank Araceli Cortes, Carmen Varela, Olga García Echeverría, Bamby Salcedo, Jennicet Gutiérrez, Esther Portillo, Tracy Zhao, Karla Mejía, Ruben Reyes, Kandree Hicks, Tasha Hawthorne, Mario Garcia, Jorge Gutierrez, Alfredo Lee, and my cheering team, Amy Tam Reyes, Anitra Grisales, and Larry Garrett.

While in Honduras many family members supported me in myriad ways that I do not have the space to recount, but I especially thank my aunts, Gloria A. Barnica Villeda, Irma del Transito Villeda, and Elvia Elisa Portillo; my uncle, Walter Chinchilla; my cousins, Javier and Delmy Chinchilla, José Antonio Barnica, Zobeida Portillo, Melissa Zepeda Tejada, Kepler and Hjalmar Chinchilla, Odette Villeda; and their families, for offering *posada*, meals, company, and rides around town, and for enduring late nights of work with the lights on.

I thank Eileen Ma for her unwavering support for this project, for me personally, for always challenging me in all my work as we "change the question" (in the words of Audre Lorde), and for being a true comrade in all of the ways that matter. I thank my immediate family, who set an example for me to work hard and care about the society we live in and the country we come from: my mother, Olga E. Garcia Villeda Chinchilla, for teaching me to fight for my rights and for putting me through school at great sacrifice; my father, Jacob S. Portillo Chinchilla, for teaching me how to read and appreciate history. I am indebted to my stepfather, Pedro Garcia Perez, for sharing his heart and teaching me to dance to Cuban music. Thank you to Gabriel Magrane for his support and many rides to the airport. I am thankful to my siblings Edgardo, Gerardo, and particularly, Marlom Portillo, whose life experience, knowledge, and sacrifice for our country is profound, and who spent countless hours translating contexts and history. My niece, Andrea Portillo, was a joy to talk to about the archival digs and history as they happened, always over pasta dinners. My nephews, Luis and Ernesto Portillo, Justin and Harry Portillo, and the younger generations of my family are always on my mind. They are among the many young Hondurans who I hope will read this book to know their history. Finally, any errors are my own.

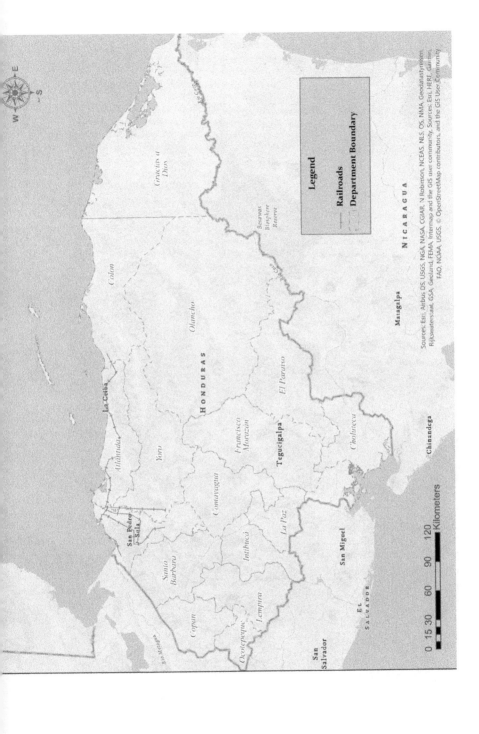

Legend

Railroads
Department Boundary

HONDURAS

NICARAGUA

EL SALVADOR

Gracias a Dios

Colon

Olancho

Besawa Biosphere Reserve

La Ceiba

Atlántida

Yoro

Francisco Morazán

El Paraíso

Comayagua

Tegucigalpa

Choluteca

Santa Barbara

Intibucá

La Paz

San Pedro Sula

Copan

Lempira

Ocotepeque

San Miguel

San Salvador

Managua

Chinandega

0 15 30   60   90   120
Kilometers

ROOTS OF RESISTANCE

INTRODUCTION
HONDURAN WORKERS—NEW VOICES,
OLD MEMORIES

Honduras trod a path of national liberation at the end of the twentieth century that was distinct from the revolutionary movements of Nicaragua, El Salvador, and Guatemala in the 1980s in Central America. Often Honduras is cited as the country most dominated by the United States' anti-communist and counterrevolutionary agenda—"The airport to the right wing!" as it was called by an activist in a solidarity meeting I attended in 2009. The justification for the country's "lack" of a cohesive revolutionary guerrilla movement is deeply rooted in the neocolonial relationship with the US State Department and military. Honduran campesinos did not embrace an agrarian reform movement in the first half of the twentieth century, as did Guatemalans and Salvadorans. Likely, such a movement would have led to the formation of a national liberation program in the latter part of the twentieth century as it did in these neighboring countries. Instead, working-class Hondurans chose to engage in a monumental labor struggle that challenged foreign capital and, more importantly, consolidated a working class, despite repression and obstacles placed in their path by the banana companies and the US Embassy. I contend that leftists of the time waged a labor struggle as a step toward addressing the larger question of agrarian reform in the future; it opened the path for a longer-term strategy. Each generation of Hondurans since the 1954 banana strike has built a movement with the resources it had and by creatively circumventing repressive state practices. These movements have cross-pollinated one another over time. Instead of asking why Hondurans chose a "labor" strategy versus "agrarian reform," or why there was no national liberation strategy, I invite the reader to look at the moments when cross-pollination occurred among movements, leaders, and the masses and how focused and targeted strategies have led to a form of sustained resistance and historical memory, despite repression. This book tells of one of these moments.

On May 1, 1954, banana workers on the north coast of Honduras brought the regional economy to a standstill in a labor strike that invigorated the labor movement and reverberated throughout the country. These actions precipitated the largest labor strike ever to influence Honduran workers' movements and national politics. The strike gave voice to a series of complaints and demands against the north-coast banana industry, embodied by the Standard Fruit Company and the Tela Railroad Company, a subsidiary of the giant United Fruit Company (UFCo). In total, over 25,000 workers flooded the streets of small north-coast towns. The strikers effectively paralyzed the trains, which sat idle in the absence of operators and mechanics. Ships remained empty and docked in the ports, and fruit hung from the stems of banana plants waiting to be picked.

According to the traditional narrative of these events, the strike began in the port of Puerto Cortés, when workers stopped loading ships to demand the rehiring of a coworker who had been unjustly fired. The news of the work stoppage spread throughout the rest of the north coast and to major cities, where it gained sympathetic support from the public and local newspapers, eventually resulting in a general strike. Factory workers throughout the country first protested in solidarity and then made demands of their own employers; more work stoppages ensued when these were not met. In solidarity with the banana workers' bold actions, service workers, maids, cooks, and independent vendors joined the strike. Students, women's groups, teachers associations, and others in the capital city and elsewhere contributed to the strike. National sentiment in support of banana workers spread, and even merchants showed sympathy by donating and giving credit to striking workers in need of assistance.

Accounts in the historical literature present the strike as a proud moment of national unity that changed the country, a moment when all Hondurans stood together. As Honduran historian Marvin Barahona explains:

> In the context of the strike, the nationalist spirit spread to all social strata with the projection of an image of an unequal struggle between a powerful foreign company and thousands of defenseless local workers. This image could only generate gestures of solidarity animated by

nationalism, without which the 1954 strike could not have lasted for so long or garnered so much sympathy and popular support.[1]

The strike was transformative for workers and brought national attention to their issues and lives on the north coast. Ultimately, the strike dramatically challenged the export economy and resulted in improvements for workers. It brought respect from a previously recalcitrant Honduran government that was reluctant to challenge foreign domination, and it generated momentum for the labor movement and the continuation of liberal reforms. More importantly, the banana-worker strike and the general strike that followed allowed working-class Hondurans to envision a broader struggle, awakening a sense of possibility and change; the emergence of a radical politics among banana workers created opportunities for all working-class people. Among other workers, the strike movement renewed a commitment to leftist principles and ideals that had long been suppressed.

While many writers, historians, officials, labor activists, and others present varying perspectives on how the strike happened, what exactly transpired, who did what, and why it matters, most Hondurans I interviewed for this project seem to agree on at least one thing: the strike of 1954 was the most important and monumental event ever to happen in Honduras—at least at the time of our interviews between 2004 and 2009. The banana-worker mobilizations were eclipsed only by the resistance movement that arose in response to the coup d'état in 2009 that ousted democratically elected president José Manuel Zelaya Rosales. This book examines the stories and experiences of campeños and campeñas, the men and women who lived and worked in the banana fincas (plantations) of the Tela Railroad Company and Standard Fruit Company in the period leading up to the Great Banana Strike of 1954. This study traces the development of the labor movement from the workers' unique perspective and explores the formation of a banana-worker identity and culture that would influence labor politics at the national level and future generations of working-class organizers.

The bulk of this study focuses on the period between 1944 and 1957, a significant time when dissenters began to push back against both the Tiburcio Carías Andino dictatorship and the banana companies' control over workers and the north-coast territory. This is a crucial time span in which to analyze worker agency on the north coast and the banana regions dominated by US companies, but it is rarely analyzed from the point of view of workers.[2] The actions and organizing of many unheralded finca workers leading up to the 1954 strike were significant in consolidating the powerful general strike effort and securing outcomes that affected the whole nation in its aftermath, namely the codification of labor laws and the formation of the Ministry of Labor. But the worker mobilization and resistance went beyond government reforms to influence an entire generation of leftist radicals, youths, and women in the region, which is evidenced by a contemporary labor and social movement led by working-class women to be discussed later in the book. I concur with Greg Grandin that "the mass peasant and working-class movements that gained ground in the middle of the twentieth century were absolutely indispensable to the advancement of democracy."[3]

The efforts of Honduran scholars and activists to build a project to rescue historical memory has been thwarted on multiple occasions, and working-class organizers and leftists have been forced to exist in the shadows or in exile. Much of the strike's history and literature was banned from most twentieth-century Honduran classrooms and forgotten until the mid-1990s, when the Central American Peace Accords in the region ushered in a period of amnesty, which enabled those exiled to return.[4] The mid-1990s gave way to radical ideas and organizing efforts inspired by the old left yet transformed by newer generations. Groups such as the Bloque Popular, a coalition of progressive labor unions, student movements, campesino land-tenure struggles, the feminist movement of the 1990s, and other social movements emerged, and within each of these sectors there has been a vibrant and political feminist intervention. This culminated in the movement that emerged to protest the unconstitutional ouster of democratically elected president José Manuel Zelaya Rosales. The organizing that ensued after the 2009 coup resembled the period leading up to the 1954 strike, an effort led by a coalitional group of leftists and Liberal Party members attempting to form a cohesive and progressive movement to take over power; the working class is the protagonist of this sketch, not unlike the 1954 strike.

Many authors have acknowledged the north coast as an important site of economic and political development and transformation for the country.[5] But often, the US-owned banana companies are almost exclusively credited with defining the economic and political culture of the region. By focusing on the workers' historical experiences, this book challenges that unilateral, banana company-centered understanding of the north coast and rescues from obscurity the collective story of the lives and labor of thousands of workers who also made the north coast an important geographic, political, cultural, and economic region. Workers' daily labor, their organizing leading up to the strike, and their participation in national reform efforts contributed to the significance of the area and influenced workers and the labor movement throughout the nation.

Perhaps most importantly, this book explores the gender, ethnoracial, and class constructions on the north coast of Honduras linked to the daily practice of work, which created the conditions of possibility for the strike. This study delves into the history of life in the campos (banana labor camps) and the nature of work and labor organizing in the fincas. In the labor camps, workers—both men and women—negotiated relationships and tensions with one another, the banana companies, foreigners, immigrants, the natural and work environments, and the work itself. Their lives reveal how workers created community and adapted to work and living conditions, how they resisted pervasive company control, and how their organizing efforts set the stage for the 1954 strike, future organizing efforts, and, ultimately, radical politics in the region. Within this narrative, I hope to tease out the gendered lives of workers, particularly women workers and their informal economy, which supported the formal economy of the region, including their roles in the banana export economy and the strike. For men, the development of a particular kind of masculinity, one tied to ethnoracial identity, gave them access to work and survival and ultimately helped create solidarity among the working-class people of the region.

This study originally germinated from the question of how the strike of 1954 in Honduras consolidated a powerful labor movement when previous efforts had been unsuccessful. While this question has been partially answered in numerous political analyses and literary works, what is still missing is a better understanding of workers' day-to-day lives and experiences at the time, and how those daily events contribute to and influence a culture and legacy of radical-left politics in the region and the country. The thousands of workers who participated in the strike were the central actors during a monumental period in Honduran history, yet we know them as faceless symbols or archetypes, rather than as real, complex social agents and actors. This book collects and analyzes their oral histories in an attempt to rescue and reintegrate alternative narratives of workers' lives. This includes previously ignored histories of the workers on the north coast like the patronas (women cooks who ran eating establishments) and their ayudantas (assistants), or the Garífuna and Jamaican workers, who faced ethnic and racial discrimination. Close analysis of workers' experiences can produce a labor-movement history that is textured by the contradictions, challenges, and possibilities of the working class.[6] Working-class identity and culture are constructions of the workers themselves, as much as workers are products of their environment—in this case the repressive enclave economy of the north coast and the Honduran government.

LABOR AND GENDER IN HISTORICAL ANALYSIS

Most workers claimed an identity as campeños, finca workers employed by the banana companies in the plantations. These were the coveted and respected jobs that drew people to the north coast to become a part of the formal export economy that the banana industry created. Agricultural workers were and are seen as prominent, central figures of the north-coast community. In general, the term campeños only refers to finca workers. Others, such as independent women workers, stevedores (dock workers), townspeople, and anyone else not connected to the company, were essentially marginalized, no matter their role or contribution to the culture and community. This is particularly striking in the case of women workers, who played an integral part in sustaining the primary workforce through their development of a robust informal economy, but generally were not considered in the realm of banana workers.

A gendered analysis, one that thoroughly addresses both men and women workers, is essential to an understanding of the north coast. Women workers' roles in particular must be understood within a social-reproduction framework—that is, one that analyzes their role in reproducing the working class and society through their work and labor.[7] Important works in Central American history have focused on the suffrage movement in order to understand the role of women in society.[8] However, the suffrage movement was dominated by middle-class and elite women in the cities and company towns; it rarely, if ever, infiltrated the lives of the women of the campos. I join other labor historians and scholars who are rethinking how to examine workers' roles and women's and men's gender roles in society.[9] The efforts to engender history are predicated on the notion that "the ways in which societies perceive and reproduce sexual difference are a result of processes."[10] These directions in labor history and endeavors to engender history have influenced my approach in this study.[11] The untold stories of the men and women banana workers provide critical illustrations of how the workplace is gendered, and they allow us to analyze how workers'

lives and relations inform larger societal constructions and macroeco-
nomic structural formations.

In the labor movement's traditional historical narrative, women
are absent because they are largely unseen in the workplace, and thus
in organized labor, too. To explain their "absence," traditional analyses
characterize their labor and exploitation in the workplace as a relatively
contemporary phenomenon resulting from the growth of industrialization.[12] More recent scholarship provides a different perspective, noting that women have been part of industrialization processes since the
late 1800s.[13] Labor history and the overall field of history are similarly
trying to make gender a critical tool of analysis along with race. As
Joan Wallach Scott advises, the challenge to "de-ghettoize" the study of
women "is, in the end, a theoretical one. It requires analysis not only
of the relationship between male and female experience in the past
but also of the connection between past history and current historical
practice. How does gender work in human social relationships? How
does gender give meaning to the organization and perception of historical knowledge? The answers depend on gender as an analytical category."[14] My own study of the patronas shows that their lives and work
in the banana campos completely changed the historical narrative of
the region—challenging the very notion that there was an absence of
women workers—and conventional understandings of masculinity and
work in the north coast.

In *The Gendered Worlds of Latin American Women Workers*, an edited
volume on gender and labor in Latin America, John D. French and
Daniel James refute the past practice of simply inserting women into
the traditional framework of labor history, which has focused mainly on
male workers. Their work refuses to "ghettoize and segregate" women
from men's labor history; rather, French and James claim that the study
of labor history needs to be reconfigured to truly reflect women's lives,
not just add their participation as an afterthought:

> The challenge facing labor historians is to explore the articulation of
> gender and class in the lives of working-class subjects, both male and
> female. In this nonessentialist approach, gender is understood as a rela-
> tionship rather than a thing; it is viewed as a verb rather than a noun.
> It must be seen as a social process of construction in which meaning
> is ascribed to sexual difference, which is reproduced by and within insti-
> tutions (such as the family, factory, or polity) that generate and sustain
> gender hierarchies and patriarchal ideologies.[15]

This framework allows us to look at women in history as well as to reconsider men and their gendered relationships within the workplace. More research in microhistories is needed to develop this approach within different Latin American countries, as well as in different rural and urban industries. By focusing on the north coast's agricultural worker culture within the banana enclave, my study contributes by revealing the gendered relationships among men and women, as well as informal and formal workers, and how their local work and organizing reverberated nationally.

It is equally important to explore masculinity in the context of work and progressive movements in history. Deborah Levenson-Estrada analyzes the particular behavior of male union members in a Guatemalan factory based on oral histories and explains that women were only accepted in the union leadership after exhibiting several characteristics that the men deemed necessary; she refers to this dynamic as "masculine," perhaps to be understood as a masculinization of women.[16] There may be a useful application of this theory in Honduras, where it was mostly men who held leadership positions in labor organizing, although with some exceptions. Women like Graciela García in the 1920s and Teresina Rossi Matamoros, a labor leader who was active in the 1954 strike committee, are remembered for their roles on mostly male committees. In Rossi Matamoros's process of *concientización* (consciousness raising) two factors predominated: the terrible working conditions she witnessed workers suffering in the campos and outside the offices of the company, and her curiosity for further study and knowledge. At the time, her ability to take the initiative and join the ranks of the Alianza de la Juventud Democrática Hondureña (Alliance of Honduran Democratic Youth) was perhaps an indication of some privilege even among women at the time.[17] Only certain women, and perhaps women of a certain class, penetrated this protected male space. She describes her interaction with working-class women, the wives of the workers in the study group:

> It might seem strange that I don't mention women in this account. I did know the wives of my comrades, but perhaps because of my strong personality—and it's not that I wasn't feminine; I was, and I am—I preferred to interact with men. They seemed to me less complicated, less gossipy, less given to intrigue. This is what most motivated me to be in the committee meetings—and there were meetings in which the only thing the wives did was serve coffee.[18]

Later, Rossi Matamoros would find a role within the strike organizing committee and join a workers' study group, while most other women, the wives of workers, were relegated to what men considered secondary status as supporters—making food, taking care of children, and leading food-bank efforts during the strike. These varied contributions and important forms of labor performed by women, who I claim were crucial to the success of the 1954 strike in Honduras, must be recognized and restored to labor histories and memory. The work of Levenson-Estrada and others suggest ways to do so.

Writing about Honduras, I have been challenged to consider how best to conceptualize the intersections of gender, class, and ethnoracial constructions in a particular time and place. Existing scholarship on the banana industry in Central America, such as the work of Lara Putnam and Aviva Chomsky on Costa Rica, has sought to chart these intersections in other contexts.[19] In my work, I found myself coming back time and again to consider three factors that stood out as themes in workers' lives and the social structure of the north coast: masculinity, mestizaje (a racial construct used by the nation to homogenize citizens), and working-class identity. These were recurring concepts throughout the interviews I conducted with former workers, just as they are in existing narratives and histories of the period. Indeed, they were promoted as part of a dominant nation-building project. At the same time, these dominant themes by themselves felt inadequate to explain the actual lives and the unfolding of events of the period. This book suggests, rather, that the undeniably male, mestizo character of the north-coast working class was only part of the picture. This identity only existed because it was in dialog with the "Other" (i.e., Garifuna workers, other Black workers, women workers) and was only powerful because of these "Others." I further suggest that the context and events of the north coast can only be understood with an appreciation of the ways in which these identities collided. Ultimately, the culture and history of the north coast, including the strike, must be understood as a result of the very complex negotiation of these different identities and actors in a dynamic environment. Thus readers will note in the following chapters a recurrence of these dominant themes, as my sources and interviewees made fairly consistent reference to these ideas, presenting male, mestizo finca workers at the center of most narratives.

Masculinity was a valued quality in male workers in the banana fields of the 1940s and 1950s, defined by an ability to endure extreme physical hardship in work and life, and to remain productive despite unhealthy conditions in order to fulfill the role of provider to a wife, children, and/or parents (even if these family members were not on the north coast). Men defined their strength, skills, and knowledge of the work in the banana fields as masculine. Life in the campos was often fierce and physically brutal, but male workers also shared camaraderie through work and social time. The concept of masculinity was also informed by interactions in the local company towns, the Honduran stores, and with brothel owners, whose enterprises relied on the banana workers' wages. Company-town locals often derogatorily called banana workers *manchados* (stained people), a slur used to denote their lower- and working-class status, because workers wore shirts of *manta* (white cotton) that were stained with the tar of the banana stems.[20] But workers preferred to be referred to as campeños, which reflected their life in the campos, and rejected the term *manchado*, which only defined them as subservient to the company and its policies. Masculinity was identified with the narrative of a "productive worker"; he who had money and was paid was seen as a campeño. While work defined them, subservience to the companies did not. When the labor organizing began in 1945 and 1946, the men's perception of masculinity became intertwined with the notion and practice of demanding improvements in the workplace. Masculinity was tied first to survival in a harsh environment in the campos, and then to fair treatment and respect as workers. Masculinity was imposed on women and partnerships in different forms. Many women who were wives and daughters developed a sort of dependence on male workers and men's access to living areas. For patronas and women cooks, though the relationships were informal, women had more independence in choosing other partners.

MESTIZAJE IN HONDURAS

While male mestizo finca workers are traditionally positioned at the center of the north-coast community and social structure, this book suggests, in fact, that the history and events of the north coast were the result of the tensions and dialectical engagement between the dominant group (i.e., male mestizo finca workers) and others. It was the very negotiation between these groups that made the north coast such a dynamic place, one where the 1954 strike was possible.

The popular image of the triumphant Honduran campeño was mestizo, indo-Hispanic—possibly racially mixed, but not Black or Garifuna, as Blackness had no claim to the national identity. Even though descendants of Afro-Hispanic origins have had a presence in Honduras since the colonial period and founded many important north-coast towns, workers refer to themselves as indios, which in most contexts refers to Indigenous people.[21] In Honduras, however, it is used to denote that they are natives, born in Honduras and therefore nationals and mestizos. It does not indicate or acknowledge indigeneity, African roots, or Black identity. Rather, it claims an imagined indo-Hispanic background, which negates Blackness.

The conflation of race and nationality by banana workers during this period proved useful for them in finding work in a hierarchical company system. For instance, workers who called themselves "indio," meaning by this native to Honduras, would likely be prioritized for hiring above Black workers in the fields. Furthermore, the Carías Andino regime policed difference and race in immigration. The company recruited and hired West Indians, but the Honduran government opposed it, and Honduran workers saw them as competition.[22] This xenophobia was felt so intensely that even in the negotiations with the company during the strike a clause was added requiring that work first be offered to Hondurans.[23] For male finca workers of the midcentury, being Honduran and indio meant the same thing; it was understood by workers and company supervisors that this group would receive priority in hiring because they were nationals and they were not Black.

By the 1940s, there was a system and understanding in place that was clear for workers, both men and women. Survival was easier for workers who identified as indio, or Honduran, a definition that devalued immigrants and Black workers, both men and women. The mestizo identity became a currency that bought an easier life within the enclave and invited participation in the organizing work of building the union and the nation. It enabled access to work and also made mestizo workers visible in the company hierarchy. Naturally, the story of the labor movement has been thought of as a story of mestizo men.

NORTH-COAST HISTORY, WORKING PEOPLE'S LIVES, AND THE ARCHIVES

The small but growing body of literature on the north coast and its people builds on the initial work of Honduran sociologist Mario Posas and historians Victor Meza, Marvin Barahona, Mario R. Argueta, and Darío A. Euraque. These authors have traced the economic, political, geographic, and cultural importance of the north coast in relation to national and foreign economic domination. Posas's *Luchas del Movimiento Obrero Hondureño*, as well as his subsequent works on the labor movement, and Meza's *Historia del Movimiento Obrero Hondureño* are important studies of the labor movement in Honduras. Both published in the 1980s and 1990s, these works provide a sweeping history of the labor movement, beginning with the craft unions, the importance of land concessions, and the role of workers in unionizing efforts that were transformative to the nation. Posas's work is critical both in its documentation of previous strikes and land concessions and as a political history and analysis of the conditions leading up to the strike of 1954. Mario R. Argueta has also made essential contributions to Honduran historiography, in part because his books *La Gran Huelga Bananera* and *Bananos y Política* both draw on US State Department records regarding the fruit companies' operations on the north coast. His recent work, *Un Desafío al Tradicionalismo Político*, documents the important role of the Partido Democrático Revolucionario Hondureño (PDRH; Honduran Democratic Revolutionary Party) in challenging the bipartisan system, yet the role of the organizers as they built broad support over a Communist party is still a bit of a mystery in the records. What was sacrificed and why? What might those debates have been like? How did organizers interpret the constant persecution and the forced clandestine agenda?

More recent studies by historian Barahona—perhaps the first labor historian to use oral histories to explore labor issues and to uncover the role of worker organizers during the 1954 strike—provide more insight into workers' agency and their interactions with the state as persecuted workers and as negotiators.[24] In particular, he has written about the leadership of the 1954 strike, bringing to light the critical role leftists played in the organizing efforts, and problematizing the relationship between the Liberal Party and other organizations—such as the PDRH, launched to challenge authoritarianism.[25] In his subsequent work on national identity, *Evolución Histórica de la Identidad Nacional*, Barahona reached back to the colonial period to elucidate the twentieth-century project of nation-building, demonstrating the fissures inherent in the process and the fractured nature of national identity. In a later work, *Memorias de un Comunista*, a book Barahona compiled on the life of former Communist Party founder Rigoberto Padilla Rush, demonstrates the richness and audacity of the men and women who built the Communist Party and challenges us to think about the terror of persecution and exile and what could have been. In *Honduras en el siglo XX*, Barahona provides a broad history of Honduras in the twentieth century, in which he spotlights economic investment and foreign interests in the north coast and connects more recent history to the construction of the liberal period of the 1880s.[26]

Rina Villars's *Porque Quiero Seguir Viviendo . . . Habla Graciela García* is an important biography that uncovers the life history and political organizing work of Graciela García, a labor activist in the 1920s in the Federación Sindical Hondureña (FSH; Federation of Honduran Unions), one of the more radical labor organizations that sought to build power for workers. García was exiled to Mexico for her labor activity during the Carías Andino dictatorship (and remained exiled until her death) but always supported the labor militancy in Honduras. The book raises questions about the fissures between liberals and more radical members of the FSH, who saw the north coast as an important site for organizing. Villar's more recent work *Lealtad y Rebeldía* is an homage to Juan Pablo Wainwright, a leader often forgotten in salutes to the nation, a founder and builder of movements during a period when the banana was king.

Euraque's works, both in English and in Spanish, look beyond nationhood and national political analysis. His book *Reinterpreting the Banana Republic* focuses on the development of a political and economic class in the north coast. According to Euraque, the north coast is important because "it developed a liberal and defiant political culture that cut across class lines and that served as a basis for distinguishing Honduras from other Central American countries."[27] His most recent studies explore the history of race and ethnicity in Honduras, analyzing the perceived "threat of Blackness" as one of the motives for the construction of national identity around indo-Hispanicity.[28] His study of mestizaje relies on a critical understanding of the construction of the nation and the marginalization of the community of Garifuna (also known as Gariganu) people and other Indigenous and Black communities through the prioritization of indo-Hispanicity.[29] Euraque has conducted oral histories, especially in his work on the Garifuna community and their involvement in the labor movement in the north coast.

Both Elisavinda Echeverrí-Gent's dissertation "Labor, Class, and Political Representation" and Glen A. Chambers's book *Race, Nation, and West Indian Immigration* have sought to uncover the complicated role of West Indians in the banana industry and their relations to Garifuna and other Black populations in the north coast.[30] These primarily Honduran authors have established a strong historiographical foundation for this study, particularly on race, political parties, and leftist efforts. The agricultural workers' lives—particularly working-class women's lives and labor—have remained largely in the shadows.

Roots of Resistance is also in dialogue with several recent works in the United States that highlight Honduras and the banana regions in innovative ways. John Soluri's Banana Cultures has exposed an additional dimension of the north-coast banana industry—that of environmental transformation.[31] His ecological focus reveals the role of the poquiteros, small banana producers, who were the first to cultivate bananas and significantly alter the ecology of the north coast.[32] Jason Colby's meticulous work uncovers the racial terrains the company carved out in Central America, exposing the underbelly of the banana empire in the early twentieth century. Philippe Bourgois's fascinating work compiling company records on persecution of workers gives a unique look into the role of surveillance and anti-communism within the enclave economies that have been forbidden and chilling for so long. Kevin Coleman's exploration of Rafael Platero Paz's photography and his role in the town of El Progreso, Yoro, a town made radical by banana workers' bold organizing efforts, grants us a view into workers' lives in a company town. The images each provide a window that includes surrounding spaces and images of the everyday Progreseño. The previously unexplored photographic archive of Platero Paz, taken with his eye for the region and the people, is stunning—a true national Honduran patrimony. Finally, James Martin's chilling account of the "American men"—the white overseers who moved from the United States to places like Honduras, conquered the "tropics," and became "banana cowboys," overseeing mostly men of color—uncovers interesting class tensions and further exposes the racial hierarchies between the employees and the company supervisors of the corporation. All these works offer important vantage points to enter into the analysis of the banana empire, its racial and capitalist empire, the ecological devastation they brought to the country, and the scars they left behind.

From this point of departure, I begin my study as an intervention to expand our view of north-coast historical actors. This book is informed by the memories of women and men who lived and worked in the north coast and participated in the 1954 strike. I conducted in-depth interviews to gather oral histories of over 200 workers and movement leaders who shared details—sometimes intimate—about their lives and the social conditions of the north coast in the 1940s and

1950s; I used 87 for this work. The interviews also provided opportunities for these men and women to reflect on power, politics, and their role in the creation of the labor movement. In the process of telling their stories, workers articulated and constructed narratives and meanings about the strike, the north coast, their work for the company and in the campos, and their daily lives during this period. As a group, the interviews suggested certain recurring themes, as I noted above, that guided my thinking. Another source of information came from conversations with local organizations and Honduran scholars who gave time and energy to answer my sometimes-difficult questions and to ask their own of me in turn.[33]

My reliance, though not exclusive, on these oral sources invites an interrogation both of why these are appropriate, even necessary, sources for the recovery of this history and of the value and challenges of this approach. In constructing this history of the finca workers of the north coast of Honduras, I have also reflected on the use of oral history as a method for this work. First, I position oral history vis-à-vis the testimonio (literally, "testimony") literature of Central America. Second, I think of the construction of history from oral histories as a departure, in some ways, from testimonio literature. Third, I reflect on the role of memory and consider the ways in which this method is imprecise yet valuable at the same time.

The practice of oral history is crucial to the rescue of the historical record for Honduras and Central America, particularly for the twentieth century. There are many holes in the historical record of Central America and Honduras in particular, especially when it comes to the story of the working class, women, and ethnoracial minorities. Oral histories challenge and recontextualize poor archives and scant historical records. Archival collections in Honduras are incomplete, and funding for their conservation is limited. The surviving documents are kept by the state in the capital, Tegucigalpa, and in several municipalities where authorities have prioritized work on the conservation of colonial records. Many of the early twentieth-century documents are suffering from deterioration and are in need of rescue and conservation. Others simply no longer exist.

The process of rescue and conservation itself presented a challenge to my research. The judicial records I consulted in San Pedro Sula at the Poder Judicial de Honduras's (Judicial Authority of Honduras) Centro Electrónico de Documentación e Información de Justicia

(CEDIJ; Electronic Center for Legal Documentation and Information, now known as the Archive of the Judical Authority of Honduras) were in the process of being cleaned, cataloged, and archived. Given the immediate needs of the court system, archivists were beginning with the most recent records and working their way back to earlier years. The period of this study, the mid-twentieth century, falls outside of the prioritized conservation efforts in Honduras, between the rescue of colonial and nineteenth-century records and the contemporary or near-contemporary records. Most of the records I reviewed while at the CEDIJ archive were stored at random. I sorted through documents, finding only an occasional piece related to my period and topic. Still, some records I found at the CEDIJ were useful in documenting workers' lives, the discussion of alcohol and violence, the reliance on the train, and life in the north coast. There were no company records on workers, either in the United States or in Honduras; my requests to companies were never attended, and I often did not get past the reception desk at their headquarters.[34]

My project focuses on workers and labor organizing during an era when the persecution of labor leaders and Communist Party leaders was commonplace. This has proved detrimental to retaining a complete record of clandestine newspapers and leaflets.[35] For instance, very little can be gleaned from Honduran archives about the important labor leader and Communist Party founder Manuel Cálix Herrera. Most of what we know has come from US State Department records or the work of Philippe Bourgois recovering UFCo records in Costa Rica.[36] In the CEDIJ archives two habeas corpus petitions were found demanding due process in the case of Cálix Herrera, who in 1929 was arrested for protesting at the US Consulate in the north coast against US anti-communist policies. Perhaps the process of conservation and cataloging would bring to the surface more cases that would help in piecing together a lost history. Other archival holdings that could have provided information on the workers' perspectives have been destroyed by hurricanes and other natural disasters, including Hurricane Mitch in 1998.[37]

Finally, the largest impediment for archivists in Honduras is the lack of funding, equipment, and training for the processes of conservation. During my research, unfortunately, a common sight in any archive was a room full of papers, folders, and newspapers haphazardly stored, stacked, and not cataloged. Consulting such records involved rolling up my sleeves to help clean, file, and/or at the very least put documents in a box—all the while reviewing them for my own work.[38] All these ongoing archival challenges conspire to limit the available historical record in Honduras.

Oral history collection, however, is critical to understanding Honduras and Central America because it grants a role for the working classes and thus balances out who gets to narrate it.[39] I was able to collect oral histories and use them as primary sources in piecing together a picture of life on the north coast and a worker history of the 1954 strike.[40] Oral histories are recognized as a legitimate source but debates about them do exist in the field of history, particularly about the imprecision of memories and the inequalities inherent in the process of gathering them.[41] Even as they provide an intimate portrait of events otherwise silenced or absent from the archival record—and present voices that may challenge dominant narratives—oral histories also raise questions about the construction of memory, who is speaking and for whom, and the relationships and power dynamics between interviewer and interviewee.[42] This "oral archive" of histories embodied in workers was imprecise and methodologically challenging yet essential and, I assert, a needed contribution to Honduran historical practice.

AN ORAL HISTORICAL PRACTICE

First and foremost, oral history collection in Honduras must be situated within the larger context of the Central American oral tradition, and especially the history of testimonio literature.[43] In Central America, testimonio arises from an existing oral tradition, a history of labor and land struggles, and the urgency of articulating the demands central to these struggles. It has been an intentional collaboration among middle-class and literate working-class poets, writers, artists, and journalists working with people who want to retell an experience of coming together at a particular time and place determined by urgency and hope of survival. John Beverley, who has offered the most comprehensive definition of testimonio, states:

> By testimonio I mean a novel or novella-length narrative in book or pamphlet (that is printed as opposed to acoustic) form, told in the first person by a narrator who is also the real protagonist or witness of the events he or she recounts, and whose unit of narration is usually a "life" or a significant life experience. Testimonio may include, but is not

subsumed under, any of the following textual categories, some of which are conventionally considered literature, others not: autobiography, autobiographical novel, oral history, memoir, confession, diary, interview, eyewitness report, life history, novella-testimonio, nonfiction novel, or "factographic" literature.[44]

Beverley provides a succinct way to look at testimonio but refuses to confine it as an established form of literature; rather, he sees it as a genre that exists at the crossroads of various disciplines.[45] The rise of testimonio literature in Central America is political in nature and intimately attached to upholding the human and civil rights of the narrator and/or of a particular group. Testimonio's propulsion into the international arena is commonly attributed to two significant events: the creation of a prize for the category of testimonio by Cuba's famous publisher Casa de las Américas, and the positive reception of both Truman Capote's *In Cold Blood* and Miguel Barnet's *Biografía de un Cimarrón*.[46] In Beverley's opinion, testimonios drew on the idea of "direct participant observation." Works such as Ernesto "Che" Guevara's *La Guerra de Guerrillas* (*Guerrilla Warfare*) "inspired in Cuba a series of direct participant testimonios by combatants in the 26 of July Movement."[47]

Testimonio highlighted the role of the women who participated in the armed struggle and in the later development of Cuba. Works such as Margaret Randall's testimonial compilation of women's experiences in *Cuban Women Now* were influenced by the oral history tradition of second-wave feminists in the United States.[48] Randall's later work, *Sandino's Daughters*, came at the behest of the Frente Sandinista de Liberación Nacional (FSLN; Sandinista National Liberation Front), which asked her to conduct oral history workshops in Nicaragua—capitalizing on an oral tradition and a history of labor and land struggles—to bring international attention to the genre and thereby to the stories of so many working poor long ignored by political historians, literary canons, and the international community in general. These movements themselves promoted the genre, forming a dialogical relationship between literature of resistance and the articulation of politics. For the FSLN, the collaboration with Margaret Randall was a way to document its struggles but also to advance its goals of mass mobilization and *concientización*.[49] Testimonio is rooted in a historical practice that places texts like *I, Rigoberta Menchú* (Guatemala), *Sandino's Daughters* (Nicaragua), and *Don't Be Afraid, Gringo* (Honduras), as well as earlier works such as *Porque Quiero Seguir Viviendo . . . Habla Graciela García* and *Páginas de Lucha* (Honduras), within a continuum that is constantly redefining and challenging our understanding of the historical moment and the master narratives.[50]

The question of veracity (i.e., "Is it true?") and audience (i.e., "To whom is this document speaking?") of testimonios is a point of contention among North American scholars. For example, when David Stoll challenged the veracity of *I, Rigoberta Menchú* by engaging in a fact-finding mission on the life events Rigoberta Menchú Tum described in her narrative, the ensuing international controversy was linked to the struggle for human rights and Indigenous rights in Guatemala.[51] Stoll's work was perceived as an attack on the struggle for justice in Guatemala. Authors such as John Beverley, Arturo Arias, and Lourdes Martínez Echazábal, among others, defended the genre, concluding that the importance of Menchú Tum's contribution is her reliance on the collective memory of the Mayan Quiche people during the civil war period.[52] Menchú Tum, they claimed, speaks for and from within a collective, a communal practice for Mayas. The academic debate over the role of truth in testimony precipitated attempts to define and question testimonio as a genre committed to the struggles out of which the protagonists/narrators emerged.[53] The discussion provoked discourse, and the debate over the primacy of "truth" and "scientific fact" in collective memory remains ongoing.[54]

Oral traditions inform both testimonio literature and oral history, and these genres share methods and tools of the trade, but there are points of departure as well as convergence. Both testimonio and oral history gathering, in the context of Honduras and Central America, are rooted in efforts to uncover historical memories, privileging the voices of sectors of the population or particular groups that the "official" history and historical record have omitted. They are also rooted in the oral tradition, congruent with the cultural and political history of the alienated groups. Like testimonio, oral history gathering in Honduras faces some challenges when considered as part of the historical record. In the context of Honduras, oral histories are testimonials of survival, but they differ from the literature of testimonio in certain key places. While testimonios have a preoccupation with political and social conditions, they are contemporary, often using the present conditions and struggles as the point of departure for the past. Oral histories document the past, as the narrators remembered it.

Contemporary historians' use of oral histories gathered from workers has been influenced by the literary tradition of the social realist novels set in the banana regions of Central America. Many of these books were the works of authors deeply committed to the working classes who strove in their fiction to make connections between the living conditions of banana workers and a national reality.[55] Many also labeled the foreign-owned companies as the culprits for the ills of the working class, favoring a story from below and inside. As Ana Patricia Rodríguez explains, "Banana social literature concerns itself with the extreme exploitation of laborers on the banana plantation"; the "US 'gringo' characters in banana social realist literature are represented as villainous corporate heads, enclave foremen, plantation expatriates, and unscrupulous adventurers."[56] Novels such as Ramón Amaya Amador's *Prisión Verde* and Carlos Luis Fallas's *Mamita Yunai*, both with testimonial qualities, were written to tell the story from the point of view of the workers.[57] In these novels, banana agricultural workers are the protagonists, and the writers themselves are former workers or organizers. The novels' overtly political context and content explain the power relations to the reader and function as a counterdiscourse to other movements of the time.[58] These works are differentiated from Miguel Asturias's *Men of Maize*—a novel that is about, but has not emerged from within, the working poor and Indigenous in Guatemala.[59] The value of these works—which seem a bit dry, are less stylized, and perhaps are perceived to be overly driven by a political message—may be in that their largest readership was among the working classes involved in popular movements. Written for them and perhaps retold in oral form back to working people, these books present an interesting subversion to a canon of accepted literary works. Almost every worker I interviewed remembered and identified with the narrative of work and life in the north coast as told in the story of *Prisión Verde*, the newspapers *Vanguardia Revolucionaria*, *Voz Obrera*, and the infamous "La Carta Rolston," which was published in *Vanguardia Revolucionaria* in 1949.[60]

Orality and the oral tradition are important in Honduras, first because the elite and the banana companies have dominated the official record, and second because schooling and literacy are twentieth-century phenomena that had not reached most working peoples of Honduras. Testimonio is still practiced in Honduras today. Examples include such lesser known works as Agapito Robleda Castro's memoirs of the 1954 strike in *La Verdad de la Huelga de 1954 y de la Formación del SITRATERCO* and Mario Benítez's account of his life in the north coast in *Nicomedes en los Bananales y las Tierras del Tío Sam*.[61]

Oral history, and its use as a primary source, differs quite significantly from testimonio literature. In testimonio, as John Beverly and others argue, the narrator can be the speaker and eyewitness for a community or group, thereby speaking for the collective memory of a people. Oral history, as a primary record, relies on a collection of memories from various narrators. It is a process of constructing a collective memory from individual memories of past events; it is an analysis of not merely what is said but rather the meanings and symbols constructed by people's own memories.[62] Oral histories written by scholars such as Marvin Barahona, Cindy Forster, Daniel James, Steve J. Stern, and Jeffrey L. Gould rely on contested sources, yet these sources are crucial, as they, in Horacio N. Roque Ramírez's words, "can produce political texts able to question institutions, and make public records of stories not privileged in dominant narratives."[63] This is certainly a necessity in the history of Central America, where civil war, US intervention, coups d'état and military governments have not valued archival sources or prioritized their maintenance but have often sought to destroy the historical record.[64]

Honduran historian Marvin Barahona provides examples of the use of oral histories as primary records. In *El Silencio Quedó Atrás*, which draws on (but keeps separate) both archival materials and oral histories gathered from the surviving members of the 1954 strike committee, Barahona tells the story of the strike and the political persecution of its leaders. His subsequent book *Memorias de un Comunista* also draws on the oral tradition, recounting the life history of one individual, Rigoberto Padilla Rush, a founder of the Communist Party in 1954.[65] Here he interweaves both archival and oral sources in a dynamic story of a political movement told through the eyes of the participant Padilla Rush.

The collection of oral histories allows not only for the corroboration of events by multiple narrators, but also a scrutiny of memory. An individual's collection of remembrances and the dialog among various individuals' remembrances make for a robust narrative that allows historians to tell a fuller story and give more information about history than previously available. Oral history collection also challenges the historian to evaluate an individual and a collective memory—how an individual worker sees himself/herself within the aggregate of workers and how collective beliefs are formed to represent a momentous period. For this study, collecting oral history was perhaps the best way to capture everyday workers' memories and accounts of their roles, and not just those of union leadership or party leaders. Also, oral history collection was perhaps the only way to uncover the hidden history of gender relationships and women's work on the north coast. While judicial records document the presence of women in the region, oral histories revealed the nuanced world of women workers.

Oral history as a primary source has been contested, primarily because of the challenges in verifying the memories of narrators. Alessandro Portelli's book *The Death of Luigi Trastulli* explores the gathering of oral history in Tierni, Italy, and Harlan, Kentucky, providing insights into the phenomenon of working-class collective memory.[66] For Portelli, what makes oral history different from other primary sources is that "memory is not a passive repository of facts but an active process of creation of meanings."[67] Historians learn not only from the collection of facts but also from the "narrators' effort to make sense of the past and to give a form to their lives, and set the interview and the narrative in their historical context."[68] In his research in Tierni, Portelli came across the story of the most-remembered event for the workers there: the death of a worker named Luigi Trastulli during a political protest in 1949.[69] It is *how* this event was remembered and the stories that workers told Portelli that are of use, and the same principle applies to the history of workers in Honduras.

First of all, in Tierni, there were police reports and newspaper accounts based on oral testimony that revealed competing narratives about what happened and how. These "strategies of official memory" are based on oral sources that are taken as hard facts when, effectively, they are just as faulty—if not more so—than the workers' memories.[70] Portelli discovers that the movement leaders were very precise about dates and focused on large national issues connected to the political party rather than workplace issues. Rank-and-file testimonies departed from these larger claims and were much more spontaneous and colorful, and they reflected, even if imprecisely, a collective memory of the death of Trastulli that also conflated it with another important event that affected the workers—massive layoffs in 1953.[71] In his search for the root of this conflation, Portelli explains, "The causes of this collective error must be sought, rather than in the event itself, in the meaning which it derived from the actors' state of mind at the time; from its relation to subsequent historical developments; and from the activity of memory and the imagination."[72]

Portelli interrogates this event to uncover the ways in which people remember, how they reorganize chronology to fit a collective memory of a symbolic event, and how the narrator places events and experiences in time and context in the larger collective memory—one that avoids defeat and demonstrates collective power. Portelli determines that memory "manipulates factual details" in three modes: (1) symbolic, where an event comes to represent another event in the working-class experience; (2) psychological, which allows the narrator to find healing; and (3) formal, where the oral histories shift the story to accommodate for time and space.

Using Portelli's framework in thinking about the 1954 strike on the north coast, we can deduce the following: For the workers of the north coast, the 1954 strike has been the single most important event in the twentieth century. For average workers who lived and endured it, the strike was transformative and became etched in their memories, perhaps in different ways than it was for organizers or activists. Workers who endured the 69-day strike against the Tela Railroad Company (11 days for those striking at the Standard Fruit Company plantations) remember it as a time of strife and suffering.

Initially there was excitement among workers, both men and women, when they spoke about the large number of workers on strike. But the sheer excitement quickly gave way to memories of suffering and hunger due to the company's refusal to yield. In the first days of the strike the workers were receiving donations of food and cattle from local Honduran merchants in company towns and San Pedro Sula, the largest city in the north coast. Toward the end of the strike, in the last weeks, workers waited in long lines to receive rations—first with beans, and then later just boiled green bananas on banana leaves, with coffee. In the early days of the strike, some male workers purchased food from *patronas* nearby, but toward the end they also ran out of money. This strife and sacrifice resulted in major changes to their wages and, ultimately, in company policies. Workers won rights that they had never before experienced, and everything in the *fincas* changed. Following Portelli's thinking, the "emblematic" narrative of the strike, the story is one of suffering, strife, and change, as well as excitement and even elation.[73] Rank-and-file workers and *patronas* remarked on the masses of people who participated in the strike, how they slept outside, hanging from their *hamacas* (hammocks) in the Ramón Rosa Park in El Progreso or the Campo Chula Vista in La Lima. This narrative is the "symbolic" memory manipulation that Portelli presents. This is the central theme in the memory of the strike for the everyday worker; it is part of the lore of the north coast.

For strike organizers and PDRH leaders such as Juan Bautista Canales, Teresina Rossi Matamoros, Julio C. Rivera, and local finca organizers such as Daniel Madrid Guevara, Agapito Robleda Castro, and

Sylvia Robleda—as well as others within the union movement—their memories are of strife and struggle, fear and repression, but ultimately of wonder that they were able to pull off such a well-organized strike, which successfully changed their lives and Honduras. In their interviews, they were concerned with setting the record straight about the work that was done to build the movement of workers, the effort to get workers out to strike, and the work to sustain the first Central Strike Committee as an independent entity.[74] They remark on how well workers observed the rules the Central Strike Committee imposed, that they did not drink or engage in violence, and how the vigilance committee maintained the peace and kept workers out of the workplace, making the strike a success.

While these two sets of oral histories—those of the rank-and-file and those of the leadership and organizers—both consider the event as monumental in their lives and for the north coast, symbolically the strike represented different things to these two groups. People rationalized what happened differently according to their personal involvement, their role in the strike, and the violence they faced after the event. While rank-and-file workers not intimately connected to the leadership cadre may have gone back to work with some notable improvements in pay and company comportment, many of the leaders were persecuted, incarcerated, or exiled, their agency obscured from history.

The second point Portelli highlights in the manipulation of memory is the psychological aspect of workers' collective memory, which attempts to make sense of what happened and the differences "between the official motives of the protest and the initial motives of the workers that attended."[75] On the north coast, this inconsistency in remembrances is evident in the memories of the details of the strike's organizing and leadership. Party leaders and strike committees shared a great deal about changes in who occupied the various leadership positions and how workers were led during the strike and in later days. Workers, on the other hand, conflated various entities and people and generally shared a relatively untainted and idyllic view of those details. Leaders' and organizers' interviews reflected a preoccupation with the complexities of these events and a desire to set the record straight, challenging the emblematic narrative of the strike.[76]

The last consideration Portelli offers in memory as history is what he calls a formal mode, whereby a "horizontal shifting of the event endows it with an adequate time-marking function" upon which workers' memory hinges.[77] Important events and memories become markers of time and chronology in people's memories—moments that are vividly etched in people's minds and around which others are centered. In thinking about the 1954 strike in Honduras, all workers, including the PDRH organizers, arranged their memories, life stories, and narratives in two epochs—before the 1954 strike and after. For instance, before the strike, work was inhumane and perilous; after the strike, conditions and wages improved. Jeff Gould, who studies organizing among agricultural workers in Nicaragua, found that in retelling the story of Nicaraguan campesinos, they "reconstructed their past by using two distinct sets of oppositions: before and after the agro-export boom and before and after the revolution."[78]

As Portelli observes, it is not merely whether the recollections are fact or truth but rather how the workers organize them collectively that tells us about not only the event but the tensions and negotiations within it. As Portelli reminds us, "The discrepancy between fact and memory ultimately enhances the value of the oral sources as historical documents. It is not caused by faulty recollections . . . but actively and creatively generated by memory and imagination in an effort to make sense of crucial events and of history in general."[79] Without these sometimes-contradictory narratives about the 1954 strike we would know less about the tensions and negotiations that transpired.

I conducted my oral history gathering using a snowball method. First I went to existing organizations: the unions Sindicato de Trabajadores de la Tela Railroad Company (SITRATERCO; Tela Railroad Company Workers Union) and Sindicato de Trabajadores de la Standard Fruit Company (SUTRASFCO; Standard Fruit Company Workers Union); nonprofits such as Coordinadora de Sindicatos Bananeros y Agroindustriales de Honduras (COSIBAH; Coalition of Banana and Agroindustrial Unions of Honduras) FESTAGRO (Federation of Agro-Industry Unions); now called Centro de Derechos de la Mujer (Center of Women's Rights); Comité de Jubilados (Committee of Retirees) in La Lima and El Progreso; Radio Progreso and Equipo de Reflexión, Investigacion, Comunicación y Acción (ERIC; Team for Reflection, Investigation, and Training), as well as well-known scholars, such as Barahona and Posas. Once I introduced my project, and myself, I was given some ideas of whom I might interview. Once I contacted or interviewed people, I asked them for other recommendations, people who might still be alive from that era. I also attended union meetings and gatherings, where I was able to collect names and addresses for potential interviewees. Sometimes I was able to find a place to sit and talk to the person; other times I made an appointment to visit them at home.

When I did make an appointment to visit their homes I tried to set our appointments between meal times; households were poor, and I did not want to eat food that could have been for the interviewee's family. When they did offer food or drink I accepted gladly, as is Honduran custom. When I knocked on workers' doors to ask if I could interview them about the strike and their lives, many said yes because they wanted to "help me with my project." Many of the workers did not interrupt their daily routine while they talked to me. Olimpia Edelmira Figueroa, for instance, cooked an entire meal throughout our first interview, frying chicken and potatoes and cooking rice for her grandchildren's lunch. I interviewed Doña Lidia Aurora Lezama on the last bus from El Progreso to her home in the campo, in the outlying regions between El Progreso and Tela. We were interrupted periodically by the bus driver's assistant asking us to pay our fee, and by local acquaintances of Doña Lidia stopping to greet her. Interruptions were the norm during these interviews; daughters and sons wanted to share their stories, remembering how they originally learned them. Other interruptions were related to the work the interviewees were doing, and for frequent pauses to have a drink, *un fresco*, to quench their thirst in the stale heat of the banana regions.

The interviews were long and emotionally charged. Our initial discussions were superficial, but courtesy and basic demographic questions eventually gave way to meaty and dense conversation. The stories my interlocutors told began with the usual local lore about the 1954 strike, recounted in general terms. Then our conversations went deep into their archived memories. Narrators eventually lost track of what they were doing, focusing more and more on the stories they were telling, stretching to remember dates but confident that the story they told was what they experienced. When I asked about something that they did not live or witness, they said they did not know.

The stories became more and more an act of "testifying," as Roque Ramírez observed in his work "A Living Archive of Desire." Marginalized groups' "testimonios about their existence are critical acts of documentation," for them as much as for the recorder or historian.[80] Most of the narrators who inform this manuscript *wanted* to speak to me; in fact, workers were eager to tell their stories and almost all chose to use their real names.[81] Workers told me their personal experiences as a form of proof that they had witnessed a great event. Many times they told their stories disjointedly and perhaps out of order, with distractions that took us through the more exciting parts first, leaving us to explore the rest of the details later, often with my prodding. Their testimonies, if one were to listen to them, may seem to be random conversations like any other, with no special narrative, starting point, or end. But careful scrutiny unveils the geography of memory logically attached to what they knew best: work and a desire and motivation to act for better wages.

These oral histories then surface as an important "living archive of evidence" that can be utilized to amplify the voices of the north-coast workers who may have fallen outside the margins of the government, the elite, and their official records.[82] Worker stories do not just fill in the blanks left by the absence of written records; instead, they actually shift the course of history-making and the interpretation of the archives that are in existence. As Roque Ramírez found in the story of Teresita, a transgender woman in San Francisco, the testimonies become "narratives of opposition," those that cannot be silenced and insist on being told.[83] As Ramírez observed of his heroine, oral testimony became a "tool for telling history."[84]

The oral testimony of María Antonia Perla, a worker I met at the retired workers committee in La Lima, Cortés, articulates the need to construct history in this way: "Es la historia de mi vida . . . y mis hijos en el futuro, aunque no tenga [lleve] mi nombre, [la lean y] digan, se parece a la historia de mi mamá" (It is the story of my life . . . even if it does not bear my name, someday my children will [read it and say] it resembles my mother's story).[85] My exploration of workers' memories of the strike has contributed profoundly to my understanding of the strike, and this book seeks to share what I found and what I believe banana workers wanted to share.

HAUNTED

Workers' stories were so intense that I became haunted by them, consumed by workers' stories, their lives, and their losses. So many of the people included in this narrative have already passed. I have come to understand that the loss of those who are now dead, whom I could not interview and whose stories may not be told, will weigh on me for a long time. What it might have been like in 1954 tugged at me when I visited the banana region as the company was dismantling the barracones (worker barracks) and moving people out of the campos in 2004 and 2006. A piece of history was disappearing right before my eyes. There, people's entire lives were disappearing with those broken slats of wood, stories that would never be told. As an insider and a Honduran, I observed these situations with familiarity and pain. As an outsider, a scholar trained in the United States, I had a certain anonymity that also brought immense loneliness and memories of loss of country and a more distant, objective recognition of change. Honduras had changed and I missed it all. In many ways I realized that this was also a search for self and "the country under my skin."[86]

ROOTS OF RESISTANCE, CHAPTER BY CHAPTER

An important goal of this book is to offer readers a bottom-up view of the strike and the seminal period of Honduran history that followed. Chapter 1, "Intersecting Projects: Contested Visions for the North Coast," provides historical and political context for the rest of the book. It traces the history of the Central American region within Latin American historiography and in relationship to US empire and local elites who may have colluded with the banana companies. Chapter 2, "Revolutionary Antecedents to the 1954 Strike: Liberals, Rebels, and Radicals," details the various efforts that led leftists and workers to organize the north coast, to build a national labor movement and challenge US hegemony in the region; this chapter also analyzes the political backdrop to the strike—namely, the beginning of the Cold War in Central America. Based almost entirely on oral histories, chapter 3, "Life and Labor in the Banana Fincas," tells of the grueling work of harvesting bananas through the eyes of formal agricultural workers, the campeños. I describe labor-camp living arrangements and workers' perceptions of one another and the work, and I highlight the compañerismo (camaraderie) among laborers, which helped organize the strike and build the culture of resistance with national implications. Chapter 4, "The Making of a Campeño and Campeña Culture: Race, Gender, and Resistance," delves into the ways in which the company and the work schedule, leisure time, and workers' relationships to women shaped masculinity and race, and vice versa. Looking at the consumption of alcohol and prostitution, the chapter illustrates the forging of a north-coast culture and campeño/a identity, critical to organizing both the strike and resistance to company control. Chapter 5, "'Mujeres que cuidaban hombres y vendedoras ambulantes': Gendered Roles and Informal Work on the North Coast," provides a never-before-told history of the pioneering women cooks and street vendors, critical lynchpins in the workers' communities between workers and company control. I create an original portrait of the informal economy by exploring the lives of women workers—including cooks, vendors, kitchen helpers, street vendors, and sex workers. Chapter 6, "¡La Gran Huelga del 1954!

Labor Organizing in the Banana Labor Camps," details the day-to-day actions in the banana camps leading up to the strike and the growing swell of workers that supported the strike, including women, across the north coast, resulting in the largest worker mobilization in Honduras in the twentieth century. I also discuss the influence of various political parties and organizations on workers' efforts to organize a union, the contradictions they confronted as the strike unfolded, and the impact of company interests via actions from the US Embassy that redirected the outcome of the strike. And to conclude, chapter 7, "Contemporary Movement Leaders Reflect on the Legacy of the 1954 Strike," explores how recent generations and social movements remember and utilize the memory of the strike as a symbolic and generative moment in Honduran history, which might inform both the content and direction of their organizing. These new movements, led by social actors who do not conform to traditional gender and race scripts, roles, and norms of the past, deploy memories learned from oral traditions in their current contexts.

As of this writing, Honduras is in the throes of struggle in the prolonged aftermath of the coup d'état of 2009, which has been marked with egregious injustices and human rights violations. Ten years later, there is an exodus of migrants steadily leaving Honduras for the north, because the north coast now "is uninhabitable," they say. As this refugee crisis unfolds right on US soil, the borderlands, I cannot help but think about the immigrants that were so useful to the US banana companies in their heyday in Honduras—the same immigrants who tamed and organized bold and powerful labor movements despite repression.

CHAPTER I

INTERSECTING PROJECTS

CONTESTED VISIONS FOR
THE NORTH COAST

The United Fruit Company
reserved for itself the most juicy
piece, the central coast of my world,
the delicate waist of America.

PABLO NERUDA[1]

The north coast of Honduras has been the site of negotiation among US investors, successive Honduran governments and national elites, and campesinos and banana workers throughout much of the twentieth century. Traditional scholarly accounts of the north coast have commonly focused on the hegemony of the foreign banana companies, a top-down analysis that often silences the voices of workers and obfuscates their role in the construction of the labor movement, and thus have only explored part of the story of the construction of the nation. Banana workers were critical to challenging the US companies' agenda in the region, exploitative company labor policies, and the role of the US State Department and its support of the banana companies.[2] Workers clamored for better working and living conditions in their daily lives; these claims reverberated in national appeals and their demands resonated beyond the banana groves and local interests to varied industries.

The evolution of the north coast is best described as a site of overlapping intersections, where state projects, capitalist interests, worker and campesino interests, and ideologies roll over and grate against each other. At one end of the ideological spectrum, the interests of liberal reformers and foreign investors converged in the north coast to create conditions that were favorable to foreign-inspired agro-export and transnational capital development. The partial alignment of the US economic expansionist agenda with that of the liberal reformers[3] during the early twentieth century facilitated the development of the north-coast banana empire. At the other end of the spectrum, worker-led organizations, including the PDRH and the Communist Party, engaged in building the labor movement to challenge capitalist development on the backs of the poorest campesino migrants in the banana regions. Between these poles, domestic small-scale growers and others elided by a government that favored big companies in the first half of the twentieth century found common ground with agricultural, railroad, and port workers in the banana industry who sought to improve their own working conditions. A booming informal economy sustained the foreign companies and workers in the areas surrounding the banana enclaves, where campeños and campeñas formed a part of an ethnically and racially diverse working class with an identity that engendered multiple forms of resistance to capitalist control and other adverse conditions. Looming large over all these actors was the emergence of US-driven Cold War politics and US State Department intervention in multiple sites of contestation.

An examination of the interplay of these multiple projects illustrates the relations between the Honduran state, the banana companies, and labor. The company's need for an ample supply of workers to support the industry attracted significant labor migration to the north coast, from other areas of Honduras and El Salvador, as well as from throughout Caribbean.[4] Along with this worker migration came a rise in the number of merchants who set up shop on the north coast.[5] With the population growth in the region, the experiences and struggles of banana workers became central to the discourse surrounding modernity and development in the north coast, as well as the discussion of Honduran national identity.

This migration of laborers forms the backdrop for the construction of the labor movement. The labor organizing that emerged in the north coast from 1912 to 1954 was radical and militant. The labor conditions and misery in which workers lived made the region a prime target for organizing. Political parties also sought these workers' votes, and the region would eventually become contested territory between Marxists and the main electoral parties: the Liberal Party and the Nationalist Party. From these origins, and in the face of harsh repression, labor organizing persevered, informed by practices reflective of a unique heritage that originated in the north coast and the banana lands.

First, organizing tactics embraced a clandestine militancy that emerged in response to severe repression of workers, including extremely poor working conditions, daily company surveillance of workers and worker leaders, and interference and manipulation in workers' lives. Second, leadership emerged from workers' ranks, building a worker-led movement in opposition to the US capitalist enterprise. Third, workers' actions determined an organizing strategy that targeted the United Fruit Company (UFCo) and Standard Fruit Company not only as fitting proxies for the US state but also notably as a means, an interim step, toward larger demands and transformative goals, including quests to recuperate land through land reform and, ultimately, to achieve a more democratic government. An analysis of the interstices and intersections of these divergent interests, and their contested claims, shows the north coast to be a unique and important region in the development of radical politics in Honduras.

This chapter is a partial introduction to the historical and political context for the rest of the book. It offers a sketch of the north coast's evolution from an underdeveloped rainforest conceptualized as the "tropics" in the US frontier narrative, to a banana empire, to the locus of the nation's liberal dream, to a contested political arena, and finally to the site and symbol of struggle for thousands of workers. Of course, the path was not entirely linear; rather, these intentions and developments overlapped, diverged, and intersected at different moments in time. But together they paved the way for the strike of 1954—an antecedent to future movements and an important marker in the historical memory of organizers in the region and the country, despite its exclusion from the official national history.

THE NORTH-COAST GARIFUNA
AND INDIGENOUS ROOTS

Indigenous people have inhabited the north coast since before the colonial period, yet during the nineteenth and early twentieth centuries the territory was considered virtually unpopulated. The region has been written into history books as the land of swamps, with no inhabitants, least of all Indigenous ones, and if there were references to Indigenous peoples, they were represented as nonproductive members of society. In the view of foreigners, in line with the analysis of Honduran liberal elites, its primary value lay in the potential ports of Puerto Cortés and Trujillo. The large stretches of land in between them were considered uninhabited and "savage."[6] Foreign surveyors and liberal reformers[7] coincided in their analysis: the north coast lacked "modernity" and was "unexplored."[8] The north coast has thus been imagined from the outside by travelers, and from the inside by Hondurans, as a land free for the taking.

This narrative, reproduced by Honduran mestizos and foreigners alike, effectively erased the well-established Afro-Indigenous Garifuna population that arrived beginning in 1797, and the Miskitus, Pech, and Tolupanes who inhabited not just the coast but also the mountains towering beyond El Progreso and La Ceiba, and who farmed and fished near rivers and the ocean.[9] An entire coastal culture thrived among Garifuna communities, but the area was and has been mostly ignored by the state, which did not invest in developing any infrastructure there. State interest and engagement came first in the port cities in the early twentieth century, and then later with banana companies in the 1920s on the mainland, though John Soluri notes that Bay Island banana production was thriving by 1880, and a large portion of the population of Roatán was Garifuna.[10] From the start, the state—and the banana companies—sought to dominate the territory for their own national agenda, to the exclusion of Indigenous interests.

Ultimately, state engagement with the north coast resulted in the absorption of the Garifuna people into the banana export economy. In the early part of the twentieth century, the government granted to UFCo, Vaccaro Brothers and Company (later Standard Fruit Company), and Cuyamel Fruit Company access to land in the north coast with significant populations of Garifuna communities. Indications of racialized interactions among these historical actors were already apparent in these days. UFCo recruited Black workers, who were perceived to be "stronger" and able to resist the maladies of the tropical climate. Among these Black workers, Garifuna workers were perceived to be "exceptional" workers "despite their [B]lackness,"[11] a view held by foreigners that clashed with mestizo conceptions of Garifuna communities. Honduran mestizos in the mid-twentieth century described Black workers, perceived to be Garifuna, as "lazy" and "slow." Both of these racialized views of Black and Garifuna workers, those of the American companies and those of the mestizos, coexisted in the region and explain differences in racial understandings constructed in the north coast. Notably, both of these essentialist perceptions were useful to banana companies and their empire. The Standard Fruit Company and its diverse local industries also hired Garifuna workers, mostly men, in the docks and some women primarily in the production of palm products for their vegetable oil factory.[12] Garifuna women also worked in the informal industry cooking and selling food in the Standard Fruit Company regions well into the 1960s.[13] Dr. Luther Castillo Harry, a Garifuna leader, reflects that in his hometown of Tocamacho, east of the Bajo Aguán region, elders told him stories of how they migrated as young men to work, at least for a stint, in the banana fields of what at that time, possibly in the 1920s and 1930s, was the Aguán Valley Company, a subsidiary of the Standard Fruit Company.[14] Some retired there and never came back to the community.

> There are these elders of the generation of my grandfather, Patricio Suazo, and Don Colón, who migrated to work in the banana companies [and region]. In my own case my grandmother, her younger brother, Pablo Palacio, worked in the banana fields and retired there. You would find that many Garifuna families lived in Palo Alto, Palo Verde, Coyoles Central. During that period the only way to find a job was for people to migrate to the banana regions, and that is why we see so many Garifunas who were actually born in the banana regions. My [other] grandmother lived there with her adoptive father, Patricio Fuentes; he worked for the banana companies, so she was raised in the banana regions for a long time. When my mother was small, my grandmother took her to live in Palo Alto, and then Palo Verde, there near Coyoles Central; they knew those communities.[15]

Garifuna and Black migrants broke ground as builders and workers of new plantations in the region of Costa Arriba, working for banana companies. Once the bananeras dominated the region, the land and lives of the Garifuna people were inexorably altered. But they still retained their own community interests and aspirations, some in alignment with other workers and north-coast inhabitants. They passed down, through oral traditions, stories of survival and organizing while employed by the foreign-owned enclaves. They also told stories of migration, as many working in company shipyards and on schooners were able to travel, generating long-standing social networks of Garifuna migration.[16]

POQUITEROS

In the early 1880s, well before UFCo and the Standard Fruit Company were the main draw for laborers, local poquiteros[17] (small-scale planters) were already employing handfuls of locals and cultivating bananas in the north coast, and workers "suitable for agricultural work" were migrating there.[18] These landowners and small-scale producers dominated banana production and sales to US company-owned schooners. Poquiteros sustained a local trade economy and a local labor force. By the turn of the century, the north coast boasted 30,000 inhabitants and a "floating population" functioning as a reserve army of labor.[19] According to Soluri, male workers were coming to the swamps of the north coast to work in either logging or banana cultivation as peons. This points to labor migration from the interior or Garifuna villages to work in the pre–UFCo banana zones of the poquiteros. Thus there was not only an existing banana trade in the region but also a preexisting, seasonal labor migration. A US consul described "four kinds of ethnic laborers, including *Garífunas* [*sic*], two Indigenous groups of Honduran Mosquitia,"[20] and described the largest group as the "common 'mozo' or peon of the interior."[21] The "peon of the interior" probably refers to a mestizo but may have also been an Indigenous person from the interior.

Recovering Indigenous peoples' history in Honduras is still a project with many gaps, and original inhabitants are completely unincorporated into accounts of the early Honduran national liberal project. However, their practices and land usage—namely, for growing bananas and coconut—undoubtedly influenced the region. Soluri notes that US schooners would stop by ports, such as the island of Roatán and Omoa on the mainland, to purchase bananas and coconuts from local producers, whose methods resembled a subsistence economy using agricultural practices that may have been Indigenous to the region but were absorbed by international trade. Plantation density and land ownership was reflective of local needs, though major income of local producers was generated by trading with US merchant schooners.[22] The landowners in the mainland who operated on communal lands (*ejidos*) were most likely caudillos (charismatic strong men, land owners) linked to the liberal elite and local government structures. Antonio Canelas Díaz found that many of the poquiteros from the southern department of Olancho who enlisted Garifuna workers in the mainland were often tricked due to their illiteracy and alcohol consumption when it came to signing contracts with the Standard Fruit, often losing everything or owing everything.[23]

In a short period, however, at the behest of government and elite actors, the country then began a fast transition from a "society of mostly craftsmen (*artesanos*) [and] campesinos, where the predominant work was local and familial" to an economy based on "foreign capital investment that rushed a national process of development to establish the agro-export economy and forced the country to mold itself to world market needs."[24] During the initial period of land concessions, the Honduran government attempted to control the parceling of land in alternate blocks. Distinct regions of the country, including largely campesino economies and parcel holders, were not all ready for (or even necessarily supportive of) the liberal reforms. The 1895 Agrarian Law stipulated that "land use would be conceded in alternating lots to those who made a commitment to exploit them, one for the beneficiary and another one that the government would either retain or sell."[25] For instance, plots of land for banana cultivation were distributed to Honduran planters, as well as the banana companies, in a checkered pattern along the north coast.[26] The government's intention was to secure trade for domestic producers, while simultaneously allowing for foreign investment. The banana companies, however, obtained land illicitly by either buying out the poquiteros or ousting them from production by not purchasing their product and forcing the local planters to sell cheaply. Domestic Honduran planters and even some Honduran government interests, at least publicly, often protested when huge land areas or control over territory was ceded to the companies.[27]

In one case, local landowners attempted a legal defense to keep their land in Villanueva, Cortés; Nicomedes Fajardo sued Samuel Zemurray, and his associates, in a case that spanned almost 20 years to annul the sale contract of over 504 acres of land (300 hectares).[28] Fajardo was acting tutor for the children of Justo Pineda, a local landowner of the area known as "El Valle," land to the south of the Ulúa River, who under unclear circumstances "sold" a reduced number of acres in 1910. By 1917, there were three sale transfers of larger acreage between well-known landowners and Cuyamel Fruit Company business associates, including Zemurray himself, ending in a final transfer to the Compañía Bananera de Santiago.[29] Although the record is in poor condition and incomplete, the case demonstrates the power of the landed elite in the region and the opposing persistence of Hondurans to fight land theft utilizing the local court system. The men named in this case, including would-be president Juan Manuel Gálvez, an attorney for the banana barons before running for office, also appears in the list of business partners Zemurray worked with in Honduras—allowing him to own land to plant in Honduras and evade taxes in the United States.[30]

The transfers of land among landed elites created a smokescreen to hide the owner, Zemurray, who never presented himself to the court or answered evidence presented by Fajardo, despite court orders. These owners were not concerned about this case or local court orders; in fact, Luis Melara, Zemurray's lawyer, did not seem to appear at all in the court records, allowing Leonardo Romero to appear instead as owner of the Compañía Bananera de Santiago, represented by Juan Manuel Gálvez.[31] Fajardo, the accusing attorney, charged them of stalling the case, which lasted well into 1922 without a favorable result for the local landholder.[32] This case shows the power and privilege of transnational bananera investors, with the support of Honduran liberals and elites, over local and Indigenous claims to land and entitlements. Many local banana producers would ultimately suffer under the collaboration of Honduran elites and the banana companies during the liberal reform period and well into the concessionary period in the early twentieth century.

US CAPITAL AND EXPANSIONIST AMBITIONS

The north coast first caught the attention of US business and political interests as a potential interoceanic route between the Caribbean and the Pacific in the 1850s, and subsequently as a potential investment site for export companies in the 1880s. Portrayed as a potential trade route that would reduce distances between the Atlantic and the Pacific Oceans, the isthmus acquired notoriety in mid-nineteenth century.[33] By 1899, banana companies had established successful operations in places like Colombia, Costa Rica, Cuba, Venezuela, Ecuador, and Guatemala, and they came to Honduras hoping to find pristine, disease-free land that was near waterways. But Central America and the banana fruit entered the US imagination long before the arrival of banana companies in 1899.[34]

Various travel narratives dating from as early as 1854 through the 1970s maintained a facile analysis of the north coast, which invariably depicted the region as a dangerous and raw environment where malaria, yellow fever, and dysentery represented hazards to personal health. At the same time, these narratives noted the region's available and fertile land, awaiting US ingenuity and imagination, which would later materialize in the form of industrial advances brought to the region by UFCo.[35] Travel authors remarked on the politically unstable governments and the threat of disease as major drawbacks to investment in Honduran territory. At the same time, the promotions presented a stimulating challenge for some investors who believed US ingenuity could conquer all.

Ephraim George Squier, a New York businessman, was one of the first US investors to write about Honduras in 1854 in order to persuade other investors and politicians of its strategic location for an interoceanic canal.[36] Squier had attempted to build an interoceanic route in Honduras between the Atlantic and the Pacific Oceans, devising an elaborate journey by land and water.[37] He enticed US investors by claiming that Honduras "has artificial wants, and no winter to provide against or to interrupt [building] . . . labors."[38] Although Squier's proposal ultimately did not succeed, his view of the country prevailed. Squier's idealized descriptions of Honduras "led to a romantic tradition of viewing Honduras as a kind of Garden of Eden, with inhabitants as innocents."[39] His views of the people of Honduras as languid and "vacuous" served to represent the "tropics" as open land ready for the taking by "industrious" and modern businessmen.[40]

By the 1880s, the potential trade route attracted adventurers, transient entrepreneurs and soldiers of fortune looking to get rich quick after the California Gold Rush and the failed exploits of westward expansion in the United States. Notions that Hondurans did not have a domestic industry that exploited their own natural resources served as further justifications for US presence and investment. For US private investors, portrayals of the north coast as pristine, undeveloped, and available supported claims that the "unexplored" territory could be transformed into productive, useful land. Those in the United States who read travel accounts conceptualized Honduras as either a "primitive paradise" with "untapped and unclaimed wealth"[41] or a dangerous and disease-ridden, barbaric place. Indeed, US conceptions of the "tropics" were useful in building and justifying the banana empire at the turn of the century.

North Americans traveled south to the newfound "tropics," many aboard the ships of UFCo in the early 1900s, for adventure, to determine business possibilities, or to observe with fascination as US companies extracted raw materials from Honduran mines.[42] Journalist Richard Harding Davis in his 1896 account of his adventures[43] renders a fascinating portrayal of the "tropics" as a mesmerizing place of possibility, notwithstanding the "sleepiness" of its people, the lack of industry, and an unfortunate predisposition for war and revolution.[44] Davis similarly presented the country as backward and uncivilized and therefore available to enterprising, industrious foreigners who could make this land more productive:

There is no more interesting question of the present day than that of what is to be done with the world's land which is lying unimproved; whether it shall go to the great power that is willing to turn it to account, or remain with its original owner, who fails to understand its value. The Central-Americans are like a gang of semi-barbarians in a beautifully furnished house, of which they can understand neither its possibilities of comfort nor its use. They are dogs in the manger among nations. Nature has given to their country great pasture-lands, wonderful forests of rare woods and fruits, treasures of silver and gold and iron, and soil rich enough to supply the world with coffee, and it only waits for the honest effort to make it the natural highways of traffic from every portion of the globe.[45]

By using this phrase, "dog in a manger," Davis means to say that Hondurans were wasting space and resources by not allowing access to others, like US industry, who would know better how use it.[46] The use of the dehumanizing term "barbarian" is also a justification and a call for more civilized industry.

A writer commissioned by UFCo, Frederick Upham Adams, cited political instability as the reason, and perhaps fear, for the lack of exploitation of the "wonderful tropical resources" of the region.[47] But by 1912, US investors, businessmen, capital speculators from Washington, and soldiers of fortune, along with Honduran elites, had begun to transform the north coast into a vast and dominant banana-export empire.[48] With easy access to Caribbean trade routes, in close proximity to the US ports, the north coast drew the attention of US entrepreneurs, who traded with local banana producers to expand their profits by selling tropical fruits in the United States.

Morrow Wilson in 1947, Galo Plaza and Stacy May in 1958, and John Melville in 1976 all believed that achieving modernity in the "tropics" could only be achieved by changing the terrain and incorporating the "modern" practices that US businessmen and steamship companies would bring.[49] This American exceptionalism would continue until well into the twentieth century. US American narratives about Honduras can be read as "racial projects of US imperialism" during the first half of the twentieth century that reflect an ideology that conceives of the region as languid "tropics" complete with docile inhabitants, undoubtedly a counterdiscourse to the fearsome tales of political instability, violence, and civil wars.[50] Such depictions in travel narratives served two purposes: they alerted US investors to the possibility and feasibility of business investment, and they reinforced both the Honduran elite's fear of the north coast and their own racial assumptions. They also reinforced the belief that outside investment was the only way to bring development to Honduras, and particularly the unruly north coast.

The travel narratives and US travelers' portrayals of Honduras also provided racial and ideological characterizations of the north coast embraced by the Honduran elite in the capital, who were themselves wary of the north coast, and who looked to foreign companies to develop the region both economically and culturally.[51] Honduran elites mostly resided in the capital of Tegucigalpa, and they had sought to invest in mining projects near the capital, expecting these would industrialize the rest of the country.[52] They were slow to turn their gaze toward the north coast as an engine to drive development nationwide or to recognize the potential of the region as a center of a Honduran export economy. Thus the focus of the domestic elite investing class remained in Tegucigalpa, as a robust north-coast economy developed under control of foreign-owned companies and their complex cultural and political interests in the region. The western gaze of "tropical Honduras" gave way to the banana companies building their empire. Honduran liberals opened the path for the companies.

LIBERAL HOPES AND DREAMS FACILITATE THE RISE OF THE BANANA

Prior to the 1870s, Honduran politicians urged caution against foreign investors from the United States. Two-term Honduran President José Santos Guardiola (1856–1862), known for regaining control of the Bay Islands from the British Empire and for the capture of William Walker, issued a protectionist statement against Squier's plan for complete control of the proposed Honduran canal that would give free passage to US citizens and company employees.[53] Concerned about overreliance on or excessive concessions to foreign investors, President Guardiola in 1854 alerted the nation's legislators and representatives: "Be cautious, after all; keep in mind the example of Mexico, Texas and California; if there are Hondurans that ignore it, let them learn from travelers, and let them seek out information in the newspapers about the luck that befell those unfortunate peoples."[54] Guardiola refers to the US-Mexico War and Mexico's loss of its northernmost territories to the United States. He warned that the United States had their own interests in mind in taking over Honduran territory.

But these views gave way to the liberal reform period, beginning in 1876 with the election of Marco Aurelio Soto (1876–1883), during which liberal reformers engaged in and promoted capitalist economic development in order to build the nation. Following in the steps of their elite Guatemalan counterparts attempting to seek national unity and reform, Honduran liberal reformers also had plans for the north coast.[55] Reforms came laden with homogenizing projects, including the construction of a railroad system that would end the region's isolation and integrate the country's disparate provinces. The era of the "liberal dream" opened the doors to the rise of the banana-export economy and capitalist industry, dominated by foreigners, in what Mahoney calls an "aborted liberalism."[56] The intention of the liberal reformers was to develop an internal infrastructure and to end the warring among political factions through industry, transportation, and modernizing and developing a strong economy. The reality was that the foreign-owned companies retained the advantage and carried out their own agenda for profits, which did not advance Honduras's national development.

While liberal reforms had already taken place elsewhere in Central America—namely, Guatemala and Costa Rica—Honduras languished under a system of regionalism and a leadership preoccupied with local caudillo infighting rather than with building national consensus and instituting reforms.[57] President Soto and his cousin Ramón Rosa (1876–1883), who acted as General Minister during Soto's presidency, drew inspiration for liberal reforms while serving in the Guatemalan government.[58] Soto and Rosa saw the reforms as the only way to expand the Honduran national economy and enter into modern trade networks. Liberal reformers believed that modernity in governing would set the stage for industrialization and that this would be possible through the development of an agrarian export economy.[59] The urgency to find a new export crop to rescue the economy was fueled by a drop in sales of the country's main exports, cochineal and indigo, as chemical dyes were introduced in Europe. Soto focused on the economic reform agenda while Rosa developed the ideological and political philosophy platform that would expand their liberal reform ideals.[60] Rosa, Soto, and later President Luis Bográn (1883–1891) promoted liberal reforms and opened the door to foreign capital.

In 1876, Soto's administration issued a set of far-reaching legal reforms that aimed toward building an economy that would compete in the emerging world market.[61] "He revamped budgetary processes; secularized marriages and cemeteries; developed a system of free public primary education; formulated civil, penal, military, commercial, mining, legal, and customs codes; and attempted to centralize control of the military."[62] These reforms, Soto thought, would form the groundwork to expand his political power and bring "modernity," defined essentially as a nationwide rail and road system, governmental reforms in primary and middle school education for its citizens, and an overall prioritization of free markets.[63] Note that underlying this concept of modernity was the racial construction of an indo-Hispanic nation and mestizo subject as citizen. Soto wanted to guarantee that campesinos would get access to a family plot of land, at low cost, for those who planted sugar, coffee, or other crops specified by the government.[64] With no way of distributing land to campesinos, the Soto government left the task of distribution of land to local municipalities. Ultimately, the initiative resulted in little change in land ownership, yet it also encumbered the local municipalities with labor issues, as workers were to be paid for their work.[65]

By 1899, Nicanor Bolet Peraza, a Honduran delegate to the International Business Congress in Philadelphia, openly encouraged attendees to do business in Honduras.[66] Bolet Peraza tried to assure potential investors that civil wars were the result of internal factions and that foreign investors had nothing to fear. He presented a capitalist opportunity: Hondurans were harming their own business interests within the interior of the country, "leaving foreigners as exclusive owners of the industrial field." He went on to tell the assembled businessmen that the Honduran government "respects and protects them and the revolutionaries do not attempt to bother them."[67] Foreign capitalists were encouraged to invest and were invited to develop their businesses without reservation, and they were given access to the country and control of national assets, including transportation, customs processes, and ports.

In 1901, Honduran delegates to the Pan-American Exposition in Buffalo were impressed with US forms of agriculture. Upon the delegates' return to Honduras, both the Minister of the Interior and local elites concluded that an export economy with the foreign aid of the United States would help develop an agricultural infrastructure in Honduras. This echoed the aspirations of earlier liberal project reformers, Rosa and Soto. The notion that exporting agricultural commodities would develop local infrastructure was reasonable, since at the time, in the early 1900s, most of the banana growers and producers were Hondurans and members of the local petite bourgeoisie, who would benefit from expanded trade and an international market. Liberals hoped that the export economy of bananas would lead to the advancement and development of a larger export economy, including domestic producers.[68]

This partial alignment of liberal reformers' goals and US economic expansionism would be a portentous one, and a model that would be repeated throughout Latin America. The Honduran state project, the companies' capitalist interests, and US corporate expansionism, along with worker and anti-imperialist efforts, intersected in meaningful ways during the first half of the century in Honduras to influence the country's development.

CAUDILLOS AND REGIONALISM THWART THE LIBERAL DREAM

At the turn of the century, Honduras lacked a national railroad, and roads outside of the capital were virtually nonexistent. This lack of infrastructure contributed to a lack of communication and transportation within and between three distinct, autonomous regions in the country: the western region, the capital city and central-southern territories, and a third area that would effectively become the north-coast banana regions and ports. This regionalism led to competing local and parochial interests, fomented civil wars, left the country without a shared infrastructure, and lent itself to the creation of caudillo nuclei within each of the regions, which hindered the consolidation of the nation and the development of political structure and political parties. Political interests revolved around regional issues and seemed tepidly concerned with building a national cohesive government.[69] The liberals believed that the local caudillo structure would assist in consolidating the nation. Caudillos, however, sometimes acted in opposition to liberal reforms and on behalf of their own regional economic and political interests, building their "alternative network[s] of rural political power."[70]

Geographic and physical space also challenged the liberal reformers' plans to develop agricultural exports. They simply lacked the money to bridge the gaps and distances—physical and conceptual—across the nation. The regional divide demonstrates the ways in which national politics seldom managed to penetrate regional interests and vice versa, creating a disjointed nation that struggled to consolidate its national identity among competing interests. This gave the capital centralized power, but it also gave distinct regions the ability to challenge central power or to simply ignore it. The efforts to consolidate a national identity thus did not come from a central power, such as the capital, but would later emerge from the bottom up, in the form of striking workers.

The tripartite geographical divide, the liberal quest for a capitalist economy, and the void created by a lack of national groups to challenge a nation of oligarchs or to impede the domination of international interests all contributed to a weak central government unable to enforce economic policy and protect its sovereignty and interests. At the same time, Honduran government officials and the elite of the period benefited from the lack of consensus and cohesion, which allowed them to manipulate foreign investment to their advantage. The elite had a clear class project and merely hoped that US businessmen operating unhindered in Honduras would serve them well. This free-rein liberal project in Honduran history set the tone for US-Honduran relations during this period, as well as the formation of an elite consensus that ultimately favored US capital and involvement in the nation.

Presidents José Policarpo Bonilla Vásquez (1895–1899), General Manuel Bonilla Chirinos (1903–1907; 1912–1913), and Miguel Rafael Dávila Cuellar (1907–1911), oversaw the largest concessionary periods to foreign investors, and after the Pan-American Exposition in Buffalo, they conceded much land for the building of the railroad and declared US investor Vaccaro (later owner of Standard Fruit) exempt from taxes in a privilege similar to that conferred later on UFCo.[71] Barahona claims that this is the key period that generated the banana enclave economy. Indeed, this era saw the marriage between interests of the liberals to enter the international market with the banana companies' emerging banana trade in Honduras. All subsequent foreign investors benefited from this dynamic turn of events. By 1911 Zemurray's Cuyamel Fruit Company was planting large tracts of land.[72] The banana companies owned the ports and shipping system and controlled the customs offices because the Honduran government allowed it. Thus the liberal reform project, a national project for Honduras, in its drive for modernity and prosperity also ushered in domination by foreign industrial interests and the development of an export economy, ultimately failing to bring about its goal of building a nation for all and bridging regional interests.

POQUITEROS GIVE WAY TO US BUSINESS

The growth of the diverse banana-planter class of poquiteros was fueled by foreign market needs and industrialization in Europe and the United States.[73] Between 1870 and 1912, early banana production and export relied heavily on poquiteros from the local areas, who cultivated primarily for export through contracts with the banana companies.[74] The poquiteros were thus important in the process of developing a local merchant class. John Soluri demonstrates that there was already a booming banana economy in 1899, when 70% of the poquiteros' fincas took up 1,700 hectares, or 28% of the arable land.[75] He specifically notes that there were 1,100 local banana producers in Omoa, El Paraíso,

Puerto Cortés, San Pedro Sula, El Porvenir, La Ceiba, and San Luis.[76] According to Soluri, these small farmers were the first to transform the north coast, both ecologically and socially. They were also important to the Honduran government, which conducted the census showing elite interest in the banana industry.[77] The majority of these regions would become part of UFCo and the Standard Fruit Company by the 1920s. In 1900 there were about 1,000 who were considered poquiteros, and by 1932 they had altogether disappeared.[78]

The small-scale planter class would rapidly be replaced by an ex-traction model of trade propelled by the agro-industrial production sys-tem that the banana companies promoted. The companies capitalized on and expanded the industrial production processes already established through the order, expertise, and skill of the preexisting local planter class on the north coast. Very much like the sugar mill of the colonial period, the land could not be separated from those who worked it. The banana plantation itself was organized around the goals of production; workers were expendable, interchangeable, and seen as a homogenous class by the producer.[79] Transnational companies easily usurped this planter class, and their processing and production, by controlling the transport and quality of the bananas before paying the growers. They did so by using company trains, but also by dominating various stages of production, which emerged into a vertically integrated system over time.

The US businessmen who established companies on the north coast and the investors who traveled there to purchase land in the 1890s acquired tremendous influence in the region. Two companies, the Cuyamel Fruit Company (Cuyamel), established in 1911,[80] and the Vaccaro Brothers and Company (Vaccaro), established in 1899 and in-corporated as the Standard Fruit Company in 1924,[81] wielded power over national political affairs. The companies exploited the vulnerabili-ties of the Honduran government leadership by taking advantage of lo-cal skirmishes between the Liberal Party and the Nationalist Party and their candidates running for office, often with the assistance of the US Embassy, to position themselves favorably and achieve their demands.[82] They negotiated for access to land and for control of labor, set import and export taxes, built their own railroads and ports, and insured their deals would remain in place with incoming elected officials. In this ear-ly phase (1899–1910) Cuyamel and Vaccaro both sought to defend their own narrow interests, including access to land, products, and seaports. While the companies did not have a common agenda, they both at-tempted to absorb Honduran land and acquire a competitive advantage.

A merger between the Boston Fruit Company and the Tropical

Trade and Transport Company in 1899 created the United Fruit Company. UFCo built a transnational business that was vertically integrated, including the domestic coordination of production, from the point of growing and cutting the product to the point of shipping to and distribution in the United States. With its fleet of steamboats known as the White Fleet of the Caribbean, plantations throughout Central America and the Caribbean, and a distribution network in the United States, UFCo acquired unrivalled power. The rise of UFCo had an immediate impact in most of Central America, but the company did not expand into Honduras until 1911–1912. When it did arrive in Honduras, UFCo competed and clashed with Cuyamel and Vaccaro. Cuyamel owner Samuel Zemurray, an investor from New Orleans, and a fierce competitor with UFCo's subsidiary, the Tela Railroad Company, had effectively established relationships with local elites and caudillos. By 1910–1911, he had gained a foothold and some influence over President Manuel Bonilla Chirinos to support his company. In 1929, Cuyamel merged with UFCo, and Zemurray became their largest stockholder, ending the rivalry between Cuyamel and the Tela Railroad Company. Unlike Zemurray, Vaccaro remained a UFCo competitor. Like most operators during this period, Vaccaro relied on local planters to supply the bananas it exported while at the same time expediting the displacement of the poquiteros.[83] Vaccaro eventually incorporated as the Standard Fruit Company and lobbied presidents in Tegucigalpa to support its operations. Despite their competition, the companies were aligned in seeking favorable government policies to benefit their businesses.[84]

Businessmen like Samuel Zemurray, although challenged by local planters and workers, had the support of presidential administrations and became powerful players in national politics. Zemurray regularly intervened in presidential elections, first aiding Bonilla Chirinos in taking power by force in 1911 and later trying to prevent Tiburcio Carías Andino from becoming president.[85] Once in power, Bonilla Chirinos granted huge land concessions to Zemurray. Most importantly, Zemurray succeeded in gaining control of customs, ensuring favorable tariffs and taxes on imports such as machinery and tools for cultivation and the export of bananas, ensuring success for his enterprise.[86]

Unfortunately, national government officials were disconnected from local and regional interests. For instance, the Honduran officials granted concessions, as mandates from the central government, in the form of public land granted to the banana companies without consulting regional or local leaders. Honduran government officials hoped that conceding public lands to the banana companies would result in economic development, which would eventually consolidate national economic and political interests. When elites in the capital negotiated concessions of the north-coast territory with foreign investors, poquiteros were at a disadvantage and eventually disappeared, replaced by the robust multinational banana export economy.

LAND FOR RAILS: CONCESSIONS TO THE BANANAS COMPANIES

The best example of the intersection of the objectives of the US fruit companies and those of Honduran liberal reformers is the land-concession period of the first half of the twentieth century, when the banana companies anchored their foothold in the north coast. During this period, Honduran liberal aspirations for a national infrastructure were deferred, even as the country developed a prosperous banana economy with the investment of US capital. What could have been an effort to incentivize and attract investors to develop the economy as a part of the liberal reforms in the late 1800s would become a Honduran government practice utilized by elite oligarchic leaders for their own benefit. In turn, US capitalists saw that they could influence and enact any practice or policy in the country that benefited their economic interests.

"Land for railroads" agreements between the banana companies and the Honduran government hastened the banana companies' domination over the country's most fertile land and its largest export crop.[87] Companies such as UFCo (which began cultivation between 1910 and 1912), through its subsidiaries the Tela Railroad Company and the Truxillo Railroad Company, and the Cuyamel Fruit Company and the Vaccaro Brothers Company (which became the Standard Fruit Company in 1924 and Standard Fruit and Steamship Company in 1926), obtained land from the Honduran government and local planters in three primary ways: (1) from land concessions granted by the Honduran government with the agreement that the company would build a railroad system, (2) through lease and/or purchase of land from local planters, and (3) through direct coercion.[88] The "land for railroads" agreements consisted of government land grants of between "250 to 500 hectares for every kilometer of rail" that the companies agreed to build.[89] As an incentive for building the rail line, the companies also profited from the raw materials found within these land concessions—including lumber, petroleum, and coal—which these companies used for daily operations.[90]

Between 1905 and 1915, Honduran government officials and US fruit companies signed four key contracts with the important goal of obtaining a rail system.[91] In 1906 and 1910, the Honduran government signed two contracts with Vaccaro (transferred to the Standard Fruit Company in 1924). In 1912, the Honduran government signed two other contracts, one with the Fairbanks Syndicate of Indianapolis and another with H.V. Rolston of Cuyamel (transferred to the Tela Railroad Company and the Truxillo Railroad Company respectively, in 1913).[92] The contracts proposed rail systems with various points of origin. All the contracts coincide on the main points. The Honduran government granted the US companies the right to cut wood and extract gravel in any section of national territory. The companies also had the freedom to exploit rivers and sources of water, had free use of national territory to build service areas for the railroad system, and were exempt from paying taxes on imports and exports or paying for the maintenance and operation of the railroad.[93] These initial contracts led to others as the companies became larger and greedy.

Beyond land concessions and tax incentives, the foreigners desired even greater influence. They vied for control of the ports and sought to control taxes on imports and exports—even full control of the industry, costs, quality, and distribution. Control of the trade tariffs and ports was so important that the companies felt US State Department appointees should engage in negotiations in order to maintain a fair price for US companies. These actions also reflect the lack of trust US investors had in the local governments in the north coast and their desire to dictate the terms under which they would conduct business.

To foreign investors, the geography of the north coast, with its deep-water bays and rail possibilities, was particularly suited for the construction of ports. They invested in building the wharves where their ships had priority docking as well as complete control of the routes to the ports. They could also control the speed and efficiency of the local banana suppliers, who would be completely dependent on the companies' timetables for purchase and distribution. Companies that controlled the wharves also controlled local taxes paid on imported and exported goods. Controlling tariff prices benefited the companies because they often imported goods and equipment from the United States that were indispensable to maintaining production in the banana fields—everything from machinery and sanitation equipment to the supplies that filled the shelves of the company commissaries.[94]

With the rise of UFCo and Standard Fruit Company, the banana industry replaced mining as the primary industry in the country and powerfully influenced the Honduran economy. Honduran presidents continued to approve land grants to the banana companies for the first half of the twentieth century in hopes of building a railroad, prioritizing the banana companies over local producers as a singular source of industrialization and development. Those companies, however, were not interested in developing the internal infrastructure of the country. Consequently, the bananeras developed intricate loops on already existing east–west rails to the main towns where they had fruit-producing centers and other subsidiaries. Instead of a national railroad, they created a railroad system that would benefit their plantations in the north coast. The land concessions led to the construction of rail lines, but they were limited to transporting bananas, and the system was strictly under foreign-company control. Other potential export crops, such as coffee, became dependent on these rails for transportation, as well as on the ports and ships owned by UFCo or the Standard Fruit Company.[95] The railroad project that liberals imagined would unify the nation and generate trade had failed, deferred to the interests of the foreign banana companies. The capital city of Tegucigalpa would never be connected to the ports by train.

THE INTERSECTION OF US CAPITAL, THE STATE, AND WORKERS' ASPIRATIONS ON THE NORTH COAST

The dynamic, evolving economic and political development in the region was not all due to the banana companies or the Honduran state. Banana workers, labor organizers themselves, some of them leftists, were influential in the challenges from below. Labor organizing among banana workers—who remain the most commonly overlooked historical actors in the country—was a critical strategic form of protest, and its study provides context for the years leading up to the 1954 strike. As the intersecting projects grated against each other, the emergence of worker labor activists was the least expected to transform the nation. Workers' obstinate desire to achieve basic labor rights, and to be connected to international movements for dignity, would drive Hondurans into a course of history that would change their lives. The next chapter will explore in detail the efforts to bring about a labor movement constructed by and for Hondurans.

CHAPTER 2

REVOLUTIONARY ANTECEDENTS TO THE 1954 STRIKE

LIBERALS, REBELS, AND RADICALS

The misfortune of this bourgeois homeland, homeland for the rich, it inhibits us from thinking freely, but it is not possible to stop ideas, or incarcerate them, because ideas do not have criminal jurisprudence.

MANUEL CÁLIX HERRERA, 1929[1]

Confronted with the designs of fervent liberal reformers and avaricious US investors, Honduran working classes were not passive victims of foreign and domestic capitalist exploitation. To the contrary, evidence of contemporaneous organizing efforts shows signs of worker agency as early as the turn of the century.[2] The roots of the labor movement in Honduras can be traced to the efforts of leftists who worked closely with agricultural and mining workers to build consciousness through newspapers and associations that challenged bipartisanship and sought to link up to the ideals of the Bolshevik revolution. Despite anti-communist persecution and imprisonment, workers' organizing activity (including strikes and newspaper distribution), created a vision for organizing by critiquing the foreign transnationals for their abuses and calling for improved working and living conditions, wages and overtime work, and access to health care.

Previous strikes reflected power struggles between the workers and companies through which workers were successful in raising issues and stopping work. Transformative organizing emerged with collaborations between labor and nascent leftists in the area. Honduran government mediation often reflected alignment with the companies and urgency in resuming production schedules, suggesting collusion of company power with a complicit Honduran state. Workers did not gain the right to organize a union but did gain piecemeal changes, positive outcomes that remained in place thanks to worker vigilance and action. Though the evidence is dispersed, historians have documented several strike efforts in Honduras that highlight worker efforts to improve their labor conditions.[3] (See table in appendix G.)

According to historian Mario Posas's description of the earlier strikes, the demands were overwhelmingly centered on wage increases, particularly during the strikes in 1920, 1925, 1930, and 1932.[4] The strikes also made quality-of-life demands around access to health care and lower prices for goods in the company commissaries.[5] The demands addressed issues and conditions in the workplace. Regionally specific demands never led to a labor contract (contrato colectivo) or the formation of an organization, such as a labor union, and although leftists often called for overarching labor protections in their newspapers and leaflets, banana workers' demands remained localized, with small gains from strikes but no further organization of a union or success establishing a labor code.

During the strikes that preceded the 1954 strike, workers exhibited a great deal of restraint, demonstrating organized and disciplined action without violence. The company and the cabos de comisariato (local company security forces), in collusion with the state, including military forces, were violent and prepared to act in response to worker complaints and strikes. Perhaps the experience and stories from the 1920 (Vaccaro Brothers Company) strike, which ended in a massacre, served to suppress organizing or at least set back efforts.

In earlier strikes the workers who mobilized and negotiated for power were campeños, or finca laborers, but railroad and port workers were critical in building leftist power. Worker committees in San Pedro Sula and Tegucigalpa understood that finca workers were an important sector of the population with the potential for organizing and the power to shut down production.[6] The link between the banana regions and the emerging leftists occurred slowly during this period (early to mid-1920s), held back by lower literacy rates limiting the readership of papers; the persecution of leftists, which hampered their circulation of newspapers; the challenging distances between regions, given that there were no roads that connected the cities; and the vigilance and surveillance of the company agents.

The early efforts of the 1920s and 1930s were fundamental to the subsequent building of consciousness and organizing principles around wages, the eight-hour workday, and other demands eventually concretized in the 30 demands of the 1954 strike. But the persecution against workers, including the murder of their leaders, also laid bare the consequences of organizing for workers and the lengths to which the companies would go to protect their businesses. The banana fincas and wharves experienced smaller strikes—sometimes wildcat strikes—that revolved around immediate workplace demands. These actions reflect workers' consciousness about their conditions and set the stage for other workers, primarily younger ones, to exercise their leadership and learn to make demands to improve labor conditions and to promote solidarity. These earlier strikes exposed North American companies and called on the Honduran state to demand better wages and rights in the workplace for its citizens. Labor strife demanded local responses, and local craft organizations in the cities grew in the 1920s and 1930s. So did a small cadre of leftist radicals who aspired to form a Communist Party.

Organizing in the banana fincas on the north coast effectively challenged the companies. Euraque points out that the "history of the working people also promoted a social and political culture that broadly contrasted with that of the interior. The elite and nonelite processes of class formation on the north coast affected one another in ways that together produced a different civil society, especially by the 1950s. However, that history was linked as well to events and developments in the 1920s and 1930s."[7] Their actions revolved around San Pedro Sula and the north coast, where worker organizations developed an oppositional consciousness against the foreign-owned companies.[8]

THE WORKING-CLASS LEFTIST FOUNDATIONS
FOR THE 1954 STRIKE

The history of the first worker organizations, and particularly the events of the 1920s, indicate the development of a national labor movement, one that would later be caught between the ideological politics of the Liberal Party, leftist radicals' and workers' astuteness, and Nationalist Party domination. Earlier organizations ranged from mutual aid societies and cultural centers to more radical unions that challenged the banana companies.

The Federación Obrera Hondureña (FOH; Federation of Honduran Workers), founded in 1921,[9] eventually aligned with the Confederación Obrera Centroamericana (COCA; Central American Workers Confederation), which was founded in 1921 in Guatemala[10] and linked to the Confederación Obrera Panamericana (COPA; Panamerican Worker Confederation), an organization created by the American Federation of Labor (AFL) in the United States.[11] The FOH was reformist in scope, yet it nonetheless moved influential labor proposals and made gains, such as company-provided infirmaries for sick workers and housing with screens on windows to keep out malaria-ridden mosquitoes in the living quarters. The FOH also provided a safe cultural space that served as an outlet for workers and their families. Within the FOH, the Sociedad Cultura Femenina (Society of Feminine Culture), a women's organization, began providing classes for children of workers and ran literacy projects for adults.[12] Another organization that was part of the FOH was the Federación Sociedades Obreras del Norte (FSON; Federation of Societies of Workers of the North), which was always critical of "worker-employer" relations and was moving away from a mutual aid model.[13] Together, these organizations comprised a faction within the FOH that was largely responsible for the creation of a *Constitución Obrera* (worker's constitution) during a Regional Congress of Workers and became a program for the organizations in the country in 1926.[14] This constitution established that workers in the organization would affiliate not with the already established political parties, the Liberal Party or the Nationalist Party, but rather with newly created ones that answered to workers' needs.[15] North-coast workers, grouped under the larger FSON, called for an agenda that reflected workers' real lives and needs in 1926.

Radical workers wanted to move toward syndicalism and away from mutual aid groups. The north coast thus became the site of radical origins in the labor movement. Inspired by a few erudite, studied Leftists, these seeds would sustain a radical worker agenda through the mid-twentieth century. Leftists in the north coast had identified the banana regions, particularly the US enclaves of UFCo and the Standard Fruit Company, as important organizing targets because they contained the largest concentration of workers in the country.[16] The north-coast organizations pushed the debate on mutual aid societies, making radical demands for changes to existing legislation that prohibited mutual aid societies from engaging in political and militant campaigns.[17] North-coast organizations were also successful in moving the COCA to develop a united worker platform that would then be adopted by all worker organizations in the country.[18] Their influence was felt at the meeting of the COCA in 1926, when they managed to move the membership to adopt a syndicalism system, rather than the mutual aid society model, in the newly drafted worker constitution.[19] Proponents sought to unite organizers around a labor union program for the country, considered more radical than conciliatory mutual aid societies. Actively engaged in worker struggles, individual members of the FSON produced newspapers in which they proposed concrete demands of the government on behalf of workers' rights. These efforts opened up space for unifying the labor movement, all the various societies and worker groups, and the banana-industry laborers in the first half of the twentieth century.

Starting in 1926, tensions arose in the organization, and the more radical organizers attempted to turn the FOH into a more political organization—one that sought to educate and politicize workers. When the FOH leaders participated in local bipartisan elections, violating one of the collective principles, radicals like Manuel Cálix Herrera challenged them, leading to his expulsion. After that, most radicals abandoned the FOH.[20] The Sociedad Cultura Femenina also decided to leave the FOH and joined the more militant FSH, under the leadership of Graciela García, one of the leading women organizers within the radical wing of the FOH and the FSH. Her role as a woman and a leftist is usually overshadowed in the historical memory of the labor movement. She would later be forced into exile in Mexico by the Carías Andino dictatorship. The FSH's largest contribution to the labor movement was its proposal for a union that would represent all workers in all sectors of the banana plantations. In this effort, the FSH formed *comités sindicales* (union committees) among workers at the docks, transportation centers, mechanic shops, and fruit centers.[21] For the first time, a workers' organization proposed an agenda that challenged the Tela Railroad Company and Standard Fruit Company, rather than working with the boss for menial gains (as the FOH had done for years).

In 1929, the FSH was founded as the culmination of the Asamblea Obrera y Campesina (Assembly of Workers and Campesinos) held in Tela on May 1 of that year; also during that event they decided to join the Confederación Sindical Latinoamericana.[22] Among the delegates to the new grouping were Juan Pablo Wainwright, a local business owner of mixed ancestry who had been a militant in the Communist Party of El Salvador in 1928 and had been exiled from that country back to Honduras for his activity, and Graciela García, a Salvadoran teacher who would be among the communist leaders in the years to come. The goals of the Asamblea Obrera y Campesina included the formation of a federation and agenda specific to the north coast and the incorporation of Black workers, because "delegates knew that the element of color displaces the worker compatriot because labor is so cheaply paid."[23] While at the same time calling for the companies to respect immigration law, and perhaps stop migration, they also called for organizing to "develop an intense campaign to agitate until we make the Black element come to the organization so that we may discipline and lead him to the struggle for emancipation."[24] The Asamblea Obrera y Campesina also called for the organization of campesinos and the female proletariat, as well as the creation of a newspaper to be named *El Trabajador*.[25] The FSH was led by well-known leftists, such as members of the Sociedad Fiat in Tela, García in Tegucigalpa, Wainwright and Cálix Herrera in the north coast, and Zoroastro Montes de Oca, a railroad worker leader in La Ceiba. The FSH wanted to educate and politicize workers and join the international cause.

THE FIRST COMMUNIST PARTY

Inspired by the Bolshevik revolution in the Soviet Union, the newly formed Comintern, and regional leadership of Communist Parties, a small group emerged in Honduras to engage the aspirations of the working class. The railroad workers were seen as the most militant workers within that iteration of the Communist Party. As early as 1923, inspired by Mexican revolutionaries, Guatemalan Communist Party members alongside Honduran and Salvadoran counterparts aimed to build a Central American Communist Party. In 1925, a delegate from the Partido Comunista de Centroamérica (PCCA, Communist Party of Central America) attended the Third Congress of the Mexican Communist Party. Various Honduran leaders, among them Cálix Herrera, Wainwright, Montes de Oca, and García, along with García's brother Felipe Armando Amaya, led the formation of various aforementioned organizations that culminated in the first Communist Party between 1928 and 1929.

According to Argueta, a Socialist Party was founded in March of 1927 by Montes de Oca and Cálix Herrera, and this party was subsequently "converted" into the Communist Party.[26] In Rina Villars's biography of Juan Pablo Wainwright, she cites a report to the Comintern written by Armando Amaya (under the pseudonym Ruiz Valdez) stating "the Party was founded in 1928"[27] as PCCA, with a manifesto authored by Honduran Cálix Herrera.[28] Cálix Herrera along with the leadership of Wainwright and Montes de Oca in La Ceiba, formed a progressive mutual aid society called "El Progreso," which would be fundamental to building unity between craftsmen and local railroad and banana workers.[29] Due to the clandestine nature of this history, poor documentation, and persecution, the precise founding history of the first Communist Party in Honduras is unclear. But evidence indicates it existed from 1928 or 1929 until 1932, when it was suppressed by Carías Andino's dictatorship, and it was reconstituted again clandestinely in 1948[30] and later openly in 1954.[31]

Persecution of Cálix Herrera and his comrades started around 1926; the organizers had identified the north coast as the target of organizing, given the abuses of UFCo, the Standard Fruit Company, and the Cuyamel Fruit Company.[32] The fear that the Mexicans were inspiring the Central Americans was of concern to US businessmen in Honduras and the US State Department. Workers and leftist organizers faced anti-labor repression by the government and by businesses with US interests. The Communist Party was severely repressed by fruit company pressure on the Honduran government in 1930.[33] Wainwright's report to the Comintern in June–July of 1930 noted a "Red Scare" that brought torture and repression on those caught and jailed. The repression came as a response to the leftists calling for a general strike—to protest the conditions of the bananeras, or banana companies—to take place on July 4, 1930.[34] While these efforts were severely repressed by the company and the state, it is evident that some level of activity took place. On October 6, 1932, the *New York Times* reported on the detonation of a bomb in an automobile, killing three people, in a series and that the group reported to have attempted an attack on the barracks at Tela was captured. They were said to be Communist.[35] The news article continued to link communists to violence on the eve of the upcoming elections.

Despite repression, the Communist Party did rebuild, and in October of 1930 it had 100 members, with six sections in the port cities of the north coast and one in Tegucigalpa; they also claimed to have 1,000 members in the FSH who were sympathetic to their cause.[36] The party had four cells, two in Tegucigalpa and two in San Pedro Sula, with the central committees based in San Pedro Sula. In terms of "composition, 3% were workers, 2% agricultural workers, 2% employees, 5% craftsmen, and the remainder industrial laborers between the ages of 20 and 34."[37] In 1932 the party participated in presidential elections, garnering about 700 votes, with Cálix Herrera as its candidate along with a slate that aimed to represent the interests of workers and campesinos.[38] During this period and despite repression, organizers gained greater traction with banana workers in the north coast, using election issues to build consciousness about conditions under the banana companies and to incite a larger movement on a national scale.

During that time several strikes were initiated, but party members did not express a highly developed political-ideological analysis.[39] They were young, and many relied on newspapers and leaflets to discuss these ideas. This may have been in part a product of a highly stratified Honduran society heavily influenced by US foreign policy, internal political factions and tensions during the period, and a lack of basic education and literacy, especially for most of the working-class leaders. Graciela García remembers that in 1930 Ricardo Martínez, a Venezuelan and representative of the III Communist International, came to Honduras to meet with the Honduran leftist leaders and to assess the party.[40] Martínez felt there was a contradiction between the reports and what he saw in their party: "a set of activities carried out by Honduran communists 'with great enthusiasm,' but without their own characteristics of a communist party."[41] Martínez concluded that the Hondurans needed to form the Honduran Communist Party as such, and not use other names for the party. Previously, the Partido Obrero Hondureño (Honduran Workers' Party) served as a front for the Communist Party of Honduras. Organizers had done this to perhaps "mitigate or minimize the reaction" from the state and companies, and also due to the "political backwardness of the masses,"[42] to which Martínez responded, "The name will never hide from the fruit company the real character of our activities."[43] Martínez also offered a second critique related to the absence of agricultural workers from positions of leadership. Most organizers could not report on the conditions facing these workers, and Martínez considered this failing to be an indication of organizers' lack of training resulting from not attending the Communist conferences, from which syndicalist movements surged.[44] The Comintern message was clear: to "come out" as communists and to connect with the hardest sector of the working people in Honduras, the campesinos. These recommendations changed the priorities and direction of the party and may ultimately have prompted the communists to begin pushing for a strike in 1932 and later.

Workers perceived to belong to the Communist Party were persecuted by the banana companies, particularly by UFCo through its Tropical Division managerial team. Leftist organizers were constantly under the scrutiny and watchful eye of the US Embassy during the McCarthy era of the midcentury. They faced accusations of being communists and therefore "enemies of the nation." Demonstrating resilience in the face of continued repression, the party remained virtually dormant for several decades until its reconstitution in 1948 and 1954.

The Honduran government took its cue from the US Embassy and also persecuted "labor agitators" such as Cálix Herrera, who was also editor of the worker newspaper *El Martillo* (The Hammer) and who frequently criticized UFCo and the United States.[45] More importantly, the newspaper served as a vehicle for the dissemination of national and international news for and about workers.[46] Reading these newspapers was considered so subversive that they were often prohibited in the fincas, and workers themselves were careful not to be caught in possession of them.[47] Despite the clandestine nature of organizing and the cautious dissemination of worker newspapers, literate workers passed information along to other workers. *El Martillo*, one of the most effective papers of the 1920s, in fact, had the tag line: "Periódico Obrero Campesino: Órgano del Grupo Defensa Proletaria" (Worker and Campesino Newspaper: Organ of the Group for the Defense of the Proletariat), clearly stating its commitment to workers and the working class. The newspaper's ideas may have been new to north-coast workers, most of whom were campesinos.[48] The newspaper called all workers and peasants to unite under the banner of the working class; in the June 1929 issue, *El Martillo* asked readers to support the 500 mine workers of the Rosario Mining Company, who had been surrounded by the military when they gathered to strike.[49] Though the event took place near Tegucigalpa, the banana workers of the north coast were able to read about the strike and the repression that ensued.[50] News of the actions at the US-owned Rosario Mining Company served to demonstrate that a local struggle to organize and stand up to banana companies was possible. Workers were also able to read about and debate the political climate, as well as understand the need for clandestine organizing work. Finally, identifying with other workers at a distance gave workers a sense of camaraderie and engagement with causes outside of their own, building courage and consciousness around working-class issues.

The newspaper became a threat to the company—serving to empower and inform workers, who in the past had been completely dependent on information from company-controlled communications, such as movie screenings in the fincas or direct communication from supervisors, overseers, and other company employees. The worker newspapers were often the only source of national news that workers received in the fincas,[51] and these often attacked US-owned businesses' practices. Cálix Herrera, the public figure behind the newspaper, thus became *persona non grata* with the companies and the US Embassy, which led local Honduran police to imprison and disappear him in 1929 for three days, assigning him a special guard that would stay on site day and night.[52] This was the first of two arrests in the same year. To avoid being shut down, the newspaper moved from Tela to La Ceiba during this period. Cálix Herrera was arrested a second time for delivering a letter to the US Consulate in La Ceiba in protest of the Sacco and Vanzetti court conviction in the United States. He was accused of offense and insult against the vice consul of the US Consulate in Tela.[53]

UFCo had its own system for profiling worker organizers who were associated with the Communist Party in the 1920s. In one internal memo from Tropical Division manager Arthur A. Pollan to the General Offices in Boston, a picture of Cálix Herrera was included. The following profile was attached to the report:

> This man is an agitator of the worst type; anti-American, extremist, given to writing and preaching Red, Bolshevist, and Comunistic [*sic*] Propaganda. He has recently been the principal organizer of a Bolshevist move originating on the North Coast of Honduras. It is possible that as his activities have been restricted in that country, he will move to other fields, and you should be on the lookout for him.[54]

Alongside the note and photo was a physical description of Cálix Herrera as "quick and alert, and rapid in his movements. Usually dresses without coat or necktie, and a straw hat, with one side turned down with a rakish fashion. Personal habits: drinks occasionally, sometimes to excess, given to frequenting low resorts."[55] The internal memo also went to the other Tropical Division managers, warning them about Cálix Herrera's work and ideas and the danger of their spreading. They were suspicious of his travel to other fincas in the isthmus. The compiler of the documents, Philippe Bourgois, deduces that the collection makes sense within a "bureaucratic logic of monopoly capital" and provides "vibrant testimony to the repeated and diverse attempts by workers (and occasionally host-country governments) to organize in defense of their rights on the plantation."[56]

Cálix Herrera tried to fit in with the demographic of the banana campos. He needed to be able to organize and to understand the conditions in which workers were mobilizing. There was a distrust of immigrants who came to work, and a significant dose of nativism in the campos; if he were not seen as native to Honduras (or indio, native to the region), this could have compromised his organizing efforts. Cálix Herrera's efforts and effectiveness at blending in with workers was a tactic of clandestine organizers during the era, and would serve as a model for later generations of organizers.

Later, newspapers such as *Vanguardia Revolucionaria, Voz Obrera, El Chilío,* and *La Pulga* were influenced in the 1940s and 1950s by *El Martillo*[57] and Cálix Herrera's work. This is important in a period when Latin American leftists looked to the international worker as a symbol of democracy and freedom from oligarchic rule. The newspapers were the main forum for leftists to communicate and for workers to air their grievances. Their power was evident in that the company cabos de comisariato hunted down known organizers who were distributing newspapers and repressed them.

Juan Pablo Wainwright was a well-educated and well-traveled Honduran merchant (exiled from El Salvador), living in San Pedro Sula, where he participated in building the city's Communist Party and the progressive FSH in 1929. In 1932, against the backdrop of the situation facing Central American nations, when the Communist party was organizing with banana workers, and while running for the presidency, Wainwright was captured not just for being a Communist but also for his "profound knowledge of the meaning of Communism."[58] Wainwright was important to the Salvadoran and Guatemalan Communist parties as well. He was an organic intellectual in his own right, and he was killed in Guatemala City at the hands of dictator Jorge Ubico in 1932 for helping to build the Communist Party in that country. A journalist who spoke with him recounts, "He will die convinced. He is, however, in the threshold of death; the prisoner Wainwright demonstrated he is a rebel and does not deny his Bolshevik ideas." The report goes on to say that when he heard that Ubico was sentencing him to death, Wainwright yelled at the top of his lungs, "¡Viva La Soviet [*sic*], único gobierno que debe imperar en el mundo! ¡Viva la revolución social!" (Long live the Soviet Union, the only government that should be an empire in the world. Long live the social revolution!).[59]

The same report noted blood all over, where apparently Wainwright had cut himself and with his own blood had written on the wall "¡Viva la Internacional Comunista!" (Long live the Communist International!).[60] While these news articles and reports on communist leaders contained an element of shock value for the audience, they also indisputably painted the labor movement efforts as communist, and therefore against the company and the state. Wainwright was portrayed as an extremist in his embrace of a violent way to achieve political change. The news coverage in the *New York Times* about the car-bomb detonation of which Cálix Herrara was accused and the misleading story of Wainwright's capture in the Honduran newspapers were incendiary stories in a Catholic society of the time. Catholicism had profound links to the values of decency and capital, and the communists were presented and perceived as aberrations and abnormal.

Beginning in 1933 and lasting throughout the 16 years of the *Cariato*, the dictatorship of Carías Andino, there was a complete shutdown of public life and protest. Leftist newspapers were shuttered completely. In response to civil-society opposition, Carías Andino created a climate of terror by abrogating most civil liberties, such as freedom of the press and even the ability to form social clubs.[61] Labor organizers were also persecuted, forced underground. Martial law, persecution of Communist Party members, and punishment for workers who dared to organize became routine. Members of the Liberal Party were especially brutalized, forced to suppress their activities for the entirety of Carías Andino's rule.

THE ORGANIZING YEARS: PARTIDO DEMOCRÁTICO REVOLUCIONARIO HONDUREÑO AND THE COMMUNIST PARTY

The dictatorship of Tiburcio Carías Andino (1933–1949) propelled the growth of the banana companies during his *caudillista* government, prolonging the lack of unity in the country and among Hondurans. Carías Andino was practically hand-picked by the bananeras, which used their influence and money to manipulate the election process to put him in power.[62] Once in office, Carías Andino thanked and repaid them with many concessions, among them the reduction of taxes, land grants, and an open door to his presidential office.[63] The *Cariato* was marked by increased state repression that benefited the companies. Many organizations fighting for popular democracy and civil liberties were forced to organize clandestinely or to leave the country.[64] Under the selectively permissive eye of Carías Andino, the foreign-dominated corporate economy grew dependent on the export of a single crop.[65] Carías Andino was willfully negligent to the needs of workers and was often quoted as saying "Honduras [does] not suffer any social problems."[66] While many countries' labor movements flourished in the face of military repression throughout Latin America, Honduran workers' efforts were stifled by repression, imprisonment, torture, murder, and exile. During this period and before the general strike, "existing legislation [was] based on the Napoleonic Code, [which] considered labor a commodity, subject to the laws of supply and demand."[67] Much of the organizing of the Liberal Party, the more progressive Partido Democrático Hondureño (PDH; Honduran Democratic Party) and Partido Democrático Revolucionario (PDR; Revolutionary Democratic Party)—later to become the PDRH—and the leftist Comité Coordinador Obrero (CCO; Worker Coordinating Committee) happened clandestinely in the country and abroad by exile networks. The CCO was "constituted in 1950 to promote syndicalism principles in the major industries of national production (mining, banana industry, railroad workers, ports, textiles, construction and others). This organization proposed fighting for universal demands like a labor code and a social security law."[68]

Carías Andino repressed workers and those perceived to be part of the Communist and Liberal Parties. During this period, the ambassador and the chargé d'affaires of the US Embassy reported to Washington that there was little or no labor activity in 1943.[69] The Carías Andino dictatorship squashed organizing efforts in two significant ways: first, by persecuting and incarcerating organizers and eventually forcing them into exile and, second, by empowering local and regional governments to persecute people seen to be in opposition to the dictatorship and the National Party. The PDRH and the Liberal Party—which organized in opposition to the Carías Andino regime but were repressed by it— would later share the stage during the 1954 strike with the CCO and the Comité de Lucha Obrera (CLO; Worker Struggle Committee).[70]

The left-leaning PDRH was founded as an alternative to the bipartisan system.[71] The new party brought together people of different ideological leanings, from centrists to Marxists. The inspiration behind the creation of the PDRH was the October Revolution in Guatemala (1944–1954). As Julio C. Rivera, a member of the PDRH, recalls, "The Guatemalan revolution of 1944 was for us one of the most impressive events happening in the international arena in those years. The information that we received from Guatemala was not very fluid, but we knew what was happening in the neighboring country."[72] The fall of Jorge Ubico in Guatemala was the most significant event of the decade for Central Americans and gave working people in the region hope that one day they could also bring down their own country's dictator.

Authoritarian governments also feared this reality.[73] The events in Guatemala gave Liberal Party members and Marxist organizers the courage to defy the Carías Andino dictatorship by protesting publicly in San Pedro Sula in 1944, a rally that ended in the bloody massacre of unarmed men, women, and children.[74] The rally attempted a powerful demonstration of public dissent against the *Cariato* and would not be forgotten by local residents and fueled their desire to organize. Outraged and like-minded individuals, young radicals and progressives who had been exiled in Guatemala, began to organize against dictatorship both in Guatemala and also upon their return to Honduras. The PDRH was a fusion in 1947 of two committees formed after the 1944 massacre: the PDH, founded in San Pedro Sula in 1945, with the newspaper *Vanguardia*,[75] and the PDR, founded in Tegucigalpa in 1946, with the newspaper *Democracia*. The PDH had as one of its goals to break with "caudillismo político," and they were adamant that "this party is born out of the national life ... free of any links to foreign influences."[76] The program of the party called for "unidad social" (social unity) for sectors of society beaten into submission by foreign interest:

> This visible and unjust dependency of Honduras moves various sectors to NATIONAL UNITY to fight democratically so that the country can improve its economics, politics, and international condition and enjoy the rights that correspond with being an independent and sovereign nation.[77]

The call for unity for all the sectors that opposed dictatorship was important in bringing down Carías Andino, but what is more remarkable is that liberal progressives and emerging Communist Party leaders came together in a project that proposed a national shift, uniting all sectors. The epicenter of this organizing was the north coast, though their membership came from towns all over the nation.[78] The PDRH party platform had a program of action that included the concerns of a wide swath of the population with national demands and demands informed by various sectors of society. The national demands included industrialization, agrarian reform, communications and transportation, a national bank, public health and literacy programs, and the revision of international contracts. Likely of particular concern to the banana companies were the revision of concessions and international agreements and the taxation reforms.[79] Also likely of concern to the banana companies were the individual sector demands, which included a labor code and the right to organize unions, state protection of campesinos' access to credit, and commercialization of their products.[80] The most radical and significant worker demands were the creation of a labor code and the call for substantial agrarian reform. Workers felt that the state had the responsibility to spearhead these actions because up until that time the state had been on the side of the banana companies and not its citizens.[81] Overall, the program the PDRH put forward was comprehensive and had something for various sectors, from workers to landowners, merchants, bankers, students, and children. It is worth noting their commitment to women's rights and suffrage for all women: "The PDRH is not proposing that only elite women conquer their political rights, but aspires for working women (*mujeres del pueblo*) and women workers to conquer those same rights, too."[82] Everything about this party proposal seemed youthful and fresh during this period, a new proposal to bring Honduras, "un país atrasado," into national unity and democracy. Certainly this was a moment of political opportunity for building a democracy led by workers.

Most union-organizing efforts by leftists and Liberal party members continued clandestinely through underground networks throughout the dictatorship of Carías Andino. Two major efforts were the 1940 TACA Airline strike and the effort to organize in the banana fincas by radicals in 1946, both of which sought enforcement of the eight-hour workday and overall labor rights, and both met repressive ends. Winning the eight-hour workday was an important and ongoing effort among workers.[83]

In other industries, concern about fair pay and work hours were commonplace. Local worksite-specific efforts to increase wages and improve working conditions were frequently initiated by workers in San Pedro Sula, as late as 1946. This same year a worker society, La Fraternidad, sent a worker delegation and letter to the political governor of Cortés to have the eight-hour workday law respected: "To request that the governorship require compliance with the constitutional law referring to the limiting of the workday to eight hours, Mr. Gonzales Aragon reinforces his petition by providing some examples of the abuses [of the law] in various industries."[84] To this request the governor of Cortés responded, "Almost all the companies observed the eight-hour workday but there were a few companies that surpassed the limit by half an hour or an hour." He explained that his office had taken steps to investigate the matter and further circulate the information to the various local companies.[85] The worker society, La Fraternindad, demonstrated urgency in securing a process or some mechanism by which workers could report law violations to the governor's office or the police. The governor suggested that workers should report to him to enforce compliance instead of resolving the issue through the use of organizations, such as La Fraternidad, perhaps because such groups were perceived to cause more antagonism with the employer. Accounts of this discussion demonstrate the government's paternalism regarding workers' lives and concerns. Their issues were not resolved. While the government claimed it would investigate the matter for workers, the reality was that the law was not observed and mechanisms were not in place to penalize employers.

By the early 1940s, worker associations had already submitted a petition to the National Congress demanding a national labor code, which they also presented to the governor of Cortés. To this petition, the governor responded that a full study of the situation needed to be conducted and presented to the National Congress, thereby putting the responsibility on the national body.[86] Actions like these, on behalf of worker committees and associations in San Pedro Sula, kept the issue at the forefront and further exhibited worker agency within an ineffective process. It also demonstrated that workers' rights and respect for the eight-hour workday were contested points, despite existing legislation, and workers had to stay vigilant and push forward. Prior to the strike of 1954, universal demands for a labor code had become commonplace among the more progressive worker committees and associations.

Publishing *Vanguardia Revolucionaria*, the newspaper of the PDRH, was one of the party's main activities.[87] The PDRH organizers had two major tasks: to distribute the paper clandestinely to the banana fincas and to develop a committee in each region and department where workers would begin to discuss the ideas and principles of organizing.[88] The newspaper was essential in the fincas where workers began to identify their issues, denounce their problems, and write letters to the editor asking the paper to print their issues and demands. It was a place where they could report on the abuses they endured. Soon, workers began to ask PDRH members to help them by drafting petitions to their supervisors to solve some of their individual workplace issues. Julio C. Rivera affirms that "on an infinite number of occasions [workers] approached us to write notes addressed to a particular departmental supervisor of the company, asking for better wages."[89] The Tela Railroad Company never responded to these petitions, but the repeated letter-writing to the supervisors and company continued. The PDRH organizers helped workers write the petitions as often as they wished. Eventually, Rivera explains, "workers came to the conclusion that this path was not going to obtain the results they wished; they continued to meet and began to organize."[90]

The organizing objective, according to Rivera, took many years. There were about five members of the PDRH who were engaged in building clandestine organizing committees—small, secret study groups. Among the organizers were Julio C. Rivera, Juan Bautista Canales, Teresina Rossi Matamoros, Ventura Ramos Alvarado, and Cesar Agusto Coto. PDRH members may have initiated their organizing work well before 1948, before the committee constituted itself, with the objective of strengthening the party membership numbers and building consciousness among workers about working conditions. "In these meetings, the agents [of the PDRH] explained to workers that it was necessary to organize and struggle in an organized manner to obtain results. That is how some departments in the banana company managed to get organized, constituting their very own directive and leadership."[91]

The US Embassy perceived the PDRH organizers as communist agitators, though their membership was mixed. The US Embassy attempted to curtail travel between campos and recorded and tracked the presence and "danger" of groups such as the PDRH. Standard Fruit Company workers were perceived to be less dangerous than the Francisco Rios group in Tela.[92] They were persecuted and forced to meet secretly and sporadically. Often workers would walk to the edge of the finca, meet the PDRH organizer, and walk him to the meeting location. After the meeting they would then walk them back to the town. Meetings with workers consisted of no more than four or five people, as larger concentrations would raise suspicion. It was not until right before the strike that organizers witnessed a meeting of one hundred or more people.[93] PDRH members and worker organizers met for hours in the dead of night and walked long hours to bring propaganda and newspapers. The workers took and disseminated them eagerly in the fields for fear that they would be discovered. Because organizing worker committees was highly penalized, PDRH organizers had to be careful and highly selective in finding workers who were in solidarity and were reliable. Supportive workers attended meetings and came up with their own goals.[94]

The incessant persecution of labor organizers who were perceived to be communists compelled the covert development of new labor leadership among skilled workers and party organizers. Organizers recognized the need to understand the plight of campesinos by working in the fields and being as close as possible to the lives of finca workers. This notion of organizing from within the ranks of workers can be traced to the earlier work of Manuel Cálix Herrera, Juan Pablo Wainwright, and others in the early 1920s. Left-leaning PDRH organizers later formally founded the Communist Party in 1954.

THE SECOND COMMUNIST PARTY

The second Communist Party was founded in 1954 by PDRH members who felt that they could not continue working with the PDRH, arguing that liberals within the party had become reformist. Before 1954, however, there appeared to be an effort to form a Communist Party, as evidenced by the existence of party statutes of 1948,[95] perhaps the only available written record of Communinst Party activity in Honduras that year. The party statutes provide a window into the structure of the organization in the country. It is unclear if those who drafted these statutes in Tegucigalpa might have also been involved in the PDRH or in the formation of the 1954 Communist Party. This document, not unlike those of other Communist Parties in the region, proposed a national structure of local, regional, and national committees that coalesced under a central committee. The statutes suggest that the communists of the time prioritized the need for unionization and organizing campesinos and proclaimed that Communist Party members ought to be "the first fighters in the workshops, factories, plantations, businesses, mills, farms, for a better more dignified life for workers."[96] Members were to do this by organizing themselves and others and by spreading the message through "collaborating in the sale of the newspaper, the organ of the Party, and all its literature."[97] The date of the document coincides with the emergence of organizing efforts by those who had experience in Juan Jacobo Árbenz Guzmán's Guatemala and who were suppressed by Carías Andino's iron rule. As early as 1948, Rigoberto Padilla Rush remembers being introduced to study groups by doctor Rodolfo Durón: "He considered himself a 'communist' and he spoke with enthusiasm of the social experiment that was taking place in the Soviet Union. . . . [W]e began to read books about socialism in foreign language editions."[98]

The 1948 Communist Party statutes and Padilla Rush's memories indicate that clandestine radical organizing might have been taking place before 1954, inspired by the October Revolution in Guatemala, where many of these radicals gained valuable training as journalists and organizers and were inspired to envision a different world for Honduran workers. The statutes may have been written by exiles upon their return to Honduras, perhaps even clandestinely, but no evidence has surfaced of any organization or active-party activity resulting from it. The party structure, the detached local committees, and the persecution and exile of radicals may have prevented the party from forming as a cohesive group at this earlier time, prior to 1954.

It is the 1954 Communist Party for which there is clearer evidence. In this era radicals attempted to pick up where they left off in 1933, when they were exiled during the rise of Carías Andino, organizing banana workers in the north coast. Many of the new Communist Party members had been organizers of the strike under the PDRH and now had the knowledge and the following from workers to once again rebuild. Evidence is scant here, but it appears there was a complex web of interests at play in the banana regions during and after the strike. While Liberals and leftists worked together in the first strike committee trained by the PDRH, liberals ended up in control of a process that had been shared. The liberals were close to seeing their candidate, Ramón Villeda Morales, gain power through elections. The persecution and exile of the more radical PDRH's leadership created space for the Liberal Party's ascension. Regardless of the reasons, many of which could very well have been ideological, the PDRH met its end in 1954, giving way to a more militant Communist Party.

Liberal Party members were persecuted as much as PDRH and Communist Party members were. The Liberal Party was persecuted under the Carías Andino regime for its opposition to the Nationalist Party, a tension that was palpable well into the 1950s. Both groups, the PDRH and the Liberal Party, had distinct agendas, but the government and police saw them as one and the same, and thus as an equal threat. The Carías Andino dictatorship put a straitjacket on any worker movement or demand for a labor code. Despite their exile, organizers and intellectuals continued their efforts; in fact, many reentered the country illicitly, walking across mountains and rivers from nearby Guatemala, to continue activities that would eventually lead to the Honduran worker strike.[99]

The Communist Party was perceived by the company and the state to be "unpatriotic" and instigated by "outside agitators." As Julio C. Rivera recalls, "In those times, organizing workers was a crime that could be punished with death; it was an act of conspiracy, not just against the banana companies but also against the state."[100] The same claims were not made of the Liberal Party, where leaders used the persecution of more radical workers to their advantage in mobilizing support for workers who were Liberal Party sympathizers. In a letter to the Latin American labor representative Serafino Romualdi, Ramón Villeda Morales, Liberal Party presidential candidate, wrote on behalf of workers, "As you know, in these tropical lands it is customary to label "communist" all of those who fight for human rights and for the rule of social justice."[101] This is complex. Villeda Morales is advocating for workers not to the Honduran state authorities but to the Organización Regional Interamericana de Trabajadores (ORIT; Inter-American Regional Organization of Workers), a US anti-communist organization advocating "free labor." The poststrike leadership of the workers, which was in the process of being purged of communists in 1956, was warned by the state not to strike anymore, or "any strike would be disbanded with machine guns." In the same letter, Villeda Morales explains that he was issued a citation by the military to appear to "take responsibility for the activities of workers." While it was beneficial for the state to equate liberals with communists, in this letter Villeda Morales makes a distinction between the two, perhaps to appeal to US operatives who were at that moment holding hostage the Liberal Party victory in the presidential election.[102]

By August 15 of 1956, Villeda Morales was writing to Romualdi notifying him that elections were not respected by the Nationalist Party and the military, and that many liberals were exiled in various local embassy locations: "and we, the leadership of the Liberal party, are in exile, victims of expulsion ordered by the de facto government."[103] In his letter, Villeda Morales once again asks Romualdi to advocate on his behalf, and on behalf of the party, before the US State Department.[104] Romualdi's response demonstrates support for his cause, and he explains that after his discussion with the US State Department he has "the impression that they consider the situation to be 'very transitory'" and "expect a quick definition" or resolution of the situation.[105] Romualdi wanted to make clear to Villeda Morales that the American Federation of Labor and Congress of Industrial Organizations (AFL-CIO) supports "free elections" and reminded him "to move prudently so as not to give pretexts to the enemies of the working class to retaliate against the unions of Honduras."[106] In speaking of protecting unions, Romualdi was likely referring to Honduran state collusion with the companies and certainly referring to communists, who were seen as enemies of free labor. In a memo written on September 4, 1956, by

Andrew McLellan, at the time a consultant representative to the ORIT and on the ground in Honduras, explains:

> In a cross sectional poll among a considerable number of workers in various fields, I learned that the Liberal Party has the greatest support and undoubtedly could win easily any democratic election, and while it claims some 80 percent of the popular vote, I would agree that it does have the sympathy of the largest segment of the labor vote, and an absolute majority of the popular vote.
>
> Dr. Villeda Morales, exiled in July, is not regarded as the titular head of the Liberal Party, in spite of the newspaper reports to the contrary. He was the Liberal Party candidate, and according to all reports from within the Party, wields no influence whatsoever over the Central Executive Committee.[107]

This report landed on Romualdi's desk in September, with information that Villeda Morales probably did not have about his own party. In a 1957 speech titled "To the Workers of Honduras," Villeda Morales once again tells workers:

> Let nobody continue speaking of communist infiltration within the democratic syndicalist movement of Honduras. Let there be immediately an investigation to ascertain whether there are Marxist agents disguised as workers within its ranks and, if there be any, they should be forced to leave the labor organizations, because they are obnoxious, contrary to the democratic principles which we all love and share in America. The workers of Honduras are able to settle their problems with our own democratic devises [*sic*], and if they are to get any help to improve their standard of living, that help must come from those who work and prospere [*sic*] in the free world.[108]

Villeda Morales's pledge to oppose communism in his message to workers shows an attempt to prove to the US State Department his allegiance in exchange for their support of his ascension into power. He also portrays communists as foreigners, outsiders to the country and to the liberal cause. Although liberals faced persecution and exile during elections at the hands of the nationalists and the military, liberal leaders and members could exist somewhat publicly, run elections, and reach out to US operatives. The Communist Party did not have that freedom. Their different organizing roles in the banana fields explain the power dynamics. After the more radical strike committee was jailed and exiled, the Liberals came to power in the worker organization and dominated the process of building the union committee structure during and after the strike. Later they would also dominate in the negotiations for a labor code.[109] These documents reveal multiple forces at play here against leftist workers and communist leaders: the Liberal Party, the Nationalist Party and the military, the US State Department (and presumably the US Embassy), and the ORIT. These were all harbingers of free labor in opposition to the more progressive leftist Confederación de Trabajadores de América Latina (CTAL; Latin American Confederation of Workers).

The 1954 strike actors inherited three organizing practices from the PDRH and emerging Communist Party organizers. First, organizing in the workplace was a clandestine activity, and if found out, a worker could not only lose his job but also end up in prison or exile. Second, organizers were not outside agitators as the companies claimed; they either were banana workers or became workers during the organizing process.[110] Third, organizing in the banana fincas in the north coast was the highest priority. By 1944 the site of struggle was clear to Honduran organizers: the Tela Railroad Company and the Standard Fruit Company fincas and camps. Although none of the strikes in the early years forced the transcendental changes that resulted from the 1954 general strike, they set a historical precedent for confronting exploitative working conditions and unbridled company power. They planted the seeds of a new, more powerful labor movement. Workers and their militancy, often forgotten in the discussion of the transformation of the north coast, dramatically changed the region. Their cultural, political, and economic influence was crucial to the construction of a labor movement. The workers, the principal actors of this story, posed the most powerful challenge to the Honduran elite and the banana companies' domination, ushering in nationwide civil and political changes and the most radical worker mobilization movement seen in the country to that point.

ANTI-COMMUNISM, COUNTERREVOLUTIONARIES, COLD WAR POLITICS, AND HONDURAN WORKERS

The US State Department's collaboration with labor leaders such as George Meany of the AFL and Serafino Romualdi of the ORIT was focused on eradicating individual communist leaders in order to stop their larger objectives. The US State Department and the ORIT benefited from each other, both financially and by providing justification for the imposition of "democracy" on another country. The collaboration was reciprocal: the ORIT reported on communist activity, even if communists in Honduras were few and suppressed, and the US State Department pressured the Honduran government to persecute organized labor. The free-labor movement influenced by the ORIT earned more members by having federations align with the Confederación Internacional de Organizaciones Sindicales Libres (CIOSL; International Confederation of Free Trade Unions) rather than the more radical CTAL, and the US State department granted them funds to pay for travel, trainings, and recruitment. The ORIT set itself in opposition to "communists"; this may have been necessary to keep US State Department support. In an undated note, which could have been written between 1950 and 1951, Romualdi wrote:

> I went to Honduras, a country that had absolutely no labor movement and was ruled by a more (or) less semi dictatorship. . . . With no great industry in the country, they were just artisans, handicrafts makers, shoemakers, carpenters, etc. . . . I met with two or three so called labor leaders. . . . All of them denied being communist. But then, I started to talk to them about certain things and suddenly one said: You are not for Chiang Kai Shek are you? . . . The first thing I said to myself was: "How come this fellow from Honduras, a backward country, way out in Central America, is worrying about Chiang Kai Shek?"[111]

Romualdi remarks on the "backwardness" of Honduran organizing efforts he perceived in his early visit, perhaps compared to larger countries in Latin America, such as Venezuela or Mexico. The striking part of this note, however, is Romualdi's observation that leaders existed and demonstrated a concern about international politics and perhaps the potential for leftist progressives to exist in the country at this time. Romualdi also missed the banana workers and the banana regions altogether, especially if he only went to Tegucigalpa, not remarking at all on the over 30,000 workers laboring there.

Tracking down Communist Party members and "labor agitators" was a large part of the work of the US Embassy in Honduras, and later in 1957, after the strike, the State Department designated a labor attaché, Barney Taylor, who reported to the US State Department regularly.[112] During the strike the detailed labor memos by agents of the ORIT reported on labor union "communist" activity and which unions embraced free labor. The labor attaché worked closely with

ORIT representatives not only to track union activities but also to assist unions in building their leadership structure, conducting negotiations with the government and companies, and resolving internal disputes. The ORIT agents traveled throughout the Central American region and would often check in with the US Embassy upon arrival to Honduras, yet they also pretended to have independent relationships with worker unions. ORIT promoted a specifically US style of trade unionism—free labor, as they called it—an anti-communist vision of building labor to ascend to the middle class while still working with supervisors and companies to achieve labor goals.

The US Embassy's strategy to combat the "communist threat" was to train leaders in the newly created Honduran Labor Bureau "to bring democratic labor organizational techniques and know-how into Honduras to cultivate the field as a preventative [means], so to speak, against Communist Labor agitation,"[113] and to nurture US-dominated labor institutions. The US labor representatives—Arturo Jáuregui from Peru, Romualdi from the United States, and Augusto Malavé Villalba from Venezuela—on behalf of the ORIT, became trainers and advisors to the Honduran government and at the same time to the emerging leaders of the labor unions. The US Embassy connection and reliance on the ORIT, and vice versa, was meant to be kept secret and downplayed.[114] The big enemy of the Americans, and Hondurans in government, was communism as they understood it.

The ORIT saw its advantage in training and education along those lines. In a press release in August of 1954, George Meany, who was president of the AFL and said to be a critical lynchpin in getting the strike to stop and encouraging the company to negotiate, reported that "Romualdi, who has just returned from Honduras, said that he had never witnessed a more enthusiastic reception to trade unionism" and that "the University of Honduras has organized a seminar in cooperation with the ORIT to develop trade union leaders; six young trade unionists are being sent to attend an ORIT seminar in Monterrey, Mexico, next month, and 12 are going to the University of Puerto Rico seminar and then to the United States through Point IV."[115] By 1954, after the strike, Romualdi's attitude toward the banana region shifted, and he recognized that the only way to keep workers away from communist ideals was to provide trainings on trade unionism at the national university. These trainings were not unusual in Honduras, as Truman's Point Four Program was already in place there to improve not only public education and health care but also police and secret service training. Those who seemed to benefit most were recently graduated young men, attorneys, teachers, doctors, and the leaders of the newly emerging unions.

In 1955 Patilla Chinchilla, a recently graduated teacher, was able to qualify for travel and training in Puerto Rico, after an arduous exam. Though he had recently graduated as a teacher from the Centroamerica Normal School in Comayagua, he could not find work, nor could he enter the university for further study due to his debt to the government. It did not help that he was a Liberal.

> Because of the political situation, there was no one to recommend us [working-class Liberal Party members], we had to present the certification of study to continue studying in the university but had to pay the scholarship first. There was a law during [the presidency of] Gálvez that said that those of us who received a scholarship to study to be a teacher had to pay the state back by working in schools for four years, but when I received a teaching assignment in Jesús de Otoro, it was taken away by local Nationalists. . . . Many of us started studying Commerce at the Institute of Pineda Ugarte and looked for jobs elsewhere.[116]

When he ended up finding work it was with the Ministry of Treasury and Public Credit, and after arduous tests, he was chosen to attend training in Puerto Rico on a variety of topics including fraud detection.

When he was in the Normal School, Chinchilla had come into contact with the North American organization Servicio Cooperativo Interamericano de Educación (SCIDE; Inter-American Service Cooperative of Education), because it helped to run the curriculum for teacher training. But it was not until his work for the Ministry of Treasury and Public Credit that Chinchilla was able to ascend into more training in Puerto Rico. Though Chinchilla does not explicitly say it, it is probable he received training through the Point Four scholarship, meant to aid developing nations, which may have in fact been useful in promoting anti-communist institutions in Honduras due to its deep reach into education, health care, and institutional trainings of state offices. The Point Four program sought to develop self-reliance in developing nations by bringing "international technical assistance—one that would alleviate poverty, ameliorate living standards and thwart the growth of Communism."[117] For many Hondurans of the Liberal Party looking to earn a living after graduating, these programs offered possibilities for advancement not available to them from the Honduran government in Tegucigalpa.

In a US Embassy memo, written to State Department officials in February of 1953, an aide explained that the CTAL would be holding their worker congress in Chile in March of 1953 and that editors of the newspaper *Voz Obrera* and other leaders would seek visas to attend.[118] The memo was intended to prevent the paper's leadership from obtaining visas to travel to the gathering by colluding with Honduran state officials. José Argueta Urquía and the CCO were under constant surveillance due to their weekly newspaper *Voz Obrera*, which was widely read in the banana fields, and also for the organization's perceived connections to the CTAL. An extensive Labor Report (1952) by the US Embassy in Tegucigalpa to the US State Department cited efforts by the Honduran government to create a Labor Bureau and change the existing labor rules and regulations.[119] But the biggest perceived threat in the area of labor was a trip that activists, including Argueta Urquía, took to Asunción, Paraguay, on behalf of *Voz Obrera*.[120] The US Embassy explicitly identified *Voz Obrera* as "strictly leftist and apparently completely financed by the CTAL from Mexico."[121] The same memo insinuates that these worker papers were "anti-administration" newspapers:

> [They] mentioned the perennial chant of exploitation by the United Fruit Company. In most cases attacks were made against the company's policy of labor turn-over and accusations were made that the company was dismissing two to three thousand employees at a time. In many cases the accusation is true but the company really cannot be accused of any exploitation since the labor turn-over on the farms and the wharves is seasonal or when the opportunity applies and most of the workers whom the company is accused of dismissing ordinarily are rehired within a short period in a different place or are occasional workers to start with.[122]

In reality, in the banana companies' fincas and on the wharves, workers' contracts lasted as long as the work demand lasted. Worker job security and seniority were nonexistent concepts for companies, and even for Honduran government representatives. Workers, however, were already starting to demand better pay and job security. These demands were made not only by banana company workers but also by workers in other industries in San Pedro Sula and Tegucigalpa. By 1952, Honduras was ripe for change, at least in workplaces, both national and foreign-owned.[123]

While the memorandum identified that the CCO was doing the bulk of the labor organizing, a smaller organization called Sociedad Esfuerzo y Cultura (Endeavor and Culture Society) was cited as having connections to the CTAL through its representative Angel Castillo, who traveled to Mexico City.[124] Castillo and his group were perceived as dangerous because of their internal labor organizing, and the US Embassy in Tegucigalpa was especially preoccupied with their international connections, as they were concerned that funding came from more developed labor movements in countries such as Mexico or Argentina. These small labor committees demonstrated the spark of new labor organizations in the country as well as the continuity of older efforts. At the same time, the Federación de Asociaciones Femenina Hondureñas (Federation of Honduran Feminist Associations) was attempting to gain suffrage for women, but its efforts were not perceived to be as threatening as the working-class organizing happening around the American enclaves.

As the Carías Andino dictatorship came to an end in the early 1940s, the transition to a bipartisan electoral model emerged. Though liberals and leftists were still persecuted, the period held promise for a political opening, a moment of opportunity for those who disagreed with the Nationalist Party and its close relationship with fruit companies. A resurgence of leftist organizers, many of whom were exiled during the dictatorship and alienated from the original founding of the Communist Party in 1929 and other leftist organizations, seized this chance to oppose the *Cariato*.[125] More importantly, they saw the potential to challenge US domination, despite the continuity of the Nationalist Party in power through Juan Manuel Gálvez, Carías Andino's chosen successor and a former attorney for UFCo. Organizers believed that UFCo, and especially the Standard Fruit Company, represented US dominance in the region.

Honduras, along with most Latin American countries, faced a new phase of US empire building following the end of the Carías Andino dictatorship in 1944 and in the wake of World War II.[126] The US State Department was engaged in covert operations to provide "technical" assistance—including the use of military aid, planes, and pilots and training for Honduran pilots in the United States—to combat communism in nations abroad. Yet Central American nations had been slow to engage in surveillance and counterintelligence tactics and social control. As the October Revolution (1944–1954) progressed in Guatemala, the United States began to coalesce a group of like-minded generals and military men around the issue of surveillance and social control—which resonated with governments, especially during a period of political opening and emerging worker protests.[127]

UFCo and US Embassy cooperation took on a new meaning in the post–World War II McCarthy era in the United States, and American citizens living and working in Central America were asked, and some took it upon themselves, to engage in anti-communist projects of surveillance and documentation.[128] The Cold War period marked the transformation of the liberal oligarchic system, established during the liberal reform period, into a system in which the elite ruling classes began to function as a "dominant bloc"[129] against the working class. The Honduran dominant bloc intersected with the US State Department's modernist agenda, which tended to "reduce political or moral problems to questions of mere technology and management, a results-oriented mentality associated, by the 1950s, with a belief in the value-neutrality of social science."[130] The severe repression of workers by the US State Department and the banana companies was legitimized by the Honduran dominant bloc in power. This is fundamental to understanding the Cold War era in Honduras. The national elite saw repression as an almost necessary evil, as the path to modernization and prosperity, which at that point was embodied by UFCo and the Standard Fruit Company in the region. These companies had become the emblems of a US-style of modernization, and elite efforts for "modernization" were thus aligned with the US State Department, regardless of the ethical issues.

The involvement of the ORIT would cripple any Honduran worker-defined democracy and justice in 1954 and prioritize free labor according to US State Department ideology. The involvement of US labor operatives, such as Romualdi and Jáuregui, limited Honduran workers' self-determination.[131] The detailed memos of the ORIT show how workers and leftists were manipulated by the company, the state, and the ORIT representatives—who presented a friendly face providing technical expertise while also exchanging information with the US State Department, and who always seemed to be on hand for the formation of union statutes and federations and for feuds among workers. The ORIT representatives grew to distrust the legal advisor to the emerging worker unions, Gustavo Zavala, who, since the labor code was not in place yet, assisted them in dealing with the government in Tegucigalpa. McLellan explains in a lengthy memo why he distrusted him so deeply:

I checked on the trade union situation in Tegucigalpa, and found the Lic. [Licenciado] Gustavo Zavala controlled practically all of the unions in the capital. It was through his organizational efforts that most of the unions in Tegucigalpa were organized, reportedly, Zavala as Legal Advisor for some eleven different unions. It is quite apparent that Zavala is exploiting these organizations for his own purpose, as his entire law practice is built around the unions, whose members he represents in the courts for substantial fees. He has publicly disagreed with the ORIT policy, and has been critical of ORIT on a number of occasions.[132]

The memo explains that Zavala was making a profit off of workers and was fearful that the ORIT would investigate him. They felt he should not be organizing in the capital but rather ought to dedicate himself to building the north-coast union jurisdiction first. Clearly by now the main target for organizing was the north coast. The role of ORIT, however, was to ensure that they had the control, rather than any Honduran. By using another attorney, Santos Reyes Ayestas, they made sure to "weaken" Zavala by splintering his group:

> The strong hold which Lic. [Licenciado] Gustavo Zavala has maintained on the labor groups in Tegucigalpa is being slowly weakened by Lic. Santos Reyes Ayestas with the aid of the splinter elements which have already broken with Zavala. Zavala, as reported by me August 1956, was operating a vicious type of protective (unreadable) with the pseudo trade unions which he had helped to organize.[133]

Zavala was accused of being greedy and stealing from workers' union funds. The level of detail paid to the cases of Zavala and Ayestas gives us a glimpse of how much workers' lives were being watched and manipulated. After the 1954 strike ORIT would document not only communist activity but any activity that could jeopardize the ORIT's positioning among workers and their emerging labor unions.

There was a close relationship between the repressive years of dictatorship in the 1930s and the years of political freedom in the 1940s. The demands of workers in the latter period "clearly emanated from the lived experience of as well as from the impact of the Allied commitment to the 'Four Freedoms' and the existence of a historical 'window of opportunity' for some three years before the onset of the Cold War."[134]

In the Guatemalan context, in 1944 and the years that followed the October Revolution, there was a resurgence of leftist collectives and parties and the emergence of union-organizing efforts. Yet Honduran radicals exiled in Guatemala, where they experienced the October Revolution firsthand, were eager to bring to Honduras the spirit of organizing for agrarian reform and building worker power against UFCo. Honduran exiles were inspired by the project of the October Revolution: "Through politics it offered a vision of participatory democracy, a vision in which individual activists were able to engage the state while remaining connected to their local communities"[135]

In the early 1920s, working-class efforts in Honduras focused on forming unions in the mining industry with some concern about foreign domination. In 1944 organizing efforts all but exclusively advanced the agenda of forming a union to weaken the dominion over workers by UFCo and Standard Fruit Company specifically. Counterrevolutionary efforts embraced the agenda of the US State Department and the notions of free labor and democracy, and ultimately sought to curtail workers' self-determination. As in Guatemala, in Honduras anti-communism was a banner embraced by a broad swath of the mestizo elite population, who in tandem with US interests justified the persecution and removal of worker organizers and did not oppose the various forms of persecution employed: imprisonment, torture, exile, disappearance, and death. In this context, any worker action that critiqued or challenged US companies was deemed "communist." Thus the politics of the "internal enemy" gained traction in the midcentury and would play out throughout the rest of the century, marking workers and farmworkers in particular as the targets for repression. This is the climate in which the 1954 strike was organized and executed. It is also the enduring context for the United States' ongoing Cold War intervention in Honduras and the region.

THE HEAVY HAND OF US INTERVENTION BEFORE AND AFTER THE COLD WAR

While studies of the Cold War in Central America have focused on the contemporary relationship between the US State Department and Honduran government, their relationship actually dates back to the turn of the century, when the State Department was a protectorate for US business in the region and in Honduras specifically. Cold War studies on Honduras focus on the era of civil wars in the 1980s, perhaps the most violent years in Central America and the years in which Honduras served as the training ground for the United States' counterinsurgency tactics. But it is the mid-twentieth century that set the stage for the 1980s. While the US State Department protected UFCo in Honduras, boasting an embassy and several consulates throughout the north-coast region, it was after the strike and the 1954 coup d'état in Guatemala and after the 1959 Cuban Revolution that the Cold War politics expanded their reach into Honduras, as it did in the rest of Latin America.

US involvement in Honduras focused on redirecting labor strategy through the ORIT and protecting US assets through the US Embassy and its contacts with the Honduran government. At the same time, Honduras provided a central launching point for US operations in the rest of the region. While UFCo, in cooperation with the US Embassy, followed workers perceived to have communist and leftist leanings and traced their whereabouts, fearful of regional cooperation, there seemed not to be a well-developed Honduran government intelligence department capable of surveillance. But for the United States this was a priority. Robert H. Holden explains that as far back as 1950 there were already a number of agencies and individuals affiliated with the US Embassy submitting reports on Honduran citizens, "for example, the State Department's labor attaché in Mexico City, Ben S. Stephansky, reported on August 23, 1954, on 'three or four Hondurans possibly attending Lombardo Toledano's *Universidad Obrera*.'"[136] The Toledano school was seen as leftist and the most important group to oppose the free labor agenda proposed by US officials. This report, dated after the end of the 1954 strike, was written at the same time that members of the original Central Strike Committee were persecuted, exiled, or jailed. In any case, the document points to increased, concerted surveillance of Hondurans outside of Honduras—a technical and financial impossibility for the Honduran government at the time. The cooperation of the Honduran government with US surveillance, coercion, and persecution of its citizens was actually a dangerous aspect of the Cold War from its inception: it allowed for the US State Department to dictate its strategy, and the data collected would serve the United States' Cold War policies and purposes.[137] Though Honduran government protection and solidarity with UFCo and Standard Fruit Company date back to the early part of the twentieth century, the government first entered into a diplomatic relationship with the United States in two instances: the 1947 Rio agreement and the 1954 bilateral military agreement.[138]

As the fear of communism rose in areas where the United States was operating, the United States became more involved militarily, and their surveillance and coercion led to the endorsement of military leaders. According to Holden, Central American nations would not have been able to build their "surveillance capacity" if it were not for US support in the name of the Cold War.[139] Developing surveillance mechanisms against perceived communism was the core philosophy of those entrenched in the US State Department's Cold War practices, though in the United States they referred to it as "modernization and security." Elites who ran Central American nations and were ideologically aligned with the US State Department sought collaboration and resources to develop such surveillance and security.[140] The relationship between the elite, military rulers, and the US State Department provided a means of delivering US "technical tools for surveillance" that ultimately modernized military authoritarian rule, rather than cultivating a democracy.[141] The convergence of the US strategic agendas of modernization and security manifested on the ground as a heavy-handed approach that superseded morality and ethics.

The Cold War in Latin America had dire and profound consequences for worker organizers, turning efforts to organize and moments of great possibility for lasting democratic change into killing fields,[142] all throughout the twentieth century and into the twenty-first century with a coup d'état in 2009. The currently emerging political and cultural resistance, despite US capitalist intervention, suggests the possibilities of a resilient Honduran worker movement that recasts Honduras as a self-determining republic, rather than a pawn of US capitalism and imperialism without agency. The roots of this lie in the early and mid-twentieth-century labor and leftist resistance, most importantly in the north-coast banana fields.

CHAPTER 3

LIFE AND LABOR
IN THE BANANA FINCAS

Walking through Nuevo San Juan, a recently formed neighborhood of banana workers in the outskirts of La Lima, Cortés, is eerie. You can almost imagine what was there before: neat rows of bright-green banana trees, their majestic, wind-stripped, rectangular leaves, and the famous barracones, the company houses on stilts, with the busy kitchens of the patronas. You can almost hear the train whistling amid the bustling life of the campos, the rails that once served as a gateway for the company into the north-coast region. Over time, this region evolved from a series of small, isolated hamlets amid vast fields of bananas to a web of plantations with important connections to established towns and even cities. This growth was due to the banana companies and the capital with which they recruited immigrant workers, imported machinery, and imposed a wage-labor system in the country. It is on this land that Nuevo San Juan is built, on the old grounds of the former banana fincas (plantations) and campos (living quarters) such as San Juan, La Curva, Copén, and Tacamiche.[1]

The growth of the large banana plantations began after 1912, when the Tela Railroad Company first began production in Honduras. The first few hired workers had to break through jungle with only their machetes to clear the land for planting. They worked without living quarters, slept near the rails, cooked for themselves over makeshift fires, and dealt with the environmental hazards of the Caribbean lowlands as best they could. Times would change in the midcentury. At the heart of all this change was the development of small villages, like La Lima, into big cosmopolitan hubs—a product of the train and abundant capital introduced into the region by the Tropical Division,[2] as the United

Fruit Company (UFCo) called its production zones in Latin America. As production increased, the growing number of workers outside of the villages and towns like La Lima needed housing. The barracones in the campos became essential to the survival of the workers; more than mere housing, these became homes for migrant workers from all over Honduras and even regions beyond its borders. The campo became a complex and racially diverse community.

Over the last half of the twentieth century, the company endured highs and lows in profits and production, including devastation from hurricanes, lawsuits for illegal use of pesticides, and stiff competition in the Caribbean market. These challenges led the banana producer and exporter Chiquita Brands—a reincarnation of the notorious UFCo, the former owner of the Tela Railroad and Steamship Company—to divest from Honduras. The consequences of these changes started to become apparent in 1994, when the Tela Railroad Company began to close down the plantations and adjacent living quarters that had been home to the campeños for more than eighty years.[3] In order to appease workers, they offered either severance pay or the option to transfer to another plantation to work.[4] On the very location where Nuevo San Juan now stands, banana workers had fought to keep the land they had worked for so many years, only to be ultimately evicted by 600 soldiers, by order of the president, who sided with the Tela Railroad Company. Men and women defended the old wood planks that held their life histories, including stories of migration to work the banana lands of the north coast. But the company won, and the fincas and campos were dismantled in old San Juan, Tacamiche, and adjacent campos. For workers who lived on those very lands, the company's decision to tear down the campos did not make any sense. Tearing apart the barracones when their residents were at retirement age felt utterly violent, like a *desalojo* (eviction). With the evictions and destruction of the barracones went years of connection to the land. It was an abrupt end to a way of life for banana plantation workers and their families.

Until the *desalojo*, the banana fincas and campos were vibrant places of work, life, and resistance, where workers strained against the company's prescriptive order and constructed homes. Workers' housing arrangements, coupled with company policies and practices of paternalistic control over their workers, contributed to the radical transformation of the culture of work and life in the north coast over time, which included eradicating subsistence economies and replacing them with a wage-labor system. The stories that workers told me about the community they created and how they spent their social time in the campos reveal how through their own creativity and despite the company's controlling policies they built a space they could call their very own. Workers adapted to the harsh work environment, coped with and confronted the companies' desire for control, pursued their own aspirations, and grappled with sometimes conflicting or uneasy interactions with other workers. Their interpersonal relations in the fincas and campos, while working and during leisure time, reflect their negotiated identities, lived experiences, and the reasons they joined in the effort to organize the great 1954 strike. Among their demands were improved living quarters, schools for their children, improved services in the campos, equitable access to healthcare, and adequate wages. Their testimonies and experiences provide a far more complex and nuanced understanding of these workers than either the iconic images that have come to symbolize the strike or the simplistic stereotypes circulated in local folklore of the north coast.

MIGRATION, LABOR, AND THE MAKING OF THE NORTH COAST

The north-coast banana fincas and campos where the agricultural laborers lived and worked were geographically removed from the small towns and hamlets inhabited by empleados de confianza (trusted company employees), skilled workers and those who arrived from the United States to work for UFCo. While the fincas and campos were part of the corporation's enclave, these areas did not benefit from the amenities reserved for the "town" workers, who could attend movies and dances regularly, play golf, have their trash picked up, and access products brought in from the United States. Instead, agricultural workers created their own lives, in rural lands, developing a set of social rules and diversions, a mishmash of customs from the various regions from which they had migrated.

From a bird's-eye view, the banana region resembled a long rectangle on the north coast of Honduras, with the railroad tracks connecting all the fincas and adjacent campos. The train connected them to the small company town centers of Puerto Cortés, La Lima, and Tela, as well as the hamlets in between. Roads were not built until the mid-1950s, so the main means of transportation was the same for people and goods as it was for bananas: the train. The campos were the lifeblood of the entire banana operation, which revolved around the successful harvesting and transport of bananas from the plantations to the shipping centers on the north coast of Honduras, and eventually to the United States.

UFCo organized itself into Tropical Division in Latin America, boasting subsidiaries in Mexico, Cuba, Guatemala, Honduras, Costa Rica, Panama, and the South American countries of Colombia and Ecuador. Within the subsidiaries lay a web of departments that reported up the chain of command, from the plantation to the Tropical Division, then to the main company headquarters in Boston.[5] The web of departments that comprised the all-encompassing Tela Railroad and Steamship Company in Honduras met a range of operational needs: the Medical Department boasted a hospital, nursing staff, and doctors; the Materials and Supplies Department served as a warehouse, receiving supplies and dispatching them to other departments; the Engineering Department oversaw everything from the rails to the maintenance of the trains and all technology running the fincas; the Construction Department was responsible for the construction and upkeep of buildings; the Sanitation Department collected town-dwellers' trash and also fumigated throughout the company's regions with pesticides to combat diseases such as malaria; the Chemical Department was tasked with figuring out how to eradicate disease in the banana plants and spray pesticides; the Research Department worked to insure that bananas would be resistant to disease and also conducted other experiments; and the Agricultural Department, the subject of this chapter, and by far the largest department, consisted of the workers who harvested and pruned the fruit. Superintendents, often Anglos from the United States, were responsible for overseeing the larger departments. Below them was an efficient and regimented hierarchy of supervisors, such as finca captains, overseers, and timekeepers. The main office for the Tela Division was in La Lima, a company town on the outskirts of the larger city, San Pedro Sula, Cortés. Just beyond, between La Lima and the nearby small towns of El Progreso and Tela, was a patchwork of banana fincas and campos. The campos sat alongside the fincas, usually divided by the railroad tracks, which connected each of the fincas to the small towns in a linear formation that ended at the port of Puerto Cortés.

The organization and hierarchy of the Tela Railroad Company reflects UFCo's vertical-integration model of production in the first half of the twentieth century, a system that sought to control every aspect of production in order to coordinate more dependable delivery and preserve the quality of the product.[6] This system was only possible because conciliatory governments, such as the *Cariato* in Honduras, conceded land and benefits to the company, as noted in the previous chapter. In the postwar period, the company was in flux, shifting its production model to adjust for diminishing profits as it faced competition from the Standard Fruit Company, which gained an advantage by moving away from growing the Gros Michel variety to the more disease-resistant Valery banana.[7] UFCo sought to disengage from direct production, a trend that would slowly begin in the midcentury with a push toward distribution and marketing.[8] Company changes and shifts over time would drastically affect workers' lives toward the end of the century. But during the earlier period of vertical integration, workers' adaptation and survival strategies, coupled with labor mobilizations, challenged the company's top-down control and profit model.

The north coast of the past was a cosmopolitan area where immigrant workers, merchants, Honduran growers, the Honduran state, and US banana companies and their employees contributed to the vibrancy of the region. Although the banana companies are often credited with the construction of the north coast, culturally, politically, and environmentally, the region was, and is, actually a result of the negotiations of relationships and contestations of power among these multiple players. During the period between 1944 and 1957, the north coast gained the reputation of being the best place to secure work, a land of opportunity, a place where a campesino/a, man or woman, could get a start on life or even start over. The banana companies demanded a steady migrant labor supply to keep up operations and therefore relied on large-scale migration networks that developed over time. Migrant workers to the north coast constructed a community and a banana-worker culture that fueled the labor movement and development of the working class and contributed to the dramatic transformation of the north coast. It is this worker culture that would eventually challenge the banana companies' dominion over them. Banana-industry workers, and in particular agricultural workers in the fields, had a significant influence due to their sheer numbers. Although the details of their lives and experiences receive scant attention outside of Honduran literary and academic circles, agricultural workers and their labor formed perhaps the most important sector of the transnational banana companies and arguably made the most lasting contributions to the north coast and later development of the country.

In the early part of the twentieth century, workers first migrated to the area, lured by promises of wealth from company recruiters tasked with satisfying a need for a larger workforce than the poquiteros had attracted. Although the companies recruited workers aggressively, others were drawn in by word of mouth and reports that almost always promised higher wages than those in their villages. Workers often traveled to the north coast with great hardship. People traveled from these towns to the banana regions on foot and by hitching rides on donkeys and horses. Passage to return home was expensive, and the distances were great; most people walked for weeks.[9] Paved roads did not exist between the departments of Olancho in the southeast, Valle in the south, Copán in the west, and the north coast. Olancho residents tended to migrate to the Standard Fruit Company installations on the eastern riverbank of the Aguán River or the Truxillo Railroad Company, which existed up until 1934.[10] Migrants from Copán and Valle tended to head into the Cuyamel Fruit Company. After the consolidation of the Tela Railroad Company in 1912, many went to the larger and extensive UFCo fincas.

US business scouts for both the Tela Railroad Company and Standard Fruit were sent to secure labor. Barahona writes, "During the first years of company activity they would send recruiters to the towns and hamlets to look for workers. The new salaried men would come from the central and southern regions of the country."[11] These young men, many of whom came from small rural towns and hamlets in Honduras, other Central American countries, and Jamaica, rarely left the north coast after coming to work and took few leaves of absence from their employment to return home. Rural workers came to the north coast because the company offered better salaries than what they could earn elsewhere.[12] Pay in the rest of the country was $0.50 US a day, while by 1944, banana workers (including migrants) were earning between $1.50 to $2.00 US or more a day.

Initial migration was primarily men, but from the 1940s onward more campesina women migrated north looking for work in the informal economy in the campos. Young women also migrated to the north coast, and not always with husbands; once they arrived, many found partners who had also migrated from the interior of Honduras and countries such as El Salvador, Guatemala, Nicaragua, and Jamaica. By the 1950s, however, women were arriving in the north coast on their own looking for work.[13]

At the height of the industry in the 1920s in Honduras, banana workers in the groves of the Tela Railroad Company and the Standard Fruit Company were the best paid in Honduras. This was the most desirable work on the entire north coast, but at the same time, the lives of banana workers in these fincas were marked by brutal working and living conditions. The mostly male finca workers lived virtually without any workers' rights—except the ones they demanded and enforced for themselves. Laborers created a unique working-class culture in the region, which was critical to the 1954 strike. The workers I introduce in this chapter were catalysts for major labor and political changes in the region and the nation. Work, leisure, campo life, and workers' navigation of these factors resulted in the development of their very own brand of working-class identity particular to the banana regions and north coast. The strike movement rooted itself in this terrain and cohered in a collectively lived experience in the banana fincas, and in the diversity of campeños who lived and worked there.

By 1944, banana workers formed the majority of the population of the north coast. Many faced hard journeys from their hometowns in various departments and provinces of Honduras, El Salvador, and Jamaica to work on banana plantations. Like many migrant workers of the time, they persevered and made the best of their lives and environment to survive. Campeños had been coming to the north coast since the early 1900s directly from southern and southwestern departments of Copán, Ocotepeque, Valle, Olancho, and even from El Salvador.[14] Others had spent many decades in the north coast because their fathers or mothers had migrated to these regions in earlier decades. They were not a regular and dominant presence in the company towns, however, because they spent most of their lives laboring on the banana plantations.

CAMPEÑOS AND CAMPEÑAS WORKING HARD IN THE BANANA GROVES

In the banana regions of Honduras, the working class was constructed and constructed itself, politically and culturally, in a process that was unique to the north coast. The intricacies of the construction and convergence of heterogeneous sectors of the working class in the north coast were influenced by race, ethnicity, nationality, and gender—the dynamics of which played out in the campos.[15] The process of becoming a campeño or campeña was not only an economic but also a cultural and political formation of identity. Workers brought with them rural campesino traditions that influenced the construction of new wage/contractor worker practices in the banana regions. Without the campesino understanding of land and work, banana workers in the fincas would not have been successful—nor indeed would the bananeras themselves. The majority of workers who migrated to labor in the banana fincas—and those I interviewed—were agricultural workers who expressed an affinity for working the land. They had a knowledge of and level of comfort with the tools and skills of land cultivation, and they sought to put their expertise to gainful use in the north coast. The functioning of the vast banana plantations thus relied on the availability of knowledgeable workers to cultivate the fincas; campeños were a ready and willing labor source that enabled and aided the rapid growth of the industry.

At the same time, the construction of the regional banana-worker culture was influenced by the transition of campesinos and subsistence farmers to wage work and the new operational systems that the fruit companies introduced into their lives and work. Together these adaptations formed a hybrid environment and culture, best described as a unique semi-rural, semi-urban terrain emblematic of the period. It is appropriate to note here that my analysis presents a context unique to Honduran banana workers' experience. Despite the dominance of the US banana industry throughout Central America, and some commonalities across the region, corporate practices varied from country to country, and the bananeras adapted according to the domestic practices of their Central American hosts. For instance, the contracting system was not the same in all UFCo banana plantations.[16] On the Honduran north coast, compared to other regions, there was a starker hierarchy in the relationships among workers of contractor teams who harvested in the fields. There were other differences in work processes and workers' positions as well. This differentiation in company practices may be a sign of negotiated preferences or may have been the result of competition between UFCo and Standard Fruit Company in the Honduran north coast and the Costa Rican Caribbean Coast. It may also have been the adaptation required for the industries to adjust to each country's specific circumstances, including the roles and agency of workers.

In Honduras, the specification of the small, entry-level positions and the myriad of work positions reveal a practice of providing piecework wages (*salario a destajo*), where a worker is paid for the number of tasks accomplished during a determined amount of time. In the fincas, workers received essentially a piece rate for each area harvested and the number of stems gathered during work time instead of a period rate for time worked.[17] While it may have developed differently in other areas, in Honduras, the banana industry of the time heralded dramatic changes in workers' lives and work, as well as the transition to wage work (proletarianization) in concrete ways. The worker was expected to do repetitive and menial work for a predetermined length of time and until completion of certain tasks or production quotas were met.

In Honduras, banana workers inhabited a dynamic position, transitioning from rural campesino lives in their hometowns to a state of proletarianization in the north coast.[18] In the banana regions, workers constructed their own communities, which sometimes looked very different from their original, native communities, but which reflected a sustained nostalgia for the campesino life. In interviews, workers reflected on having the desire to return home with ample earnings to buy a plot of land or build a house. For north-coast workers who lacked access to land and their own means of production, the aspiration to return home to work their own land was an important sustained dream throughout their lives in the campos.[19] There, banana workers who migrated lacked a "web of family and communal relationships" on the north coast; instead, they were forced to create other networks around the new economy, forming distinct communities in each campo and within each ethnic and racial group.[20] The constructions of community in the banana campos diverge from the theory of the peasant economy, which positions the household as the unit of analysis for labor and gender relations. In the banana regions, the unit of analysis is a broader campo that consisted of the finca and the living quarters, and not only the household. The banana workers' community consisted of physical intersections of space, activity, and identities in three major social and geographic spheres within the plantation and living quarters: the workplace, in this case the work in the fincas; the company housing units and living arrangements in the campos; and leisure and time off from work, which provided space to organize and resist company control. These various community spheres together informed the broader banana-worker identity of the campeño. The campeño and campeña resistance and resilience contributed to the building of radical politics among workers and throughout the region.

WORKING THE BANANA FINCA SYSTEM

Honduran popular writer and former banana worker Ramón Amaya Amador wrote a popular novel about the banana fincas, which was banned throughout the 1980s in Honduras due to fears that it would incite workers to revolutionary action. Its title, *Prisión Verde*, is a powerful metaphor for the geography of the finca and workers' lives.[21] The "green prison" he so aptly described was a place where workers entered and rarely left, making the north coast their home and their children's homes. Workers inhabited but also strained against the "green prison," which was framed around the work in the fincas and the negotiation of their lives in a prescribed system of work. Workers' testimonies reveal a complex system of negotiation against company control.

The fincas were neatly organized in rows interspersed with dugout water channels to irrigate the banana groves. The channels were deep and wide. Workers would hop across them daily, sometimes while carrying banana stems weighing over 100 pounds each. Everyday life and work were characterized by arduous labor. Workers faced long workdays and low pay, compounded by hazardous working conditions that exposed them to harmful chemicals, diseases like malaria, and perils like the infamous *barba amarilla* snake, which was said to kill with just one bite.[22] Poor campesino men suffered under nearly inhuman expectations that they would labor for twelve hours straight, cutting, carrying, spraying, watering, and washing bananas; cleaning fields; pruning the banana plants; and enduring extreme sun and humid weather.[23] During the late 1940s and early 1950s, workers reported earning no more than 2.20 lempiras ($1.10 US) a day, but these were still the highest paying jobs in the region.[24] The tough working conditions created among the campeños an inevitable shared experience of hardship from the moment they entered the finca to work.

Despite outsiders and townspeople's perceptions of the banana groves as a wild, untamed territory, there was an established order to things, including a company hierarchy as well as a system of work and hiring. Workers survived in part due to strong, shared connections among laborers. Often they migrated to the north coast with contacts from their hometowns, provinces, or departments, which ensured some sort of access to work.[25] Men entered finca work through a system of padrinazgo (patronage), unlike in the company towns, where references and proof of certain skills were necessary to obtain a job. A *padrino*, or a friend who worked for the company, in a particular finca or port would help someone get hired, but this meant putting themselves on the line, too. Angel Martinez recalled, "The person who recommended you was responsible for you. You had to be on your best behavior, because if you behaved badly, the person that recommended you would look bad. It was better to put up with anything [and not complain] or leave the job than to make a mistake."[26] People thus found work through immigrant social networks that they were careful to respect and maintain. Young men would often come back to their hometowns telling stories about the north coast and sharing ideas of travel. These networks offered both jobs and protection; workers watched out for one another and were careful not to get others in trouble. Campeños and the culture they built relied on a sense of solidarity with one another, built over time and through padrinazgo and other trusted networks. Each finca was its own fiefdom and offered its own distinct subculture. In the absence of clearly stated overarching company policies on worker duties, each supervisor in the fincas could establish his own labor-relations policies and practices, depending on their needs and temperament. This work process in the finca generated an interdependence among workers in the finca and between fincas and defined an important component of the local campeño identity; they needed each other to improve their own working conditions and access suitable and better-paid employment, and to survive and thrive.

The most expansive and accessible social networks were those established and supported by mestizo men, as they were both the majority and those who fit most easily into the established worker culture. Exact data on the population of mestizos and other ethnic groups that migrated to north coast to enter the ranks of the company is nonexistent, but mestizos certainly were the predominant group.

Upon arrival in the north coast, people typically started as day laborers who picked up jobs on a day-to-day basis. The goal for most was to eventually obtain any regularly scheduled job with the company and then seek opportunities to move into other preferred positions that might pay better or lead to more autonomous agricultural positions in the fincas. Those laborers came to work in any kind of jobs they could find, usually starting at the very bottom of the finca hierarchy. The entry positions for finca laborers were usually the worst paid and least desirable, and workers had little choice in the assignments they received. Changing job assignments did not typically include getting promoted into better-paid positions, but workers appreciated the freedom and opportunity to move between fincas. If they tired of certain kinds of work, they went to another finca to find something that suited their skills and training.[27]

A variety of daily jobs provided entry-level work for the company. Young men jumped at the opportunity to take entry-level finca work as a stepping-stone to better-paid positions. They would make contact with work teams, develop a skill within the team, either by shadowing workers or by being mentored by an older worker, and then either wait for a position to become available or move on to another finca to seek the same kind of work where there was availability. Some of the low-ranking entry-level positions were dangerous, like the ones that required workers to spray pesticides. Others were just perceived as more menial and less macho, because they did not require great body strength. For example, the position of *chapeador* (a person who trimmed the grass and overgrown weeds from the fincas, trusted employees' yards, and/or the campos) was seen as a low-ranking and low-paid position, typically assigned as entry-level work or a job for an elderly person who could not do the rigorous work of cutting bananas. These positions were still desirable, however, because they allowed workers to earn enough to eat for a day and gain entry into the bananeras' Agricultural Department.

Entering through low-ranking positions gave workers an opportunity to show their youth, strength, and ability to learn, all good qualities that they hoped would lead a supervisor to recommend them for a better job. Workers went from finca to finca looking for better work or heard from other workers where they were hiring. Being able to say they had previous experience helped secure new positions. The ultimate goal was to gain better-paid employment in agricultural work in the fincas, which, in addition to paying more, carried an affirmation of manhood among campeños. It was also the type of work that most closely resembled the farm work that many campesinos had knowledge of and valued back home.

Entry-level workers did whatever was asked of them. One worker, Edmundo Cabrera Williams, described how he started working in the fields at age 16. His assignment was to bag fruit, but he was asked to do many other odd jobs:

> Whatever they ordered us to do we had to do. Because I was a young man, my first job was to bag fruit. From there I went out to work in the finca; I was a fruit mulero [worker responsible for loading, leading, and tending to the mule team], a fruit stevedore, and a fruit washer, back when the fruit was washed in two large containers—one was full of acid, another with water. I had to wash the stem in the acid and then dip it in the water container. That is how the stems were sent [shipped] before.[28]

Bagging fruit was considered easy starting work for a young boy in his teens, and while doing this job, Cabrera Williams learned the process of cleaning and shipping the fruit. He could then work his way into different positions.

Workers who later graduated into higher skilled positions (e.g., in the Chemical or Engineering Departments), or became empleados de confianza of the company, also often started with varied types of work, as was the case for Oscar Rodriguez Pagoada, who explained, "My first job was in the fincas, in finca Santa Rosa. I did various jobs in the finca at that time, whatever they assigned me to do: weeding, fertilizing, any job that presented itself."[29] Rodriguez Pagoada began to work in the finca at age 14, immediately after completing sixth grade, which was considered a high degree of education at the time. He cites this educational background and his connection to other workers in company offices as one of the key reasons for his ascension into the company system of trusted employees.[30] Others worked for the capitanes de finca (captains or supervisors) and were expected to perform various menial tasks, seemingly at the whim of the capitán de finca and his family, as in the case of Eduardo Padilla, a yardero (yard worker) for an empleado de confianza in a company town.[31] Despite the specific name, yarderos did all kinds of menial jobs, including running errands, gardening, and cleaning. It was an entry-level job because it was poorly paid and often considered light work. Jesús Gómez, who also started as a yardero, explained that much of his work involved being a chaperone for the teenage daughters of his employer, a North American empleado de confianza:

> My first job was as yardero. Yardero means that I served Mr. Keller's daughters; Zoila, she is still alive, Zoila Keller. I was a yardero for that family. That didn't mean cleaning the yard. They called me this because I was in charge of taking care of his daughters. Because I was trustworthy I took care of their daughters. They, of course, had their boyfriends.[32]

The yardero position, though it included daily physical and personal contact with the employer, did not necessarily translate into better work. These were subordinate positions akin to an errand boy or servant. But for Gómez, as for others starting out in the north coast, doing errands as a yardero was important entry work because it earned him a recommendation for a future position. Gómez eventually moved on to work in the fincas, but his experience with Mr. Keller did not necessarily help him advance. Through that entry-level job, he was able to meet other workers and get an understanding of the layout of the finca and organization of work. This allowed him to make the right connections and eventually get better-paying work in the fincas.[33]

Among the riskier entry-level assignments were jobs on a *venen-ero* (pesticide) team, which included a *manguerero* (water-hose carrier) and an *escopetero* (pesticide sprayer).[34] The team carried water hoses and pesticides to the areas in need of treatment, taking turns carrying and spraying.[35] Workers were resourceful and invented ways to minimize exposure to the hazardous pesticides. "A worker that knew how to do it . . . would not even dirty his fingernails, because he would figure out the direction of the wind," Cabrera Williams told me as he demonstrated with his body, "and spray behind the wind, away from him, so that it would not drift into him. They had their ways."[36] Even so, many of the men were exposed to pesticides and chemicals, despite workers' skills and efforts to avoid the poison:

> We used to fumigate, not with an airplane but with a spray gun. Each finca had a fumigation pump. Eighty workers labored in pairs, one would pull the fumigation hose and the other had to douse the plants. Like that. That is why the bunches would stain, since the copper sulfate is blue mixed with lime. That is why we washed [the bunches] with acid, so the fruit would not get stained or dirty.[37]

Cabrera Williams, who studied plumbing in a vocational school, was forced to take any job available—including *escopetero*—until a position opened up in his trade. Later, as a plumber, he shadowed pesticide workers to repair leaks in the hoses and tubes, never ascending beyond this position.

Another position was *fertilizador* (fertilizer), which was Alejandro Ortega's entry-level position at the Tela Railroad Company in La Lima. A fertilizer prepared the land for planting.[38] Ortega recounted, "I used to work scattering salt, a black salt that you had to be very careful with because if it touched any part of your body it would burn a hole in you . . . We were 16 young men of 14, 15, [. . .] 17 years old. We would be very careful because the workers who had a hole burned in them would no longer be able to work."[39] Workers made lateral moves across these dangerous, low-ranking positions, hoping eventually to attain preferred positions where pay was consistent and higher.[40]

Workers coveted positions as contratistas (contractors), most commonly of a cortero (fruit cutter) team, or as *paleros* (canal diggers) in a cuadrilla (ditch-digging team).[41] Contratistas had the necessary skills to lead other workers and act as liaisons with the company officials and low-ranking overseers who formed and led teams of workers for particular finca assignments. The contratistas negotiated for jobs and typically secured high earnings compared to other workers. Working by contract was desirable because workers could potentially earn double the pay.[42] Workers reported earning up to 8 lempiras ($4.00 US) as contractors, higher than the standard pay of 4.40 lempiras ($2.20 US) for workers directly employed by the company.[43] Local growers and small-scale producers who operated in the vicinity of the company were also often paid less than contractors—up to 7 lempiras ($3.50 US) a day. The company's contracted wages were better.[44]

The use of contracted cortero and cuadrilla teams set up an important hierarchy within the workplace, created a shared experience for workers, and became a critical time and space for organizing agricultural workers. Worker teams created interdependence, solidarity, and trust among workers, as they relied on relationships with the contratista and one another and shared work commitments. Analyzing in detail their various positions and interconnectedness gives us a view into this process. The most sought-after work was with cortero teams, led by a contratista, at the top of the hierarchy, and a juntero (gatherer/carrier) and a mulero (mule-team driver) at the bottom of the hierarchy. The team was contracted to cover a section of the expansive finca looking for bananas ready to harvest. These were not necessarily all located in the same rows, so the team traversed the finca in search of trees with ready-to-harvest bananas. The team walked deep into the finca in a particular trajectory and then came out with the banana stems to load onto the mules. The team would set a goal of cutting a certain quota of banana bunches before the end of each day. The contratista de corte (banana cutter contractor) received full pay directly from the company and then paid the other workers. These teams were an important part of the finca workforce, and the system of contracting corteros was an essential part of the harvesting process and the efficient and timely transport of bananas out of the fields.

Other contratistas led cuadrillas of *paleros* who dug ditches and constructed canals for new fincas.[45] Teams of laborers worked in areas lacking the infrastructure that existed in settled camps, such as a company commissary and food establishments. Pay arrangements were similar to those of the contratistas de corte. The contratista led the work, based on advanced knowledge and experience, and reported to a timekeeper and mandador (overseer) or capitán de finca.[46] The timekeeper was responsible for keeping time and tracking work completed, and for calculating the amount of work and pay for the contratista. Timekeepers were respected and regarded as skilled Honduran workers who held some degree of formal education, could count, and had some knowledge of the finca work. The relationship between the timekeeper and the contratista was critical in making sure workers were paid properly for the team's completed work. The timekeeper additionally held some bookkeeping responsibilities such as making sure the right deductions were taken from workers' pay when they bought goods from the company commissary.[47]

This contracting system granted the contratista great power and provided the company with a reliable form of control over production. Maximizing earnings was a primary incentive for both contratistas and workers, and the contratista was respected as a leader who ensured that both he and the team earned more than they would if they worked independently. A contratista was also respected by his coworkers for his knowledge and experience. He occupied an elevated social standing, evident in his power to influence his team. The contratista was a worker leader of sorts among campeños. He was not an empleado de confianza or an elite Honduran in the company, and thus he played an important role in forging relationships among workers. Oftentimes, contratistas started at the bottom and had much in common with the workers in his team; they lived in the same camp and may have shared meals and time off together. Often a contratista would bring his wife into the campos to serve as a cook for workers; this is where the title "patrona" came from. In such cases, the junteros, muleros, and other lower-paid entry-level workers would virtually be required to eat in her comedor (eating establishment). This was especially common in fincas that were located far from towns or settlements, where there were more men than women. This unspoken policy would later, during the strike, become a point of contention.

The fincas could not provide everyone with contractor work or other coveted positions; the latter, as workers described them, reflected the variety of tasks required for the fincas' operations. For example, there were the *deshijadores* (banana tree pruners), who would trim the banana plant of dangerous *hijos* (literally, "sons," but used here to refer to small banana tree outgrowths that could, if not removed, drain the plant of nutrients and impede the growth of the fruit);[48] *regadores de agua* (irrigation workers), a team of workers who would water the plantation during the night shift; and *concheros*, who were responsible for collecting the various *conchas* (skins of the fallen bananas and plantains as well as pruned banana leaves after the harvest). *Concheros* were responsible for bringing the skins to the *rejillas*, flatbed train cars with spaced slabs of wood on the sides for loading merchandise in the fincas. The skins served as a cushion for the fruit to make sure there would be no damage to the Gros Michel banana that was shipped for export at that time.[49] These positions were acknowledged among workers themselves as critical steps to obtaining better positions, a network and process of advancement within campeño lives that allowed them to be part of a respected community within the campos.

In the company towns, the work positions and assignments differed from those in the interior of the fincas.[50] The treatment of workers also differed, since most in the company towns were considered to be more highly skilled than the finca workers. They also enjoyed a higher status that workers refer to as "second class." Workers who considered themselves indios (those who were born in Honduras or who could pass for being born there, but not necessarily Indigenous) also had class differences among them. According to Juan Bautista Canales, finca workers were classified as unskilled and therefore third-class employees. Second-class status was given to skilled indios or *criollos* (those of Spanish descent, born in America) and Hondurans who identified as mestizos, and first-class status was reserved for the North American supervisors and captains. Differences in status were apparent in the company clubs and hospitals, where certain classes could not enter or were allowed only in separate sections of the buildings.[51] Company towns, or small cities that sprung up around company fincas and regional offices, such as La Lima, El Progreso (Tela Railroad Company), and Olanchito (Standard Fruit Company), as well as the port cities of La Ceiba, Puerto Cortés, and Tela, also provided various forms of labor in railroad workshops and warehouses (*talleres*). Workers repaired company machinery and handled construction or mechanical work, like cutting wood for homes and buildings. For these jobs within the confines of the company towns, workers had to give proof of their skills—for instance, by presenting a vocational certificate from a training school.[52]

When workers moved to work for another finca, company, or grower, they then started at the bottom despite their potential skills. Angel Martinez, for example, worked in a skilled position in the Materials and Supplies Department of the Tela Railroad and Steamship Company but moved up the coast and became a fruit cutter for the Standard Fruit Company: "In the M&S [Materials and Supply] department the work was to cut wood with an electric saw to make 7-foot columns; from there I left for finca El Tigre, and from El Tigre I went to the Standard."[53] Opportunities for promotion or pathways for advancement were virtually nonexistent for banana workers. Few went from finca work to second-class employment in the company towns. More commonly, finca workers would find frequently temporary and thus precarious labor work as yarderos, gardening for a finca captain living in town. It was not a promotion; yarderos, like other agricultural workers, would have rather worked in a contractor team and have the freedom to move between the campos.

The company's hierarchy was implemented and enforced based on literacy skills, country of origin, race, ethnicity, and gender. The hierarchy denoted status for workers based on these categories and was not necessarily indicative of wage differences. For instance, Juan B. Canales, a worker with a certificate in mechanics and electricity from the Escuela Nacional de Artes y Oficios (National School of Arts and Vocations) in Tegucigalpa, was hired for a job that was considered better than other finca work not because of better pay but because of its classification within the company hierarchy. Instead of working as a harvester, one of the lowest-ranking jobs in the finca hierarchy, in 1947 Canales worked as a toolmaker in the repair shop for the railroad system, securing a wage of one lempira per hour ($.50 US per hour).[54] Edmundo Cabrera Williams, who came from the rural western part of the country, despite his formal training as a plumber, was hired as a field worker to do various jobs for 2.20 lempiras ($1.10 US) a day in 1945.[55] Although both young men brought technical skills to their jobs, they were valued differently because Canales came with a letter of recommendation attesting to his literacy, while Cabrera Williams had to begin from the bottom of the hierarchy. They also came from different regions; in the hiring process the more skilled workers who came from the city center, like Canales, were prioritized over the workers perceived to be from marginal rural areas, such as Cabrera Williams, who came from a regional provincial area.

Jesús Gomes, before securing a better job as a *bodeguero* (storage shopkeeper), a position that demanded complete company trust, was asked to demonstrate that he could read, count, add, and subtract. It was understood that workers who lacked these skills would be relegated to the physically demanding jobs of finca work.[56] Amerto Lagos and Rodriguez Pagoada recalled that their knowledge of, and experience in, finca work was not valued when they started working in the Chemical Department, which hosted various teams of US scientists and experts who conducted experiments to produce disease-resistant fruit.[57] In the

process of working with the visiting experts and scientists, Amerto Lagos and Rodriguez Pagoada had an opportunity to demonstrate their
knowledge of the plantation and the banana. They shared their basic
knowledge of plant life, weather conditions and their impact on the
agricultural process, disease characteristics, and best practices. They often "taught" the professional scientists about the banana plant. Their
knowledge was recognized only after scientists made several mistakes
after ignoring their suggestions. When the company finally saw the utility of these workers, they were hired in the department, and they then
worked in the company town, La Lima, and their living arrangements
also changed.[58] In this uncommon case, company supervisors and scientists subjectively identified workers as having high potential to contribute. These workers were then hired out of the finca and into the experimental departments—a rare instance of apparent internal promotion.

Overall, banana workers were regarded as "unskilled laborers." The
labor system and general structure outlined above reflect the experience of most finca workers—mostly Hondurans, mestizos, and workers
for the Tela Railroad Company. The process of gaining access to finca
work in cortero teams, the grueling work itself, and learning to live in
the campos with one another generated interdependence and solidarity
among workers. Agricultural workers who referred to themselves as
indios formed a dominant majority, and their experiences of work as
campeños informed their organizing, militancy, and the construction
of working-class identity that sustained their survival in the workplace.
The Tela Railroad Company workers' challenge to the company set an
example for Standard Fruit Company workers and other workers in
the cities—who would eventually join a general strike in support of
the banana strike, but also fight for their own workplace rights. Their
living arrangements also proved to be an important area of negotiated
shared space among different ethnic and national groups, which made
the campeños and the campos unique when compared to the rest of
the country. Although the fincas were "green prisons" for workers, the
campos, where they lived, were complex communities formed out of
necessity and resistance.

BARRACONES: LIVING IN THE CAMPOS

Workers' experiences and identities were formed and influenced by
learning to share space with workers who migrated from different regions. Their housing and living arrangements both generated tension
and forced solidarity. The interactions with one another, their notions

of masculinity and work, and the power dynamics developed in relationships to women were critical to the construction of the campeño
identity, as much as they were influenced by the harsh environment and
the company's workplace practices. During the first half of the twentieth century, no one would venture into the territory of the campos
unless they worked or sought work there. The lack of roads and limited
availability of passengers trains severely hampered entry into and exit
out of the campos. The only way in, besides on foot, was the railroad
line. Most of those who came either walked or took the *machanguay*,
pasajero, or *mixto* trains, which ran only a few days a week into town and
back.[59] Next to the fincas were the banana campos and the barracones, the wood-slab company worker's quarters. The rectangular buildings sat on stilts that lined up almost parallel to the railroad tracks, and
one building could contain up to six rooms. Angel Martinez explained,
"Our work area was very close to the living quarters. The only thing
was that the rooms were small; four or five men [slept there]. Look, on
the floor there were many people sleeping on straw mats (*petates*), above
there were men in hammocks, and higher up there were men in bunks
(*tabancos*)."[60] Single men lived in close quarters, sleeping on hammocks
in dirty, overcrowded barracones. Most workers found them undesir-
able. Alejandro Ortega was one them: "The company had us build a
barracón with six rooms; six of us slept in each room in hammocks.
. . . I didn't like it [because] some of the guys were really dirty. I would
reprimand them and they would get mad.'No, man, get those shoes out
of the way.' Or they would get to the bedroom too drunk to bother
[taking off their shoes] and [step on] someone who was resting."[61]

Production needs determined the number of workers in the fincas
and thus the living and eating arrangements. Depending on the campo
and the level of production, the rooms for single men would have as
few as six or as many as 20 men at a time. Jesús Gómez worked at a different finca than Ortega, and he had to endure living with many more
men.[62] "They would crowd as many in as possible; 16 of us lived in one
room. You have no idea how those barracks were. . . . Many people from
different regions of Copán liked tobacco. . . . They chewed tobacco,
smoked cigars."[63] The walls were often stained with homemade cususa
(illegal alcohol) or chewing tobacco spit—a habit that workers developed to maintain their energy.

While jobs were obtained through networks, living arrangements
were assigned. Workers could transgress these assignments, however, and
make their own arrangements by selecting roommates of their own

choice. Many workers coming from the interior, with very tenuous networks of friends or coworkers, had little choice but to make the best of singles' housing assignments, or find a female partner to get on the list for a new *cuarto* (room within a barracón) assignment in the family barracones, which were perceived to provide better conditions.[64] Or, as Ortega explained, "What I would do is switch barracones, I would go to the Salvadorans' barracón because they got along and they were clean."[65] Coexisting with workers from other regions and countries, and dealing with one another's cultural understandings of home and each other, was usually a challenge. Angel Martinez found this to be one of the biggest problems that often led to violence, either at bedtime or first thing in the morning. Martinez remembers lodging with Olanchanos and Salvadorans, two groups that did not get along.[66] If one worker walked into the barracón late at night and woke up another, a fight would often ensue, and then no one would get any sleep that evening.

> Someone in a bunk above would come down, and there would be a serious situation because there were all kinds of people [in the barracón]. Salvadorans, people from Olancho [a region in Honduras]—no offense, but it was a delicate matter if you woke them up [Salvadorans or Olanchanos]. When they would come in to sleep it was bad, too; they would walk in with their machetes and cut the ropes off a hammock, and to the floor it went. You couldn't say anything because you wouldn't get out of there—or only in pieces. Sad. . . . It was like living with pigs.[67]

The proximity of workers in the barracones fueled fights and exacerbated tensions. The lack of cleanliness and the enclosed environment of the *cuartos* in the barracones were excruciating for many workers, who may have come from single-family campesino households. In the singles' barracones, the bachelors did not bathe or take care of themselves except on Sundays, when they would sport their best outfits to visit the company town bars and brothels.

The most violent confrontations between men happened in those singles' barracones. Workers brought their daily frustrations from work back to their rooms, and those frustrations were then compounded by tensions over their regional and cultural differences. Workers' prejudices were particularly exposed in these living arrangements. Black workers often had to sleep outside on the porch.[68]

Compañerismo (camaraderie) among male workers had its limits and was often utilitarian. Workers may or may not have been friends or friendly with one another, but if they were from a particular region or country they helped each other based on their common origins. While these ties endured, it is important not to romanticize workers' level of connection with one another. Often, Hondurans did not get along with even other Hondurans.[69] Workers' actions and tensions in their living situations demonstrated the newness of the wage-work system, job hierarchy, and race and gender norms, as the company brought workers from different origins into close proximity. The tensions in living arrangements led workers to room with groups they identified with or find women to partner with whenever possible. Otherwise, they learned to live together despite tensions and even build certain affinities with one another and create a bustling, tight-knit community.

HOUSING AND GENDER: RELATIONSHIPS BETWEEN MEN AND WOMEN

Women laborers were excluded from the male mestizo padrinazgo, as the company's labor positions in the finca were reserved for men. Young women had different networks that connected them to the north coast—sometimes they were made up of older women or women who had more experience in the north coast.[70] But they did not expect to get work with the company in the fincas. The formal company structure of finca labor relied on primarily single male workers and did not recognize the contributions of women at all. This exclusion made women dependent on relationships with male workers to cement their housing and strengthen their chances of obtaining work. Those partnerships, envied by single men, also reinforced the construction of "codes of manhood"[71] that equated masculinity with providing for the family, but also saw possession of women as central to a man's value. During the period between 1944 and 1957, worker narratives also suggest a shift from what was once a single, male workforce toward a family-oriented one, which increasingly included male workers with women partners and extended family members. Banana workers, men and women, adapted to the available living arrangements in the campos and reworked them into their own notions of home. Many were able to work and raise their children outside of the constricting tradition of dowries and wedlock that characterized the middle classes in the cities and company towns. The rules of marriage and partnering were constantly being reformulated to meet the circumstances and to make sense of their distinctive campeño community.

Most men sought to marry or partner with women in order to request company housing for families. Some solidified relationships they already had with girlfriends to be able to at least have their own home. Others created arrangements of convenience, as was the case with Daniel Madrid Guevara, who partnered with a woman for mutual, practical support: "I had no interest in loving her, just in helping her," he said.[72] Alejandro Ortega explained, "It was so sad to live [in the singles barracón], crowded on top of one another."[73] He wanted out, so he requested to be put on the wait list for a room in a family barracón. Then he set out on his search for a woman to partner. This dynamic had important implications for women, as many were "taken" (sometimes against their family's will) into marriage by force, while others made arrangements with their husbands, as was the case with Daniel Madrid Guevara's first wife.[74] Women were seen as useful to men because they could do the cooking, and the men would no longer have to pay a patrona to feed themselves. The woman partner might even become a patrona and cook for other men or wash clothes (for the household and for hire), bringing in additional income and eliminating many extra costs that single men had.[75] Edmundo Cabrera Williams remembers that at first men with wives also slept in the communal barracks: "Before there were no little houses, only barracones. . . . There was one barracón building where singles slept on one side, and the other side was for men with wives who made the food. But it was just one barracón."[76]

Women sought to partner with men in order to have access to a kitchen and other support and opportunities for livelihood; men sought women as partners to leave the singles barracón for a family *cuarto*. The assumption was that the women in these relationships, or arrangements, would do the cooking and washing. This utilitarian partnership marked the power dynamics between men and women and is woven into the campeño/a construction of gender norms, rules on sexuality, and conduct. While men had access to women, women also had access to men's possessions to make their own lives and businesses thrive. If it did not work out, they each moved on to a different partner. It is important, however, not to downplay that sometimes the breakdown of family units involved the eviction of women from the campos and, even worse, violence. The division of labor between men and women persisted in both single and coupled households. A single worker, for instance, would have to either cook his food and wash his work clothes or purchase these services from a patrona and a *lavandera* (hired washer woman) for a monthly fee. A coupled worker would have his wife cook the food and carry out domestic duties, such as washing clothes. While the coupled worker assumed that his wife would do the domestic duties and he would provide the income, the female partner would frequently do extra jobs to earn cash, such as wash laundry for others, or sell bread or other food. Cabrera Williams's wife took in laundry to make ends meet and would sometimes make more money than her husband did.[77] María Ángela Cardona, along with her children, sold food:

> I used to make food, too; yes, I would cook it and then go sell it in Coyoles. I used to sell cooked spiced pork or chicken. . . . I would buy the pig's head, and people really liked the pork ears. . . . Before they used to call that kind of food "burra" [a quick meal to go]. "Give me a burra," they would say. It was a plate of rice, salad, tomatoes, cabbage, and one pork ear. I charged forty cents.[78]

The family's ability to earn wages varied even among conjugal partnerships if the wife engaged in casual work. The extra income would go to clothes and the children's education, and part of it would be reinvested to make food that the women and children sold to workers on payday.

Oscar Rodriguez Pagoada, who cared for his mother, was more fortunate. He was given a *cuarto* in the family quarter's section of the barracones, "I lived in the campos [family living quarters]. . . . Yes, the campos were enormously big; each could hold 150 families and they had singles barracks. I lived there, but not as a single man because I had my mother and they gave me a room to live as a family."[79] Rodriguez Pagoada's mother, however, did not just live there; she also participated in the banana economy by working as a patrona. He explained, "At certain times she used to make food for some of the single workers, she took care of people."[80] Rodriguez Pagoada saw this as temporary work that mainly helped to subsidize their food in the household, since patronas often got good deals on food from the company and from their relationships with local merchants. Her work allowed her to purchase extra goods for herself and the household. Even so, men saw this type of women's work as supplementary to theirs, and this was reflected in the strike movement as well. Formal male workers were seen as the leaders, while women were in supporting positions. This, too, was a defining feature of the construction of masculinity.

Men proved their masculinity not only by doing arduous agricultural work that demanded great physical strength but also by fighting for access to women. Madrid Guevara explains that bringing a woman into the campos helped him get his own barracón, but it created a whole slew of other problems with the other men who saw her as a potential partner, given the competition for women in the campos in the early 1940s. The woman, Juana Marquez, was from the same region, and their connection was platonic; they coupled to help each other. She had three children and no husband, and he wanted out of the singles' barracón. Every single man that lived in the campo was courting Marquez. But she was candid with Madrid Guevara and explained that she could not do her job as patrona because she had too many suitors trying to make her acquaintance, and she was afraid. Marquez told Madrid Guevara, "Look, I don't know these people, and I know you; I prefer to be your woman and not end up in the claws of another."[81] Marquez's story demonstrates that although men often chose their partners to get a room in the barracón, women also wanted to be partnered. At the same time, her cautious statement reflects a fear of ending up in a violent or repressive situation or facing exploitation with no opportunity to work—and finding work was one of the primary reasons women migrated to the north coast during this period in the first place.

Women were only seen as inhabitants in the labor camps by happenstance and primarily because of their relationship to the men. When a woman entered into a partnership with a male worker and became a regular in the campo community, she became an object of interest. Alejandro Ortega remembered that women were a cause of tension between men when they were brought into the campos: "In those times there weren't many women; there were more men, and if they saw a woman there regularly, they would bother and court her."[82] Women were highly sought after in the campos, and it did not matter whose wife she was—she could be "stolen" by another stronger, fiercer man.[83] Angel Martinez explained, "When a woman landed in the campos she was like a piece of gold. Everyone desired her, and the one with the most courage [or guts] would take advantage of her [court her, try to bed her], and she would have to get used to it."[84] Men heckled, engaged in catcalling, courted, and dueled for women—not necessarily just because workers wanted to make a home, but because this was a part of male fraternizing that also reinforced masculinity. Men saw women as potential partners and as accessible commodities that could be "stolen" by a stronger and more macho worker. A worker's ability to "obtain" a woman and keep her amid a sea of "needy" men depended on his own masculinity, his ability to provide for the woman and kids while in the barracón. In return, the woman was expected to serve and not be disloyal. But once the campeño was ready to leave the woman, he would claim their space and the woman would be expected to leave. As in Olimpia Figueroa's mother's case, men often changed their minds and moved other women into the barracones, kicking their partners out whenever they felt like it.[85]

> We women were so humble that we did not make any noise so others would not find out. My mother told me that my father met another woman, and since my mother did not have anything, and he was a Comanche [pseudo–police officer appointed by the company], the boss helped him get rid of her. And what do you think my mother left in? With me, a baby in her arms, and pregnant, he sent her off in a fruit train that was transporting fruit to go dump her over there by Cortés, so that he [her father] could move the other young woman into his room where they lived.[86]

Figueroa's mother and her children were kicked out of their barracón and sent to another campo so her husband could move his new partner in.[87] This was typical of how partnerships were dissolved, with men having the final say. It illustrates the power men had over women, and how their relationships were often akin to that between a boss and a mistreated subordinate worker. These were fierce codes of manhood that often ruled over women's labor, bodies, and lives.

AJUNTADAS AND AMACHINADAS: INFORMAL MARRIAGE ARRANGEMENTS AND LIVING QUARTERS

On the north coast, the word *amachinada* means *ajuntada*, or partnered with a man, without official marriage. It connotes that women were not married into formal arrangements. Though the origins of the word are not confirmed, its composition suggests a lot about these informal partnerships: *ama* refers to *amarrar*, "tie," or even *ama de casa*, "housewife," and *china* refers to a domestic worker, usually Indigenous, in the popular lingo in the region.[88] *China* is a racialized term denoting that the woman may also be india (or of Indigenous ancestry). According to Heidi Tinsman, the "terms *india* and *china* indicated women of low and mixed caste, by definition women of little sexual virtue; *china*, in particular, was associated with sexual flirtation and concubinage."[89] The word, *amachinada*, aptly reflects these marriage or partnership arrangements, those of convenience, both for men and patronas, who could have space for work in the kitchen and make a makeshift comedor. The male worker also benefited immensely because he could have a steady source of services, such as cooking, laundry, and sex, without having to pay for them—as was the case for single workers.[90]

The adoption of informal marriage arrangements resulted at least in part from the lack of state presence, such as a municipal office, to grant marriage licenses, combined with the absence of the Catholic Church to set the norms for conjugal relationships.[91] At the same time, marriage was expensive for workers, with little transportation and access to the institutions and churches. While marriage ceremonies were celebrated monthly in the American Zone (la Zona), finca workers and the women laboring in and around the campos did not partake in this ritual, which was only for *los de la Zona* (those from la Zona). As Olimpia Figueroa explains, "There were many marriages; the poorest people were the ones who did not get [officially] married. In the [American] Zone I would see weddings every month, there with that little drummer [procession]. It would start from there where the Hotel Sula was."[92] Informal arrangements were common.[93] The fluidity and informality perhaps reflect that workers may not have intended to remain in the banana camps to live long-term. It is likely that many banana workers, women cooks, and vendors came to the north coast to work and thought they would earn some money and return home, making temporary arrangements as they went along. The reality, however, is that once settled in the area, very few workers actually returned to their hometowns; they stayed on the north coast and made new lives for themselves and new familial and partner relationships and remained indefinitely.

In other Latin American contexts, less formal arrangements were common among the working classes, and especially in enclave settings. Thomas Miller Klubock found evidence that in El Teniente mine in Chile, women's arrangements with men were "fluid" and that "many men and women never intended their relationships to end in monogamous marriage, despite men's claims of control over women's sexuality and men's indignation at *empleadas*' assertion of the right to be nonmonogamous."[94] The fluidity that was embraced in Chile's mining towns corresponds to the fluidity and sexuality found on the north coast, where many arrangements were possible in order to work and earn a living. In some cases women had several partners without formal arrangements over time, until they settled with someone. Olimpia Figueroa, who lived in the campos most of her life and was not formally married, remembers the day her father decided he was done with her mother and the family, and wanted to bring another woman into the barracón. Memories like this formed a living archive of experience for women that was reproduced and passed on to younger women. Relationships with banana men were tenuous, and the women always had to watch out for their survival and that of their children, including keeping some of their profits hidden from their partners to cover the children's expenses.[95]

The informal arrangements often clearly did not benefit the women, but somehow they found the resilience to make arrangements work or walk away from them. Figueroa had two marriage-like arrangements—the second one was lasting. Asked whether the absence of a marriage certificate was beneficial to women, Figueroa explained that even with a marriage certificate, it was never a good situation for women who had less power in these domestic arrangements:

> No. It did not work for you, or anything; you see, they alone ruled over us. Only the men had a say—her, nothing. Then, no, if you did not have power, no matter what you had, you had no power. Look, if a man partnered with you, he gave you your water bucket, your washer board so you could do laundry, because before we did not do laundry with a *pila* [large indoor sink]; he would give you your pots and pans, and if you wanted to leave, he got mad and sent you away naked. He would take everything away from you, because according to him, he had given you everything and it was his.[96]

While romantic love figures as one justification for these arrangements, violence and coercion were also imposed on women to obtain favors and control over women's sexuality.

Women's positions in the camps, especially those of younger women, made them vulnerable to abuses of power, including by male workers. The Honduran state had no protections for women in such cases, and it often even pardoned rapists if they married the victims.[97] While this may seem extremely cruel, Tinsman found that in campesino communities in Chile "female sexual activity and men's marriage promises historically had been closely linked in concepts about honor."[98] María Antonia Perla was not officially married in the campos; she returned to her hometown of Villanueva to get married. In Perla's case, the only option she had, and it was the one her family gave her, was to marry (which really meant to partner with) the man who had raped her.[99] She evaded him by running away to work in another campo but was found. Between 1953, the year of her rape, and 1957, she avoided actually partnering with him. But eventually, her family forced her to go to her hometown of Villanueva and officially marry him.[100] She endured domestic violence most of her life: "I ran away many times. . . . Once he had me thrown in jail for abandoning the home. I spent eleven days in jail."[101] Perla remembers that she was also generally responsible for the kids, remarking that other than providing her with his check for the month, he took no part in their children's upbringing or education. Perla's options were limited, and diversion was scant. If she went to dance by herself, it was considered inappropriate, and she would suffer discrimination. Perla's story reveals two dynamics: men's power over women's lives, often sanctioned by the state and the company, and the complicity of married women in enforcing gender and sexuality codes on younger women in the community. In Perla's case, it was not the violence against her that was of concern but her honor and the potential harm to the working man, who could be accused of rape and lose his job. The patrona who served him, Perla's grandmother, would lose a paying customer. Her grandmother's actions in actuality prioritized protecting the man, the customer, and ultimately her own finances rather than her granddaughter's well-being, even if the rhetoric of morality itself served as the pretext to require the marriage as a resolution. As a consequence of the family's insistence, Perla felt as if the rape had been her fault and that the family's actions were about saving her honor.[102] Her case brings to light the place women held in the campos and the primacy of the male worker, the formal company employee, as well as the social codes that condoned male workers' violence against young women and older women's complicity in enforcing some norms that legitimized this violence. Perhaps the older women enforcing rules on younger women spoke more out of fear of the burden that would have befallen the family if a young woman like Perla had gotten pregnant and had a child without a partnership. At the same time, these older women may have wanted more responsibility placed on the man to take care of the situation, reflecting a concern about men's sexual irresponsibility in the campos, a preoccupation that would be evident in later years in demands for the child support for children abandoned by fathers, to which the company responded by garnishing wages by court order.[103]

Male workers often remarked in interviews that there were few women in the campos, perhaps meaning there were few young women whom they could partner with, and that this somehow made partnering and being with a young woman coveted and desirable. In other words, a woman's perceived rarity and unavailability made it permissible to take her body by force. Perla's story demonstrated that she was not a "simple victim," and as Tinsman has argued, that violence between husband and wife reflects their different and unequal positions, both socially and culturally. In society, she argues, "men do not invent ways to dominate women, but act within the parameters of proper male behavior established by state policy, religious ideology and community tradition."[104] The banana enclave labor system instituted by UFCo and Standard Fruit Company and their policies on worker housing, as well as the living conditions, shaped and altered the understandings about gender and sexuality among men and women workers who migrated to the region. Some of these partnerships were of necessity, for both men and women.

Despite the problematic implications of informal arrangements for the women and children involved, and in the absence of church or state laws, informal arrangements, although dangerous, did provide women with certain flexibility in their lives and work. María Ángela Cardona had a husband who did not provide for her family. Every time he returned home, she would find herself pregnant after he left. Her partner's absence and lack of responsibility made her and her children work long hours, selling food outside the brothels and on paydays. She became the head of household and as the years went on relied less and less on her partner.[105]

While there is an archival silence on women and patrona's mutual aid societies or informal groups that provided communal support, patronas did turn to their campo communities, to other women workers, and to wives. Perla remembers that in her worst moments she had somewhere to go: "Life in the campos was free, community oriented, people worried about you."[106] Although Perla ran away many times from her abusive home, her barracón, she found community in the campos more generally. She was from the campos and did not want to leave them altogether, and so she ran away to another campo. She lived there among the campeño community, despite her own lack of safety with her husband in her individual barracón.

Men and women were not equal partners. The male banana worker's relationship to the company gave him access to the barracón, the company commissary, and passes to take the *machanguay* train (the merchandise train used to transport people off the finca into town);

therefore, the man legitimized the presence of the woman partner in the campo. The male's role in the formal economy of the banana industry determined the nature of the partnership, and the campeño codes of manhood dictated the circumstances of his relationships to women.

This limited view of women in the campos—then and now—affirms the predominance of the male mestizo worker narrative of survival in the campos. But in actuality this represents just one part of north-coast culture. In fact, it is more important to recognize both men and women as banana workers. The men most often worked as formal employees of the companies, while the women functioned as informal workers in and around the plantations. The construction of workers' communities in the campos owes much of its survival and vitality to the informal economy, in which women outnumbered men.

CONFRONTING COMPANY CONTROL: PERFORMING MASCULINITY OFF THE CLOCK

Finca workers' lives, partnerships, and workplaces reflected a constant balancing act between company control and worker autonomy and resistance. Their leisure time—the third sphere of the campeño community—was similarly dichotomous. During their unpaid, nonwork time, workers developed their social networks, which began with camaraderie formed through working closely together, and negotiated a constant tension between the company's efforts to control workers and workers' resistance to that control. Even during nonwork hours, workers were within reach of company policies and dominion, a reflection of the fact that the company's priority was protecting workforce productivity. Workers' free time was policed in different ways, which also led to the defiance of certain company rules. The company's need to ensure a consistent supply of workers in the fincas led to the coordinated, localized surveillance of workers' lives and activities, including alcohol consumption. In the banana regions there was no Welfare Department per se. Instead, workers were policed by local comandantes (police commanders) or cabos de comisariato and auxiliares (volunteer police, usually select workers in the campo).[107] Cabos de comisariato were essentially small-town policemen, often assigned to their posts by the Gobernación Política (departmental governor), who understood they were there to protect the company's interests.[108] These policemen had a dubious official relationship with the Honduran government as representatives of the state; they worked in favor of and in cooperation with the company that subsidized their wages and gave them free rein to surveil workers' lives in the campos and their visits to the company towns. The company employed cabos de comisariato and chose auxiliares from among the workforce to aid the police, sometimes without extra pay, to oversee other workers' behavior in the campos and during leisure time. Many accepted these roles for their perceived power and respect in the campo. The cabos de comisariato, the auxiliares, and the comandantes exerted power over the campos and workers, interchangeably functioning as company security guards, law enforcement officers, private police, and even government inspectors.

The head of the police in the early 1950s, Guayo Galeano, a local who was designated chief by the local state authorities and paid by the company, was stationed at a river crossing between La Lima and the campos, to the disdain of workers; they had to pass by every time they crossed the Ulua River.[109] The makeshift police checkpoint was near the train station, just as workers entered or exited La Lima from the fincas. Guayo Galeano's checkpoint enabled him to monitor workers traveling on foot in and out of town.[110] Workers experienced abuse and persecution in their everyday lives at the hands of these policemen, at times because they were suspected of being from the opposition political party, and at other times they were accused without proof of political activity. According to the workers I interviewed, Guayo Galeano and Matías Aríaga, the comandantes of El Progreso were members of the Nationalist Party and attempted to recruit workers who identified with that party.[111] Galeano and his men monitored finca workers daily and in particular on payday, but according to Madrid Guevara, they were at their worst during election periods and would especially terrorize Liberal Party members.[112]

Madrid Guevara was a self-proclaimed Liberal Party member who was persecuted by cabos de comisariato and auxiliares loyal to the Nationalist Party. On the way back into the campos after a good Sunday in town, Guevara and other workers would face the threatening inspections from the cabos de comisariato. If they smelled of alcohol, they would be thrown in jail until they sobered up, ensuring that they would report for work on Monday sober. Many times, these pseudo-policemen harassed workers for sport, often incarcerating men who had not had any alcohol.[113] The holding cells of Galeano and Arriaga's prisons in La Lima and El Progreso were often packed on Sundays at sundown. While many had drunk alcohol, the primary fear was that they would return to their campos and continue drinking illicit alcohol that would then prevent them from showing up for work on Monday. Workers almost always showed up to work, however, even if they did not sleep well or consumed alcohol.[114] While the next chapter will delve further into an analysis of the social construction and use of alcohol in campeño life in the north coast, it is important to note here that the workers' rejection of the company's total control is evident in just how prevalent alcohol consumption was during leisure time, even in the face of severe company surveillance and restriction. The paternalistic surveillance translated into officials treating these fierce men as if they were children and literally corralling them to provide an example to others.

Despite the company's efforts and interests, the ways in which workers spent their nonwork time in and out of the campos—playing cards (*naipe*) and gambling (*chiviando*), forming soccer (*fútbol*) leagues, and even consuming alcohol—all defied the overreach of company control and proved their masculinity and virility. Workers enjoyed leisure time mostly right after paydays—the weekly Friday payday, the ten-day payday, and the monthly payday.[115] Leisure-time activities included playing dominoes, cards, or soccer; attending dances; drinking at the *estancos* (small makeshift bars) run by patronas; going into the company town on Sundays to hang out at the brothels, local bars, and parks; and buying supplies in the busy commerce districts. Workers have fond memories of the abundance of goods, food, treats, and alcohol (beer, aguardiente, and cususa) in an almost fair-like atmosphere on paydays. Alcohol was not only important for surviving the daily grueling work, it was also a critical factor in the formation of campeño masculinity; to work hard, men had to drink hard.

Workers' existence and activities during nonwork hours influenced the work itself and the formation of the campeño working-class identity. During these times, workers who did similar kinds of work spent free time fraternizing and building trust with one another. These interactions helped determine their allies, who would be instrumental in future efforts to organize the union. During their nonwork time, workers challenged company control, sometimes in small ways and other times in overt and confrontational ways, like the 1954 strike itself. Organizing for the 1954 strike happened, in part, in these moments away from the finca, though not exclusively. Workers describe a strengthening of compañerismo and the formation of social and labor networks (based on hometown, nationality, ethnicity, and work position) during their leisure time. They also adapted to company policies and sometimes directly confronted or resisted company control, actions that can be seen as antecedents of the strike.

One example of workers' rejection of the company's prescription was the formation of campeño soccer teams, which existed as an alternative to the company's promotion of sports such as baseball, golf, bowling, and cricket. The company organized sporting events and activities for trusted employees and those who lived near or in the Zona Americana (the American Zone), but workers reported feeling uncomfortable there and not wanting to attend these events.[116] On one fourth of July, Madrid Guevara remembers feeling resentment at being forced to attend the company picnic because the ticket price was already deducted from his paycheck. Elaborate sporting leagues were prevalent throughout Honduras during this period, but in the banana campos workers played soccer with others from nearby campos, for both distraction and entertainment.[117]

Writer Wilfredo Mayorga recounts in his novel that players in *Club Vida*, founded in 1938 in La Ceiba, lacked essential funding, despite the team deriving its name from Vincent D'Anthony, owner and founder of what would become the Standard Fruit Company.[118] Soccer teams did not necessarily get funding and financial support from the companies, but workers embraced their teams because they represented where they lived, their community, and the sport they loved. It was remarkably different from gambling, which relied far more on individual gains and harsh penalties to prove one's masculinity. Teams existed in each of the campos, and they played against one another in regional leagues. Journalism and literature in Honduras, when it referenced soccer, usually focused on the national team, and even then often in a humorous manner. Rarely would stories focus on the working class and their favorite pastime, perhaps because it was such a prevalent leisure activity, which transcended differences in ethnicity, nationality, job positions, and status.

Soccer was so common in the campeños' daily routine that they often failed to mention their nearly daily practice. It came up only in interviews with pointed questioning, and then consistently as a staple in campeños' lives. They simply saw this part of their life as completely outside of their work life, as something of their own. Soccer was a revered sport for workers. Whether they played or went to watch other workers play, this was an important pastime. Despite extreme exhaustion during the day or weekend, this was the one thing workers had time and energy for—a truly important activity that was theirs. The subject of many fables and the trade of storytellers, soccer and its players created a sense of belonging in the campos. Locals who remember their soccer days retell the best plays in a mixture of memory, imagination, and truth, a magical realism of love and loss but also, in unexpected ways, perseverance.

Through these sports narratives, workers organically acknowledged race and class. Mayorga's story about two great strikers nicknamed Campeón and Chuña (a derogatory word meaning barefoot, often used to describe a poor person who cannot afford shoes), who could have played on any team but stayed with their home team, and who were "able dribblers and strong shooters who attempted to make goals, despite their small stature and apparently fragile complexion,"[119] harkened to a very interesting racial dynamic, perhaps between indo-Hispanic players and Afro-descendants in the region at the time. The players in his story are probably mestizos and their "fair complexion" only fair within the degrees of brown to Blackness in the north-coast banana regions.

Players' nicknames often described their abilities and challenges on the field, but also characteristics of their race and ethnicity, a tradition that would carry over into the work of the campeño, where men were known for their nicknames. "Chuna" or "Chuña" is perhaps one example laden with implied meaning. The nicknaming tradition also demonstrates that workers spent a lot of time together, as players on a soccer team would, sharing space, knowing each other's work practices and personalities, abilities and mishaps, developing camaraderie and constructing "codes of manhood." But it is clear that this leisure sport became another form of belonging and home for workers who migrated from multiple locations and who were racially diverse. In Argentina, soccer allowed immigrants to challenge dominant national narratives and forge their own identities; it was a way for men to belong, build a home, be visible in a positive way, and perform acceptable masculinity, along with sometimes violent behavior, with one another.[120] The campeños' relationship to soccer mirrors the Argentinian case: the sport allowed them to create community among workers from different regions of the country and compete with other campos. More importantly it stood in direct contradiction to company-sponsored baseball games and other American sports introduced by the company.

CAMPEÑOS LIVE AND DIE IN THE GREEN PRISON
These hard-working and hard-drinking men spent their lives in the "green prison." They partnered with women there—multiple times, more often than not—bore and raised children, and worked until old age. The campos had become more than just company housing; they had become home. "Campos" became synonymous with small hamlets

in the minds of campeños. They made a community there that held together the fabric of survival and perseverance, despite and in resistance to company policies and surveillance. Rarely did these campesinos return to their villages, sometimes not even if a parent died. They simply became campeños, and the only way the company would remove them was by demolishing the barracones, as they did in old San Juan, Tacamiche, and nearby campos in the early 1990s. The companies would sporadically close down fincas and campos up through the early 2000s, when all workers were evicted from the former banana regions they called home. Ironically, a transnational worker campaign for redress (for harmful use of pesticide) scared the company and contributed to their *desalojo* (eviction) from the only home many knew. Workers would now have to relocate to far-off neighborhoods in the outskirts of the city, leaving behind the open space of the campos.

Nuevo San Juan of 2004 was flat and dusty. The homes resembled the quick pop-up homes brought in during Hurricane Mitch; with small, thin walls made of concrete instead of wood planks, they were filed closely together in a row and were indistinguishable from each other, except perhaps for an added fence or garden. At one point these flood lands were prime banana land. Water for irrigation once flowed in channels where dusty streets now break up the rows of small houses. This is where banana workers who qualified for home loans between 2004 and 2006 could afford to move to, as bulldozers tore down their campos.

A fateful turn of events in the early 2000s motivated workers in another region of the fincas and campos adjacent to La Lima to stay, resist eviction, and escape relocation to the old Campo San Juan, now renamed Nuevo San Juan. This historical practice of resistance would be seen again in 2004–2006, when families refused to be evicted from the campos. In Finca Indiana, Don Leandro Bautista, a former 1954 strike leader and retired banana worker, remained in the barracón despite efforts to forcefully relocate him to Nuevo San Juan. He refused to retire and voluntarily leave his entire life behind.[121] Ultimately, Don Leandro, alongside other men of his generation, received eviction notices. As he told me, "The company wants to kick us out; they came to threaten us with rifles, groups of soldiers, but it has never been able to kick us out of here."[122] Despite the threats, Don Leandro Bautista and forty other people remained. "What the company has done is cut our electricity and water. We are isolated. We have to go get water from far over there. We, however, need to demonstrate strength."[123]

He spoke with nostalgia for the past, a bygone era when the company had paid for electricity and provided potable water for workers. This man, who arrived in the north coast when he was 18 years old from Yamaranguila, Intibucá, in the south of the country, never left. He worked as a mulero in a cuadrilla in Finca Copén, one of the very campos that was evicted and demolished in 1994, in what may seem like an interrelated set of macabre events that best explains the relationship of the enclave to the nation, even now. Today, for UFCo's successor Chiquita Brands, the past is irrelevant. Its imperative has been to cut costs and divest from the country, following a neoliberal trend throughout the region. The fight to preserve the campos and the barracones, even though they are relics of a paternalistic company, was important to workers because they had constructed a distinctive culture and identity in the region. They built a livelihood there.

In 2006 Don Leandro's personal belongings consisted of the tools he had always relied on for work and survival as a mulero and, later in older age, a *chapeador* (weeder) in the banana plantations: a sharp machete, a hammock, one or two shirts, one or two pairs of pants, a straw hat, and a *candíl* (oil lamp). These modest possessions, and his life and livelihood in the campos, were threatened by the impending demolition of his barracón. His life and home now rested on the balance between old company policies, international labor lawsuits, Honduran agrarian law, and international environmental standards in free-trade times. Don Leandro's story is a fitting end to this chapter, as his life and experience in the campos from the strike era until now show the sustained power and resonance of the campeño identity throughout a lifetime of work and survival. The times and circumstances have changed, and the future is uncertain, but the campeño culture of resistance and adaptation remains, with its roots extending back to the previous era. In the next chapter, I take a closer look at the intersection of working-class cultures, masculinity, race, and leisure time through the consumption of alcohol and prostitution, deepening the analysis of a north-coast campeño/a identity that became critical to organizing the strike and resistance to company control.

CHAPTER 4

THE MAKING OF A CAMPEÑO AND CAMPEÑA CULTURE

RACE, GENDER, AND RESISTANCE

Not just any overseer would talk down to a worker,
because the worker had nothing to lose and could turn
him into ground meat [with the machete].[1]

ANGEL MARTINEZ

The complex geography of gender, racial, and ethnic relationships and negotiations among social actors, among working-class men and women in the midcentury north coast, shaped not only the workplace but also a unique and radical campeño/a identity in the region. This chapter examines the development of a unique working-class campeño and campeña identity and culture in the north coast that was informed by the power dynamics of gender, sexuality, and class and racial regimes. It explores the construction of race and gender values, masculinity and femininity, and how they operated in the north coast. This culture and this identity are products of the campeño/a role as agricultural worker and influenced by the location of and living conditions in the campos, by workers' connections to the company, and by their migrant condition, as much as by male workers' hypermasculinity, gendered notions of work and the household division of labor, and their ability to earn money and purchase food, alcohol, sex, and goods to sustain their families. At the same time, campeño/a culture and identity were marked by adaptability, resistance to control, and working-class solidarity and unity, enabling the 1954 strike.

Despite the undisputed diversity of the population of workers in the region and in the industry, it must be emphasized that the predominant experience and culture was defined by male mestizos who self-identified as indios.[2] This is important for three reasons: it explains the workers'

agency within the paradigm of Honduran nation-building that was oc-
curring at the time; it acknowledges the significant exclusion and marginalization (though not an erasure) of different ethnic-racial groups and
women; and it explains a dominant worker culture, imbued with a specific masculinity, that enabled resistance to the banana companies.

The sentiment captured in the quote at the start of this chapter
communicates the spirit of transgression and resistance ingrained in the
campeño/a identity that ultimately transformed the north coast and
its working-class culture. Angel Martinez's almost passing remarks, in
fact, suggest the multitudes contained in workers' identities: there is a
reference to an overseer, a tacit acknowledgment of a subordinate role,
yet pride and braggadocio as a worker and a man; there is fatalism, nihil-
ism, and implicit anger about having nothing to lose; and there is overt
threat or potential of violence. The oral histories revealed the same nu-
ances. Workers' own self-images and identities were complex, reflecting
often contradictory, dichotomous understandings of themselves: as dedicated, hard workers, but also fierce, violent men; as providers and wage
earners, but also squanderers, gamblers, and alcohol consumers. These
identities were forged dialectically with their environment, the culture,
and other inhabitants of the north coast of the time.

North Americans, elite mestizos, and *criollo* empleados de confianza
living on the north coast found the banana fincas and accompanying
campos inhospitable. Workers of elite status in the companies would
only enter the plantations by train or train-cart (pulley) to monitor the
work. They confined their stays to near or around la Zona, or the American Zone, a "tamed," well-developed area equipped with traffic lights,
dancing clubs, *burdeles* (brothels), and cantinas; plenty of shops for edible
goods, clothing, and tools; a company hospital; company offices; and even
an elementary school. These towns, like La Lima, a hamlet of San Pedro
Sula, were essentially created by the banana companies but were markedly different from the banana campos. These communities felt exclusive
to workers, who felt that they could only venture into these towns—La
Lima, El Progreso, Tela—looking spiffy and well dressed; otherwise they
would risk being called *manchado* (stained one), a derogatory name used
by local company town dwellers to refer to finca workers. Creole Hondurans from the capital or nearby cities saw the north coast as a violent
region, where workers were illiterate, machete-wielding, working-class
ruffians, who drank hard, gambled, and engaged in prostitution—all seen
as promiscuous, immoral, and inferior behaviors. Banana finca workers
were characterized as men to be feared and distrusted, who exhibited

violent behavior in part because of their excessive alcohol consumption and perceived bad character. For the campeños, this "hard" reputation also informed their sense of identity and masculinity.

First and foremost, campeños were workers in the banana fincas. Finca workers built lives and leisure *a lo pobre* (poorly) in the campos of the north coast.[3] While the fincas were viewed as unsuitable and uninhabitable for North Americans, thousands of workers struggled and succeeded against the odds to live modest, dignified lives there. They constructed their homes and community and adapted to the environment and the work. An analysis of the everyday lives, working conditions, environment, and leisure time of primarily male finca laborers in the banana groves shows varied experiences among male workers based on ethnic, racial, and other differences, along with unconventional gender relationships that deviated from the indo-Hispanic mestizo and elite/dominant understandings of gender. These experiences and the realities of workers' lives and self-perceptions are juxtaposed with both the company-imposed identities and societal expectations and assumptions about banana workers. The misconceptions and false, often negative, perceptions actually served to promote unity among workers across differences, including non-indio immigrants and workers, mostly Salvadoran, Garifuna, and Jamaican workers.

Ultimately, even in their diversity, north-coast workers shared a common experience and were unified in their desire to thrive and achieve better conditions, as evidenced by the strike itself. Workers' oral narratives portray the strike as a result of ethnoracially diverse workers negotiating their lives on the north coast, not a state project or an orthodox party-led institutional action. The banana-worker identity allowed for other racial identities, despite preoccupation with an indio worker identity, and reflected very particular class constructions in the north coast. The construction of a working-class, male, banana-worker identity allowed workers to transgress status-quo power dynamics and resist company control. A mapping of the power relations and gender and racial constructs in the banana plantations and campos puts into sharp relief how the campeño identity, imbued with an adaptability and willingness to resist, was critical to the collective worker identity that led to effective organizing.

MESTIZO ORIGINS OF CAMPEÑO IDENTITY

There is no disputing from the outset the dominant presence of male mestizo workers and the construction of a banana-worker identity around their lives and experiences. The campeño identity developed with a mestizo character, and indeed with a projection of masculinity, that existed in alignment (and sometimes contention) with the national project of mestizaje. In interviews, campeños/as consistently referred to themselves as "indio/a," which they used interchangeably to identify as mestizo/a and as native to Honduras, but not of indigenous descent.

Narratives of the north coast throughout history presume that Honduras is a predominantly mestizo nation. Banana workers' racial and ethnic self-identification during the first half of the twentieth century was influenced by the national project of mestizaje. The wide use of the term "indio" among the banana workers to describe themselves may be understood as an indicator of the resonance of this movement to make Honduras a mestizo nation.

The nation-building project of mestizaje took hold over the years of 1890 to 1940, the objective of which was to cement the notion that Honduras was an indo-Hispanic mestizo nation.[4] For the nation's elite and government, two projects in particular were important in the forging of a mestizo national identity: first, the naming of the national coin of Honduras after Lempira, the mythologized Indigenous leader of the resistance against the Spanish incursions during the process of colonization, and second, the construction and development of the Mayan ruins in Copán as a historic preservation site with the support of the United Fruit Company (UFCo).[5] The influx of foreign labor, especially West Indian migrants, linked to the banana industry and the north coast, prompted xenophobia and increased support for the implementation of mestizaje.[6] Promotion of racial homogeneity was embraced as a way to consolidate the nation during a period of strife, further complicated by the influence of North American company's capitalist ideology and racial hierarchies.

In 1926, after a contentious debate on the naming of the national coin after either Lempira or Honduran independence hero Francisco Morazán, the Honduran Congress selected Lempira. The Indigenous leader became a resonating symbol for the nation-building process and, simultaneously, a rejection of Honduras's Black and African heritage.[7] In the 1930s and 1940s, during the dictatorship of Carías Andino, UFCo under Sam Zemurray and his US-educated daughter, Doris Stone, promoted what Euraque calls the "Mayanization" of Honduras.[8] This period actually made Indigenous peoples invisible to the nation while rescuing a form of their civilization through Mayan mythic symbols and ruins. An *Indigenista* movement with "certain elements of North

American archeology and the banana companies' hegemony in Honduras advanced efforts to incorporate postcolonial discourses on national identity."[9] The Honduran *Indigenista* movement resonated with intellectuals and fit well with Stone's archeological writings and UFCo's efforts to discover a version of the Indigenous past—a heavily Mayan one, even though the Maya were not the largest Indigenous group in Honduras. An added incongruency is that Lempira is commonly theorized to have been Lenca (another Indigenous group), not Mayan.

The liberal reform period was also key to the construction of the mestizo nation, since the economic opening given to the foreign banana companies led to increased West Indian migration to the region, which in turn strengthened support for mestizaje. Honduran liberalism was inspired by Europe and the United States and their "modern scientific" approaches to nation-building that relied on exclusion, xenophobia, and racism.[10] Blackness was read as foreign due to the banana companies' recruitment of Black West Indian workers. Roaring immigration debates of the time centered on efforts to curtail the threat of foreign Black immigration from the West Indies, as well as Salvadoran and Arab immigrants. These migrants and their diversity presented a challenge to the consolidation of a Honduras as a mestizo nation, yet at the same time reinforced it, as mestizos unified to counter the influx.[11]

Honduran intellectuals, under the banner of patriotism, challenged West Indian migration "to promote the interests of the Honduran worker."[12] *Indigenista* intellectuals promoting mestizaje, such as poet Froylán Turcios (1875–1943), were inspired by the *Indigenismo* movement in Mexico. While Turcios (once closely aligned with Augusto César Sandino) promoted sovereignty and resistance to foreign-owned companies, his patriotism was imbued with racism and xenophobia.[13] His writings, for instance, claimed, "The Honduran worker, who is of a race a thousand times superior to Black people, is more intelligent and apt for agricultural work. The majority of Hondurans cannot imagine how pernicious they have been to the country, these Black people from strange origins who work in the north coast fincas."[14] Research shows that Turcios saw West Indians as British subjects and allies of the foreign-owned companies, which he criticized in his writings, and their abilities as workers and as citizens were subject to doubt.[15] They were considered by *Indigenistas* to be an obstruction to the nation-building processes in an imagined homogenous community.[16]

The national debates among government power players and elites on issues such as the national coin and immigration to the north coast filtered down to workers through Liberal Party newspapers and fliers advocating worker support, and through institutional leaders and social policies.[17] Prejudicial sentiments were also prevalent in the emerging labor movement. For instance, the FOH played a role in introducing legislation against the migration of Black and Chinese workers in 1921.[18] FOH also sought the deportation of such workers already in the country. Euraque explains that the British Embassy, the US Embassy, and the companies supported this law in tune with the elite and the government's anti-migration and anti-Black sentiments at the time. Black immigration was in direct opposition to the mestizaje aspirations, and the rejection of Black workers demonstrated a form of patriotism at the time. The national project relied on the homogeneity of mestizaje to consolidate the nation, but also consciously embraced gendered and racialized strategies of exclusion that aligned with elite interests and subordinated marginalized interests.

CAMPEÑOS EMBRACE "INDIO"

The north coast was never homogeneous as the Honduran government and elites conceived it in their promotion of a mestizo national identity. Though this nation-building process was influential in workers' lives, at the same time, the workers' understanding of themselves as indio reflected their own constructions of an ethnoracial identity important to work and life in the campos. In their narratives about the north coast, workers often referred to themselves as indio to describe that they were natives of Honduras. This indio identity was an instrumental ethnoracial descriptor in the everyday work and life in a multiracial and multinational north coast. The indio identity embraced by workers had two important functions: on the one hand, it differentiated one from other nationalities—such as Salvadorans (perceived to be mestizos)—and, on the other hand, it strictly defined one as not Black—like Jamaican immigrants (inglés)—or from the Garifuna community.[19] The codification of an ethnoracial identity as Honduran, native, and Indigenous was advantageous for banana companies, as it created a potentially competitive division between Black and mestizo workers.

This indio identity was useful to the state project of mestizaje and continues to evolve today. During the colonial period indio was not a desired identification. As Marvin Barahona reminds us, "During the Independence period, the word "Indio" (Indian) acquired a pejorative meaning among ladinos [mestizos] and had a connotation that invoked adjectives such as 'ignorant,' 'poorly educated,' and 'stupid,' etc."[20]

Barahona dates the process of mestizaje to the colonial period, when there were "three racial influences, the Spanish, the Indigenous, and the African."[21] These influenced later understandings of nation during the independence period, informing questions of race and ethnicity, which according to Barahona became an instant preoccupation for Honduran *ladinos*, or mestizos, after Honduras achieved independence from Spain (in 1821).[22] By the 1940s and 1950s, the term indio gained currency again, but this time during a period of heavy immigration control. Mestizo is a contested category that has taken on various meanings. Originally, it referred to racial mixture—not necessarily between Indigenous and Spanish, but any racial mixture. Gradually, mestizo came to signify indo-Hispanic, eradicating the possibility of other interpretations. "Indio" originally referred to Indigenous ancestry, particularly in the colonial era, but campeños used this term to mean they are native to Honduras and not immigrants or Black. These terms, however, were charged and imbued with social meaning, as mestizo took on meaning as a potential national identity for Honduras, marginalizing Blackness and Indigenous altogether.

Honduran worker narratives, their memories of the strike, their lives in the campos, and their self-identification as indios are markers of resistance to the Honduran state's project of mestizaje and the process of constructing a national mestizo identity, as well as indicators of workers' own identity construction in the contexts of work and life in the north-coast banana fields.[23] The campeño contruction of indio identity came to encompass a broader, less exclusive diversity of identities. In addition to native Honduran workers, Black workers, Salvadorans, and other immigrants strategically identified with the term in order to keep their jobs and live in the campos. Social constructions of identity, ethnicity, and race were adapted by campeños to suit their lives. Identifying as an indio became a claim to belonging in Honduras and the north coast, used advantageously as a component of ethnoracial identity among campeños during the 1940s and 1950s. Campeños were not, however, merely passive recipients of state, company, and elite ideas of national identity; they also constructed their own understandings of ethnicity and race as workers and embraced indio identity because it allowed them access to work and to survive within company and state control and to gain better work and housing.

For Honduran workers, indio was not just used and understood as a racial identity;[24] identifying as indio signaled that they were native to Honduras and not foreign, Black, Jamaican, or Garifuna. Many

Salvadorans could also pass for indio, especially those who lived on the north coast for a long time. The term was loaded with racial, ethnic, and xenophobic meaning that was advantageous to mestizo workers when obtaining work and living arrangements. Calling oneself indio—even for Black workers—was a claim of belonging to the dominant culture, to the majority, and all the entitlements that came with it.[25]

Worker narratives show that many workers from the same regions or countries helped each other to access work and make living arrangements through the system of padrinazgo (patronage). Workers from El Salvador tended to stick together and sought padrinazgo from their fellow countrymen, often going to supervisors from their own town or region. Efraín Hernández Maldonado remembers that in work and life in the campos, at first "one would find one's way from others."[26] At the same time, the padrinazgo system may have excluded workers who were from different groups; it was most effective for the majority mestizo workforce. Padrinazgo thus served to reinforce indio identity in the campos by favoring indio workers for jobs and advancement over others. One worker explains that he knew a company worker, a timekeeper and helper who selected the work team, and he himself was chosen in this way.[27] Some mestizo stevedores had gained the confidence and trust of certain *capataces* (overseers) and were chosen immediately and made a little more money or were given lighter work for the same amount of pay. Lighter work, for instance, involved counting the stems as they were loaded onto the chain stem holder.[28] The contratista system of work also allowed for discrimination. In La Lima and El Progreso, contractors were often identified as indio even if they may have been Salvadoran, and they often looked for a crew of workers within their own network or hometowns, resulting in privilege for those who identified as indio or were read as indio.

Anti-immigration decrees issued in 1929 and 1934 sought to restrict migration of Black Jamaicans and Arabs, among other immigrants. In 1929, a law decreed "Arabs, Turks, Syrians, Armenians, Blacks, and Chinese had to post 2,500 dollars before entering the country."[29] Similarly in 1930, an immigration law prohibited the migration of "Blacks, Chinese, and gypsies," and the other races and ethnicities—"Arabs, Turks, Syrians, Armenians, Palestinians, Czechoslovaks, Lebanese, and Polish"—were not permitted to enter unless they showed proof that they came to work in "agriculture or to promote new industries."[30] Based on these laws, the companies increased their vigilance over immigrant workers, which meant that workers had to prove that they were native Hondurans to ensure access to work. At the very least, workers had to pass for Honduran, which many mestizo Salvadorans could do. The banana companies essentially stopped recruiting and hiring Black workers in 1933.[31]

RACIAL EXCLUSION AND INCLUSION AMONG CAMPEÑOS

The first two decades of the twentieth century proved to be an especially dangerous period for British Jamaicans and other West Indian laborers at the hands of the mostly mestizo workers, who saw them as competition or a company ploy to replace workers who attempted to organize. Labor organizers at the time demanded their deportation.[32] The xenophobic actions by labor organizers and mestizo workers were driven by racist views about British West Indians and other Caribbean Black workers; West Indian workers, for instance, were perceived by some as competition for work and beneficiaries of favoritism by US companies due to their ability to speak English.

Padrinazgo often resulted in the exclusion of the minority Black workers from well-paid finca work, even in the ports of Tela, La Ceiba, and Puerto Cortés, the most racially diverse centers of the north coast where thousands worked as stevedores. Mestizo, Garifuna, and Black workers worked together on loading docks, railroad and on company grazing lands in the ports of Tela and Puerto Cortés, but racial tensions are evident in the historical memory of workers and reflected in company policies and acts of favoritism toward mestizo workers.[33] Gerardo Pery Laredo, a Garifuna worker, painfully recalls, "Before, the indio [mestizo] did not like to intermingle with Blacks. If a group of indios came together . . . we [Black workers] were not included in there. They were rude because of the color and all."[34] Pery Laredo eventually found alliances with other Garifuna workers from Tornabé, a Garifuna village outside of Tela, and would spend almost every weekend with them or in the community.

The stereotypes about Garifuna and Black workers that circulated among mestizo workers could not have been farther from the truth. Mestizo workers frequently remarked that Black workers could not handle hard labor—that of finca work—despite their representation in high numbers as hard laborers on the loading docks.[35] Some felt that Black workers had privileged, "easier" positions, such as timekeepers, hotel employees, nurses (usually Jamaican women), or work supervisors, an impression created by company hiring preferences, in this case, for

English speakers.[36] Company hiring policies and the bananera employment systems were discriminatory toward Black workers and relied on stereotypes to explain why they had restricted access to regular employment in the fincas. The company had an unspoken hiring policy that privileged English-speaking Black workers in the absence of mestizo workers. Supervisors propagated contradictory narratives about Black workers: they were strong enough to load and carry stems onto the ships but not strong enough to withstand labor in the fincas day in, day out.

Discrimination against Black workers in the ports was blatant, as witnessed by Juan Canales while working in Puerto Cortés—especially in the demeaning process by which dockworkers were forced to compete for jobs every day.[37] Garifuna workers and *ingleses* (Jamaican workers, so-called because they spoke English) were relegated to and vied for limited work on the docks. Loading at the docks was irregular, temporary labor, fluctuating with product demand and local labor needs.[38] These workers, the stevedores, loaded banana stems onto a chain contraption that would carry the stem onto the ship. To get hired for the day, workers presented themselves at the gates of the shipyards ready to load bananas. A supervisor picked workers arbitrarily at first sight and gave them a ticket with a number on it to designate that they had been chosen. Workers showed up daily, especially when there was *corte* (cutting of fruit) for work. Of course, only certain people were chosen; others were turned away. Black workers were often turned away from work. Juan Bautista Canales, when prompted to talk about his knowledge of Black workers, explains: "Sometimes [workers] would come back and say 'they did not give me a ticket for work.' They did not work; it was an unfortunate life . . . facing being fired, certain kinds of discrimination, whether you're Black or mestizo."[39]

Race is a complicated issue in Honduras. While many workers I interviewed may have been phenotypically Black or racially mixed, they did not self-identify as such in oral interviews. Once employed, Black workers experienced differential treatment in the campos. For example, Black workers did not have the same hospital benefits as finca workers, they often had a harder time securing jobs on the finca, and their job security was more precarious.

Pery Laredo migrated from Trujillo, Colón, to La Ceiba to look for work. Not finding it there, he traveled further west to look for work in the Tela Railroad Company fincas: "I could not find work. . . . They would tell me they did not need workers . . . they had workers."[40] This may have been because he was a Garifuna worker and also because he did not know anyone to help him get a job in a finca. He eventually ended up in San Pedro Sula working in a bakery before he gained a foothold within the Tela Railroad Company as a yardero.[41] Once Pery Laredo became a finca worker he remembers being the only Black (*negro*) worker among mestizo workers.[42] Pery Laredo explains that indios had stereotypes of Black workers, including Garifunas: "[Mestizos used to say] that we were not good people; they said that we were bad. . . . Then the others, [the Black workers] would respond that the situation they all faced [the labor conditions] was the same between the Blacks and the indios [mestizos]"[43]—meaning that they should be treated equal. His memory reveals the racial and ethnic negotiations around work on the finca. He explained that campeños held stereotypes about indio and Black workers, usually that Black workers were *luchadores* (fighters) like the indios. While mestizo workers held harsh stereotypes of Garifuna and Black workers, Black workers also defended themselves, their work, and their identification as campeños, a category Pery Laredo also considered as indio: "Yes, indios [are campeños]. There are some from here [referring to the village of Tornabé] who are also campeños. [To be campeño was] to live in the campos, to grow corn, grow plantain, grow manioc [yuca], and work in the finca too."[44] Despite differences in perception, interestingly, Pery Laredo still identified Garifunas with the term "indio" for those who worked in the fincas based on the work they did for the company. For him, "the majority of campeños are indios," but they were also Garifunas because of their relation to the agricultural work of the finca and their knowledge of working the land in general. For him, these were non-race-based factors of being a campeño.[45]

COMPAÑERISMO AND CAMPEÑO IDENTITY TRANSCEND DIFFERENCE

Pery Laredo strongly identified as a campeño despite his non-mestizo origin; working in the finca and living in the campo were important to defining that identity for him. Despite being from a village near Trujillo, he worked near the Garifuna village of Tornabé. He met a worker who invited him to the village on days off; he integrated into a Garifuna social and familial network away from home.[46] He speaks to a sense of unity and common experience, despite the stories workers shared about the different levels of inclusion and exclusion in their social spheres and others. Workers' experiences on the north coast varied based on numerous factors, including the workers' own origins, race, ethnicity, skill level, and gender, but they shared a common experience as workers struggling to survive in a challenging environment and in a competitive labor market. Constraints on workers' opportunities and the types of available work resulted in an increased reliance on compañerismo (camaraderie) among finca workers for their livelihood.

Despite the hierarchy of different positions and the differential treatment of workers in various finca work positions, there was a common experience that drew workers together. In the workplace, or the finca, workers developed camaraderie and worker solidarity throughout their work hours and workdays. Many workers labored in teams with at least one other worker. This everyday contact through both leisure and work time fostered a sense of connection and community based on place of origin and race, or based on the type of duty they performed, whether or not they got along or shared race or ethnicity. A sense of camaraderie and compañerismo helped workers survive.

Despite diversity, or perhaps with diversity as an integral component, compañerismo created a sense of unity, enabling effective organizing and transgression of company control. The entry process into the work of the fincas and the precariousness of many positions, coupled with a lack of social mobility and stability, were experiences most finca workers shared in some variation in their lives and histories of work. The workplace was a site of shared experience and compañerismo for many, certainly most finca workers. Still, indios, campesinos, mestizos, Garifuna, Black workers, and women all had vastly different experiences in the north coast.

DIVERSITY AND ADAPTABILITY AT THE HEART OF CAMPEÑO IDENTITY

While there was a dominant banana-worker culture, many workers' experiences diverged from the common narrative, and these, too, became part of the north-coast culture. The campeño/a identity provided flexibility and allowed for exchange across difference. Remarkably, the workers' diversity, and gendered and racialized differences in particular, did not prevent cohesion and in fact became a part of the character of the community and the strike movement.

Oral histories of workers reveal various facets of workers' constructions of their own identity in resistance to brutal working conditions and company control. While workers sometimes repeated the myth of being outsiders, often eliding women workers' own accounts of the banana worker–campeño community, they were by far more diverse in their incorporation of race, ethnicity, gender, and nationality, in contrast to the national ideology of mestizaje. The campeño/a identity resonated with workers across ethnic, racial, and gender lines, despite the different types of roles they were guided into based on these traits. Rural workers who came to work in the fincas from the interior of Honduras, for instance, had markedly different experiences from those of Jamaican, Garifuna, and Salvadoran workers. Most mestizos found work in the fincas through their networks, while most Jamaicans were drawn to the English-speaking jobs in hotels or hospitals. Garifuna workers returned to their villages after a stint of work; they rarely made the campos of the Tela Railroad Company their full-time home. In contrast, Salvadorans formed migratory networks, housing networks, and work alliances, and rarely returned home.[47] Women workers tended to participate in the informal economy within the campos and work as vendors or women town dwellers worked near the banana finca. Workers' lives and communities were shaped by these differences in their regional and social networks, experiences informed by ethnoracial identity, and roles and opportunities in the fincas.

GENDER AND CAMPEÑO IDENTITY AND CULTURE

Male workers' lives in this terrain on the north coast provide evidence of the formation of a working-class masculinity that was integral to work, survival, and dignity. Men's lives were typified by violence, projections of manhood, and resistance. The dominance of campeño masculinity in the historiography has often led to the marginalization of women from the narrative. Traditional narratives create an impression that only male workers lived and labored in the banana fincas during the first half of the twentieth century. But to understand the campeño identity of the 1950s requires examining the experiences of both men and women within the banana enclaves, as this identity was shaped by the interplay and tension between campeños and campeñas, revealing an ongoing and evolving set of codes of comportment and race and gender performativity that also provided opportunities for subverting company and state control.

Despite a glorified masculinity in the north-coast culture, campeño identity made room for women. Women worked hard in the north-coast campos, and their relationships to men and the state were complicated. Town dwellers cast campesinas as "loose women," and the company saw them as expendable women, though it relied on their informal labor extensively. But when there were only a few women in the campos, they were also seen as commodity and could be pursued, and even coerced, by finca workers.[48] Men and women often maintained relationships of convenience in which men used their power over women to obtain sex and services, like receiving food and goods. In other ways, women held considerable power in the fincas and within company control because of the important role they played in feeding and taking care of men. Overall, men and women worked hard alongside one another, and the ever-present surveillance of their lives and activities by the company and the state was shared by both. They were affected in gendered but analogous ways; while women sex workers were corralled and pursued by authorities under company control, men were often thrown in jail and then released just in time for work. Together, and based on their living conditions and camaraderie, men and women enacted a resistance to company and state control, which ultimately contributed to the strike. These indicators of shared resistance can be seen in the sale of illicit alcohol, which both men and women did, during the leisure time spent in the brothels, and later in their collaboration during the strike. The culture of campeño masculinity permeated even leisure time and contested spaces, as exemplified in workers' use of alcohol and engagement in prostitution, and it could be wielded as resistance to company and local authorities. These were areas of life—use of alcohol primarily for men, and prostitution for women—where campeños/as submitted to a measure of control but also transgressed and resisted in common ways, forms of resistance that would later inform them during the organizing of the strike.

These examples demonstrate both the extent of company control and the creative power of workers to subvert it. While workers' actions may not suggest deliberate or coordinated resistance in these arenas, these activities show a degree of freedom, outside of regulation, created of their own agency and perhaps as an adaptation for survival. Despite attempts to control men's lives beyond the finca and women's lives perceived to be in the periphery, these campeños/as were able to chart a new path for themselves, one that challenged gender and racial constructs and roles in the indo-Hispanic nation. Their subversion of company control was daily, local, and complex, sometimes happening in unexpected places, and together these small acts of subversion allowed for workers to build resiliency into their common campeño identity, which allowed the strike to flourish as powerfully as it did in 1954.

The spheres of the campeño community—the plantation, the living quarters, and leisure time—in the campos allowed workers to build a distinctive collective identity among men and women, of the banana regions.[49] This community and identity based on shared work, life, and leisure melded together many people from different regions or countries. It superseded identities as mestizo, indio, Black, male, or female, etc. It was not always a haven, but workers made it work. Even in times of violence and strife, workers saw themselves as part of the north coast and a community of campeños, campeñas, and transgressors.

MEN'S USE OF ALCOHOL AND WOMEN VENDORS ON THE NORTH COAST

Alcohol figured prominently in the social sphere of the north coast. Alcohol consumption was both a predominant pastime for workers and a useful and often-used tool of social control for the company. Alcohol production and consumption could also be seen as a form of resistance by the banana workers against strict company control, as well as an adaptation used to survive the grueling labor and a form of economic and physical survival day to day. Beer and aguardiente (hard liquor) could only be legally purchased from the company in the commissary of the campos, and these were the only permitted forms of alcohol consumption.[50] In addition to buying beer at the commissary and drinking in the campos, however, workers would ride into the local towns on the margins of the company territories and purchase beer at the brothels perched on the edges of the river and near the train depots. In the campos, men and women food vendors earned a living by providing alcohol to workers, regardless of company policies. Workers could buy aguardiente from a patrona who may have brought it from her shopping trip in one of the larger towns of La Lima, El Progreso, La Ceiba, or Olanchito. Patronas would sell aguardiente illicitly out of their eating establishments in servings of eighths, or *un octavo*.

In addition, workers had their own homemade liquor, cususa, that was made and consumed in secret throughout the campos, despite the company's prohibition. Also known as *gato de monte* (mountain cat), cususa was moonshine made with fermented corn, water, and sometimes sugarcane and other additives.[51] The *cususeros* (cususa makers) set up *fábricas*, makeshift distilleries, and cususa-making equipment composed of simple containers and distilling equipment that were not easy to obtain in company stores. María Celea Ardón Torres inherited her tools from a *cususero* who had passed away. She learned how to make it from her father, who was also a *cususero*.[52] The process itself involved taking corn, rice, or wheat and fermenting it with water and sugar for as long as six months, using the grains as the base for the liquor. The *droncito*, a small tin can or barrel, is used to boil the substance, the top of it closed shut with the *serpentina*, a long copper tube (or sometimes made of clay) that sticks out of the top of the tin can and coils around the tin can or container.[53] As the mixture boils, the steam travels up the tube and clear, shiny liquid drips out the other end. The mixture can be flavored with a variety of ingredients, from cinnamon to tropical fruits. The first batch, the strongest essence, is then mixed with second batch to make the *cususero's* signature drink.[54] During the Carías Andino dictatorship, which was violently repressive, conservative, and puritanical, the use of alcohol was condemned.[55] In fact, both the fabrication of aguardiente and the act of drinking it were seen as transgressions, and this societal value was sustained well after Carías. Drunkenness comprised 42% of all recorded crimes in 1945.[56] The *Police Magazine* characterized these techniques of liquor production as "villana profanación" (villainous desecration) in which the "beautiful fruits of the earth" are converted in "contaminated mud."[57] Drunkenness and gambling were crimes for which people were prosecuted as fiercely as "political censure against Liberals and Communists and prostitution."[58] But there was a distinction in class; while elites were consuming more dignified imported cognac, whiskey, or brandy,[59] the working classes drank the locally distilled, homemade forms of alcohol—not only the vile cususa and basic aguardiente but also *chicha*,[60] a traditional Indigenous drink made from fermented maize and fruit. So even the consumption of alcohol was gendered and racialized for the campeños of the banana regions.

COMPANY CONTROL

The company and the local inspector from Hacienda Pública, the local public health office, were at odds with the vendors. The company preferred that workers buy all goods from the company commissary. The company also relied on workers' continuous productivity and thus monitored excessive drinking, which was assumed to lead to violence and work interruptions. The local authorities aggressively enforced the alcohol prohibition, for both consumers and vendors, to protect the company's financial interests, including their profits from alcohol sales in the commissary. Honduran law and the company cabos de comisariato leveled harsh penalties for consuming cususa.[61] Men or women accused of cususa production (*tener fábrica*) faced legal charges or confiscation of their equipment if caught by local cabos de comisariato, who operated under the directive of the company and the government's Department of Public Finance and Police (Departamento de Hacienda

Pública y Policía). In the case of Tomás Calderon from El Ocotillo, Choloma, Calderon was apprehended in his home and accused of possessing contraband alcohol.[62] Among the cususa-making equipment found in his possession were two empty 1-liter bottles, one of which was said to have held aguardiente belonging to the state.[63] Ardón Torres and her live-in partner, Lorenzo Cerna Martinez's *fábrica* was also raided in the hamlet of Majaine in Choloma, a company train depot. Inspectors surprised Ardón Torres at five in the morning about 1.5 kilometers from her house, near a creek (*quebrada*) where she had set up her distillery. Her makeshift distillery was described in a report on her arrest: "Said operation was on a cliff, near a creek, and it was composed of a *droncito* full of *chicha* [probably cususa], a *serpentina*, and a bottle and a half of alcohol."[64] Ardón Torres explained that she was forced to work because her husband had abandoned her; she had to feed her kids.[65] While she was caught red-handed with the *fábrica de cususa*, her defense was that she did not know it was illegal to produce it ("ignoraba que era prohibida") and all she did was ferment an "arroba de maíz" (25 pounds of corn).[66] Although Ardón Torres confessed to making it, she was not prosecuted, perhaps because she was a woman or may not have had a prior record; instead, the local authorities prosecuted Cerna Martinez for two years from the date of the original infraction.

Despite the risks, workers and unauthorized vendors adapted to these conditions and maintained this alcohol consumption as a part of life and leisure in the north coast. While drinking alcohol was not the only leisure-time activity of workers at the time, the prevalence and casualness of references to alcohol, its use, and availability in interviews with workers is noteworthy. For them, alcohol consumption was not a vice, as the company saw it, but a retreat from the work, and a well-deserved reward for a life of hard labor. To enjoy this particular leisure activity, workers learned to deal with policing by company agents in the company towns and the fincas. Cususa-makers and patronas learned to exist in spite of persecution and heavy policing of alcohol sales in the campos.

Workers also suggested that, beyond prohibition and restriction, the company in some cases used alcohol affirmatively to control workers. An overseer, a *capataz*, would offer a worker a swig of alcohol to encourage him to work faster.[67] Given the characteristics of the north-coast enclave, a region under strict surveillance and prescribed social codes for workers, this method of control is not surprising. Authors have noted how widely colonial powers utilized drugs and alcohol to promote work and as a tool of control.[68]

In the north-coast region of Honduras, the manipulation of alcohol to exert control over workers is evident in the infamous letter from H. V. Rolston of the Cortés Development Company to Luis Melara, a Honduran company lawyer, on the subject of acquiring more land from the Honduran government:

> It is indispensable to capture the imagination of these subjugated peoples, and attract them to the idea of our agrandisement [*sic*], and in a general way to those politicians and bosses that we must use. Observation and careful study have assured us that a people degraded by drink can be assimilated to the demands of necessity and destiny; it is in our interest to make it our concern that the privileged class, whom we will need for our exclusive benefit, bend itself to our will; in general, none of them has any conviction or character, far less patriotism; they seek only position and rank, and on being granted them, we will make them hungry for even more. These men must not act on their own initiative, but rather according to determining factors and under our immediate control.[69]

The organizers of the 1954 strike made this letter available to workers, and ever since it has taken on importance as a document that is emblematic of the US-based companies and their role in the banana industry of the north coast. Workers cite this letter and condemn the companies for the unjust representation of workers and their lives in the north coast and the oppressive power of the US companies' dominance in the banana industry. That the company would blatantly and disrespectfully manipulate them struck a bitter chord for many workers. If Amaya Amador's *Prisión Verde* epitomizes the story of the harsh life of the banana worker, the Rolston Letter represents, for workers, evidence of their antagonist in the story, the cause of their hardship: the companies that hired them.

RESISTANCE AND ALCOHOL

In looking at the use and restriction of alcohol in the north coast we can see a fluid, unstructured, and arbitrary negotiation of workers' relationships with company control, as well as workers' creation of alternatives to company policies, which affected worker culture and identity. The negotiation of their lives around alcohol provides an example and microcosm of workers' resistance and adaptation to company control. Alcohol, as a result of its use by workers and its policing by the company, accentuated a culture of violence in the north coast. Cususa was known to be potent and have the potential to make men so inebriated that it could lead to serious violence. Some women vendors recall that this homemade liquor "made them crazy" (*los ponía locos*). Despite the consequences of drinking alcohol, whether purchased from the company alcohol or illicitly obtained, workers did not abstain from engaging in public drinking. And for the most part, it did not prevent them from showing up to work.[70]

One case involved Antonio Orellana and Paulino Alemán, two friends who were drinking together in Campo Guaruma Uno when they met up with two other men, Felix Orellana and Benedicto Dubón, a Salvadoran. Felix Orellana and Benedicto Dubón attacked Antonio Orellana and Paulino Alemán, seriously injuring both men.[71] The two workers were unable to work for at least twenty days due to injuries, and Antonio Orellana was left with a mutilated hand and gashes on his arm and head. As soon as the fight was over, Dubón tried to escape to the neighboring Finca 12, where he was caught.[72] The testimony from witnesses and workers in and around the barracón who heard the commotion failed to establish who the instigator was. Everyone attested to Dubón's disappearance from the scene of the incident, but no other information was forthcoming. All that was certain was that all workers involved were consuming alcohol and were drunk, two were armed, and the incident occurred in the barracón. In this case, both Alemán, the injured worker, and Dubón, the accused, used the consumption of alcohol and their state of drunkenness as an excuse for not being completely aware of what exactly happened. According to the police report, "He claimed that he did not remember if anyone saw the aggression because he was drunk."[73] Being drunk was presented as a common and acceptable excuse for the violence that occurred, and claiming drunkenness was presented as a credible defense for workers against auxiliares and *cabos de comandante* (local police that served the company) and in the courts. I want to draw a parallel between alcohol use, the acceptability of inebriation, and masculinity here, and the ways in which the state assumed this evil was necessary, permissible even, for the functioning of the banana harvesting.

This case may also show a collective rejection of company control. Witnesses reported not really seeing Dubón commit the actual crime, an important fact in declarations that eventually led to Dubón's release after appealing in the courts of San Pedro Sula. The victims relied on the auxiliar to testify as to what happened, but without witnesses it was not a strong case. It is unclear whether or not workers saw Dubón commit the crime, but it is likely that campeños were protecting one another in the context of the local courts. Workers may not have disclosed all the information they had to support the court prosecution system. The campo, as we have seen, was a place where workers knew and shared information with each other. It seems unbelievable that workers would not have known what caused the altercation, at the very least. Typically, these incidents became topics of conversation during leisure time, in comedores, or while playing cards, especially among workers who worked closely with those involved. In this case, there is no indication of testimony as to any reason for the altercation, and in fact, the resolution of the incident does not seem to have been important for bystanders. The violence, despite the dramatic circumstances and horrible injury, seemed to have been treated as a regular or ordinary occurrence, unworthy of special attention.

Company surveillance, monitoring, and prosecution of workers perceived to be engaging in illicit activities often led to violent repression. This brutality was commonplace and became an accepted part of workers' lives. Company watchdogs, cabos de comisariato, tied alcohol consumption to violent behavior. One example of company brutality was a case from Campo Verde, where two cususeros, Cupertino Garcia and Manuel Mejia Portillo, were caught by the cabos in the act of making cususa and implicated Eulalio Perez Garcia, the owner of the cususa fábrica. Perez Garcia was then tortured by the police to reveal the location of the fábrica and to admit that he was the owner, and "Eulalio Perez confessed to trafficking in alcohol and that the alcohol he made he sold it in the campos."[74] He was confronted at his home and confessed to police after the previously arrested partners in the business were tortured. "When he woke up they captured him and they whipped him on his back with [the flat side of the] machete and they tortured him by putting sticks in between his fingers and then squeezing his hand. They told him to give up the location where he had his equipment."[75] When Perez Garcia gave up his fábrica and equipment, the police forced him to make the infamous cususa drink and then took the liquor and the equipment with them. Such physical coercion and violence by the local police against male cususeros was typical of the campos and their surroundings. If the men did not provide information it would be coerced from them through corporal punishment. Abuse of power was common against workers who consumed alcohol as well as producers of cususa.

BANANA WORKERS' CODES OF MANHOOD: THE GEOGRAPHY OF MASCULINITY AND WORK

Masculinity in the north coast was constructed through the upholding of contradictory gender roles and norms, forming a very specific set of codes of manhood and solidarity among the working-class men of the region. In the north-coast campos and fincas, even though both men and women were a part of the making and distribution of alcohol, alcohol consumption was regarded by workers as an act that took place primarily in the male social and public sphere. Men were the primary targets of surveillance and arrest for alcohol consumption.[76] A gendered culture developed around alcohol that was reflective of how they mobilized in other areas of the living and work environments of the campos.[77] Codes of manhood were constructed and observed in campos particularly during leisure time, and these included alcohol consumption and confronting company restrictions.[78]

Male workers' codes of manhood were critical to their survival. Some of these codes were notions they brought with them from their hometowns, and others were made up on the spot, as they engaged with one another in the finca work, and during leisure time away from finca work at the end of the day. US and foreign company employees in the American Zone read campeños as violent men, prone to alcoholism and womanizing, who used their machetes—their work tools—as weapons. Workers' lives, and the construction of working-class masculinity, drastically challenged the dominant culture of the period in the country, including the narrative of violence and murder. In fact, the strike itself is remembered as an extremely "disciplined effort" on behalf of workers who insured that there would be no damage to company property and the finca while they were on strike.[79] How could such violent men lead such a disciplined effort? It was precisely through these codes of what it meant to be a decent, hardworking man in the north coast.[80]

For banana workers, drinking alcohol in the banana campos and in the company towns was a public act, a social time in which workers could engage with other men. Drinking in public was where men could prove their masculinity and transgress the rules of the company and social norms. Leisure activities during non-work-time also formed a masculine social space where men were able to recuperate their dignity. Spaces where workers consumed alcohol, publicly and clandestinely, were places where they transgressed company control on repeated occasions. These spaces inscribed their lives with elements of maleness and macho attitudes, and they also differentiated workers from women, company control, and the Honduran legal system. There was power in sharing their lived experiences as men doing "masculine" work, helping them see themselves and cope with the insurmountable obstacles they could not change. Alcohol, gambling, and other forms of leisure were tied to violence and interruption of work, yet these activities actually bonded workers, making them *compañeros* just as much as working together did, and allowed them to form a collective identity, in resistance to company control.[81]

Ultimately, the most notable element in the construction of identity and codes of manhood is that of transgression or resistance. Workers' responses to their environment were forms of reclaiming dignity in the context of the brutal work and unhealthy living arrangements that were recounted by workers I interviewed and an intentional response to unwelcome and unreasonable company control.

What may have seemed simply to be a violent outburst or uncontrolled altercation may actually have been a reaction to a constraining environment. Perhaps by engaging in brawls, disputes, and angry responses, as workers frequently did in the campos, they were also challenging codes of behavior prescribed and enforced by company supervisors and a web of social controls imposed by the industry. Workers who ended up in bloody machete fights were subject to serious consequences. They were arrested and processed for trial, first through the local auxiliares and then by the local comandante in the company town. Bloody altercations, murder, and/or theft from the company were tried in the local courts. Appeals processes, seeking to overturn initial convictions, were laborious and often costly in financial and human terms. But these acts of violence, I suggest, were one part of a larger process of worker empowerment that enabled the strike. The "passive," objectified campesino, or subsistence farmer, became fierce, in control, and powerful in the context of the banana fincas.

MERETRICES Y CLANDESTINAS: PROSTITUTION IN CAMPEÑO CULTURE

To be a man in the campos, as we have seen above, required a complex set of codes of manhood that relied sometimes on the partnership with women and, at other times, on the objectification and commodification of women. The company and the state also relied on the suppression of women to maintain control over the male agricultural workforce.

Within this complex hierarchy, women found autonomy and agency despite their dependence on campeños' ability to purchase services, sex, or alcohol. I claim additionally that in Honduras, the prioritization of the racial identification of mestizo also excluded women of all races from the national project.

The now-classic poem "Poema de amor" (Love Poem) by Salvadoran poet Roque Dalton is perhaps one of the only poems that references the infamous brothels frequented by Salvadoran migrant workers, as well as all banana workers, in the Caribbean basin in Central America on paydays:

> *las que llenaron los bares y burdeles*
> *de todos los puertos y capitales de la zona*
> *("La gruta azul", "El Calzoncito", "Happyland")*[82]

> the [women] who filled the bars and brothels
> of all the ports and capitals of the zone
> ("The Blue Grotto," "The Little Panty," "Happyland")

Dalton was referring to the north-coast banana regions of Honduras in this particular verse. While most of Dalton's poem immortalizes male Salvadoran workers, in the excerpt above he refers to workers with the feminine pronoun (*las que llenaron los bares y burdeles*). While use of the female pronoun hardly qualifies as a notable effort to include women, these lines—which acknowledge the prostitution of the time—hint at how leftist organizers and writers perceived the region during the most affluent period in the banana regions: as a place of debauchery and lack of discipline brought on by the foreign banana industries and capitalism. The poem also hints at how other women sex workers from Honduras and other countries existed and worked in the brothels and streets of the banana towns.

Women came from rural areas in Honduras, nearby countries like El Salvador, and places as far as Brazil in order to forge a livelihood in the north coast, the booming center of Honduran economy at the time. Leftists, liberals, and conservatives alike, in fact, saw the foreign-owned companies as the culprits behind the booming prostitution industry in and around the banana region. In my oral history gathering, the common narrative of exploitation went something like this: exploited men left their hard-earned money in the brothels, where exploited women worked for meager wages while the foreigners got rich off their labor.

This narrative was plausible and may have been equally pertinent to the north coast of Honduras as to all the banana regions in Central America. But this is only a part of the story.

The north coast, though perceived to be under complete control of the foreign-owned banana companies, was the site of a dynamic creation of worker agency. It was a region where power, positioning, and relationships were highly contested among workers, both men and women—particularly those who worked as local merchants, street vendors, cooks, domestic workers, owners of *estancos* (small makeshift bars), and prostitutes, among others. Prostitution, which became an important industry in the north-coast company towns of La Lima, El Progreso, Puerto Cortés, La Ceiba, and Olanchito, was a significant factor in the lives and livelihoods of the banana workers of the time; this was acknowledged by both workers and the company. The system of prostitution matched the culture of the north coast; like the banana work itself, there was significant company and state control attempting to regulate this aspect of workers' lives.[83]

Prostitution was regulated by the Venereal Prophylaxis Regulation of 1920, which sought to control not only brothels but also clandestine sex workers.[84] During the Carías Andino dictatorship, in 1938, the Department of Venereal Prophylaxis was formed as part of an effort to combat disease and eradicate prostitution from the public parks in the urban areas.[85] Sex workers had to enroll in a national registry, including a picture and listing their nationality. Sex work went from the public sphere, in public parks, to brothels at the outskirts of city and into working-class areas of the city.[86] This attempt at persecution and controlling public morality has been called a "secular puritanism" by Honduras scholars.[87] There was a double standard, though: upscale night clubs also emerged during this time, such as the Copacabana Night Club in San Pedro Sula, inspired by the banana companies in the mid-1930s.[88] In 1950, the government of Juan Manuel Gálvez enacted the Public Hygiene and Public Sanitation Regulations, through which the government sought to prevent prostitution by learning more about the lives of the sex workers. This new regulation and the Venereal Prophylaxis Regulation of 1920 were used to regulate sex work. In addition, the 1950 reform also created a Sanitary Police Department within the police department.[89] A study conducted of 50 *meretrices* revealed that many women were between the ages of 15 and 20 years old and were exposed to sexual relations as early as 9 years old, and the majority of sex workers were Honduran and doing this work for economic survival.[90]

No such document exists for the north coast, where sex worker demographics might have been more diverse.

Women and men in the north coast, however, operated outside these controls. In judicial records from La Ceiba, Atlántida, in 1929, a period of great affluence for the banana companies,[91] and in oral testimonies of women who worked in brothels, I unmask the complex life and work of *meretrices* (women who worked in the booming prostitution industry of the banana regions) in the first half of the twentieth century. During this period, male banana workers had a few options to purchase sex: they could visit the brothels; brothel owners would visit them in the banana fields, where they would set up makeshift tents from banana leaves; or they could pay for sex with a *clandestina*, or clandestine prostitute. Beyond uncovering the existence and operations of prostitution, I examine the triangle of power and control that was created between the state's Sanitation Department (*Departamento de Sanidad*), the brothel owners in the local towns, and the companies—both the Tela Railroad Company in the northwestern towns and the Standard Fruit Company in the northeastern towns. These three interests sought to regulate prostitution and the practice of sex work outside of any morality or honorability norms. At the same time, women workers challenged the control over their bodies, and many exercised clandestine prostitution outside of the triangle of power that sought to contain their labor neatly in brothels or brothel excursions into the banana plantations. Documents for the year 1929, for example, reveal how the practice of "clandestine prostitution," as opposed to state-regulated prostitution, was exercised by women as a means to resolve their economic hardships. Their activity defied the efforts to contain their work in brothels and allowed for a degree of self-determination in choosing when and how they worked.

My intention is not to say that "clandestine prostitution," the term by which it was known, was a better option for women. There is reason to believe that women suffered under this system. Documents suggest that there was exploitative trafficking of women, where men brought women from their hometowns and pushed them into prostitution in the north coast. This was the case for Victoria Ayala Yanes, a woman from Nacaome, Valle (in southern Honduras), who arrived in La Ceiba with a man, Francisco Anariva. She worked as a prostitute clandestinely until she was captured and put in a brothel.[92] Esther de Young, a migrant from Brazil, also suffered the same fate in La Ceiba; both partnered women were forced into the work of prostitution "clandestinely."[93] According to

Article 20 of theVenereal Prophylaxis Regulation (Reglamento de Pro-filaxis Venéreas) from the Department of Sanitation, a woman was said to be a *clandestina* when she could not prove her good health through a certificate that stated she was free of venereal diseases, specifically syph-ilis and gonorrhea. A woman who proved or certified her good health with the department would be allowed to register herself as a *meretriz*, or prostitute, in the Libro de Meretrices (Book of Prostitutes), the city's Sanitation Department log.[94] If a woman was perceived to be soliciting work on the streets and was found not to be registered, she was im-mediately arrested and taken to the Hospital de Venéreas (Hospital of Venereal Women). If she was free of disease, she was sent to the nearest brothel. If she was ill, she was kept in the Hospital de Venéreas until she healed, after which she was sent to a brothel in the city. The only way out for a woman in this position was either to run away from the hospi-tal or brothel to another town, or to have someone in her family, usually a parent, demand her return to the family.

This transfer of custody and the historical judicial records related to this process provide an indication of the conflicted positioning of women. In legal documents supporting women's return to the fami-ly, arguments were made as to the truth or falsity of charges that the women were prostitutes. On the one hand, families made arguments about the women's married status, family relationships, demure char-acteristics, and other qualities to provide evidence that women were not *meretrices*. On the other hand, arguments suggested that unaccom-panied, unmarried women were more likely to be *meretrices*. This was a common practice by police and health officials in other Latin Ameri-can countries, as Donna Guy's study of Buenos Aires in the late 1800s reveals.[95] There, the state was interested in having prostitutes registered and preferred that they worked in brothels. Guy explains that the po-lice and Sanitation Department generated a "witch-hunt" for women who may have behaved unacceptably.[96] Between the 1920s and 1940s, the banana towns were cosmopolitan places with a robust immigrant population and social networks ordered according to a racialized hi-erarchy. Women sex workers were categorized based on their racial attributes as European, *pardas* (a Spanish caste-system term meaning "racially mixed"), or mestizos by brothel owners and the consumers themselves.[97] As Guy's study finds in Buenos Aires, "Any woman sus-pected of prostitution was accused of operating an illegal bordello,"[98] and the police and local authorities closed down any establishment that was not registered. Similarly, though in a very different geographical and cultural context, in Honduras *clandestinas* were hunted down and forced to conform to a system in which their bodies would be under state control.[99]

In Esther de Young's defense, her attorney claimed that there was a lot of corruption in the Sanitation Department and that workers in that department would "frequently attempt to court honorable women, and when they [didn't] accept their advances, they [would] report them as prostitutes."[100] The commonplace nature of this indiscriminate persecution and classification of women is also evident in this statement: "Married, single, and even young women whose honesty was never doubted have been recorded as prostitutes [in the Libro de Meretrices] and forced to adhere to the rules [i.e., the Sanitation Department's Rule of Venereal Prophylaxis] and forced to enter the mud of the brothel system, all in the name of a false interest in public health."[101] De Young was freed because the Sanitation Department workers had no witnesses to attest to their claims, and the inspector of the Sanitation Department had basically just taken their word for it. She was provisionally written up into the Libro de Meretrices by these men and was therefore taken into custody when she was perceived to be violating the law. De Young won her case in the court, which prevented her deportation, because of the absence of witnesses that could claim she was a *meretriz*.[102] In fact, few witnesses ever came forward in cases like this with the Sanitation Department.

In Victoria Ayala Yanes's case, her honor was more in question. She had come to La Ceiba with a presumed partner, Francisco Anariva, who then left her. She was picked up for clandestine prostitution and was then released to her father, Eduardo Yanes.[103] Victoria Ayala Yanes then partnered with another man, and upon separating from him, she was once again picked up and accused of clandestine prostitution; upon physical examination, she was determined to have gonorrhea and was forced into confinement in the Hospital de Venéreas. When she recovered, Yanes was taken to a nearby brothel, from which she then escaped. She was probably held in the brothel against her will and forced to remain in peonage to the brothel owner, a common narrative for which there are rarely archival sources. She was turned in to the authorities of the town of El Porvenir, where she was hiding, and then once again forcibly taken to the Hospital de Venéreas to be treated for "ulcers in her uterus." Her father's appeal, attempting once again to gain her release, was denied. Her venereal disease was accepted as adequate proof by the Sanitation Department and the judge who, gave the delegate of the Sanitation Department permission to confine Yanes for treatment in the hospital. This was an accepted policy used to contain the spread of venereal diseases.[104]

From these two examples it is clear that there was an effort to move women who were perceived to be *clandestinas*, regardless of whether they were in fact prostitutes at all, into the brothel system. The Sanitation Department was accused of getting kickbacks from particular brothels if they brought in women. The relationship between the state and the brothel owners was important to the company, in this case the Standard Fruit Company. The state sought to control the women in part to ensure company operations ran smoothly. The company regularly paid workers at the end of the week, every ten days, or at the end of the month. Workers often migrated to the north-coast towns alone without their wives or partners. These same workers often visited the nearby town of La Ceiba, arriving in company trains from the nearby banana fincas and campos for fun, diversion, and liquor. In these visits workers visited brothels, bars, and *estancos* (small makeshift bars), and it was beneficial for the company that these workers made it back to work on time on Monday. Local police commanders policed workers' leisure time, sometimes even holding men in cells until they sobered up for work.[105] Policing their sexual behavior was also part of ensuring the workforce would be available and ready for work the next day or on a Monday. If a worker was sick with gonorrhea or syphilis, the company suffered the loss of that worker until he was well enough to work. The company and the Sanitation Department colluded to insure workers would make it to work while also creating a system of debt peonage for women as sex workers.

RACE AND THE GEOGRAPHY OF THE BROTHEL

The banana companies settled in La Lima, a village of the larger city of San Pedro Sula. Oral testimonies of women and men who worked and lived in La Lima, Cortés, during the 1940s and 1950s reveal a complex narrative around sex work, selling sex, and the men who purchased it. Workers explain that La Lima was a banana town divided in two, La Lima Nueva (New La Lima) and La Lima Vieja (Old La Lima). La Lima Vieja, the original hamlet, is where the sex industry thrived; near the Tela Railroad Company banana plantations there was an area that agricultural banana workers visited on Sundays to shop, drink, dance, and purchase sex.[106] It is here where medical and sanitation laws were deployed against women, violating their bodies and rights to work. In

La Lima Vieja the evidence of a triangle of power between the company, the Sanitation Department, and the brothel owners is clear. What is not so clear, however, is how women ended up working in brothels or as *clandestinas*—but here the choice was to survive or die of hunger.[107]

Rosaura Garcia or Rosa La Negra—who also was nicknamed, against her will, *chorro de humo* (which is how I found her in La Lima)—first worked as washerwoman, then as a *trabajadora* (live-in maid), and later as a *cantinera/cajera* (bartender/cashier). As *cantinera*, she was responsible for watching and making sure that the men on the cantina floor would invite the company of women and that they purchased drinks from the bar. When the man and the chosen woman were ready to have sex, Garcia would be their *cajera*, handling all money transactions through the purchase of *fichas* (plastic coins). She would also keep track of the amount owed to the woman after services were rendered. Rosaura Garcia prides herself on being trustworthy to both women and men. The women would go to the back of the cantina to the brothel rooms knowing they would be paid correctly, and the workers would leave their wallet with Rosaura to protect their money from the women; the men feared that after sex, in their weakest moment, the women would steal money from their wallets or pants.[108]

Race in the brothels of La Lima Vieja—situated out of sight of North American eyes in the American Zone in Lima Nueva—was determinative in setting the price of the woman. While Black women were perceived to be accessible, the light-skinned women from the interior were deemed desirable. Rosaura, a dark-skinned woman who identified as india and was known for chain-smoking cigarettes (perhaps the source of the nickname *chorro de humo*) and for being a good dancer, lived and worked alongside *mujeres de negocio* (sex workers) and managed the business of sex transactions for them.[109] Her duties often included accompanying women on the bar dance floor, ensuring that men paid them for their work and were served enough drinks, and accompanying women to get checked by the local health clinic every Wednesday. The brothel owner would pay her 45 lempiras a month and a few kickbacks, though she never clarified, despite my inquiry, if she herself also participated in "the business." These women, *las rojas, las amarillas, las azules* (the red ones, the yellow ones, the blue ones), all had a different price and were color-coded according to the colors of the plastic coins or *fichas*.[110] But in reality the plastic coins may have represented skin color and a racial hierarchy that prioritized lighter-skinned women.[111] Rosaura kept a tally of the money they made from making the men buy drinks and a tally of the money for going to the back, to do "their business." The money earned from drinks was not the women's money to keep. They only earned when a man agreed to go back with them, and Rosaura would charge minimum of 5 lempiras each time—but not overnight; that was extra.

The taller women and lighter-skinned women from the western part of the Honduras were kept at a higher price by the brothel owners, and they were worth more to the workers paying for her. The brothel and the cantina were connected—a worker would enter, be entertained by a *cantinera*, like Rosaura. There was a *cantinera* in each brothel, and they tended to be either *trigueñas* (caramel brown),[112] like Rosaura, or Black. Rosaura recalls other *cantineras/cajeras* who were also referred to as Black or *trigueña* for example, *La Negra Heroína:* "Nos decían negras porque eramos trigueñas" (they called us Black because we were caramel-brown color). Rosaura noted that light-skinned women were preferred but that Black women also worked in and out of the brothel, like Nora La Negrona, who would come to the brothel to dance: "Pero si llegaba a bailar Nora La Negrona, pero es que le gustaba bailar" (But if Nora La Negrona came to dance, it is because she liked to dance).[113] Nora La Negrona, confirms Rosaura, was Black; what I infer from Rosaura's memory of conversations about her friend Nora is that she may have worked clandestinely but befriended Rosaura in order to gain permission to come and dance in the cantina, a place where she could certainly secure work.[114] While oral history does allow for the rescue of some of this story, the reality is that many women who engaged in sex work are now dead, many living and dying in impoverished conditions, and some without family and with no state retirement support; they just vanished in time and from history. One woman who was "rescued" from the brothel by a worker who married her to make her "a decent woman" did not want to speak on the record. These stories demonstrate that women workers not only existed at the margins of the banana enclave informally; they were central to the economy and life of all campeños, and in their own lives transgressed not only company control but Honduran morality codes of the period.

WOMEN'S LIVES AND DECENCY

Similar to records for the clandestine sex workers of La Ceiba of 1929, in the 1940s and 1950s women had to demonstrate that they did not have diseases in order to work in the brothels of La Lima Vieja. They themselves paid the 5 lempiras for the exam that would clear them for work. Rosa La Negra would take these women and be their confidant; she would often hear their stories, be their friend.

Many women who made 5 lempiras per session with a man were often indebted to the brothel owner for up to 3,000, 4,000, and sometimes even 5,000 lempiras, depending on how much of her daily wages she applied to her debt. The debt was incurred for the purchase of food and basic life necessities, as well as lipstick, dresses, shoes, or treats, or hiring Rosaura to clean their room and launder their clothes and bedding (if they did not want to do it themselves). The women essentially paid for room and board to work there, paid for clothes, and paid to eat. Rosaura remembers that she was very good with the women, and that is why they did not challenge her: "Yo era buena con ellas por eso nunca me hacían un daño." The harm (*daño*) she refers to is running away from the brothel—this would be charged to Rosaura, including the runaway's debt.

Here I have provided a snapshot of an industry within an industry, a group of unacknowledged workers within a well-known, nationally acknowledged class of workers, militant workers. Prostitutes were dealing with the triangulation of power and control of the worker-company-state. This framework allows us to see the ways in which the company and the state cooperated to control the labor force.

The banana enclave was itself a complex place to live and work, a myriad of power relationships and everyday forms of resistance, enmeshed in codes of manhood and race, that allowed workers to survive and even thrive in the face of extreme cruelty on the job. Women's lives were just as complex as men's lives; they worked just as hard, but the enduring masculinity narrative for the region had completely erased them. The codes of manhood and the hypermasculinity of the north-coast agricultural worker that allowed for the strike organizing to succeed also relied on the suppression of women actors.

CHAPTER 5

"MUJERES QUE CUIDABAN HOMBRES Y VENDEDORAS AMBULANTES"

GENDERED ROLES AND INFORMAL WORK ON THE NORTH COAST

Olimpia Edelmira Figueroa told me about her work as a patrona in the banana camps while she was making lunch for her grandchildren, who were about to get home from school in Colonia Sitraterco in La Lima, Cortés. She cooked the emblematic fast-food meal of the region, fried green bananas, fried chicken, flour and corn tortillas, and fried potatoes. Her story was no different from that of many other young women who came to banana zones and camps early in their lives. She worked as an ayudanta—a kitchen helper—and would eventually have her own kitchen, marry, and have children who would all work for the same company.

My recorder hung around her neck by a string and the tiny microphone was clipped to the neckline of her homemade *delantal* (apron) as she moved seamlessly between the sink and the stove. A pot of blazing hot oil crackled, frying noises littered the recording, and her laughter and stories provided the background for an exploration into the lives of women cooks and food vendors who, like Doña Olimpia, staked a place for themselves to work and earn a living in the banana campos. Doña Olimpia, a campeña, brought the patrona to life, and her story is an unavoidable and important piece of history.[1] Her oral testimony illuminated otherwise obfuscated social actors: women who were subject to complex rules on domesticity, women who engaged in gender mixing in the campos, and women who broke some rules while conforming to others. She spoke of the subjugation of women as well as their ample freedom to partner and repartner, to re-create their lives, to forge new ones, and even to break gender norms in both subtle and overt ways. The north coast gave women an opportunity to form new working-class identities and redraft existing notions of women into values that could be applicable to working women's lives.

This is the story of women workers' experiences in the campos bananeros—in particular, their role in the informal economy of food vending and preparation. Women cooks, known as patronas, and their makeshift eating establishments, comedores, were critical to the construction of a collective worker identity, which allowed for successful organizing for the 1954 strike, yet their role has been completely elided in the archival record.[2] By focusing on their lives and work in the informal economy surrounding the banana industry, I demonstrate the process by which these women influenced and constructed a working-class campeña "working woman"[3] identity in the north coast—long before women entered the company as formal workers in the packinghouses in 1962—and how gender ultimately influenced the working class and the work itself.[4] I claim that the patronas existed within a campo hierarchy created by the company for the purposes of efficient and unhindered banana production, but maintained and shaped by all those who lived and participated in it, including workers, vendors, company supervisors, and local government police.

Neither the company nor the Honduran government had a plan to feed the over 25,000 workers who migrated to work in the north coast during the first half of the twentieth century. There was no populist project by the Honduran state to embrace this working population, as was the case in some South American countries at the time; in fact, in this era, the state was not equipped to provide food and sustenance for its workers. While the company did have commissaries stocked with provisions and work tools, it did not provide eating establishments or hot food for agricultural workers in the banana groves. Women workers and their makeshift eating establishments stepped in to fill that gap, creating a space where working-class men could eat and drink in places they felt comfortable and at home.

After the long and grueling labor of harvesting bananas, agricultural workers retreated to the patronas' comedores every day and engaged with the community of workers, cementing camaraderie and ultimately building a unique a working-class identity that differed from the rest of the country. Campeños and campeñas in the region had few mixed-gender oases for social interaction or for resting after a hard day's work in the campos, which were often located far away from the local towns by foot, and the trains did not run at night. The comedor became akin to the *parque central* (central park) in the campo—the place where people came to mingle, eat, socialize with one another, drink some aguardiente, and perhaps even play a game of *naipe* (cards) outside the comedor. Oftentimes a cuadrilla (ditch-digging team) would eat together, maybe even with the contractor, making it a place of reflection on the day's work. Patronas, along with their comensales, contributed to the creation of a sense of community, a campeño culture of resistance and radical organizing.

The patronas made a space for themselves, both physically and socially, in the campos and, in doing so, became critical lynchpins between the company and worker. Gendered relationships among workers in the campos, then, were crucial to organizing and an integral part of the formation of working-class consciousness that not only made labor resistance possible but was also key to its radicalization. These gendered relationships, I argue, were formed through shared visions around work, life in the campos, and solidarity with workers in the fields, as well as through leisure time and nonstandard family arrangements. The makeup of the campos and the social infrastructure that the patronas helped nurture through the comedor easily served the purposes of organizing and became instrumental in sustaining the strike. Paul Drinot notes that in the 1930s, Peru's *restaurantes populares* were welcomed solutions to "material and moral needs," and places where identities were constructed and reaffirmed.[5] While the patronas' makeshift comedores were not sanctioned or supported by the state, they existed within the neatly demarcated finca and campo system in which working-class values were respected, valued, and reproduced, allowing for the construction of a working-class campeño identity.[6]

It is important to view these women as workers, albeit informal ones, and not just as secondary strike support. The patronas transgressed normative gender roles of the time; they existed in the public sphere and were remunerated for their labor. Patronas had agency in the campos and wielded this power in the gender hierarchy; they were not regulated by the company, or by the state, and they existed in the public sphere with men, unlike the middle-class suffragists of the time.[7] The comedores positioned women in the camps as wage earners and made them indispensable to banana-industry productivity on a daily basis. During the strike, they would be essential to sustaining the labor movement. Without the patronas and the infrastructural support that they provided, the strike likely would have collapsed. Women's participation in the 1954 strike and, more generally, in the north-coast economy and labor organizing is critical to understanding the entire trajectory of labor history in Honduras in the second half of the twentieth century. The story of working women, though informal, in the banana campos provides a dense history of women's participation in the labor movement. Today, subsequent generations of women are now in union leadership positions and leading popular movements.

THE INFORMAL ECONOMY AND WOMEN'S WORK ON THE NORTH COAST

Women migrants to the north coast faced various challenges in finding work and resources in the campos bananeros. Like the men, women migrated to the north coast for a variety of reasons and from a variety of backgrounds. They came from nearby areas—villages and hamlets in and around the banana plantations—looking for work, or they came with family members, usually their mothers or grandmothers. Many arrived following the male migration trajectory from outlying departments such as Olancho, Valle, and Copán; some came alone, others with their husbands or partners. Later, in the 1950s, many more women began to come alone to work. Doña Olimpia Figueroa recalls her first experiences finding work:

> I was very young when I came. We lived here in La Lima, but I went to work far away [pointing toward the fincas] where we would find work. That is where I started to work with those men; how to tell you how hard those men worked . . . I saw how the union was formed in 1954; I was a 20-year-old woman.[8]

Her first job, as a domestic worker, was in the house of the captain of a finca; he was responsible for building canals in new banana plantations.

> They needed a maid and so I went with them . . . I washed their clothes and they would give me my room and board. I had to share with the cook; two of us shared a room. They only paid me 1.25 lempiras a month.[9]

The company provided families of trusted employees funds to hire a washerwoman, like herself, and a cook, like her roommate. For women, then, earning a living in this booming banana economy was even more difficult. Their exclusion was deemed natural because of their sex, as most women could not handle the excruciating, extreme physical labor of cutting and carrying the more than 100-pound stems from the banana tree to the mule-driven carts and then onto the rail cars.[10] Labor and gender historians of mining and textile industries in Latin America have found that this gender classification of workers and its justification conveniently aligned with the cultural and social constructions of women's place in Honduras and the prevalent attitudes among the US company bosses.[11] Women were simply not strong enough, at least within the conceptual framework of "enduring masculinity,"[12] where common understandings about men and masculinity served to mask not only the roles of women in the camps (and in the industry more broadly) but also the historical constructions of gender and sexuality.[13] The notion that banana harvesting was not women's work did not mean women did not work in and around the banana industry.[14] This trope, that women were not strong enough, or simply were not there because of their sex, was repeated time and time again in interviews with male workers and others in the region. In light of the limitations they faced, women had no choice but to create viable work alternatives, utilizing their home-making skills to make ends meet.[15] Women, then, tended to work in the informal economy in and around the campos and nearby towns.

"*Mujeres que cuidaban hombres*"[16]—patronas, *vendedoras ambulantes* (street vendors), and *vendedoras con puestos* (vendors with stands)—were women who made a living selling food in and around the campos bananeros to earn a living. These women cooked for the single or unaccompanied male workers, and ayudantas and cuques (cook's helper)[17] supported the patronas in their kitchens. Other women worked as street vendors in and around the finca and living quarters and in public spaces where men congregated. Some women (and sometimes men) had *puestos*, designated spaces in the campos to sell foods and goods. Many individuals performed one or several of these work activities at different times. Other vendors came into the campos bananeros from nearby towns such as La Lima, El Progreso, and Olanchito on paydays to sell foodstuffs and goods. In this chapter, I focus on women cooks and food vendors who lived and worked within the campos bananeros as a special group of entrepreneurs who operated in between the company store, the commissary, and the local Honduran merchants of nearby towns, creating their own niche for work. All these forms of informal labor created intricate relationships among workers and helped balance the needs of life, work, and banana production in the campos.

Patronas often held informal oral contracts to cook for their comensales—single men or men who were not accompanied by a female relative (a mother, wife, sister)—and were paid a weekly, biweekly, monthly, or even a daily fee. The agreement ranged from 16 to 30 lempiras a month, or 1 lempira a day.[18] Often patronas did not get paid immediately, as many men relied on a system of credit (*de fiado*) to eat. But in general, the pay was good, and it often meant that patronas made more money than men did. If they did not make ends meet, then they might seek additional income by stocking and selling aguardiente and special foods on paydays, or by sending their kids out into the campos to sell food.[19]

In the best-case scenario, patronas whose partners worked in the company were assured some income. Husbands provided the necessities: a home, the very basics for the household, and access to their company benefits with the commissary and with the milk and meat train. While this mirrors a family-based labor organization system, the company only supported partnered workers by granting them a *cuarto* in the barracón system. Women found themselves partnering with men sometimes out of necessity for a place to live and work, or to benefit from the company.[20] Yet the benefits were limited, and patronas, women vendors, and others had to figure out how to make ends meet—often by doing extra labor outside of the comedor, such as cooking specialties their kids could sell in the streets, washing clothes for workers, and selling illegal homemade alcohol. The women had to earn enough to pay for their children's clothing and other needs: "We had to sell to sustain our children and their schooling," explains Casta Figueroa.[21] In a more common scenario, patronas only relied on their partners for housing; they could then use the kitchen to set up their comedores.

Mujeres que cuidaban hombres and *vendedoras ambulantes* worked as a family unit in the informal economy within the formal work structure of the banana-export economy.[22] Patronas held status as heads of the family enterprise and managed the kitchen and labor roles within it. A well-functioning kitchen was crucial to the operation of a patrona's comedor. The comedor was usually located in the back or side of her barracón, next to an open-air kitchen, where she cooked and served the meals to the men. The patrona, for the most part, determined the menu each day; it was basic and repeated weekly, though depending on the availability of resources, she would sometimes serve special meals. She managed the cooking and controlled the flavoring with her own *sazón* (seasoning/flavor), which made her food identifiable to the workers. Both the patronas and the ayudantas were known among workers for their cooking, prices, and service. Patronas cooked the meals and supervised the workers, whom they hired for tasks such as grinding corn for tortillas, toasting and grinding coffee beans, and serving during meal times.[23]

The work hours were long, and preparing meals was labor inten-
sive.[24] Patronas and ayudantas report getting up as early as 2 a.m. and as
late as 4 a.m., seven days a week, in order to make tortillas and prepare
food to serve all day. Olimpia Figueroa would spend hours preparing
for breakfast in the morning:

> Imagine that one had to grind [corn]; nowadays who will grind corn
> up to 12 times and then grind again to make tortillas for lunch? I had
> to toast coffee beans; I would toast six pounds of coffee beans every
> week; six pounds I had to toast in that fire. Then I had to grind them
> in a grinder. What do you think? . . . That was work; that is how we
> worked.[25]

The patrona typically served 5 to 30 men daily, but occasionally more,
sometimes with little help. Finca workers were dependent on patronas
for their daily sustenance. This arrangement virtually locked patronas
and ayudantas, their helpers, in the kitchens so they could provide continuous service, and it often required that patronas themselves obtain
goods on credit to sustain their services.[26]

All patronas went through a phase of working as ayudantas to a
patrona. Ayudantas were young, often single women, usually mestizas,
some of whom were related to the patrona while others were just
young women searching for work. Often the patronas hired daughters,
nieces, or distant relatives sent from other towns as ayudantas, and usually provided housing and food for them in exchange for assisting the
patrona with the cooking and serving duties. María Ángela Cardona
worked as an ayudanta before she married, and in this job she had a lot
of responsibility:

> I worked in the kitchens of the contractors *cuidando* [feeding] 15–20
> [men]; if it was ten men, it was 10 lempiras [I earned.] I cooked [prac-
> tically] all the food. The one who helped me was the son of a *morenito*
> [Black man]; [he helped] to grind coffee, to grind corn in the corn
> mill, to bring wood, and to go and deliver the lunches when there were
> lunches to be sent [to the fincas]. The young helper, we called him
> cuque [helper], and I was the maid of the [patrona's] kitchen.

If ayudantas were family, they were paid in-kind and given things such
as fabric for dresses or items they needed. The dire survival circumstances influenced how women themselves enforced gender norms

upon their daughters in and out of work. María Antonia Perla's grandmother brought her to the campos in 1953 at the age of 13 to work as an ayudanta.[27] Her grandmother and her aunt ran a comedor for 80 men in Finca Guaruma Dos.[28] She recalls that despite getting up at 2 a.m. every morning and doing everything that was asked of her, her grandmother never paid her and often physically abused her:

> She never paid me. Instead, she gave me three beatings, the first time because money was missing, and since I was the new one in the house, it [the blame] fell on me. . . . Then a clock fell and broke and she said that I did it, another beating. The last time because I told her that a man was visiting her daughter's room during the night.[29]

Perla's relationship with her grandmother became even more abusive as the days went on. When Perla was savagely raped at the age of 13 by a 35-year-old worker, her grandmother did not come to her aid.[30] Perla attempted to defend herself and told her grandmother and mother; in fact, the rape was so violent she ended up at the Tela Railroad hospital.[31] In response, Perla's grandmother, a stern businesswoman, told the worker, "Either you marry her or go to jail."[32] Perla attempted to run away from her attacker, but family pressure forced her to partner with him because she had become pregnant.[33] Perla thought that the cold shoulder she received from all the adult women in her family had to do with the benefits the comedor would receive from the partnership with the rapist: "I figured that my grandmother sold me for twenty coins, for a room in the fields."[34] Perla's case underscores the importance of company benefits, which in some cases became a commodity, allowing for the abuse of young women, an enduring sexism often imposed on younger women by older women.[35] Access to the commissary, the meat and milk delivery train, housing, and the company hospital were important benefits in high demand for patronas and their comedores, and not an uncommon exchange.

Even when helpers were not family members, patronas still wielded considerable power over their ayudantas in managing labor roles in the kitchen. Some young women unrelated to the patronas, mostly mestizas and Black women, came to the banana fields looking for work and welcomed these opportunities in the comedores.[36] As a young woman, Ricarda Fernández Sabillón was brought to the campos by a woman from her hometown in the department of Santa Barbara who helped her find work. "I worked in the fields, in the kitchen as a helper," she remembered, taking a long pause as she looked over at her husband.[37] Once on the north coast, she had to learn to make flour tortillas, but she said, with a certain pride and confidence, "The rest of the food I already knew how to make."[38] Fernández Sabillón was not related to the patrona she worked for, but her boss still abused her: "She would get mad. If I broke a plate she would charge me for it. I felt that she was not good because she charged me for things."[39] Fernández Sabillón was paid meager wages but was given food and a place to live. As soon as she could, she found herself a partner, moved into a family room with him in the barracón, and worked in her own kitchen.[40]

The ayudanta position, despite its disadvantages for those who did not earn full wages and who were often victims of abuse, provided an opportunity for women in the campos. It was a stepping-stone to becoming a patrona.[41] Women's skills were not recognized formally, and while women workers had few opportunities to become apprentices or assistants in banana harvesting, they could become apprentices in a patrona's kitchen. There the ayudanta could acquire the skills and experience needed to become a patrona herself—the basics of cooking for campeños; how much to charge people based on food consumption; where to buy produce, meat, and dry goods; how to operate the kitchen and deal with clients; and how to reinvest comedor earnings, hire help, and utilize the household for support. Thus while patronas were not considered formal employees and therefore not "skilled," in fact their work required a lot of skill, organization, and sharpness.

The power dynamics in the patrona's kitchen were clear. They worked around the workers' various schedules, which meant they worked longer hours in order to provide services to both day shifts and night shifts. In order to meet this service demand, the patronas firmly exercised their power over the ayudantas and cuques while also laboring in the kitchen the whole time and during meals. The workforce understood the value in their ability to provide good, hot food in a timely manner, as well as a space for winding down after work.

The positions in a comedor were hierarchically structured according to race and gender rules, and sometimes impacted by their position in the hierarchy of the north coast more generally. For example, cuques[42] were usually young Black men who were hired to do heavy lifting, grinding, and carrying, but they are most commonly associated with the grinding tasks in kitchens that had over 20 comensales, as María Ángela explains: "The cuque was a young boy, that is what they called him, he was responsible for grinding the corn for cornmeal, the coffee for the table, and [to gather] the banana leaves to wrap the food that was going to the fincas."[43] Gerardo Pery Laredo worked as a cuque when he could not find formal work in the fincas. He performed intense physical labor, typically from early in the morning to the evening, in order to grind enough *masa* (corn meal) for tortillas and coffee for all meal times.[44] Mestizo comensales saw the cuques' work in the patrona's kitchen as effeminate and considered them lazy, despite the grueling work they did in the kitchens. In the masculinized social structure of banana workers, the cuques were feminized and found it hard to obtain formal work in the company; this may also have had to do with the fact that they were young and Black. While racism and gender biases were clearly marked, the company also accentuated this division by promoting what Klubock calls "enduring masculinity," which in Honduras can also be called the "enduring mestizo masculinity" of banana-harvesting work, a commonly accepted understanding of what it meant to be a man and a worker in the banana regions.[45] Gender and race intersected in ways that were subtle but clearly placed people within a hierarchy that served the company's own imposed rules.

Gender, class, and ethnoracial understandings cohabited on the north coast. These factors, as well as company policies and practices, determined the work women were able to perform within the companies' territories. For instance, domestic workers needed to have recommendations to work in the American Zones. If a woman worker had just arrived, she would likely not know anyone who could recommend her. At the same time, her gender determined her role, wages, and overall understanding of herself as a member of the working class. While Olimpia Figueroa remembers that the trusted employees were given funding by the Tela Railroad Company to have cooks and washerwomen: "Tela would give them [money] so that they would pay us, and they would pay what they [deemed appropriate]."[46] Few Hondurans could claim whiteness in a multiracial and multiethnic north coast. Most workers referred to themselves as indios to mean native to Honduras, not Indigenous, white, or Black. The ethnoracial demarcations also informed the roles of patronas and street vendors, who also called themselves india to mean that they were native to Honduras.

In Costa Arriba (Standard Fruit Company areas), male workers, female food vendors, and patronas were indios, of Jamaican descent (*ingleses*), or ethnically Garifuna (from nearby coastal towns and hamlets right outside of the banana-company areas).[47] Lucilla Goodlitt, a vendor and baker who sold bread and provisions to workers in Coyoles

Central, never lost her identity as a Jamaican and retained English as her native language despite living in Honduras since childhood. Women workers lived and intermingled with one another, particularly in the campos, during work and while traveling into town. They interacted closely with people from the same regions and often of diverse ethnicities. Still, racial and ethnic lines were subtly sustained in living arrangements, even when work arrangements could not be controlled. María Ángela Cardona shared living areas with Garifuna workers in Campo Agua Buena but eventually settled in the mostly mestizo town of El Carríl after getting married. Lucilla Goodlitt, whose father was one of the initial settlers of El Carríl, remembers that her father was the only Jamaican bread maker, and they were the only Black family, for a long time in the area:

> We were the only ones that lived there on the land of Don Sarapio Reyes, who asked my father where he was coming from [when he met him], to which my father said, "I come from Trujillo to sell bread here." He asked my father why he did not live in the campos, and my dad said he did not know anyone there. He then told him, "Come here and I will give you somewhere to live." In exchange for taking care of his cattle and other animals and there, he could have a little house. We were the only ones [the only family], and eventually . . . other Jamaican bread makers, called *ingleses*, arrived and rented a piece of land next to us, from the same man, and then another family came and settled right next to them. They would send them all to that landowner who would rent to all Jamaicans.[48]

Goodlitt thus explains how her father created a niche for life and work in El Carríl alongside mestizos.[49]

In Costa Abajo, the workforce was more indio or mestizo, which led María Antonia Perla to say that "there were no Black people in the campos before" (meaning when she first arrived).[50] Black workers tended to live in either the port towns of Tela or Puerto Cortés. The accessibility of these towns from local villages, along with company policies, may have made them more attractive to Black Garifuna workers, as they could settle and work there and still easily return to their villages.[51] Patronas' historical memory of this, however, is filtered through some of their own experiences, and race and ethnoracial understandings were delicate subjects. The distinctions in experiences among women were apparent in interviews among the diverse group I interviewed, who represented the gamut of multiracial people of the north-coast society. But rarely were these interviewees forthright about racial differences and racism unless they were ethnically Garífuna or of Jamaican descent.

Perhaps in the food patronas cooked we can uncover some of the complicated terrain of mestizo and Black influences in the campos and gain a greater appreciation of the diversity of the north-coast culture and the ethnoracial assimilation in the campos. The patronas' kitchens illustrate how the workers' diet reflected the racial and ethnic diversity of the campos, a fusion of different ingredients from different ethnic groups from which the patronas derived culinary knowledge. The company provided the bulk of the food, mainly imported goods, that workers consumed. Ingredients such as oatmeal (osmíl), white flour (harina), beef, and pork, imported in abundance, shaped the north-coast cuisine, where fried foods and meals-to-go were perfected.[52] Patronas also shopped at the local almacenes (local stores not affiliated with the company) for local goods, such as corn. Their lunch and dinner menus drew on traditional staple recipes of Honduras or El Salvador (among other places), personalized with each patrona's own sazón (seasoning). Compared to the rest of the working people in the country, it seemed that banana workers had a better diet, simply because of their access to company beef, dairy, and pork from the cattle and hog farms in Puerto Arturo, Atlántida.[53] Patronas took the company's ingredients and incorporated them over time, attempting to adapt staples to incorporate new ingredients (i.e., the flour tortilla) and new influences from the Garífuna and Black cultures of the region. For example, mondongo soup (cow belly/tripe) is made with coconut milk, a staple ingredient of Garífuna cuisine. Classic Garífuna methods of fish preparations, fried or cooked in soup, were also incorporated into the patronas' kitchens. Traditional soups, such as beef and chicken soup common in the interior and mestizo areas, evolved on the north coast with the addition of such ingredients as cassava, green banana, plantain, sweet potato, and yuca, a staple of Garífuna communities and relatively easy to grow with moderate upkeep.[54]

Cooks prioritized fast, dry foods that could weather the temperature. Baleadas, large flour tortillas folded over beans, eggs, and cheese, accompanied by a cup of oatmeal usually made up the first meal of the day. While corn tortillas and coffee were also available, baleadas were the daily and expected breakfast.[55] Street vendors, wives of workers, or people from local towns would also sell sweet bread, salty coconut bread, nacatamales (tamales), and even fresh fish to workers on

ptioned "Oficinistas de la Tela RR 1954," this depicts office workers peeling
en bananas to feed strikers in a communal kitchen. (María Antonia Valle de Ven-
s, El Progreso, Yoro, 1954)

ptioned "Viva La Huelga, 5 de Mayo de 1954," this was likely taken at the Campo
ula Vista strike center in La Lima, Cortés. (María Antonia Valle de Venegas, El
greso, Yoro, 1954)

Captioned "Finalizó la huelga de 1954," this features Manuel de Jesús Valencia (midstride, in white shirt and baggy pants), a charismatic teacher in the company schools, Liberal Party member, and anti-communist, who garnered support from striking workers after PDRH members were jailed. (María Antonia Valle de Venegas, El Progreso, Yoro)

The Tela Railroad Company headquarters in Tela, Atlántida, from 1914 to 1977, before the company headquarters were moved to La Lima, Cortés, and prior to their renovation by the mayor's office. The headquarters were moved to be closer to the banana fincas. (author photo, 2006)

Julio C. Rivera, a PDRH member who was persecuted, jailed, and eventually exiled to San José, Costa Rica, in 2008. (author photo, 2008)

Lidia Aurora Lezama, a patrona whom I interviewed during a bus ride home to the campos following a retired banana workers' meeting in El Progreso. (author photo, 2006)

María Ángela Cardona, a patrona, in her outdoor kitchen in El Carríl, Olanchito, Yoro. (author photo, 2006)

retired banana finca workers' committee meeting, La Lima, Cortés. (author photo, 06)

trike of '54/The Struggle Continues/Power to the Workers," a message on the main eet leading to La Lima, Cortés, circa May 1, 2006. (author photo, 2006)

Candida Garay, a patrona, discussing her life in the campos after a retired banana workers' committee meeting in La Lima, Cortés. (author photo, 2006)

campeño poses while working at Finca Palo Verde, a Dole Fruit plantation and
merly owned by the Standard Fruit Company, Coyoles Central, Olanchito, Yoro.
thor photo, 2006)

Casta Figueroa Portillo, right, pictured with her mother and grandmother, who were also patronas and who migrated from southern Honduras to work in the banana region, El Carríl, Olanchito, Yoro. (author photo, 2006)

Francisco Amerto Lagos describes his life in the campos and his work in the chemical department of the Tela Railroad Company, La Lima, Cortés. (author photo, 2006)

Daniel Madrid Guevara speaking to retired banana finca workers in a meeting, La Lima, Cortés. (author photo 2006)

A typical cortero team with pack mules, junteros (wearing shoulder pads to protect the fruit), and muleros, Finca Guaruma, December 1946. (United Fruit Company Photograph Collection, Baker Library, Harvard Business School)

#4126-Banana cutting crew & pack mule-Gua Farm (Wimmer's trip)
HONDURAS   December

A *venenero* team member fumigating on a plantation, Tela, 1955. (United Fruit Company Photograph Collection, Baker Library, Harvard Business School)

)atrona at work in her kitchen in Finca Santa Rosa, December 1946. (United
it Company Photograph Collection, Baker Library, Harvard Business School,
46)

A typical barracón (worker housing). (United Fruit Company Photograph Collection, Baker Library, Harvard Business School)

#4131-Banana Pack Mule(Guaruma Farm)Winner's trip
HONDURAS   December 1946

Muleros specialized in driving sometimes uncooperative mule packs to work every day, Finca Guaruma, December 1946. (United Fruit Company Photograph Collection, Baker Library, Harvard Business School, 1946) paydays. Garifuna women sold fresh fish and coconut bread in and around Tela and also near Coyoles Central.[56] Sweet bread, a common tradition in Honduras, was usually made from corn or rice flour, but the sweet breads sold to workers for the afternoon coffee or during time off—for instance, *caballito* (literally, "little horse")—were made with white flour.[57]

Fast food to go, which the north-coast banana camps became known for, was sold by street vendors who merged the traditional staple corn with local north-coast ingredients, such as *pollo con tajadas* (fried chicken with fried green bananas or plantains), served with tortillas and green banana chips, and rice and beans known as *casamiento* or coconut "rice-and-beans." Small meals known as burras, meals packed to go, such as fried pork or chicken with green banana chips and tortillas, combined campesino cuisine and north-coast ingredients. Traditional fare, such as *nacatamales* (tamales) and sweet bread, a staple adopted from the indo-Hispanic culture, were served as special treats on paydays. The food sold reveals the diversity of both those who were making the food and the community in which they worked and lived. What can be gathered from vendors' and patronas' stories is that these racialized and gendered hierarchies persisted throughout everyday life in the campos, and in the other informal work women did.

It is important to note that street vendors (*vendedoras ambulantes*) and other food purveyors, while crucial to the informal economy of food provision for the north-coast labor force, held precarious social positions of less esteem than the patronas. Street vendors would specialize in one or just a few items—such as coconut bread, sweet bread, *nacatamales*, or a portion of a meal (known as a burra)—that then sold for as little as 25 centavos of a lempira in Coyoles Central.[58] Street vendors were small entrepreneurs who had some degree of independence and lived and supported their families on their own. Like patronas, they worked every day—including Sundays and holidays—and sold food at negotiated prices. But street vendors earned considerably less than patronas. Although these vendors had more control over what, when, and where they sold, their mobility made them a less routine part of the workers' sustenance. Vendors sold food and goods much cheaper than meals prepared in a comedor, but they required immediate payment at the point of sale—they did not extend credit to customers. Vendors existed at the margins of the patronas' establishments, their racial and gender makeup was diverse; for example, on paydays, Black vendors sold bread and single mothers sold food outside brothels.

Life for street vendors and their families was more precarious; every child of walking age sold the food, bread, *nacatamales*, and burras in the streets and outside the brothels. As Casta Figueroa remembers it:

> I used to sell *chicharra* [fried pork skin] with cassava when it cost 10 centavos. From one large piece of *chicharra* I would make four pieces. I would then go out to sell all night. I would get together with my sister and my friends Victoria Zelaya and Olimpia. I would come to sell to the bars, and since there were many cantinas . . . I would come to sell where the drunks were, because the drunks would buy.[59]

María Ángela Cardona also sold food near the brothels and saloons in the *champerías* (mud huts) that the Standard Fruit Company workers lived in, around what is now El Carríl.[60] Both Cardona and Casta Figueroa, along with other women, sold food all night to make ends meet. The relationships they remember were not with the workers and soldiers who visited the brothels, but with the other women workers, the prostitutes, who were nice to them and bought from them. Women shared stories of charitable and generous exchanges between the women working in the brothels and those selling food outside.[61] There were always a few problems with the company soldiers, or cabos de comisariato, who tried to take advantage of her son:

> There were company soldiers who were there for [maintaining] public order. If anybody bothered anybody else they would go to jail, and tomorrow they would have to pay bail. One day I sent my son to sell fried green plantains (*tajadas*) with fried pork (*chicharra*), and then I noticed [the soldiers took] many portions—each portion cost 10 centavos—and they did not want to pay. When the kid would go charge them, they would give him centavos, those blond coins we had before. So, I went [to the station] and the soldiers were arriving, and right away they paid the kid, who was very small then.[62]

While the soldiers did not want to pay the kid, they did pay immediately when she showed up—perhaps they were also dependent on the food vendors and women cooks, and it was important to maintain good relations with the vendors. Street vendors did not make enough selling food and had to engage in other work activities to make ends meet—"side businesses," as Cardona calls them—such as raising chickens and selling lottery tickets: "But I sold things; I had chickens; I had pigs; I had a donkeys, horses, ducks, Guinea hens. Back then one was young. Now as an old woman I don't [raise animals]. I sold lottery [*la chica*] using funds from my other vending ventures; I paid for my [lottery to sell]."[63]

Patronas, on the other hand, had fixed locations and provided credit, which made the comedores attractive to workers. When paid at the end of the month, patronas were able to invest their earnings by purchasing food in bulk for their comedores as well as providing for their household.

WORKING ON A MIDDLE PLANE OF POWER

Workers, both women and men, living and working in the fincas, existed within a myriad of power relations; workers depended on the banana-production organization but were also constrained by company policies, including supervisory staff—the capitanes de finca and cabos de comisariato—who implemented their interpretation of company policies, and a state apparatus that sometimes aided the company.[64]

Patronas undoubtedly held a position of power and commanded respect among workers in the north-coast fincas. Because their work was of an entrepreneurial nature (as was that of other vendors), they had a high degree of autonomy. They had freedom to create their own menus and meal schedules and managed their own kitchens. They negotiated relationships with clients and wielded more bargaining power than the workers did; ultimately, the patrona chose which comensales would receive her services and rejected others at her sole prerogative.[65] Typically, men would come to the patrona's kitchen and ask to be allowed to come and eat there: "'Patrona will you feed me? How much will you charge a month?'"[66] The patrona would then explain that if they wanted full portions it would cost full price (about 30–40 lempiras a month); if they wanted the meals to be less expensive (about 15 lempiras a month), arrangements could be made to serve smaller portions and less meat.[67] Edmundo Cabrera Williams's wife earned 30 lempiras a week working as a patrona for bachelors.[68] The workers' needs, wages, and work position determined the quality and quantity of food. For instance, *poiseros* (pesticide sprayers)[69] would leave the earliest in the morning and return earlier in the day than other workers because this was a grueling, entry-level position. *Poiseros* earned less than some of the other men did, and they generally paid a bit less for their meals. The agreement at the comedor was verbal and flexible, so either the worker or the patrona could terminate the agreement.

For the most part, the workers respected the patronas in the campos and saw them as an integral part of the fincas. One subtle indicator of this respect lies in the word "patrona," the name by which the workers consistently referred to the women who provided for them. Although clearly linked to the word patrón (boss), patrona seems to say less about the woman's connection to the boss than about her position as a respected steward of the worker's sustenance and survival. When patronas talked about themselves, they referred to themselves as women who took care of people or took care of men (*mujeres que cuidaban gente/hombres*). But the finca workers always referred to her as patrona. This indicated both the workers' respect for her position and an acknowledgment of her power over their lives, labor, and housing quarters. Workers understood her power in her kitchen and her importance in supporting their success in laboring in the fincas. The use of the term patrona distanced her from the prescribed gender role of taking care of or serving men's needs.

The patronas' position was not, however, uncontested within the fincas. In fact, patronas occupied a unique place: at the intersection of privilege, power, access, and subordination. I suggest the term "middle plane" to describe the position and relationships patronas held; they were fluid and negotiated, at times contradictory, and by turns supportive and oppositional to company and workers' interests. Patronas inhabited a space that straddled the world of the worker and the company, the positions of supervisor and worker, the status of business owner and laborer, boss and worker, and traditional and unconventional gender roles. They also experienced complicated relationships and social positioning that were marked simultaneously by freedom from and dependence on both workers and the company, power and vulnerability to the changes in the labor market, and, notably, personal closeness and solidarity with workers along with businesslike constraints imposed by the company hierarchy. Patronas inhabited this dynamic, sometimes contradictory middle plane of power, which was actually crucial to the smooth functioning of work on the banana finca. They achieved this middle plane by negotiating power relationships in their daily contact with workers, their own positionality as informal workers in the campos, and their own self-identity as workers based on the work they did, day in day out.

Patronas held this unique position in the finca in part because of their closeness to the workers. They linked the work in the fincas to the activities of the living quarters. Doing business in public, male spaces gave the patronas and female street vendors privileged knowledge of the laborers' lives, their long hours, and their working conditions. Olimpia Figueroa has dedicated her entire life to cooking and selling food, starting as an ayudanta for a patrona who had many comensales who were *poiseros*, who very often became ill in the course of their work spraying pesticides.[70] Cooking for the men each day allowed Figueroa to understand the nature of the work and its effects on them:

> Let me tell you, I used to get up at three in the morning to make flour tortillas. They would take two tortillas, and they would have their oatmeal and a cup of coffee. That's it. Then they'd leave with their tortilla, and I tell you, many of them got sick because they didn't have protection from the pesticide. Their lungs would get sick. The danger for them was when they sprayed [the pesticide]; that is what harmed them, because when they sprayed [the mixture] upward, the [pesticide] would fall back on them.[71]

Patronas' livelihoods were dependent on their engagement with the banana workers on a regular basis. Daily business interactions with the patrona were perhaps the most contact an unaccompanied worker had with a woman in the campos. Food was sustenance and survival, but it also guaranteed human connection in desolate work areas where one's life and world were determined by the production schedule of getting bananas from the fincas to the ports. At the same time, the patrona's work brought them into contact with the workers' lives and complaints, and their sympathies arose from this contact. The patronas saw firsthand the harshness of work in the finca, the conditions of workers after they got off work, and the challenges they faced in the mornings. The patronas' labor as cooks was crucial to workers getting to work on time and persisting through long hours. Patronas understood workers' need for money and shorter hours. They also shared workers' living conditions. Even when they were not working, finca workers engaged frequently with patronas, as many sold liquor to workers at lower prices than the company commissary. For the most part, the relationships between workers and patronas were amicable and respectful, even mutually supportive (as was the case during the strike). This was unlike the relationship between workers and bosses.[72]

Workers saw patronas as providers, allies, and witnesses to their lives, but at times, the relationships were more complex, as in the case of María Ángela Cardona, an ayudanta, street-food vendor, and self-taught seamstress who worked as a patrona for a contratista early in her life.

She came into this position through her mother, who had been a washerwoman and food vendor throughout María Ángela's childhood and early adulthood. She recounts an incident that reveals different power dynamics at play in patronas' spheres. María Ángela Cardona was unfairly treated by a worker, and her boss stepped in and sided with her, not the worker:

> One day a worker fought with me. He told me, "Angelita, send me hot coffee to the finca." But we didn't have enough coffee to give to all [the workers] at the same time, and he got mad. He insulted me, and I was not even 22 at the time. . . . "Tell the boss," he demanded. The boss asked, "What's going on here?" Another worker told him, "This guy's fighting with the cook." The boss said, "To hell with that worker." Because at that time you couldn't find a cook. Finding a cook was hard—a cook was more valuable than a man because there were plenty of workers, and cooks were not easy to find.[73]

This incident highlights at once a patrona's power over a worker, her dependent relationship on a company supervisor, and her perceived subordinate role as a laborer providing value for the company. Cardona's position was situated in between the worker, the client, and the owner of the kitchen, the supervisor. Her unique set of skills and the overwhelming need for them in the campos made her an important worker in the comedor. Cardona still fell under the paternalism of the supervisor, who exerted his authority and wanted to make sure his workforce was ready and available. Supervisors had a clear and active interest in making sure the comedores ran smoothly.

Patronas, for the most part, enjoyed freedom from company supervision. They determined for themselves the terms of their work lives and independently negotiated relationships with and among the men, workers, mandadores, capitanes, and cabos de comisariato. Yet for all the freedom afforded them in their work relationships, they lived with a fundamental dependence on the banana company's organization of the finca work, on the workers themselves, the paying comensales, and ultimately the company's pay. As with nearly everything else in the north coast, the patronas were economically tied to the bananeras—as were other women workers, ayudantas, young women family members, cuques, and other food vendors who were subordinates of the patronas.

The financial dependence of the patronas—and their power over workers in negotiations about the patronas' services—can also be viewed as an extension of the hegemonic rule of the company over the workers and their lives on the north coast. This extension of the company's power was even more pronounced in the common situation where patronas were married to supervisors, usually capitanes de finca, mandadores, or jefes/capitanes (lower-ranking bosses).[74] They were not the wives of the higher-ranking bosses, the North American employees, or elite Hondurans known as empleados de confianza (trusted company employees), who were supervisory figures.[75] The banana workers who labored under these supervisors often felt coerced into contracting services with the wives of their supervisors. Thus the money they earned went right back to the boss via the comedor operated by his wife. Most of the women interviewed for this project were not married to supervisors, but they identified this as a common circumstance. Though they acknowledged the contradiction of this role, the overriding narrative about the patronas is their critical function in providing for workers' needs—not their compromised position as supervisors' wives.[76] The patronas' position in the middle plane perhaps unwittingly included a role as a proxy for company power.

The work performed by patronas and street-food vendors was entrepreneurial. Their earnings were, in some cases better, than those of their husbands'. Being a patrona offered more financial security than being married to a banana worker, working in a campesino economy, or working in the company towns of La Lima, El Progreso, or La Ceiba. The patronas may have inadvertently carved out a space for women workers within the banana-export economy. They created an industry of women's work in and around cooking and purveying food and liquor that supported the needs of the United Fruit Company (UFCo) and Standard Fruit Company. But that system also helped create space and opportunity for other women who sold food from their kitchens or came to sell their wares in the public areas of the living quarters on paydays.[77] Theirs was an important and innovative role as a small but critical entrepreneurial class, which presented new opportunities for women workers in the north-coast economy at the time.

LYNCHPINS, WORKERS, AND TRANSGRESSORS

These women workers were essential to the formal work of the banana industry and influenced processes of working-class formation in the region. Ultimately, the industry of informal women's work in and around cooking and selling food and liquor sustained and subsidized the male finca workers of the bananeras. Their unique position is a critical and

previously unexplored lynchpin in the bananera economy that facilitated the operations of the company, the company bosses and policies, and
the lives and work of the male finca workers.

The role patronas and campeña food vendors played during the
period from 1944 to 1954 must be viewed against a backdrop of the
bananera economy, with a few notable features. First, the banana companies introduced a wage-labor system on the north coast of Honduras,
more similar to that of factories than of the labor systems used in rural
fincas. The banana companies made technological advancements in machinery, some forms of work organization, and botanical technology. In
this scenario, workers' understanding of and participation in labor transformed the previous campesino practices and rural economy rooted in
nineteenth-century notions of work to a twentieth-century capitalist
wage economy.[78] Second, the banana company's organization and policies, coupled with the demands of the agro-export economy, challenged
notions of Honduran worker identity. From an agricultural campesino
economy with independent farm laborers, the dominant worker identity became that of wage laborer in the transnational-owned fincas. The
labor opportunities created by the companies' needs and the common
perception of the banana regions as a place of ample and well-paid employment opportunities caused workers to flock to the north coast. The
system of work created by the companies, including the peculiarities
of labor contracting, in turn created conditions that were conducive to
the formation of an informal economy that sustained and supported
the work of the men who found entry into the company's ranks. This
informal economy, regulated by neither the company nor the state, existed in a middle area of power determined by the needs and workflows
of the company and worker availability.

Campeña vendors and patronas formed the crux of this informal
economy and proliferated into other sectors of the country, including state road-construction projects in 1955 and 1956.[79] Although the
patronas did not have a formally sanctioned role in the projects, and
instead worked alongside them, their role was key to the survival of
workers, and therefore to the projects. The work of preparing meals,
seen as a private household duty for women of the time, became in the
banana industry, and later during road-construction and maintenance
projects, acceptable and permissible to the banana companies and the
state. This informal employment, along with that of washerwomen
and domestic work, existed outside of the purview of debates about

women's proper place or notions of morality to which working women may have been subjected during this period in the towns, cities, and factories of Honduras and other Latin American countries.[80] It was not just earning a profit for providing meals that made patronas and other informal women workers of the banana fields unique, but also their unregulated existence within the company and the fact that they often had the most direct contact with the most productive sector of the banana industry, the finca workers. The patronas created a powerful role for themselves in the industry as an important workforce in the in-between spaces and relationships of the very people who made the industry work.

Despite their importance, patronas clearly identified as and with workers—as a vital part of the banana-zone system and the community in the campos. The conventional view of the division of labor of the time classified women's work as domestic and secondary to men's work, which was considered productive and essential to the banana economy. Yet women's lives and work as informal workers supported and even subsidized workers of the Tela Railroad Company and Standard Fruit Company.

Women clearly viewed their work as integral to men's labor. It was clear to patronas and also to traveling/street vendors that their labor was needed wherever there were male workers in the banana economy and that their labor should be remunerated. Women's testimonies show an understanding of themselves as workers and their work as equally important to that of men. Casta Figueroa saw herself as a worker:

> Yes, [I considered myself a worker]. Back then if you didn't work, you didn't eat, and neither did your kids. I had to work. By day I would sell, and in the afternoon I would come with all that cassava; 19 pounds of cassava was 1 lempira. Then I'd cook the rations and then return to the cantinas [at nights] to sell.[81]

Men, in turn, understood the work of the patronas and *vendedoras* as a service that allowed them to do their jobs in the banana fields.[82]

The process by which the woman worker became a campeña in the north coast is evident both in their multiple transgressions of formal company policies and in their redrafting of the societal norms of the time to fit their reality on the north coast. Patronas' role within the hierarchy of power, the interpersonal relationships they formed, and their own identity as workers were influential to carving out a space for the later development of a working-class feminist politic that their descendants embraced years later—and one that is in stark contrast to the suffragists.[83] Normative women's roles at the time emphasized austerity, modesty, and propriety. The lives and daily survival of the patronas made these notions somewhat obsolete on the north coast. While suffragists organized anti-alcohol leagues in nearby San Pedro Sula, some of the patronas sold aguardiente illegally and at cheaper prices than the company commissary in La Lima.[84] Others also sold burras as street vendors outside of brothels in El Carríl, near Coyoles Central. Middle-class women involved in the suffrage movement organized a "pro-moral cleansing of society" campaign to end alcohol consumption in 1930. This campaign was founded in Tegucigalpa and promptly spread to other parts of the country; it had the support of the president at the time, Vicente Mejía Colindres.

Patronas existed in the public space differently than middle-class and elite women of the time. For many middle-class women, society was structured strictly by moral codes and bounded by spaces of propriety. Patronas' comedores, however, were spaces of constant interaction with men, and they expanded outside of the domestic sphere and into the banana work. The interactions and the different notions of what defined women and men, both cultural and practical understandings, were reorganized and reworked on the north coast to create a campeña understanding of gender relations that included women's participation in public space and building a worker consciousness and a deliberate solidarity. Male survival depended on women's labor in the kitchen and outside of the domestic sphere of marriage, so these typical domestic duties were transformed into remunerable roles. Normative gender roles may have been reified in this process, but women's labor certainly challenged the typical roles of the period. Company policies and male workers shaped the ways in which women did business, and the standards by which women's work would be evaluated during the first half of the twentieth century. In particular, they participated in the moral economy of defining what it meant to be "good"—a good businesswoman, making good food, providing good service—and to exist within this new entrepreneurial class and within the economy of the company.

This privileged position of the patrona/finca laborer subverts and transgresses the prescribed roles for men and women. One clear marker of this was the exchange of money for a service, that of cooking three meals a day (and sometimes serving illicit alcohol). Another marker was that of the workers sharing the public spaces—the streets, comedores, and outside brothels—with these patronas or ambulatory vendors in a form of gender mixing not often seen in the middle classes. While the popular narrative in mestizo towns was that "indio" men were heavy drinkers who, at the drop of a hat, would slice anyone with a machete and or kill anyone with their pistol, for patronas and street vendors, these supposedly violent men were vital for survival. Though patronas recognized the workers' propensity for alcohol consumption and their often violent behavior, they also best understood their work and life-style—understood campeño life—and generally did not fear for their own safety while working. This identification was critical for the strike movement, which required support from everyone living and working in the banana-company labor camps.[85]

The construction of this campeña identity in relation to campeños, the company, and the larger societal and national positioning of women puts them in a very unique position as precursors to multiple formations of feminisms and militancy.[86] I claim that the campeña went through the process of constructing a working-woman consciousness that would endure for most of the twentieth century, one of her very own making that developed with time, work, and experience. While at the time, they did not see themselves as dismantling gender inequity or subverting patriarchal hierarchies overtly, their labor and existence in the context of the enclave did just that, and through their daily labor they challenged and reworked a system that would otherwise have taken complete advantage of them, constructed other forms of morality and honor, and reassembled what it meant to be a woman in the campos. The campeña very much identified with male harvesters as a woman worker herself; indeed, their work ethic and solidarity during the strike stemmed from their role as workers and community members. Though separate from the struggles of the suffragists of the time, they were linked to other workers by the shifts and changes in wage labor that the banana companies and agro-export economies initiated.

The patronas' very existence as a critical part of the banana-export economy operations was a transgression, for they were unrecognized and unacknowledged by the company rules, regulations, and policies. The establishment of the informal food-provision economy, without which the formal banana-export economy would have failed, is a dramatic and revolutionary repositioning of gender and labor roles, and even a restructuring of work and operations. It demonstrated that the banana enclave was porous and that other workers—informal workers—could exist within its larger system of hierarchies. Moreover, patronas transgressed normative gender and women's roles, and perhaps notions of middle-class femininity. By creating remunerable labor for women from what was perceived as a household duty, patronas transgressed expected gender roles—both as a part of the formal economy and in relation to workers—and opened up previously inconceivable opportunities for women on the north coast. The patronas were influential to the construction of the working class and the nation, despite their complete erasure from the national archival record.

The patronas embodied a working-class notion of livelihood that diverged from the nature of the middle-class, suffragist feminist movement that was prominent in Honduran towns at the time. Elite struggles for suffrage did not intimately affect these workers' lives, many of whom may have had limited reading and writing skills and lacked time to engage. Levenson-Estrada's work on working women in Guatemala reminds us that "a critical consciousness about class needs a critical consciousness about gender, and vice versa."[87] Patronas and street vendors were aware of national political debates, including women's suffrage. They describe participation in political party elections and worker issues and support for the political parties of their husbands or family members. But patronas and food vendors were not organized in cooperatives, nor did they share a common political agenda or interact with suffragists of the period. Still, as working women, they fundamentally impacted the work of the banana plantations and the construction of the working class. Patronas' private and public spheres were blurred, and more often than not they participated in political campaigns and movements, despite their inability to vote or belong to the union formally.

The patronas' participation in the strike may be seen as their ultimate transgression of company policies and normative gender roles. Their unique position made patronas key stakeholders in the complex events leading up to the banana strike of 1954, from the organizing to the actual strike itself. Their dependence on the bananeras meant that patronas had a lot to lose when the workers went on strike or when there were work stoppages or company layoffs. Yet more often than not, patronas sided with workers during work stoppages and the strike of 1954, and when workers challenged company rules. Their indirect relationship with the company gave them the freedom and opportunity to challenge the company and support the workers.

PATRONAS JOIN THE STRIKE

Women in the banana fincas also expressed their orientation as workers when they participated later in union solidarity. Patronas saw themselves as part of the striking body of workers during 1954. Casta Figueroa supported the strike because "workers wanted more work and wanted to raise their wages."[88] María Antonia Perla accompanied her partner in strike activities as well, despite not wanting to be with him in the relationship.[89] Daniel Madrid Guevara recalls that his partner at the time, a patrona, also joined the strike and helped to organize the community kitchens: "She gathered all the women together, and the same women elected her as president of the committee in charge of food. She was the one who ordered the food. She received everything and turned it over to the cooks."[90]

Patronas, *vendedoras ambulantes*, and *vendedoras con puestos* sold food and subsidized the strike, which broke out in late April of 1954 in the Tela Railroad Company banana regions.[91] The strike centers had kitchens staffed by women cooks, family members, and volunteers, but patronas from nearby areas and street vendors also sold food outside of the strike center. As women workers who engaged in solidarity with striking banana harvesters, patronas subsidized the strike by providing food, full meals or snacks, and by selling on credit to striking workers or simply by working without wages during the labor strike at the strike center.[92] Workers preferred the option of eating outside of the strike center earlier on in the strike, when they still had money and options. Soon business for women street vendors and patronas near the strike centers increased, and women made profits early in the strike, especially those selling food near Chula Vista. The workers paid until money ran out. As food became scarce in the strike center, the workers ate boiled green bananas with beans on a banana leaf for three meals a day. Patronas asked for compensation when workers still had money during the strike, and they also provided cooked meals on credit (*de fiado*), especially toward the end of the strike when food donations were scarce. Patronas hoped that once the strike was resolved they would be compensated, but many were never repaid after work resumed. The company did not pay workers for the total time out of work, and many decided to try their luck at other fincas, leaving their debts unpaid. Standard Fruit Company workers and women food vendors had different experiences, as that strike only lasted 11 days (compared to 69 at the Tela Railroad Company in Costa Abajo).[93] Street vendors struggled differently; they could not provide credit and their businesses suffered.

The Tela Railroad Company workers congregating at the Campo Chula Vista strike center in La Lima were greatly affected by food shortage near the end of the strike because the initial donations began to run out as the company continued to refuse to negotiate fairly. The losses put women in debt. Adela Sánchez, an ayudanta, would get up at 2 a.m., leave her sons asleep at home alone, and go to Chula Vista with her sister, a patrona, to sell coffee and other food to strikers. "In the beginning there was money; all the workers had money, they would buy. After, they did not have any money left to buy food, and they began to owe for the food. My sister had many who did not pay her; instead, she was indebted to the people who gave her products on credit."[94] Later the workers would ask for credit, because the strike was draining the provisions that strikers obtained during the initial stages.[95] Adela Sánchez's sister fed people on credit. At the end of the strike, the workers only received 40 days as compensation for the 69 days they were on strike. Although there were collective kitchens in the strike centers, like the ones Sylvia Robleda participated in, there were working women like Sánchez's sister who used her comedor to continue making a living during the strike.[96]

Vendors, such as Lucilla Goodlitt, supported strikers by giving away food such as bread and natural juices as the strikers passed by, to and from their duties guarding the fincas against strikebreakers.[97] Goodlitt explains:

> We would make bread, caballitos [cookies in shape of a horse]. I would make boxes. I would take 100 pounds of flour, and I would guide a helper, a man, on how to make the bread in the ovens, since I was still a young woman and my mom was a bit [old]. Then we baked that bread, and when the strikers passed us, I would give the bread to them. . . . I did not bake every day for them; sometimes I would just give them the flour sack or some juice . . . but not every day.[98]

The donation was a sacrifice for a small vendor who had recently lost her business to an accidental fire.[99] These actions were small gestures compared to the larger donations of cattle and grain from the more established local storeowners known as turcos. The sacrifice that working women—including patronas, traveling vendors, wives, and daughters—made during the strike were key to not only filling workers' stomachs but also lifting their spirits.

Patronas were also trusted allies and confidants for protesting workers. In the comedores, workers felt they could talk about their problems in the fields or with their bosses. Workers shared information on strike plans in the presence of women.[100] But most importantly they relied on these women to feed and provide for them. Women reported leaving the camps for the center of town to the gathering strike centers of Campo Chula Vista in La Lima for Tela Railroad Company and the yard of Coyoles Central for Standard Fruit Company. Vacating the camps to support the strike meant not earning money, so the patronas and vendors quickly adapted to the new, temporary situation. The women vendors' support (both material and emotional, sometimes at great personal financial cost) for the male workers' strike showed a clear working-class solidarity and a rejection of company control and helped forge relationships that carried over beyond the strike's conclusion.

After the strike was over many women were left with so much debt that their businesses floundered. Food vending resumed, for workers always needed to eat, but the business relationships changed because after the strike, the company built roads into the campos, making them much more accessible to outside traveling vendors. Also, more women made their way into the campos bananeros as wives and workers. In 1962, the company opened packing plants in each campo; there the fruit was packed in boxes for export, a process that would ensure the fruit would not be damaged in transport. The packinghouses at first hired mostly men, but demand would lead them to open the door to women. Soon women found that working in the packinghouses was a good source of formal employment in the company, making them eligible for benefits.[101] The changes in the worker-patrona relationship also had to do with the fact that the workforce itself was changing from a workforce composed of single men to a family-oriented one, in which workers were sustaining households. While the patronas' position on the north coast waned, it did not completely disappear. Many women followed the construction of the roads, providing services to workers alongside construction sites.

ARCHIVAL OMISSIONS, SILENCES, AND FEMINIST RECOVERY

Midcentury US American housewives, patronas, and harvest workers were integrally tied together in a transnational historical relationship through a chain of production and consumption that affected their lives, albeit in different ways.[102] The bananas harvested in Honduras would end up on American dinner and breakfast tables, depicted in countless cheery ads that portrayed the American wife in domestic bliss and suspended in time as the provider of nutrition and well-being for the family. UFCo is best known in the United States for its quirky twenti-eth-century Chiquita banana commercials depicting the banana as an overtly sexualized, curvy, ultrafeminine, presumably Latina woman.[103] Miss Chiquita, as most Americans knew her, is now part of the cultural and political media archive of television, film, and advertising histo-ry. Cookbooks produced by UFCo (and the parent company United Brands) and recipes reproduced in *Unifruitco*, the company magazine, could be found in kitchens throughout the American heartland.[104] The cookbooks and propaganda by United Brands were aimed at making the mainstream American woman comfortable with the consumption and presentation of bananas, turning an otherwise phallic fruit into a nonthreatening household ingredient.[105] The UFCo cookbook recipes became fundamental to the genealogy of American family recipes fea-turing the banana, to be served during birthday parties, holiday week-ends, and major celebrations, but also on the everyday dinner table.

But this narrative of American domestic bliss is "haunted" by the women cooks and their households thousands of miles away, where the harvest held a fast and steady pace. Very little has been written about the food consumed by the agricultural workers who harvested the ba-nanas eaten in the United States, and even less about the women who cooked the food that workers ate on a daily basis. Their absence is best described through Avery Gordon's frame of "haunting":

> If haunting describes how that which appears to be not there is often a seething presence, acting on and often meddling with taken-for-granted realities, the ghost is just the sign, or the empirical evidence if you like, that tells you a haunting is taking place. The ghost is not simply a dead or a missing person, but a social figure, and investigating it can lead to that dense site where history and subjectivity make social life.[106]

Patronas haunt the archival record, as omitted social actors hidden in plain sight, referenced only superficially when talking about their sup-port of the strike. This is not only the case in Honduras; the absence of women workers in the archives is pervasive throughout the Ameri-cas.[107] Patronas' everyday material presence in the public sphere of work in the campos is completely invisible from the archival and historical record.[108] The patronas' presence, and the recovery of it, challenges the very complacency and domesticity of their counterparts, the targets of the UFCo cookbooks, the perceived American housewife.

Patronas held a key role in the work and hierarchy of the campos, one often ignored by historians of the 1954 strike and Honduran history in general. Workers often remark that there were few or no women on the north coast during the first half of the twentieth century; the miraculous appearance of women came with the incorporation of their labor into the formal economy of the banana packinghouses. When talking about women in the campos bananeros, male workers talk about them primarily as cooks and as women workers. Their roles were defined by their work and function within the campos. Women were thought to be performing a domestic role, natural to their gender. This may have led historians to think of their cooking as donated, unpaid domestic labor. The failings of traditional and conventional historical narratives and the workers' historical memory locate these working women in a place that nearly erases them from the narratives.[109] But as the women themselves tell us, the patronas and street vendors not only lived and worked hard alongside men, but their labor was essential to the company and subsidized the strike efforts. Their services were so essential to workers that their relationship was perhaps a more balanced relationship of power. A gendered analysis of power in the context of the patronas and male finca workers reveals that the exchange of wages was the act that gave women independence and autonomy in their household relationships by enabling women to have material resources they could use as they saw fit. This gave them power in the campos in a middle plane where patronas negotiated various relationships among workers and company interests. Despite their dependence on male workers' connection to the company and their pay, household independence and autonomy in their work was important for their self-sufficiency.

Femininity and work, and notions of what it meant to be a woman on the north coast, were closely linked to racial and ethnic understandings of work, gender, and life. These were also shaped by individuals' campesino backgrounds as well as by emerging constructions of community brought on by migration to the north coast and the banana economy. To be a working-class woman in the banana fields represented different values from the notions of womanhood being discussed by elite and middle-class women. The patronas and street vendors, in fact, were constructing their own understandings of race, class, and gender, organizing their lives and work in the campos into their very own campeña identity. They were not necessarily beholden to company policies or to the formal work and notions of manhood around the work. The campeña narrative, then, though not acknowledged to have been as transcendental as the male workers' role as a formal, striking worker, must still be understood as a critical part of north-coast history and the national narrative. Their lives served to radicalize the workers and inform their struggle, just as much as male workers' lives did.

Although recent literature argues that feminism in Honduras evolved as a movement only in the 1990s, and that the left considered it a Western imposition,[110] the reality is that suffragist issues were introduced as early as 1894 and were a hot topic of debate among the wives of politicians and educated women, in the 1920s between anti-imperialists and those organizing around political party interests, and surfacing once again as a middle-class demand in the 1930s.[111] Others have studied working-class feminism as a dynamic movement that emerged with industrialization and state nationalist projects that brought women into the factories as workers.[112] Yet others have not ventured to call working women "working-class feminists," perhaps because it may be anachronistic or because the evidence is simply not there.[113] While in nearby Nicaragua the emergence of a strong feminist movement developed around suffragist struggles and transformed over time into a militant movement,[114] the trajectory of the Honduran women's movement has been rendered latent and fragmented by class struggles.

For instance, for elite women, suffrage was the most important struggle.[115] For working-class women it was their immediate survival that mattered. These women did participate in elections, as Madrid Guevara remembers it, often aiding men in protecting local ballot boxes from tampering during the dictatorship and beyond.[116] Yet the fight for suffrage did not have the same pull for working-class women that it had among urban educated women, primarily teachers.[117] However, some, in particular vendors, did participate in political campaigns and elections despite not being able to vote. Rina Villars notes that women wavered between activism and apathy in their engagement in war efforts and political campaigns in the first half of the twentieth century, and that their participation was clientelist in nature—not truly a reflection of democratic politics.[118] In other words, men in power have always used women actors in their own campaigns and war efforts.[119] The struggle for banana-worker rights did inspire anti-imperialist efforts in the early 1920s under the Sociedad Cultura Femenina (Society of Feminine Culture), a women's organization focused not on suffrage but on issues of class in challenging US power in the region.[120] Sociedad Cultura Femenina did not participate in the suffragist work because "the suffragist demand was for them a petite-bourgeoisie struggle disconnected from the 'proletariat redemption' and therefore of limited importance to women."[121] Patronas' activism in the strike is in line with the earlier history of organizing by women, and though patronas may not have related to the overt political ideals and ideological rhetoric of the early twentieth-century feminists, in practice they exhibited adherence to a common cause: to end the injustice facing workers in the foreign-owned banana industry. For patronas, however, ending injustices against workers meant a direct and material improvement in their wages and lives.

If we look at the development of feminist and anti-patriarchal movements as an ongoing process that relies on feminisms and feminist tendencies, we can see the generational value of there being not just one form of movement but several. Taking inspiration from Chandra Talpade Mohanty's work on rural women, I propose that there is not, nor should there be, a "universality" of gender oppression and the struggles to dismantle those oppressions.[122] Furthermore, we can appreciate why multiple Honduran feminist struggles did not emerge until the 1990s, though they have ties to class struggles from earlier 1920s movements. Yet the patronas' life and work informed labor militancy on the north coast and the working-class feminists of today.

As the stories in this chapter have illustrated, the patronas helped construct and develop working-class women political actors through their role and self-identity as workers laboring alongside men; their wage-earning capacity, with or without a man; their autonomy and independence despite their paradoxical relationship to men; fluidity in their partnerships, sexuality, and motherhood; their ability to manipulate power within relationships that did not benefit them; and, lastly, their construction of a campeña cultural and political identity that continues to evolve and inform generations of younger working women. By examining the experiences of women and the various roles they played in the bananera community and their relationships with finca workers, including during the strike, we can see the textured gender dynamics at play during the construction of a banana working class. Their lives provide new opportunities to consider working women's aspirations, and their positioning vis-à-vis the formal banana-company workforce is just one important component of women's experiences of that place and time. The years of organizing leading up to the strike were arduous and full of sacrifices and secrets, a period in which the patronas' comedores were tactically important places and their relationships to men and one another were ultimately strategically important to the success of the entire strike movement.

CHAPTER 6

¡LA GRAN HUELGA DEL 1954!
LABOR ORGANIZING IN THE BANANA LABOR CAMPS

[The union] entered into play in '54, but organizing started in '49. Three men came . . . [and looked for] five men in each campo. It was organized five by five. I would look for coworkers [to talk about the union], the more centered and conscious ones. . . . I would talk with them. They [worker leaders] gave me that responsibility . . . because we knew eight days before the strike began. Well I would tell workers, "Be ready to stop work, such and such day there will be a stoppage in all the fincas." That is how it was. . . . The plan was already in place. The strike was hard.

LEONARDO BAUTISTA, 2006[1]

In late April and the early days of May 1954, a series of worker actions exposed a collection of complaints and demands against the Tela Railroad Company that evolved into a 69-day strike. Standard Fruit Company workers also went on strike for 11 days, and in solidarity with the banana workers, many other workers throughout the nation went on strike. Merchants and students showed solidarity with workers and donated food and goods. But it was over 25,000 organized workers on strike, many of them leftists, who managed the successful work stoppage. Workers forced the company to negotiate a contract and accept the union, in spite of the company's dirty tricks and manipulation of the state against the workers.

The conventional national narrative of the strike, an indisputably monumental event in Honduran history, portrays a singular event that triggered a rapid and sudden general strike. According to reports from the United Fruit Company (UFCo) and national newspapers, the port workers in Puerto Cortés stopped work following the company's unwillingness to respond to the workers' petition and the demand to rehire a fired worker, a stevedore, whom they perceived to have been unjustly fired.[2] Firing workers for little or no reason at all was a very common practice at the Tela Railroad Company.[3] Furor over this news spread across the fincas and resulted in work stoppages and demonstrations of solidarity from workers in banana fincas owned by the Tela Railroad Company and the competing Standard Fruit Company, as well as various other industries and factories. The news of the work stoppage spread throughout the rest of the north coast and to major cities in Honduras, culminating in the general strike.[4] This conventional narrative only tells part of the story.

This chapter is based on workers' and organizers' testimonies, which reveal how the strike unfolded across multiple tracks of activity. In fact, oral histories reveal that each division of UFCo went on strike at different times and at its own pace. I argue that the strike was neither a spontaneous mass action nor a top-down coordinated action, but it instead reflected a combination of these strategies, coupled with worker-initiated actions on the ground. Workers engaged in different ways and at different paces based on their conditions.[5] Rank-and-file workers' narratives provide evidence of several significant elements of the strike's history. First, workers' organizing efforts in the years prior to the strike laid the foundation for the successful work stoppage in 1954. The strike can thus be located within a complex of workers' various experiences, which included perilous work in the fincas, traditional responses to injustice, such as strikes and work stoppages, and other efforts to address working conditions and organize in the fincas—all of which laid the groundwork for the events of 1954. Second, workers' testimonies identify five geographical points in the region of initial worker activity that led to the general strike; each of these lays claim to having originated the strike. Third, workers' oral histories substantiate an evolution and escalation from localized activity to coordinated regional activity to consolidation and eventually centralization of an industry-wide strike that garnered solidarity across the north coast and the nation. A closer analysis of their stories, then, reveals that the strike was an outcome of organizing processes led contemporaneously by the various worker committees and was the result of continuous worker activity and consciousness building. The strike spread as a series of organized reactions, rooted in a historical practice of developing worker agency and consciousness and organizing in response to lived experiences.

Workers' narratives inform this chapter's analysis of a number of issues and themes: the roles of the worker-organizers despite the perception that outside agitators predominated; the relationships among workers; the dominance of skilled sectors in the leadership of the strike movements, resulting in different experiences among finca workers, mechanics, engineers, and other company sectors; the prioritization of mestizo and male workers in the strike committee; and the different ethnoracial and gendered experiences of workers, including patronas, in the organizing efforts. This chapter also considers the conflict and collaboration between Liberal Party organizers and leftist organizers, the legacy of these inter- and intraparty relations, and the use of surveillance by the companies and the US Embassy, and the tensions that characterized the relations between the political parties and the US Embassy. While it is important to analyze the strike as a manifestation of workers' demands and intentions, it is equally important to recognize the impact and positioning of the strike in the context of Honduran national politics of the period, and against the backdrop of the geopolitical terrain of Central America.[6]

The workers' memories of the strike paint a narrative of worker agency, collaboration, and assertion, marking a moment of change that started on the north coast with the banana workers and reverberated throughout the entire country. Workers' oral histories reveal that the strike movement did not emerge suddenly or spontaneously; it was an outgrowth of previous organizing efforts, some public and some clandestine. The initiation and development of the work stoppages also varied according to the dynamics particular to each of the banana regions and local towns. The strike was also made possible by the historic collaboration among the left-leaning PDRH, the CCO, and the newly consolidated CLO, a worker committee representative of the Communist Party. These parties, particularly the PDRH and the CLO, later clashed with the Liberal Party in a tense power struggle over the direction of the strike. The activities of these organizations helped to create the context in which the strike developed.

Worker committees and craft organizations worked in coordination with the PDRH, the CCO, or the CLO. These groups, along with international labor federations like CTAL—a Marxist-leaning Latin American federation of unions led by famous labor leader Lombardo Toledano of Mexico City—sought to promote syndicalism and labor movements in the country and region. Honduras did not have a labor code or any of the labor laws that other countries in Central America had won in the 1920s and 1930s. Worker committees in San Pedro Sula and Tegucigalpa would receive and disseminate news of strikes and actions undertaken and the concessions won by the labor movements in other countries, such as Guatemala, Costa Rica, and Colombia.[7]

Banana workers were a desirable organizing target in Honduras in the 1940s and 1950s. It was a challenging task, however, because of the Tela Railroad Company's close relationship with the US Embassy and its power to influence national politics. Labor organizers who were aware of workers' conditions repeatedly attempted to gain access to banana workers to address specific workplace issues, while at the same time connecting them to the struggle over larger, universal worker conditions.[8] Many organizers linked to the PDRH on the north coast were either Tela Railroad Company workers or had recently obtained jobs in the various departments and fincas.[9] Others were local teachers and concerned members of the community who contributed by writing news stories in progressive worker papers, such as *Voz Obrera* and *Vanguardia Revolucionaria*. Worker organizers from these groups led efforts in various company departments to demand better salaries.

By the early 1950s, workers had a history of collective action at the department level, where they regularly presented petitions and led small efforts to improve conditions in their immediate areas of work. In their demands, wage increases were key, but they often also sought other concessions, such as the firing of especially cruel supervisors, improvements in the company housing, access to health care for their families, and transportation services. Although there are many narratives that posit a singular location or incident as the beginning of the strike, in reality multiple centers of strike activity emerged simultaneously. Workers identified five major areas of initial organizing activity preceding the strike: La Lima, El Progreso, Tela, Puerto Cortés, and Bataán. The first days of the strike were extensions of worker actions already set in motion in these locations days before the work stoppage.[10]

On May 1, 1954, workers successfully came together to celebrate International Workers' Day in La Lima and El Progreso, where they made demands of the most notorious banana company, the Tela Railroad Company.[11] Organizers, primarily of the CCO and the PDRH, urged banana workers to join them and march during the May 1 International Workers' Day celebration.[12] Ultimately, they also hoped to instill in banana finca workers a desire to improve their conditions in each of their work areas and to participate in a movement for working people in the national arena, promoting their demands for a labor code and the recognition of the right to unionize.[13] They were well aware that their work and the attempt to organize a May Day protest were very risky acts that could lead to severe retaliation; workers could lose their jobs or, more dangerously, face military violence and imprisonment.[14] Previously, on July 6, 1944, President Carías Andino ordered the military to open fire on crowds of unarmed people at a Liberal Party rally. But workers in San Pedro Sula and La Lima, including those who were already part of an organized group, the PDRH or the CCO, embraced this action as an opportunity to build consciousness among finca workers in the Tela Railroad Company and the Standard Fruit Company, and to raise awareness of the need and support for the labor code. They were ready to act.

At the same time, in different regions of the north coast, workers were already organizing in response to objectionable working conditions in their fincas. As workers and organizations in San Pedro Sula, as well as Tegucigalpa, prepared for the May 1 mobilization, Tela Railroad Company workers moved to address their own workplace issues. Organized worker actions that had been evolving since February were hitting their zenith by late April 1954. Perhaps the observance of May Day was an impetus for the escalation of organizing tactics in the fincas in the regions outside of the cities. By May 3, all the divisions of the Tela Railroad Company had stopped work as a way to address frustrations with their working conditions.[15] The departments of or near the company towns congregated first, but the finca workers, many in outlying fincas and desolate areas, were not on strike yet. Starting May 3, "messengers from the strikers [in the company towns] rapidly deployed to all the banana fincas and managed to get the support of thousands of workers,"[16] convening what became two major strike centers in La Lima and El Progreso.

THE LEAD-UP TO THE STRIKE IN LA LIMA
Like other localities, La Lima had a unique and specific experience of mobilization for the strike that was dictated by local circumstances, decisions, leaders, and actors. National or regional party influences or other organizational directives to join a broad movement were only part of the story. Long before May 1954, frustration with wages and dissatisfaction with working conditions had motivated workers in La Lima to organize under the guidance of Cesar Agusto Coto, one of the local

PDRH organizers.[17] Thus a strong, well-organized worker committee and base had already been established in La Lima, and workers followed this local leadership into action in May 1954.

Daniel Madrid Guevara, a member of the worker committee in Finca Tibombo, one of the outlying fincas farthest from La Lima, explains that the leaders in this finca waited explicitly for a message from Cesar Agusto Coto in La Lima to stop work and begin to mobilize at the strike center of Campo Chula Vista in La Lima.[18] They did not look beyond La Lima for leadership or command. While waiting for news from La Lima, some other men wanted to initiate a march into town to join other striking workers. But according to Madrid Guevara, these individuals were agitating on behalf of the company, which wanted striking workers to march prematurely into La Lima, where workers would potentially face *la básica* (the military). Such an encounter would destroy the organizing effort. Workers learned that the military was, in fact, waiting in Campo Dos near La Lima, prepared to stop the effort by force.[19] Fearing worker injuries at the hands of armed soldiers, organizers adhered to strict orders to wait for communication from the leadership in La Lima before beginning their march into town.[20] To thwart the disruptive efforts by pro-company employees to create confusion, and to affirm their connection to the leadership of the worker action, two women volunteered to travel to La Lima to bring news. One of these women must have been Emilia Hernández, known as La Rápida, the fast runner who volunteered to help the workers.[21] They set out across hidden paths, through back roads and villages, avoiding military posts to deliver a concealed note from local finca strike leaders to La Lima strike leaders, explaining the uncertainty back in Finca Tibombo.[22] The strike leaders in La Lima assured workers that they would not march until the troops moved from Campo Dos. Eventually, the workers marched safely to La Lima and along the way convinced workers from the fincas they passed to stop working and march with them into town. Finca Tibombo workers joined in, with their leadership at the head, and ensured work stopped in the outlying fincas, always peacefully, and moved into Campo Chula Vista, the La Lima strike center. Newspaper accounts noted the great number of workers striking and their remarkably peaceful strike movement, presenting an unfamiliar image that stood in contrast with the stereotype of the north coast as a land of fierce *manchados* (a derogatory name meaning "stained ones") wedded to alcohol and crude conduct.

A great number of workers had arrived in La Lima by May 3. Once workers congregated in Campo Chula Vista, workers organized work committees, donation committees, and *vigilancia* (security) committees. The patronas, along with men and women ayudantas, cooked for the immense number of workers there, while other men and women secured donations from local merchants and landowners in La Lima and San Pedro Sula, obtaining meat or produce for the community kitchens.[23] Men and women were integrated in the security committees that patrolled the fincas to make sure that no one was working there. If a worker was found in the finca or in the barracones, he was forced to come to the strike center in La Lima. There were two reasons for clearing the fincas of workers. First, workers intended to demonstrate unity in a *brazos caídos* (literally, fallen/idle arms) strike until demands were met. They also wanted to prevent the company from blaming workers for potential violence and destruction of company property. The strike committees wanted to make sure that the only damage the company suffered was the loss from the maturing fruit ripening on the stems.[24] Workers monitored the La Lima strike center diligently to prevent violence among workers.[25] The level of organization and thorough delegation of responsibilities indicate the discipline of an organized movement, a process that had taken the PDRH and the CLO many years to develop and implement.

EARLY DAYS OF THE STRIKE IN EL PROGRESO
El Progreso became one of the other strike centers on the north coast, and workers also tell of organizing efforts there that predated the strike. In El Progreso, Agapito Robleda Castro worked in the Construction Department of the Tela Railroad Company, which built and repaired the barracones and other company buildings and installations.[26] Robleda Castro was sympathetic to the PDRH, which touted its commitment to moving workers from complacency and fear to collective action, a principle derived from its identity as a workers' organization and from study of other political worker organizations.[27] The biggest complaints historically in this department were the construction workers' low salaries and the company's refusal to pay for workers' train rides back home for weekends.[28] Between February and May 1954, workers increased their pressure on the company to address these frustrations.[29] In response to the construction workers' complaints, the company proposed a contract system as a way to deal with their concerns and

improve their salaries.[30] The proposed solution was not satisfactory for the department leaders, but workers remained hopeful that the contract system would work for them.

Workers primarily wanted a wage increase in some form. Robleda Castro explained, "There was some confusion on this point. Many workers, hopeful that they would receive wage increases, looked at the banana company's proposal sympathetically."[31] After much debate, workers agreed to the contract system in the Construction Department, but worker leaders, many of whom were active with the PDRH, convened workers again and managed to change the vote to challenge the contract system. According to Robleda Castro, the second vote was different because workers received an explanation about the drawbacks of the contract system in the Standard Fruit Company and its failure to benefit workers there.[32] Once they made the decision to reject the contract system, a commission of workers, including Robleda Castro, was chosen to communicate the final vote to the supervisor, Alfredo Blecken, nicknamed "el Sonto." Blecken told them to accept the contract system or they would be fired.[33] Robleda Castro and other representatives made their way to the other work centers, where 139 workers labored in cuadrillas in the Fincas Pajuíl, Perdíz, Pato, and Loro (fincas known in the region as Los Pájaros) to solicit a collective decision on the matter.

On April 27, 1954, Robleda Castro and other representatives of the Construction Department, alongside the laborers in the finca, came together for a meeting to discuss their concerns in the workplace and the prospect of losing their jobs. Feeling extremely indignant about the supervisor's attitude, they unanimously voted to strike. Workers from the fincas in and around El Progreso then took over a passenger train with the support of railroad conductors and rail workers, who later joined the nascent strike movement, spreading the word to workers in all the fincas and train terminals about the strike as they passed them on the tracks. Upon arrival in El Progreso, they communicated the decision taken by workers in the fincas of Los Pájaros to the El Progreso Construction and Engineering departments.[34] In total, 2,000 workers joined the strike vote, bringing strength in numbers and debilitating the company's crucial production departments, the finca agricultural workers, and the train operators.[35] Workers marched to the American Zone in El Progreso in an official work stoppage on May 1. They congregated there, believing that President Gálvez would arrive to conduct the negotiations himself. As Jesús Gómez recounts:

There were only gringos [North Americans] there; we did not let them leave . . . anywhere. Then they complained, and the military came. They were going to shoot at us. . . . We went to the [American Zone] because they told us that Doctor Gálvez, who was President at the time, was going to come, but no, it was the military that was coming to harass us. They pushed us away from there to the park [Ramón Rosa] at gunpoint. That is where we hung our hammocks between the trees.[36]

Workers remember the scene with the military at the American Zone vividly and with some bitterness, because they meant no harm to North Americans and were peacefully gathered.[37] The North Americans and other empleados de confianza (trusted company employees) were paralyzed, afraid to leave their company housing. Their work was also disrupted, since beyond the fincas, service workers, yarderos, washerwomen, maids, and other service employees in the American Zone of La Lima had also joined the strike alongside the El Progreso workers. The situation in El Progreso escalated faster than in other towns and fincas.

In the initial days, when the multitude of men saw others on strike, it gave them a great deal of confidence to continue, despite physical threats by the Honduran troops that President Gálvez had deployed to repress them. As Jesús Gómez explained, military strongmen pushed them out to Parque Ramón Rosa in El Progreso. Gómez, who at the time worked in the pesticide storage warehouse for the Tela Railroad Company, said he was aware that workers were meeting in small committees to talk about conditions in the company, but he did not get involved immediately. His first engagement with the strike came when the workers marched to the American Zone in El Progreso.[38] There he was assigned to the security committee to make sure that workers were not returning to work in the fincas, looting, or engaging in disorder.[39]

The Construction Department workers agreed to present their demands in a petition to the company on May 3, after which they would go on strike. Between May 1 and 3, the PDRH and the CCO communicated the Construction Department workers' plans to other previously organized committees and asked for solidarity. The May 3 timeline set by the construction workers of El Progreso fueled and challenged other workers to do the same, some in solidarity and others because they had been involved in organizing efforts since the mid-1940s. As in La Lima, the activities in El Progreso evince a level of organization and structure that challenges the notion of a sudden or spontaneous strike. By May 3 and May 4, all five Tela divisions (Puerto Cortés, La Lima, El Progreso, Tela, and Bataán) were on strike.[40]

BEGINNINGS IN PUERTO CORTÉS

Juan Bautista Canales worked the night shift for two years in the tractor shop in La Lima and later became a strike leader in Puerto Cortés. While working in La Lima, he had a run-in with his supervisor, who targeted him for unjust termination. Workers during that period (before the 1954 strike and without a labor union contract) had no recourse against bad supervisors except going to the company's Labor Relations Office, where a representative would take down the details of the case. But the next day the worker would be fired. "Why go to the company in this situation?" Canales asked hypothetically.[41] But just as Canales was about to be let go, another supervisor came to his aid and transferred him to the Mechanical Department in Puerto Cortés. There, Canales found workers who encouraged his rebellious attitude but challenged him to develop a political consciousness. "They told me, look Canales, you need to understand what has happened to you. Unjust firing/transfer happens everywhere in the company; there are supervisors like this everywhere . . . it happens everywhere. We need to organize; we need to be conscious of our attitude as a working class."[42] After studying with the PDRH worker committee in Puerto Cortés, Canales was ready to combat "so many crooks stealing from workers in a desperate situation." In the years leading up to the strike, Canales became involved with this group of mostly men to produce the newspaper *Vanguardia Revolucionaria*, led by Ventura Ramos Alvarado.[43] In defiance of company supervisors, he distributed and read the newspaper *Vanguardia Revolucionaria* (of the PDRH) and later *Voz Obrera* (of the CCO) to workers. He and his coworkers in the Mechanical Department were an important part of the 1954 work stoppage in Puerto Cortés.

Events that led to the strike in Puerto Cortés had been brewing among the dockworkers and stevedores responsible for loading the ships at the port. Stevedores had been forced to work during the peak season on the Monday of Easter Week (*Lunes Santo*). They demanded to be paid time-and-a-half, but the company refused.[44] Rafael Garcia, a leader among the stevedores, suggested that if the company did not pay them, the workers should stop working. Garcia was not politically trained; he arose as a leader in response to workplace issues of excessive workload and inadequate compensation for grueling labor. He was fired after meeting with the company supervisor about workers' demands.[45]

Because this action, in Garcia's case, took place in a different department, Canales and his department were not immediately aware of the developments. But when they got to the Mechanical Department workshop for work the next day, "there was a human sea of people, there at the wharf, which was paralyzed because they had stopped work, and there was a ship waiting [for fruit to be loaded]."[46] The mechanics in Canales's shop tried to work, but the stevedores began throwing rocks at anyone still working, forcing them to come out and support the strike.

At this point, workers who had more political training began to support the stevedores' efforts, calling for the reinstatement of individual workers and for longer-term demands beyond wage increases, promoting labor protections for all workers. The information "spread like wildfire to San Pedro Sula, and the comrades began to move." According to Canales, various political organizations came to Puerto Cortés to aid the striking stevedores and Mechanical Department, and "the PDRH sent a comrade, Cardona Casaña, immediately."[47] It was then that the leadership of the broader work stoppage came together under political organizers and workers like Canales.[48] The PDRH and CCO worker committees had been working with the workers' study groups, like the one Canales joined in Puerto Cortés. These workers' committees' connections to the machine shops were influential in building solidarity with the stevedores and port workers' demands. The developments in Puerto Cortés were a convergence of worker-led actions to address intolerable conditions, with bases of politicized and organized workers built from past intentional organizing efforts.

THE BEGINNING OF THE STRIKE IN TELA

As in the other locales, in Tela we see evidence of organizing that predates the May 1954 strike. The town of Tela, once the site of UFCo's headquarters, also had a history of organizing activity prior to the strike. Many locals and teachers habitually circulated ideas and news from other labor and revolutionary movements. In Tela, the PDRH had organized worker committees, youth groups such as Alianza de la Juventud Democrática Hondureña (Alliance of Honduran Democratic Youth),[49] and the organization where Teresina Rossi, a key strike leader, began her involvement.[50] Members of these groups worked tirelessly to spread information and organize in the nearby fincas and various departments of the company in Tela Nueva. Worker organizations, including the CCO and the PDRH, intended to do the long-term work of consciousness building and developing workers' committees in each finca. In 1954, they also hoped to incite workers to participate in the May Day activities.[51]

News of organizing in the late days of April in El Progreso and in the Campos Los Pájaros (located between El Progreso and Tela) spread to other company towns, divisions, departments, and finca workers. These struggles over workplace issues in El Progreso and Puerto Cortés had already begun to escalate into serious work disruptions that were well-timed and powerful enough to stop the ships from sailing with bananas for export. The work stoppages and workers' actions to address their concerns enabled a timely convergence of the worker committees' two objectives: committee building and May Day rally participation.

Worker committees in Tela received word of the Construction Department workers' planned strike in El Progreso. The news stimulated support for the strike from office, hospital, and hotel staff, as well as nearby departments such as the Materials and Supplies (M&S) Department. While workers in Tela attempted to join the strike on May 3, they were not able to do so because local Liberal Party leaders, who were also workers, initially opposed joining the strike. Liberal Party leaders feared blame for the mobilization, which would hurt their candidate in the upcoming presidential election.[52] Teresina Rossi Matamoros explains that in Tela, workers confronted a conflict between the Liberal Party activists and those, like her, who worked with organizations with Marxist leanings and had divergent strategies.[53] Reluctant Liberal Party activists did not want to strike, and many of them held other workers back from joining the strike for at least a day. The Liberal Party had not been an organic part of the organizing process or the coordination of worker committees in the various fincas. Conflicting messages confused workers who were not sure what to do. Rossi Matamoros, a bilingual secretary in the M&S Department, and other organizers confronted this issue and worked tirelessly to urge them to go on strike and to give workers in Tela courage to respond to the organizing efforts:

> Our mission was to travel to all the barracones announcing the strike for May 1st; this was in the last days of April. We knew about the strike, but many workers did not know. Of course, we had our study groups in which our work every day was to build consciousness where we worked. [The finca workers] also had someone; they had Secundino Laínez, a very old man, older than me. He would go to the banana camps. He was a political communist; he was in charge of indoctrinating people in those times. There were those kinds of people [political com-

munists] working [organizing], I tell you about Secundino because he was the one who was closer to Tela, but they also had their people in El Progreso, La Lima. . . . He was a great leader, an honorable honest man, solid, a good communist, an honest man in the rank and file. . . . That was the dawn of the strike. I used to work in the M&S Department.[54]

Rossi Matamoros remembers that workers feared walking out but did it anyway, facing the military in Tela. Tela workers eventually went on strike on May 4, joining the effort in El Progreso. "In El Progreso, workers and their families congregated daily in the public park Ramón Rosa,"[55] and strikers set up temporary kitchens where everyone from the town was fed with food and supplies that campesinos and local merchants had provided to the strikers.

By May 4, 1954, all workers—including those from the Tela sector, the fincas, the Mechanical and Construction Departments, and railroad and service workers in the American Zone—were on strike in El Progreso or La Lima. During the initial days of the strike, workers began to develop their internal infrastructure and organization for their desired representation. The striking workers did not go home to their barracones during the mobilization; instead, they set up strike centers as places where everyone from the region would come together and stay. Many strikers slept at the strike center in their hammocks. The centers encouraged workers to remain on strike and to participate actively in demonstrations of strength in front of the military and the companies.

The gradual spreading of awareness about work actions and solidarity with workers in Puerto Cortés, El Progreso, La Lima, and other areas created a ripple effect of work stoppages along the north coast. Workers were called on to support the demonstrations and did so in large numbers—in no small measure due to the efforts of worker organizers who helped spread the strike message and the call for solidarity from finca to finca. By May 4, when banana finca workers went on strike in all the fincas, other workers and industries had followed suit. Organizers recognized a need and opportunity for leadership, but leftists feared persecutions and remained behind the scenes during the initial address to the crowds assembled in the strike center of El Progreso.[56] The need to maintain a unified strike front among workers, in the face of employer opposition during a long strike, along with the political concerns of the PDRH and other left formations, prompted the creation of an ad hoc strike. In part, the ad hoc strike committee was positioned to ensure that the more centrist Liberal Party would not dampen the movement-building work that the other organizations had invested so much in over the years. The ad hoc committee also served the important role of gathering together regional representatives of the fincas and striking workers to formulate collective demands. Thus the coordination and cooperative solidarity that marked the initial stages of the strike gave way to consolidation by previously organized leadership bodies and established base organizations. Later, it was centralized in a Central Strike Committee, which became the only recognized bargaining agent for all the Tela Railroad Company workers.

STRIKE DEMANDS AND NEGOTIATIONS WITH THE TELA RAILROAD COMPANY

By May 4, 25,000 workers were on strike. Between May 4 and May 11, workers were organizing themselves in what would eventually become the structure of the union. Workers were represented in regional sections by geographic area and in subsections by work departments.[57] On May 11, the initial ad hoc committee of worker representatives presented 30 strike demands to the company—later known as the Pliego de Peticiones (List of Demands), or simply Los 30 Puntos (The 30 Points)—which made the workers' concerns clear to the Tela Railroad Company and to Hondurans at large. The initial letter, which included the workers' list of 30 demands, also cited the Universal Declaration of Human Rights and the Inter-American Charter of Social Guarantees "in defense of their material, social, political and cultural rights."[58] The Pliego de Peticiones were gathered during assemblies with workers throughout the five divisions (Puerto Cortés, La Lima, El Progreso, Bataán, Tela) of the Tela Railroad Company. By May 11, the demands from each region, by department, were brought together under a formal collective petition for the first time in the history of worker organizing in the area.

As the strike progressed, the Tela Railroad Company did not engage with workers and instead called on the Honduran government to intervene. The Honduran government sent a mediation team to the north coast, which settled in San Pedro Sula, met with both sides, and compiled proposals based on the 30 demands the workers submitted. The Tela Railroad Company maintained a firm policy of nonnegotiation[59] and ignored the petition, refusing to negotiate with the workers or to even acknowledge the "30 points," insisting that workers return to work before any discussion would take place.[60] The Honduran government's Mediation Commission tried to engage both parties. Workers, however, feared that the mediation team had the company's best interests at heart, not theirs. They stood steadfast and did not go back to work.

The 30 demands that the ad hoc worker committee presented to the company centered on several themes of great importance to workers: wage increases, respect for the eight-hour workday, adequate access to health care for workers and their family members, compensation for transportation and work equipment (including protective gear), improvement in housing and food in the wharves for *muelleros* (stevedores), and access to education. Larger, more symbolic issues revolved around race and gender equity and respect for workers and their right to organize a union. The Pliego de Peticiones also shows that women service workers were considered part of the workforce and were taken into account in the formulation of the 30 demands.

Workers cited the existing Honduran laws pertaining to the eight-hour workday, compensation for overtime work, education, and protection for workers and women's rights to justify their claims.[61] These sets of high-priority demands by workers called attention to the fact that the banana companies often violated established Honduran laws. Both foreign and national employers regularly disregarded laws governing labor standards in order to meet the demands of the export schedule.[62] Workers' immediate demands included a substantial wage increase that would raise their wages by 30% to 72%, depending on the position.[63]

CORTEROS AND THE CONTRACT SYSTEM

Most workers perceived to be skilled and those in a workshop—for example, construction or machine shop workers—felt it was important to demand the elimination of the contract system. Agricultural finca workers (corteros, muleros, junteros), however, stood to benefit from the contract system. This is reflected in the exception carved out for agricultural work in the demand to end the contract system. For corteros (cutting contractors), the system worked. They were seasoned workers who led a team that they themselves chose, including the mulero (mule-team driver) and juntero (gatherer/carrier). The cortero was paid by the company and negotiated with the timekeeper. He served as a buffer between workers and the mandador (overseer). The cortero would agree on the goal for the number of stems needed and receive pay for the pieces or stems the team cut; he then paid the rest of the workers.[64] Management considered that three work teams of nine men performed "fast-paced and team-oriented" work.[65] Oral history gathered in the region reveals that each team was made of four to five men instead of nine, but the size had to do with the cutting needs of the day.[66] Once a cargo ship was waiting at the docks to be loaded with fruit, orders came down to every mandador and timekeeper, determining the goals for each finca.[67] The mandador and the cortero would communicate about cutting goals. The corteros had vast knowledge of the fields; they were respected for their expertise in harvesting, planting, and pruning as well as determining when it was just right to harvest the fruit before ripening. Once a goal was identified for the particular finca, the corteros would set the whole process in motion, working long hours for one to two days until reaching the limit.

Working with their own team, corteros could control the pace of the work, choose the workers, and have some flexibility and independence in the fields.[68] Oral histories reveal that this was an important way in which workers structured their finca work because the independence allowed them to "cut corners" to earn extra money for the work team.[69] Junteros and muleros saw their positions as an important step to becoming corteros themselves, the highest position within the hierarchy of the finca before the management position of timekeeper.[70] Corteros supported the demand for ending the contract system for all workers except those in the finca. This exception shows that the first Central Strike Committee had insider knowledge of the issues and was very concerned with addressing them in ways that respected the interests of workers in different roles. The first strike committee leaders took great care to address every department's issues properly, and the original list of demands clearly illustrates that. At the same time, we can see the strong role played by corteros in making these demands important to the larger strike committee.

DEMANDS TO ADDRESS GENDER AND RACIAL EQUITY

The demands also included wage increases for washerwomen and service employees, many of whom were women, in the American Zone.[71] Several points addressed the company's failure to adhere to the eight-hour workday and asked for double pay for overtime work after eight hours as well as reduced hours for nighttime employees to six hours per workday.[72] Requiring double pay would encourage the company to adhere to the eight-hour workday restriction, hire a second shift, or pay overtime. In their demands, workers sought pay schedules that reflected weekly pay and monthly pay, instead of the company schedule of a ten-day pay period.[73] Also included was the permission to miss work for medical or family emergencies; people often were not allowed to leave work to go to the hospital, attend funerals, or deal with other life or family situations.[74] Workers who wanted time off or had suffered an accident and could not work would have to leave their position entirely and hope that the job would still be there when they returned. Also of great concern for all workers, especially rail workers, banana cutters, and *poiseros* and *veneneros* (pesticide sprayers) was the right to receive appropriate health care and pay for time lost due to work accidents.[75] There were significant demands for protective equipment for workers, in addition to free transportation and work materials (at the time all workers paid for their machetes, shovels, hoes, and other digging tools).[76] Despite the dangerous work and environment, there were no provisions to ensure workers' health and safety, and the company provided no protective gear. Healthcare for family members was also a high priority. Even service workers in the American Zone did not have access to the hospital, despite working so close to the facilities. Workers proposed a 2% employee[77] contribution from their salaries for upkeep of the company hospital on the condition that their families would be treated free of charge.[78]

The demand for access to improved health care, housing, and an eight-hour workday reflected the fact that the workforce was becoming family-oriented, diverging from the company's assumption that it primarily consisted of single men. A family-oriented workforce was also evident in the workers' rebuttal on June 17 to the company proposal of June 13, 1954, in which workers demanded that dispensaries and hospitals be well staffed by doctors, specialists, and nurses who could take care of their needs, including delivering babies: "section 2E: Accepted, on the condition that the nurse is certified and has the proper equipment and that care arrives in a timely manner in contrast to what has transpired lately, including cases of childbirth in which they arrive after the child has already been born."[79]

Demands for improvement in living conditions, food establishments at the wharves, and access to education would also benefit families and women, including patronas who were not linked to supervisors in the finca. Workers proposed the "abolition of the obligation to eat in the eating establishment of the wife of the supervisor" to prevent coercion of workers in their selection of comedores for their meals.[80] Many workers made their own contracts with patronas in the outlying campos. In new areas where the company expanded its plantations, workers were commonly expected to patronize the comedor of the wife of a supervisor (*capataz*). This proposal aimed to limit the power of the supervisors and their wives and to open work opportunities for unaccompanied women, patronas, ayudantas, and vendors in new areas.[81]

According to Canales, many women also worked as service providers and nannies in the homes of the company bosses. About 100 women worked in a *banania* factory (where banana paste was produced) that was also owned by the company. Many were nurses in company hospitals. Others were telephone workers, known as *las clavileras* (the operators), and yet others were "servants assigned to the company employees," according to the Pliego de Peticiones, for whom one point demanded just compensation.[82] Several other demands addressed women's lives in significant ways, demonstrating their significant numbers in service jobs at the American Zone, the hotels, and the hospitals. There was a demand for direct pay from the company, and one for paid meals and wage increases for washerwomen. This would change the company practice of providing stipends to supervisors and first-class employees in the American Zone and Lima Nueva to pay for service workers, cooks, washerwomen, babysitters, and yarderos (often men). The stipend arrangement was not advantageous to women because they either received less pay or were at the mercy of each individual household's work needs and pay schedule.[83]

The 30 demands as a whole clearly demonstrate not only the overwhelming presence of women workers but also workers' intent and ability to advocate for women workers and family needs, including health care (as mentioned above); recognition as workers of the company, as a bargaining unit, and with access to company benefits; and fair treatment. Workers fought hard for the recognition of informal-sector service workers, washerwomen, and cooks who served trusted company employees in the American Zones. "Number 2, section D," for example, insists that, "the cooks and washerwomen should be considered employees of the company and as such should have the right to all worker benefits."[84] Workers essentially advocated for the formalization of an unacknowledged and informal workforce.

Several factors may have influenced this demand. The sheer numbers of service workers laboring within the American Zone was crucial to the strike. In the 1950s, women's participation in the Honduran labor force was uniquely high when compared to other Central American nations. Honduras's rate of female participation in the labor force was 41.8% compared to 11.8% in Guatemala and 16.2% in El Salvador.[85] Workers supported and demanded equal pay for equal work for women.[86] Even this general demand, perhaps a universal one, reflects a consciousness not present in previous strikes.

Very few north-coast working women made it into leadership positions or committees in the strike, but still their labor and role in the strike was significant. *Las clavileras*, for instance, were instrumental in helping maintain the communication flow between fincas and strike centers; their communication over the phone was referred to as "*metiendo mecha*," literally "lighting the fuse."[87] Although the organizing role of women is minimized in the conventional narrative of the strike, both Canales and Cabrera Williams allude to women's role in preventing workers from getting caught by the military. Canales's wife even went to jail and was forced to leave her children at home alone for 15 days because she refused to say where he was hiding.[88] Canales remembers that his wife kept abreast of the political plans because she was home when they would hold meetings; her participation in the day-to-day organizing, though, was marginal. Cabrera Williams's wife also saved him by disposing of the newspapers *Vanguardia Revolucionaria* just before the military came to look for him at home.[89] The women of the *banania* factory also went on strike, and others served as messengers between strike centers. Despite the obvious presence of women both in the fincas and as workers in the company towns, the everyday narrative of the strike relegated them to a secondary supportive role.

Also evident in the 30 points is a symbolic demand for both gender and racial equity. Number 11, for example, demands that "for equal work there should be equal pay regardless of sex, race, creed or nationality of the worker."[90] Company policies were extremely discriminatory against Black and Salvadoran workers, as well as women. Black workers were not allowed to enter the American Zone club, the hotel, or the bakery and were often relegated to sleeping outside the barracones if they did not have a family. In the company's hotel, neither Black nor mestizo workers were allowed to enter the bakery unless they worked there.[91] Black workers experienced discrimination at the wharves, where mestizo workers were prioritized. Black workers, who were perceived to have less body mass than other workers, according to Canales, were often turned away if there were mestizo workers ready to take up the numbers or jobs slots: "Domingo Martinez posed the problem of discrimination; in the port where he worked the same thing happened. The one that gave out the numbers for work would call such and such workers, always leaving out the Black workers."[92]

Aside from not having secure work every day, when Black workers did manage to get work, their jobs were often the hardest and most grueling of physical labor—commonly, the work of stevedores in the fincas and in the ports. The workforce of *muelleros* (stevedores) included significant numbers of Black and mixed-race workers. They were expected to unload the *racimos*, or bunches of bananas, weighing anywhere from 75 to 100 pounds. These were unloaded from the rejillas or wooden flat-bed railroad containers, onto their bare backs. Another worker skillfully used a very sharp machete to slice the stems while they were still on the carrier's back; the machete barely missed the carriers' backs. It is interesting to note that mestizo workers saw Black workers as weaker because they did not work in the fields, but they may not have been aware of company policies that actually directed workers into different departments on the basis of race. The first strike committee attempted to address workplace discrimination directly with the inclusion of these universal demands and also engaged in negotiations related to this work.[93]

During his interview, Cabrera Williams was very quick to say that Black and mestizo workers were equal in the fields. But Canales and Cabrera Williams subtly marginalized this group by glossing over the discrimination of Black workers, perhaps accepting it as part of the company hierarchy. A Black finca worker would probably present a different narrative. As Gerardo Pery Laredo's recollections have already shown, he lived through daily discrimination in the campos, as did other Black workers who worked alongside him, constantly negotiating space with mestizos.

Teresina Rossi Matamoros's testimony tells us that race was a determinant in who entered the "mess halls" or clubs. On one occasion, a friend who was *trigueña* was not allowed to enter the mess hall. The guard told them it was busy and whispered to Teresina, a light-skinned woman, that she could go in if she wanted. The mess hall was a dining room where the first-class, trusted employees of the Tela Railroad Company came to dine. Rossi's friend may not have been Black, for a mestiza could also be *trigueña*, but it was clear that ethnicity and race were policed and that degrees of skin color were important to company installations, as they were in the United States.[94] Workers' testimonies indicate that discrimination marked the lives of Black workers beyond the work-selection process, affecting their daily lives and the local worker culture in the company towns. Race and ethnicity instilled a sense of hierarchy among workers, and the 30 points attempted to address this and bring about equity.

Another strike demand, the "abolition of racial and worker discrimination in hospitals, dispensaries, ambulances, and hotels" identifies the company spaces where workers felt the worst discrimination.[95] Workers received medical care in the hospitals according to their position in the company and often had second- or third-category status when they went in for treatment. Each floor served a category in the company's La Lima hospital.[96] It was understood that finca workers were in the lowest rank when receiving services, and many feared going to the hospital except in cases of extreme emergency.

The worker committees of the emerging labor union also sought to change the culture and work organization imposed by company policies.[97] The ad hoc committee, the initial strike committee responsible for the elaboration of the 30 points, was preoccupied with larger universal demands, like an end to discrimination based on sex, race, and nationalism.[98] This initial committee had a larger vision for the union movement that did not stop at building a localized union but aimed also to change the working-class culture in the north coast. These ambitions faded as negotiations with the company began; concrete workplace policies dominated the negotiations, and the leadership and representation of the workers changed over the duration of the strike. Still, the demands on the Tela Railroad Company were made public to all workers in Honduras, setting a model for how to make workplace demands and what work policies should look like. The 30 demands served as a template not just for local workplace issues but also for broader universal demands.

THE CENTRAL STRIKE COMMITTEE AND NEGOTIATIONS

On May 17, 1954, the initial ad hoc committee gave way to the worker-elected Central Strike Committee (Junta Directiva del Comité Central de Huelga). An ad hoc committee had submitted 30 demands to the company a week earlier on May 11, 1954, and the Construction Department workers had also submitted a list of demands on May 3, 1954, before going on strike. To bring coherence and unity to their demands, the Central Strike Committee was elected. Members of the Central Strike Committee were Cesar Augusto Coto, secretary general; Juan Bautista Canales, secretary of strike organization; Marcos Santos, propaganda secretary; Guillermo Rosales, notetaker and recorder of agreements; and Gabriel David, Augusto Castañeda, Manuel Sierra, José Velasquez, Adan Posas, Cruz Melendez, Ernesto Pérez, Angel M.

Dominguez, Antonio Rivas, and Gregorio Ferra as adjunct secretaries.[99] The local strike committees in the five divisions came together, and each elected three of the leaders of their local strike committee (for a total of 15 individuals) to represent the mass of striking workers regionally and to lead them in negotiations with the company and the Mediation Commission.[100] El Progreso, seen as the place where the PDRH had the strongest support, was chosen as the center of activities for the Central Strike Committee.[101] Most of these committee members, all men, were PDRH sympathizers and some progressive Liberal Party members.[102] This leadership body was responsible for improving coordination and support among the different support committee activities.

This new leadership formation adopted the demands articulated in the 30 points sent to the Tela Railroad Company on May 11 and added seven additional demands before they would enter negotiations. The added list of demands established their function and role as the only bargaining committee for workers. Workers were well aware that the company was not negotiating in good faith and that the government Mediation Commission was often biased in favor of the company. The Central Strike Committee demanded that the Honduran government release workers incarcerated for their strike activity and for organizing across the north coast.[103] It also called for respect for the worker's Central Strike Committee, asking that J. Antonio Inestroza, the Minister of Justice, "abstain from using inappropriate language, and making inappropriate threats, during the mediation talks."[104] At the same time, it demanded that the military retreat from the banana zones, since workers had already demonstrated their ability to protect company property.[105] More importantly, the Central Strike Committee wanted an end to the intimidation of strike supporters, a tactic that was beginning to threaten the strike leadership in early May.[106] The one recourse the Central Strike Committee had in light of the persecution was to establish their body as the highest form of worker representation, and therefore the only committee with permission to negotiate for workers.[107] This consolidation would prove to be an important move for workers, as divisions and local interests were already brewing in La Lima, causing friction between two strike leaders. The powerful insistence on the committee's role as *the* representative of the workers movement made it harder for the company to divide or pit striking workers against one another.

A month after the ad hoc committee submitted the 30 demands with the facilitation of the government Mediation Commission, workers heard back for the first time from the company.[108] In response, the company, as workers expected, did not accept all the workers' demands and especially rejected those affecting service workers and the proposed abolition of contract labor. The company claimed that these service workers did not work directly for the company and therefore were not their employees.[109] The company also cited great losses due to wind blow-downs of fincas and the strike itself, both of which did affect banana production gains well into 1955.[110] UFCo's anti-union strategies and practices were similar in all the Latin American countries where it did business. UFCo initially did not recognize the demands of the workers, hired strikebreakers, denied that workers actually worked for the company, and often used national political instability as an excuse to avoid accepting the union.[111] UFCo in particular felt confident that its subsidiaries in other countries could supply the bananas needed for export until strikes subsided. Thus it "could afford to wait out the isolated strike, repress workers, or simply abandon production in particular locales."[112]

The company claimed that its workers' salaries were higher than those of all agricultural workers in the country and cited the added benefits of health care and goods, such as milk and meat, provided by the company at cost.[113] The company was not conciliatory with regard to real wage increases or overtime. It also did not accept demands on transportation or the demand for work supplies.[114] The company's rebuttal suggested time-and-a-half pay for overtime and no special shift for nighttime port workers.[115] Thus began a back-and-forth process of negotiation, assisted by the government mediation team that would eventually result in a resolution of the strike about a month later.

The workers' response to the company proposal on June 17 is perhaps the most revealing about workers' lives and conditions. Great care was taken to respond to every company allegation with detail and accuracy. Workers demonstrated two very clear points in their rebuttal. First, the company did not have policies that addressed the workers' needs, so local supervisors and overseers made up their own, often arbitrary rules in the fields. Second, the company did not understand that the workforce was changing from a mostly single, male, and migrant workforce to a family-oriented workforce, with an increased presence of an invisible workforce of women. Third, in their response to the company letter, workers also refuted the company's claims that it paid better wages than the rest of the country. In reality, according to workers' estimations, they did not.[116] Banana workers argued that while agricultural workers throughout the nation earned lower wages than banana workers did, they also had fewer work responsibilities and hours. Landowners provided tools and food for agricultural workers, whereas banana workers had to pay for their own out of their salaries. Agricultural workers in the other parts of the country also had access to national public hospitals, where they received free services. Other agricultural workers also experienced less extreme climate conditions and less grueling work when compared to the banana workers of the north coast.[117] Banana workers demanded pay for their specialized expertise, for laboring under harsh conditions, and for living in enclave economies where the cost of living was higher and fees for medical services were deducted from their paychecks. Workers' organizing around these demands gave way to new ways of thinking about the workplace and the creation of new structures to deal with injustices.

The Central Strike Committee continued to effectively develop the emerging structure that represented workers' issues and reflected regional and departmental representation. Workers were organized into five committees representing the five distinct areas of Tela Railroad Company operations. These committees would eventually become known as *seccionales*, with departments and areas of work known as *subseccionales*. Each work center made demands particular to its own region, department, and position. With a workforce of over 10,000, labor leaders were conscious of the need to prevent divisions and breaks in negotiations. The larger Central Strike Committee thus unified the diverse needs and tensions of the five sectors. It was also responsible for issuing public statements on behalf of the striking workers.[118] Also, concerned about the Mediation Commission's bias toward the company, the newly formed strike committee called on mediators to "observ[e] the due respect in the proposals presented by both sides."[119]

It is important here to note the orientation and composition of the Central Strike Committee. An evaluation of its hierarchy and the elected representatives of the sections and subsections during the strike reflects the impact of race and gender on the organizing priorities. The hierarchy privileged mestizo men in skilled positions in the leadership. The first Central Strike Committee's leadership was unique in that aside from almost all of them being skilled workers, many if not all of them had been part of a PDRH study group, and later the CLO, participating in clandestine meetings at Julio C. Rivera's house in complete secrecy.[120] Juan B. Canales and Rigoberto Padilla Rush had attended school and received training. Canales worked in a skilled-mechanic workshop. Padilla Rush worked in the Tropical Radio Division of the Tela Railroad Company. Rossi Matamoros was a bilingual secretary in the Material and Supplies Department in Tela. Marcos Bardales worked in the

Engineering Department, installing irrigation systems.[121] Another organizer, Cesar Agusto Coto, was a teacher.[122] Though many were skilled workers, their commitment to agricultural workers was clear in their participation in the organization of the movement. Rivera explains:

> That I did not belong to the popular class, working class, or campesino class did not mean that I did not have sympathy for that sector of the population. It is possible that the workers themselves may have thought my conduct strange. Under different circumstances, and if I had another attitude toward them, perhaps they would have thought me an enemy. The workers who were aware of my activities had consideration and care for my position.[123]

Rivera's personal grievance was that he had lost a parcel of land he owned to Tela Railroad Company.[124] But his overall commitment to the political work was of greater importance and is reflected in his class consciousness, his leadership of the study group, and his actions later in the strike. Aside from being a charismatic leader, his organizing and teaching ability, his resolve, his persecution, and his subsequent incarcerations proved his loyalty to the banana finca men on whose behalf he was working.[125]

COMITÉ DE HUELGA DEL MONTE

Although they had limited representation in the Central Strike Committee—the only finca worker who held a position as adjunct secretary to the Central Strike Committee was Gabriel David Galeano—workers were organized in each finca.[126] Workers in the finca had their own organization system; it was built over time and began with the recruitment of workers.[127] Edmundo Cabrera Williams, or Mundo, as he is known throughout the campos in the outskirts of La Lima, credits his "awakening" to Cesar Agusto Coto, a Honduran organizer who had just returned from exile in nearby Guatemala, where he organized with other banana workers. Coto worked with and trained Honduran banana workers on campaign strategies, giving people the tools with which to organize by conducting *charlas* (literally, "chats"; used to refer to union meetings) on tactics to avoid the ensuing repression:

> In those times there were no laws; there was nothing until a fellow *paisano* [countryman] came to awaken us, Cesar Agusto Coto. He was in jail most of the time he was here, but he had already awoken us. This is when we organized and started to hold the sessions. Look, to find out

where we would have sessions that day, we had to leave a trail of pieces of *güineo verde* [green banana]—we would find one of those *güineos* [he points to a green banana tree with bananas] and that is what would direct us. . . . That is how we did the sessions.[128]

While Edmundo Cabrera Williams gives Coto most of the credit for "awakening" the mass of workers in La Lima area, he describes the various roles finca workers took on to keep the organization going while Coto was incarcerated. Workers conducted the *charlas* themselves and determined strategy in what was known as the Comité de Huelga del Monte (Field Strike Committee): "The secretary general of the Strike Committee from the Fields, that is what we called them, his name was Marcos Miranda. . . . [The] old man was a cortero. He was the one who brought many people to the strike."[129]

This Comité de Huelga del Monte was made up of men who were all agricultural finca workers, and their role was to pass information to other workers about the injustices in the workplace and the possibility of a strike. The *charlas* were particularly challenging because there was constant surveillance and any literature found in the possession of any worker or in his barracón would be sufficient cause for death. Cabrera Williams recalls:

I would receive all the pamphlets; it so happened that one time the *jura* [military police or paramilitary] of Don Guayo Galeano came [to my house]. In those days I was in the camps of Ticamaya, now they call it El Remolino, a small village [*aldea*], . . . and the soldiers spread throughout the houses setting up their machine guns [*máquinas de patas de gallina*]. In the end they could, they influenced us. . . . We changed sessions [location], one day we would go to one place, another day to another. That is why we used that signal; we all knew that when we saw the trail of green bananas, that is where we were being led.[130]

Canales and Cabrera Williams found roles that challenged them to collectivize their personal experiences of strife on the banana plantations. But they also used tactics by leftists in the region in response to company surveillance and persecution.

The diversity of the ranks was reflected in the movement in more subtle ways. In the development of the Pliego de Peticiones, workers were invited to *charlas* or sessions by the leadership of the sectional committees and Central Strike Committee. But only those perceived to be literate or those who were in skilled job positions were identified as leaders who could engage in the most arduous study groups with Honduran intellectuals and producers of *Vanguardia Revolucionaria* and *Voz Obrera*, both linked to the PDRH and the CLO.[131] For these leaders, the strike was part of an organized plan, a step in a strategy based on their political evaluation of the country and informed by theoretical study. For workers such as Cabrera Williams, immersion in organizing was experienced differently; he relied on word of mouth. This was perhaps the most powerful and safest tactic for communication because workers could avoid discovery and potential persecution by paramilitary police.

Women were excluded from day-to-day organizing, perhaps not by design but because the effort was not made to recruit them. One woman, Teresina Rossi Matamoros, was recruited by Julio C. Rivera to participate in the study groups and was elected to the strike committee; she was a former secretary who sympathized with the workers and who quit her job and became a steady supporter in Tela and a member of the PDRH and later the Communist Party.[132] Canales explains that her main tasks were typing up the notes from meetings and what would eventually be the Pliego de Peticiones, or Los 30 Puntos. She got involved after working with Chico Rios, a strike leader in Tela. As Juan Canales reported:

> There was Chico Rios, he organized a technical executive committee, and Teresina was there. Teresina had left her job with the management office and went to Chico Rios. Chico had been training her in political study. Teresina was very active [during the compiling of the Pliego de Peticiones]. . . . Poor Teresina had blistered fingers from so much typing. Everything was typed. Well, Teresina? [they would ask her how she was doing] Let's continue [they would say]. Well then, right now we will sign the demands, because Reikoff [*sic*] was in Tela.[133]

While Rossi Matamoros held a role within the organizing committee and was able to participate in the study groups, the wives of the workers are described as secondary supporters, making food, taking care of the children, and leading the food bank effort during the actual strike. Further prodding actually reveals that this may be an issue of perception. On the questions regarding women, both Canales and Cabrera Williams speak of their wives and other women in passing, without acknowledging that these roles may have been key to the functioning of the overall plan. Canales explains that the leadership tried to maintain a cordial relationship with women workers and the wives of workers: "We tried to keep them as our friends, so that they would cooperate with us, but in study [political study groups] they hardly participated; women had another problem: taking care of the home and the kids."[134] While not all women were active in study groups or in the organizing of the strike, a great majority did join the ranks when the strike began, performing indispensable roles.

Even though the contributions of PDRH and CCO members were crucial to building the list of demands and advancing the workers' positions, not all the strike representatives were part of these groups.[135] The Central Strike Committee structure, with *seccionales* and *subseccionales*, created an effective communications system. In addition to a range of newspapers and bulletins, striking workers spread the word about the union and shared information about workers' issues through the representative structure to inform the negotiating process. Every point accepted or negotiated had to be approved by worker vote. This structure and practice constituted the antecedent to that of the labor union.

While the Central Strike Committee effectively unified workers from the different centers, divisions arose when the leadership of La Lima disagreed with the Tela and El Progreso regional strike committees. Manuel de Jesús Valencia, a charismatic teacher in the company schools and a presumed Liberal Party member and anti-communist, managed to garner support from striking workers and pro-company forces alike.[136] He became a leader and spokesperson in La Lima, and he was even featured in an anti-communist report in *Life Magazine*. The photo of him reading a communiqué against a backdrop of striking workers proudly displays the caption "strike leader Manuel de Jesús Valencia is reading an anti-communist resolution which was passed by acclamation. Valencia, a moderate with a good deal of official support, was strengthened recently when the government arrested a group of Communists."[137] Meanwhile, PDRH organizer Cesar Agusto Coto, who spent many years organizing in the fincas near La Lima, also had the support and loyalty of workers. Coto, a recognized representative in the strike committee organization, disagreed with Valencia's politics and his lack of ideological commitment. He believed Valencia was working for the company, trying to create a division between La Lima and El Progreso and trying to gain support from the regional strike committee in Puerto Cortés in opposition to the El Progreso-based Central Strike Committee.[138]

A tug of war ensued between the two leaders when the company proposed rehabilitating some of the train lines, particularly the ones between Tela, El Progreso, and La Lima.[139] This tentative agreement included the resumption of activities one day a week for train operators and commissary workers. The workers voted adamantly not to return to any kind of work until the company agreed to the 30 demands.[140] Ultimately, the fissures in the La Lima leadership were ideological. Coto's own leadership was based on a structure of worker votes and participation, while Valencia felt empowered to make decisions without consulting workers or with the input only of La Lima workers. Valencia was a complicated figure throughout the negotiation process; he had a strong following in La Lima but was heavily distrusted among workers in other regions. Coto was known to have played an active role in tactically bringing together different factions of the movement, including Communist Party and PDRH members, for a common goal. Valencia's attack on Coto in the early days of June was destructive; he accused Coto and the Central Strike Committee of being communists.[141] The accusation reverberated onto the national scene as the Central Strike Committee attempted to defend its position as the representative of a majority of the workers. This was futile, and the military descended on the Central Strike Committee, incarcerating many of the PDRH and those perceived to be part of the newly created Communist Party.[142] The first Central Strike Committee, originated on May 17, was persecuted and jailed.

The first strike committee had been elected by workers and composed of PDRH members. Their initial influence was visionary; their contributions included the initial set of universal demands for workers. In the later days of May, these members were persecuted and jailed in Tegucigalpa; many remained there until September of 1954, while others were forced into exile. The second strike committee election took place once the original strike committee leadership was thrown in jail. The election took place out of necessity; without a strike committee, the workers would not have a negotiating body. It is unclear how this second election happened, but what is clear is that the next leaders were mostly Liberal Party members. Because they organized covertly, their situation created an opening for well-positioned, well-spoken, anti-communist, and educated Liberal Party leaders. Though at first reluctant to join the strike, when they saw the successful work stoppage, they positioned themselves as spokespeople for the coordinated movement along the north coast, hoping it would benefit their party ranks.[143] The company utilized the committee's internal destabilization to its advantage and reiterated accusations that the committee did not have the support of the workers and was composed of communist leaders.

The workers were left with no choice but to elect a new committee to represent them; the strike committee reconstituted without the original members.[144] On June 7, workers reelected a second central committee. Valencia conveniently placed himself at the head of the organization, elected as representative of La Lima.

The worker response, via the second strike committee, to the company's proposal of June 13 agreed to the company's terms of negotiations. By this time, there were significant changes in the negotiations, but the 30 demands remained on the bargaining table between the new committee and the company. The new committee, for instance, negotiated demand no. 27, which stated that all workers be returned to their original positions and that no actions would be taken against workers who participated in the strike and the various committees.[145] The company's rebuttal on June 13 also made significant changes to demand no. 27, such as maintaining their right to transfer and lay off workers, and adding a provision that "worker representatives will cooperate with the company in eliminating from the company the communist elements."[146] The new strike committee and the Mediation Commission accepted this point with the company amendments during negotiations. The new strike committee, in fact, reneged on the original petition's universal demands of no discrimination based on race, sex, and nationality, by agreeing to terms, on June 25, that prioritized "the rehiring of Honduran workers and those who have worked for the company previously."[147] The newly elected strike committee was operating on the structure left over by the first strike committee, yet the larger demands in the original petition were evidently set aside. The rest of the universal demands were negotiated and symbolically included, but no processes were set up to make sure that discrimination by sex and race were avoided.[148] The negotiations with the second Central Strike Committee began on June 12, and by July 9 the contract was ratified and workers returned to work. Most other workers from the Standard Fruit Company subsidiaries (as well as cigar makers and textile workers) had already returned to work by this point.

The most memorable experience that workers related was the *sufrimiento* (suffering) they endured throughout the strike. During the first days of the strike, strike workers were optimistic, as they received ample donations of food and support. But the last days of the strike were full of strife. Donations were scant. Workers ran out of extra money to purchase food from patronas and food vendors around the strike centers. The only food available during the final weeks were boiled green bananas and beans. The early rainy season was especially grueling for workers who slept outside on their hammocks in the strike centers. The outstanding memories of suffering were compounded by financial loss for many workers who bought food on credit. After the strike, the company only paid for 40 days of work, not the 69 days that the strike actually lasted, making it impossible for workers to pay their debts.[149] Workers' testimonies focus on these challenges—particularly how poorly they ate toward the end of the strike.

To explain why workers accepted the loss of the original strike committee and its demands, the reelection of a new committee, and the conciliatory return to work, one can only speculate that the lack of food and supplies was wearing on them, or perhaps the divisions within the organization, compounded by lack of food and supplies, led to their eventual acceptance, notwithstanding any disapproval or reluctance. Other workers may have simply embraced gaining the right to organize as a pivotal success that would enable them to begin organizing autonomous unions, even though these first unions were immediately replaced or reconstructed following the company's massive layoffs and retaliation. Yet another reason may be that the first Central Strike Committee leadership may not have had the time to communicate the situation to the rest of the striking workers because they were either jailed or forced to flee. In any case, the change in the leadership altered the results of the Tela strike and movement.

STANDARD FRUIT WORKERS FOLLOW TELA RAILROAD

News of the Tela Railroad Company strike spread nationally and internationally as workers all over Honduras began to make demands of their employers in the national industries. Worker actions combined into a national strike, one that, as Barahona notes, lacked a national central strike committee.[150] The absence of a national coordinating body outside the banana fincas meant that each localized strike effort was led locally, and the outcomes were mediated between the workers and local companies. Barahona notes that textile workers mobilized in various factories owned and managed by Arab immigrants, an industry that had been organized by the CCO since 1950, and began to make demands of their employers, many going on strike: "The first strikes broke out in San Pedro Sula on the afternoon of May 18 when approximately 1,000 women from seven textile factories blocked the entrance to the factory installations and demanded an increase in wages."[151]

Inspired by the actions of the workers on the eastern Caribbean Coast, workers at the Standard Fruit Company, the largest competitor of the Tela Railroad Company, went on strike on May 7, 1954, making four major demands of their employer.[152] The primary demand was explicit: fire oppressive personnel, "the superintendent of the railway, J. A. Gridner, the administrator of the Hospital D'Antoni, Jaime Rodriguez, and the assistant to the superintendent of the wharf [muelle], Ramón Cerril."[153] The workers considered these men to be abusive. Workers also asked for increases in wages, paid vacations, and access for family members to company hospitals. By May 20, the Standard Fruit Company strike ended with an agreement on the first point but left the rest unresolved, particularly on wages, which would be increased on a scale from 4% to 8%.[154] Workers revolted in the fincas of Olanchito, particularly Lomitas and Ceibita, where they stopped a passenger train. The workers felt deceived by the negotiations and attempted to protest but were repressed by the Honduran troops.[155] Nevertheless, workers' memories of the great 1954 strike while working for the Standard Fruit Company demonstrates an important step in changing conditions.

José Narciso Duarte Cruz, a *venenero*, was on his way to work at 5 a.m. when one of the strike leaders in the Standard Fruit Company, Antonio Navarro, stopped him and told him about the strike: "'Narciso do not go to work because today we are not going to work, there will be a strike.' I turned back. I was a very young man at that time; the older men began to talk to us, explaining that the strike had started and that there was no more work until the issue was resolved."[156]

According to Duarte Cruz, older and more experienced workers led the strike effort and as others joined, they deployed themselves to the nine work centers to insist that the majority of workers join. While many voluntarily marched out and joined the strike movement, others did not; resistant workers were forced to join the strike under threat of violence. Duarte Cruz explains, "We went to the center of production, the work centers, to bring out the ones who had gone to work and the ones who resisted; the older workers would beat them with sticks because there was no . . . you had to understand, good or bad, we followed the struggle."[157] In the Standard Fruit Company strike, older workers led the strike and coached younger workers, many of whom were young or new migrants to the region and had not lived through previous strikes. By 1954, the few older workers who experienced the strikes of the 1930s still worked in the finca, and their leadership was important to the movement. Workers feared retaliation for striking and did not want to lose their employment. All, however, intimately experienced the brutality of the Carías Andino dictatorship and company control. While some had participated in presenting petitions and making smaller demands, a work stoppage of the nine centers of production was unprecedented.

The Standard Fruit Company strike lasted 11 days, officially ending on May 20, 1954. Though inspired by the Tela Railroad Company strike, the Standard Fruit Company workers' strike ended far sooner and through less extensive negotiations. The larger general strike movement also realized the monumental achievement of union recognition, spurred by the Tela Railroad Company workers' movement.

GAINS OF THE STRIKE

Workers' narratives of the strike's outcome are diverse. For many, the gains were important, especially the recognition of their labor union, which opened the door to other workers in other industries to organize their unions without intimidation.[158] Of the initial 30 demands submitted for negotiation on May 11, 1954, the recognition of the union as a bargaining body for the workers, and their right to organize a union, were among the greatest achievements. The strike also exposed the labor legislation of the time to be unsatisfactory. Additionally, the government, through the Mediation Commission, proposed the creation of a body with representation from the union and the company that would work to establish improved labor legislation after the contract was finalized between workers and the company.[159]

The positive results of the strike were monumental for the time. Although gains in wages did not reach the 50% workers asked for, the debate around wages during the strike prompted change in both the overall relations between company and workers, and consequently between supervisors and workers in the banana fields as well. It was reported that workers earned "22% in wage increases, scaled down to 10–12% for the higher-paid workers."[160] Some of the workers did not like this but agreed to return to work. The negotiation around wage increases, regularization of the pay schedule to once a week, respect for the eight-hour workday, pay for overtime work, and limits placed on the night-shift workload were all significant changes that empowered workers. Workers gained important autonomy in their daily lives, including access to improved food and freedom to choose the patronas from whom they obtained their meals rather than being forced to eat at the comedores of the supervisors' wives. Workers' families gained from the strike negotiations—access to health care, improved housing, recognition of service workers as company employees, and improved nutrition. Stevedores and dockworkers in general received improvements in pay; after the strike, they were paid continuously for shift work, a change in the past practice of withholding pay for hours during delays in work that they did not cause. Their work schedules were regularized and reflected a greater consideration for workers' lives. The improvement in food for stevedores and rail workers also meant more employment and economic opportunities for women food vendors and patronas not linked to a supervisor. These changes would make the campos and fincas dramatically different places to live and work after May 1954. Workers had more agency, and their families were recognized. After the strike, the realities of their lives and hard work were visible to the supervisors in the various areas of work, a qualitative change that workers welcomed and valued.

Beyond the powerful national implications and industry-changing results of the 1954 strike, the Tela Railroad Company strike gave other workers, and especially Standard Fruit Company employees, a model of action that would help them achieve their goals. Many workers, particularly those working for national industries, worked for very low wages that did not reflect the cost of living. During the strike, workers all over Honduras stopped work, closed their shops or factories, peacefully draped the Honduran flag in the entrance to the factories/strike centers, prevented any Honduran workers from entering, and made lists of demands of their employer.[161] The Honduran government responded by assigning the Mediation Commission, and workers then elected a negotiating body that represented the strikers. Labor contracts were unknown before this period. The Tela Railroad Company workers' model of organizing was essential for those in other industries demanding changes in the workplace in an organized way and on an ongoing basis. While some of the labor contracts cemented new practices that benefited workers, they also created limits and policies for the companies, whose power had previously been unchecked and who had imposed paternalistic relations upon their employees.

The strike also affirmed the importance of building consciousness among workers as a part of a national Honduran workers' movement. Workers organizing with PDRH had learned about other countries' labor movements. The consciousness-building process included denunciations of labor conditions in the fincas and various departments. For committees such as PDRH, CCO, and Comité de Lucha Obrera, the rhetoric of nationalism was influential and helped to instill conscious-ness among workers about their particular conditions. Organizing ef-forts also exposed foreign capital, namely the banana companies and foreign nationals, as exploiters of Honduran workers.[162]

THE STRIKE IN ANTI-COMMUNIST TIMES

Although the strike sparked a remarkable sea change for workers in Honduras at the time, its impact was ultimately limited and influenced by both the geopolitical dynamics in the region and the historical legacy of past strikes and worker actions in the nation. The fear of communism in the region, the US dominance in Latin American political affairs, the triangular relationship between the United States and Honduran governments and Honduran business interests, and the positioning and experiences of various worker organizations were determinative in the ultimate resolution of the 1954 strike. With the United States looming large in the background, the ideological and practical deployment of anti-communist rhetoric was devastating to the Honduran movement of the 1950s.

Strikers and the worker leadership committees could not avoid anti-communist rhetoric and accusations throughout the strike, as this attitude permeated regional and transnational relations. In 1954, during the gathering of the Tenth Inter-American Conference of the Organi-zation of American States (OAS) in Venezuela, the Caracas Declaration was enacted, stating a commitment to "hemispheric solidarity" against communism from all Latin American countries.[163] Guatemala refused to sign on to the OAS declaration (they saw it as excessive meddling by the US State Department) and was in response officially labeled a communist government.[164] The declaration stated that any "commu-nist government in any American state would constitute a direct threat and would automatically trigger a consultative meeting of the OAS."[165] Though the OAS declined to engage in a military intervention against Guatemala, it did not oppose US support of a subversive attack planned by Guatemalan general Carlos Castillo Armas in Honduras to depose President Jacobo Árbenz Guzmán.[166] Notwithstanding Guatemala's op-position, the Caracas Declaration was a potent message opposing com-munism in the Americas.

The Guatemalan government turned to their neighboring coun-tries for solidarity and asked the Honduran government to sign a non-aggression agreement, which the Honduran government refused to sign. Given US influence and power, Honduras instead entered into a bilateral arms agreement with the United States in 1954. This agreement granted the US government unlimited access to Honduran soil for the purposes of training and military exercises. The Honduran government agreed to pay an undisclosed sum of money to the US government for the soldiers' stay. Prior to signing of the agreement, the United States had already trained Honduran fighter pilots, and many Honduran military officers had begun to train on US soil in 1946.[167] It is under this international political backdrop that the striking Honduran workers waged their union struggle. Facing the rampant and ubiquitous accusations of communism, leaders struggled to keep the strike in the national consciousness as a patriotic Honduran effort.

Árbenz Guzmán's imminent fall and the accusations of communism in Guatemala put inordinate pressure on the banana workers' Central Strike Committee in Honduras to disavow any connections with communists and to allow Liberal Party members to engage in the strike-committee process. Taking cues from the events of the time, the Tela Railroad Company charged the workers with attempting to cause a national economic crisis and of being communists like the Guatemalans. The strike committee was understandably afraid that the anti-communist sentiment, already spreading through Honduras, would destroy the strike effort. These dynamics were particularly challenging for Honduran workers, because they were dealing not only with a resistant employer but with a transnational one that had allies in the US State Department and the Honduran government and military. These interests came together to protect the company's territory, both economically and politically. The Tela Railroad Company did not negotiate with workers until a few days before Árbenz Guzmán's government was deposed in June of 1954.[168]

The local Tela Railroad Company proceeded to work with the Honduran government to isolate members of the Central Strike Committee whom they perceived to be "communist." While the structure set up by the Central Strike Committee made it hard for the company to quash the various local strike committees individually, this very same structure ultimately betrayed the Central Strike Committee. The company used its power and influence with the Honduran government to campaign against workers who were perceived to be communist, effectively targeting the first unified strike committee elected by workers. For workers on the ground, there was little choice but to elect a second Central Strike Committee to replace the first in order to maintain a recognized negotiating body. This transition enabled teachers like

Valencia and others who had not been organically connected to the organizing process, and who arguably had less accountability to finca workers, to attain status as bargaining representatives for all the workers with the company.

THE US SHADOW LENGTHENS

Once the members of the first committee were in jail, Arturo Jáuregui and Serafino Romualdi and their consultants served as special envoys of the ORIT, who were secretly invited by the US Embassy, and heavily influenced the new negotiating process.[169] The US Embassy and the ORIT were working together as early as 1953. Jáuregui and his organizations offered to bring democratic labor organization techniques and know-how into Honduras to cultivate the fields as a preventive measure, so to speak, against communist labor.[170]

The US Embassy had determined that the "Honduran government was 'apathetic' toward labor."[171] By the time the 1954 strike was taking place, the relationships between the Tela Railroad Company, the US Embassy, and the ORIT were well established: "ORIT sent a number of organizers to Honduras. [Augusto] Malavé [Villalba (Secretary General to the Venezuelan confederation of workers and staff at the ORIT)] was stationed there for many months, helping set up unions in the capital city of Tegucigalpa and assisting in the organization of the Standard and Tela unions."[172] In one report from Honduras, an unnamed source writes:

> There seems to be widespread belief that the banana workers strike was actually started by the communists or people under their influence. President Gálvez maintains that he has correspondence that passed back and forth between Guatemalan communist leaders and the people of Honduras just before and during the first days of the strike. He maintains that the original plan of the Communists was that, when the government crushed the strike, as it was fully expected to do, the defeated strikers would high [*sic*] it in considerable numbers to the Guatemalan frontier where they would be armed by the Guatemalan communists. . . . and then would return across the border as an insurrectionary army. . . . Gálvez foxed them by not suppressing the walk out.[173]

The report continued, "The question of the organization of the strike is another mystery." The author seemingly pondered how so many workers could organize so quickly.[174] "The merchants, who don't like the company commissaries, backed the strikers. Funds were raised in some schools, . . . and the strike took on the coloration of a nationalistic struggle against the foreign company, which was not too well loved by anyone in the country."[175]

After the strike, ORIT continued the surveillance and meticulous incursions into workers organizations, searching for communists and signs of communist influence on new workers. After the strike, from 1955 to 1959, Andrew C. McLellan, a consultant of the ORIT in Honduras, wrote extensive reports to ORIT representatives, including Luis Alberto Monge, General Secretary of the ORIT, and Romualdi in the United States. These reports detailed the ins and outs of worker organizing, union dilemmas, and interactions with "communists," and he acted as an intermediary between workers, the company, and sometimes the state. Most of the organizers of the PDRH are mentioned at some point or another in the reports, identified as communists and radicals:

> The only clandestine political group operating at this is the Partido Democrático Revolucionario Hondureño, the PDRH, with whom all of the communist elements and sympathizers are working. This group has been particularly active among the campesino groups but has been meeting with little or no success. Most of their activity seems to be concentrated in the north coast, particularly in Tela and La Ceiba. In Tela the active propagandist is Theresina ROSSI, of Honduran and Italian descent[,] who has been quite active in the Bataan area where she is not only well identified as being a fellow traveler, but is well known personally. It is assumed that she is on the payroll of the PDRH or that of the communist party.[176]

McLellan was reporting on poststrike activities of the newly formed communist party or perhaps some of the last activities of the PDRH, as it is believed that the party disbanded with the creation of the second Communist Party in 1954. McLellan's informant was the US Embassy representative, and his information may not have been accurate. Rossi was an active member of the PDRH and a secretary of the first strike committee, but she was certainly not paid for her activism. Rossi was actually in the Bataán area to stay with her sister, whom she visited often; after the strike she was persecuted and subjected to finger-pointing by other women, who "spoke behind her back" in Tela; visiting her sister was a refuge.[177] It is unclear precisely who the US Embassy's informants were—perhaps company security or locals loyal to the company.

Nonetheless, the ORIT's investigation was ongoing. The long report on the Honduran labor movement in 1956 detailed a June 16 strike that failed that year, presumably by rank-and-file workers of the Standard Fruit Company and led by the PDRH:

> PDRH members within the union did manage to circulate a number of leaflets flown into the area by the proponents of the strike. . . . Among the listed as being sympathetic to the Communist Party on the north coast are, *Francisco RIOS* and *Juan B. CANALES*, both in jail, and formerly from Tela. *Luis BUESO, Ignacio Paz* of La Ceiba, all of whom worked for the Tela Railroad Co. In Progreso, *Gabriel DAVID*, a construction worker gave counsel to the autonomous union which had its inscription cancelled early in August. La Lima had *Alfonso CERRA-TO*, former employee of the Tela Railroad Co., now in Tegucigalpa. In Puerto Cortes the most active leader was *Antonio GUAJARDO*, former employee of the Tela Railroad Co. and who still resides in Cortes. There are three active workers in Tela, *Gregorio FERRERA, Juan FERRERA*, and *Theresina ROSSI [sic]*, none of whom seem to be meeting with great success with the campesinos, but who have sympathetic following in the railroad shops.[178]

The ORIT was interested in the PDRH after the strike because they believed leftist organizers had success in convincing workers to join their cause. But leftists were actually persecuted and unable to move around in the post-strike period. The ORIT memos also missed the nuance between the Liberal Party's politics and activists and those of the leftists, assessing that "there does not appear to be any well-organized communist activity in the country" and that all these activities could have been orchestrated by the Liberal Party after all.[179]

Clearly the Communist Party was founded, however, in 1954, and the PDRH was on its last legs. These leaders had to leave their home-towns to escape persecution. The Communist Party's organizing efforts revolved around organizing unions parallel to those established by the Central Strike Committee in 1954. Unions like the Autonomous Union in El Progreso led by Gabriel David[180] actually sought and were granted legal status in 1955–1956. There was also a "splinter union to the Standard Fruit Company union," which Chico Rios was advising.[181] A series of wildcat strikes was organized across the north coast between 1956 and 1957, and again they were blamed on the leftists, who were supposedly there to agitate. Despite repression, torture, jail time, and exile, these activities suggest an active, though small, communist party that was successfully leading workers in organizing them into autonomous union movements and wildcat strikes, some of which were very successful and others of which failed. Among the workers most engaged against the Tela Railroad Company were the railroad workers, the construction workers, and some of the agricultural workers nearest El Progreso. Standard Fruit Company divisions between perceived communist and free-labor leaders, mostly liberals, would continue for several years. These autonomous unions, led or advised by leftists, challenged the hegemony of the company- and state-dominated trade unions, which were sympathetic to free labor. Three things slowly destroyed these autonomous efforts. First, the state conducted surveillance of leaders and either exiled them or persecuted them until they self-exiled. Second, the ORIT advocated for dues to be automatically withdrawn from workers' paychecks and transferred to the official unions sympathetic to free labor, SITRATERCO and the Standard Fruit Union; under these conditions, autonomous unions, not recognized by the company as legitimate unions, were unable to adequately finance themselves. Third, Federación Sindical de Trabajadores Nacionales de Honduras (FESIT-RANH; Federation of Unions of National Workers of Honduras), the first labor federation created in April of 1957, put together with the help of the ORIT's technical assistance program, decided that "free" labor unions could be admitted to the federation due to their affinity with the ORIT and that body's statutes.[182] The left-leaning, communist visions for the north coast saw a decline amidst the entrenchment of free-labor politics and deference to the United States.

To Julio C. Rivera and Teresina Rossi, the PDRH gave them, and other communists and progressive Liberal Party members, a cloak of protection. Once they emerged as members of the Communist Party, severe persecution limited their abilities to work, to live, and to organize: "No me deja ban en paz," says Rivera; he had to sell his land and move to Costa Rica for good. "Tanta persecución," lamented Rossi, who moved around until she finally ended up in Tegucigalpa. The outcome of the strike for which they did so much to organize was bittersweet. On the one hand, they challenged a behemoth and won. Aside from the practical improvements in workers' everyday lives and work, the largest gain and most dramatic outcome of the workers' direct action was the shift in power relations between employer and workers and the respect for banana workers in the surrounding communities. The process of organizing the strike enabled workers to participate in the building of the labor movement in concrete ways and change the role of workers in the national landscape. Their work and successes were the building blocks of Honduran labor movement recognized after 1954. On the other hand, however, they experienced loss, persecution, and exile, as the Cold War drove them and their histories underground or into obscurity, and the fruition of their visions for a working-class movement for Honduran workers was deterred. The legacy of the strike thus includes both grand success and a disappointing aftermath, exciting progress and deferral of worker empowerment and democracy, at once constructed and interrupted by the national and foreign powers at play.

CHAPTER 7

CONTEMPORARY MOVEMENT LEADERS REFLECT ON THE LEGACY OF THE 1954 STRIKE

> *Narratives are made of silences, not all of which are deliberate or even perceptible as such within the time of their production. We also know that the present is itself not clearer than the past.*
>
> MICHEL-ROLPH TROUILLOT, *SILENCING THE PAST*[1]

> *Ha pasado mucho tiempo,*
> *ha transcurrido la vida,*
> *y sí, este pueblo no olvida lo que allí se pudo ver.*
> *Hoy, me asalta una quimera*
> *en el plan que nos convenga, armemos otra gran huelga*
> *y tomemos el poder.*
>
> MARIO DE MEZAPA, CAMPEÑO SINGER AND SONGWRITER[2]

The birth of the labor movement is said to have come about in 1954, after the workers and the second strike committee ended their strike and sat down to negotiate with the company. From this emerged the union contract and the Ministry of Labor, so goes the narrative. In fact, the labor movement was born well before 1954. As we saw in earlier chapters, according to Mario Posas, strikes emerged around 1912, in protest to the United Fruit Company (UFCo) and their quest for land to plant their bananas, dispossessing local planters and landowners.[3] In the fields prior to 1954, young workers learned from older workers affiliated with the PDRH, that organizing had to happen clandestinely and oftentimes looked to them for strategy. Children were instructed to keep meeting locations secret if they attended with their fathers,[4] and countless other acts of resistance, small and large, were undertaken prior to the strike by working-class people in the north coast and across Honduras to challenge labor exploitation and foreign and elite economic domination.

While the strike of 1954 was not the first important collective action, it jump-started the labor movement by guaranteeing the right to unionize and the formation of union federations in the country. For workers, activists, and organizers, it also created a labor, social, and political movement that set the stage for contemporary organizing in later generations. The audacity of the PDRH to organize among banana workers, of the radicals who formed the Communist Party, and of the women in all these movements who dared to challenge corporate, authoritarian, and imperial power is perhaps the most significant, lasting, and symbolic result of the 1954 strike. While the many meanings and impacts of the strike are too numerous to recount, I focus here on the legacy it has left on Honduran social movements to this day. The strike lives on in the memories passed down from generation to generation to this day, in union trainings and in political youth organizing, in the homes of banana workers, and in current resistance struggles.

The working class in the banana fincas has transmitted the memory of the 1954 strike by modeling the leftists' organizing processes, charting the formation of the movement for their children and grandchildren in stories and sometimes in nonverbal ways. The memories are shared in patronas' kitchens, in the *bajos de los barracones* (the areas underneath the barracks' stilts), in the workplace, and by workers with sons and daughters as they enter the workforce in the fincas or the packinghouses. In union halls today, the memory is passed down with pride to demonstrate resilience, survival, and triumph over injustice. The strike is also invoked with some caution to convey the power of the company, the reach of US foreign intervention, and the overzealous Honduran state, which protects the company more than workers. These memories are passed down among union members, their families, their communities, and many others, constructing a collective value and belief in justice for workers. Memories, passed down in secrets and silences, have been important to historicize the movement, develop consciousness and solidify their identity as radicals, organizers, and movement builders. The resistance movement of today is looking back to past organizing efforts as sources of inspiration and as proof that there were valiant resisters in their past, despite repression. Despite US control in the region and the years of military domination, memories persisted and were transmitted to younger generations. This concluding chapter attempts to analyze the legacy of the strike through the lens of current social movement leaders' and organizers' reflections of the past, as a starting point for an archive of memory about the strike that is not only symbolic but also grounded in organizing work that has come together in dissonance with and resistance to the Honduras created in the image of US capitalism and neoliberal policies. Persistent memories sustain and inspire leaders in resistance.

José María Martinez, a campeño and communications director and publisher of a worker newsletter (and more recently a migrant worker in the United States), wrote a piece in an educational newsletter he edited for the banana union–coordinating body COSIBAH[5] under the heading "A bit of our story." He writes:

> The Honduran workers' general strike of 1954 has been the most important social movement of our national life. The strike initiated by the Tela Railroad workers on May 1 of that year spread like a flare that burned the entire meadow, extending itself to the Standard Fruit Company, the mines, textile and clothing factories, sugar mills, the factories of cigarettes and drinks, the woodshops, the factories of soap and lard, the candle-making manufacturers, the cotton plantations, and the shoe-making factories, from the north coast to the south, from Danlí to Santa Barbara.[6]

Martinez claims that the strike was akin to a social movement in that era. Though anachronistic, this remembrance shows how leftist leaders, and not just union leaders, processed their past and derived symbols from it that influenced other workers and ultimately the national context, where power was perceived to be centralized and hoarded in the capital. This piece—written to both educate and inspire the rank and file in a beleaguered union, which was facing the changes and losses that accompanied the privatization and capital flight of neoliberalism in the 1990s—is an example of how the memory of the strike transcends the oral folklore to become a form of literature accessible to workers. By focusing on the bottom-up union effort, it claims that organizing brought about improvements to workers' material lives, including "the right to organize, as well as proposals of law such as the labor code, Agrarian Reform Law, and Social Security Law,"[7] all fundamental benefits workers now have thanks to the midcentury strike. At the time of its writing, Martinez's piece was meant to inspire workers to organize to protect earned rights. The aftermath of Hurricane Mitch in 1998 gravely affected the union SITRATERCO: the United Fruit Company, under the name Chiquita Brands, was pulling out of Honduras, and a once-strong union of over 20,000 dwindled to 2,200 in 2002.[8] As of 2019, there were fewer than 1,500 members.[9] In the face of devastation, migration, and crisis, the union reached back to the strike in order to forge a narrative of what Honduran workers had done and could do again. *Revista Visión Sindical*, the union magazine, featured pieces on women workers and participants in the strike, such as Emilia Hernández, known as "La Rápida," the woman who transmitted messages between strike committees in different regions. This piece asked the reader to "follow the example and the progressive thinking of Emilia Hernández, who left us with a legacy of consciousness, humility, love for others, the spirit of struggle, and above all the understanding that 'rights are fought for'"[10] and not given.

The memory of the strike among union members, and passed on by union leaders and thinkers, persists in union educational materials, trainings, and workshops. The pieces on women also historicize women's presence not just as supporters but also as leaders of the strike. The everyday worker could aspire to this position in the construction of his or her own history in the present. Memories of union leaders with particular leftist values and the strike were constructed and reclaimed to inspire workers in the present. Memories of the strike, campeño and campeña working-class life, and migration experiences have been important influences on contemporary worker mobilizations, fueling the increase in women's leadership in various union movements in the region[11] and even shaping the resistance to the 2009 military coup d'état in the banana regions.

Iris Munguía, a campeña and a high-ranking labor leader and coordinator of the Latin American–wide labor federation of banana unions COLSIBA,[12] and whose mother, Olimpia Figueroa, was a patrona who participated in the 1954 strike, remembers:

> The story that comrades have shared with us, because we had not been born yet, labor leaders and comrades, older men, used to tell stories about the strike; they told us that they lived in the barracones and that in one small room lived from 10 to 12 men. They told us their workday was 12 to 14 hours long, that there was no social security, and when they sprayed strong pesticides there was no protection, people did not last more than two or three years in that position. We also had men who were militants in leftist parties at that time [during the strike]; of course

they did it clandestinely, and that is how they thought to organize themselves. It was not easy to organize; there was great repression from the company. Those are the stories we heard from our coworkers . . . and also from Ramón Amaya Amador's book, *Prisión Verde*, which tells the story of how the transnational companies settled here. We as campeños have an obligation to read that book.[13]

Once Munguía turned 18, she began working in the banana pack-inghouses and attending meetings to hear what was going on and learn from the union leadership, mostly men; women were not vot-ing members of the union, though they were affiliated and paid dues. Agricultural workers led the union subsections, and the union hierar-chy in general, and there was no representation for the packing unit, where mostly women worked, which prevented them from voting.[14] Iris Munguía's formal training in the labor movement gave her a more extensive understanding of the strike: "As a rule we had a union train-ing on labor law, where we learned about the labor code, the right to organize a union, and in that training we also learned about the strike and why SITRATERCO was formed."[15] Now, as a leader, she conducts similar workshops on union organizing and conditions facing workers in the nation, especially after the coup. These workshops are critical for new union members. Iris also reflects on her children and how she taught them their history as campeños, and although they are university educated, they still identify with social-justice struggles: "For example, my daughter, during the coup d'état, when people marched every day, and when she saw marchers coming through La Lima from el Aguán, she went out with baskets full of water and sandwiches, from her own business, to give people."[16] Iris perceives a chain (*cadena*) of solidarity among the campeños, a social reproduction of consciousness, that is de-veloped over time and manifests in a tight-knit community that never forgets the origins of their struggles.

Gloria Garcia, a campeña and union leader, gained her first under-standing of the strike during a labor dispute when she was working in the packinghouses. The company mounted a strong anti-negotiation campaign, and that is when she remembers people talking about the strike. "I learned that it was a struggle, and people remind us that it was costly and difficult to build a union. There were so many dead, disappeared."[17]

Bartolo Fuentes, a former LIBRE party *diputado* (congressperson) for El Progreso and former student-movement leader from the 1980s, explains "el SITRATERCO nació chueco," literally meaning the union was born curved or crooked—that is, leaning toward anti-communist policies.[18] Bartolo and his wife, Dunia Montoya, a campeña, have extensively compiled archives and interviews with members of the first strike committee and other labor leaders—or, as locals call them, the original strike committee. In their analysis, those from El Progreso were seen as more radical and incorruptible than those from La Lima. Bartolo reflected on the memory of the strike, and in the process was making sense of the past; he explained that when Honduran president Zelaya was going to recognize the strike's 50-year anniversary, members of the original strike committee were dubious about attending the event. They did not want to be photographed with the second strike committee members:

> These gentlemen maintained their firmness; they said, "We cannot go to that recognition ceremony." Why? [I asked and Juan Canales answered the following] "Because so and so will be there . . . those leaders that worked with the ORIT. We cannot go there . . . we will be together and they are going to take a picture of us. In that moment I will be able to explain that we are one thing and they are another, but in the future people will see this photo, and they are going to think we are the same thing, and we are not the same thing . . ." After 50 years . . . these men were the original strike committee; they were [had been] jailed . . . [and did not forget]. The strike was not all marvel and wonderment, [workers] suffered repression, there were people captured, and they were held in captivity in Tegucigalpa for three months. Something that cost them eight years to organize was robbed from under them.[19]

Bartolo's reflections, based on his own interviews and relationship with the strike committee, perhaps explain the depth of grief and anger the original strike committee experienced after their capture, and a transmission of memory that was unresolved. At the same time, Bartolo, who did not experience the event, is making sense of their grief and anger and interprets them as *firmeza* (firmness/unwavering). Bartolo, and other descendants, have not inherited the same pain, and perhaps not the same anger, but he can relate to it and draw parallels that make sense for his own reality.

The man with whom the original strike committee did not want to be photographed was a well-known national labor leader who dedicated most of his career to the anti-communist cause, Andrés Victor Artiles. Artiles was a Liberal Party member who participated in the strike against the Standard Fruit Company and eventually climbed the ladder of the labor movement to the top, becoming Secretary General of the union from 1957 to the 1960s, and later the Secretary General of the Confederación de Trabajadores de Honduras (CTH; Confederation of Honduran Workers), a position he held for over 30 years with the support of US-sanctioned free-labor policies. Andrés Victor Artiles explains in his own testimonial:

> In my formation as a union leader, the training I received in the University of Río Piedras in Puerto Rico was important; it was sponsored by the ORIT, the AFL-CIO, and the US government. I attended in the second half of 1955. This training lasted six months . . . with the support of the FESITRANH. I attended in 1962 the "First Training of Elevated Union Studies," which was sponsored by the American Institute for the Development of Free Labor (IADSL) [Instituto Americano para el Desarrollo del Sindicalismo Libre].[20]

Artiles's very public and clear anti-communist politics were well known in La Ceiba and were manifested during his leadership of the CTH in Tegucigalpa. He claims that the free-labor union trainings he received in Puerto Rico and later in Washington, DC, did not teach him his anti-communist politics; rather, he says:

> When I returned to La Ceiba, I saw how the penetration of the communists was wreaking havoc on the union and decided to fight against them. This was not taught to me in the union trainings in Puerto Rico, because there they did not speak to us about communism; rather, I perceived with my own senses and my own intelligence.[21]

He recounts how he was friends with people he thought were communists, with some until they grew old, died, or were killed in those tumultuous years. He grew tired of the animosity against the "gringos." Artiles benefited from this point of view during the dictatorship years, as he was allowed to stay in the country and rise up as a union leader. The original strike committee lived in exile; their families were separated and their lives would never be the same again. Some of them are still in exile or died there. It is interesting that the *firmeza* of the original strike committee is rooted in a past not yet forgotten; they were not the victors. But to the younger generations, the recognition of the strike was an important act.

Former president José Manuel Zelaya Rosales, who during his first year in the presidency arranged the fiftieth-aniversary ceremony recognizing the strike, and who was later ousted during the 2009 coup, reflected on that ceremony in 2006:

> We were recognizing a historical moment in the country and its leaders. In the end, it was not important who formed part of the committee, but rather what is significant is the representation of what happened in that moment. History is not based on facts, but rather the causes and context behind those facts. Events can happen at any moment, but the cause or context that provokes actions, and how these affect events, is more important. The strike of 1954 provoked substantial changes in the daily life of the country, and it continues to have significance today in national life. It is especially important that we do not forget that this was happening during a strong [revolutionary] process in Guatemala and in the dictatorship in Honduras at that moment.[22]

Here we see the various vantage points from which memories are stored and shared. For original strike committee members, the ideals of that era were more important than a presidential recognition. To be seen with those workers, who betrayed the more radical union effort, would be a betrayal of their past and that for which they struggled and suffered. They held a collective memory of the past as a disenfranchised and incomplete victory. Meanwhile, for the ousted political leader, the past actions were more important than the actors themselves, and what came of it was important to the history of the nation as whole.

From the mid-1950s to 1980, the US State Department promoted free labor across Latin America, in efforts to combat communism. The ways in which this played out for workers meant that those perceived to be too militant or radical were hunted down and persecuted for having differing political views. The tales of the militancy associated with the strike, the fierce survival skills of the strikers, and the great organizing effort would continue to follow them. Books such as Ramón Amaya Amador's *Prisión Verde* and newspapers that were key to the organizing campaigns would come to be labeled subversive literature, and police could arrest and disappear workers caught in possession of them.[23] Barahona claims that the biggest threat for worker organizing and the potential development of a larger movement was "ideological anti-communism, which was and continues to be prevalent in wide sectors of the population, and this was the ally of the military, traditional electoral parties, and

US foreign policy."[24] But workers sustained undercurrents of memory, holding space that would resurface and be critical during contemporary strikes and land takeovers and to organizing movements, such as the Coordinadora de Resistencia Popular and its members, the Bloque Popular, in the late 1990s, as well as the resistance movement in 2009.[25]

THE WORKERS AND COLLECTIVE MEMORY

After the original strike committee was thrown in jail and harassed or exiled (Julio C. Rivera and Juan B. Canales, for instance), a new set of leaders from the Liberal Party took over the strike committee and sat down to negotiate. These leaders, adherents of free labor in favor of the ORIT's involvement, began a new era of anti-communist politics that aligned with the new military junta and emerging US Cold War politics in the region.[26] But the "oblivion" these bodies created did not stamp out leftist organizers and their efforts on the north coast. In fact, the same networks and organizing infrastructure created during the strike and in its aftermath actually propelled the agrarian reform movement and also facilitated the exchange of information and newspapers with one another and with emerging movements. The 1957 hurricane, which inundated most of the fincas of La Lima and El Progreso, affected UFCo as well as the Standard Fruit Company. Images from this catastrophic hurricane demonstrate the pervasive damage to the fincas, which provided a great excuse for the company to lay off workers and undercut the union contract. It also gave them cover to persecute progressive union leaders, such as Rivera and Canales, members of the original strike committee who had to face jail time and exile.

Despite these efforts, the memory and the work of the strike continued, one version reproduced by the union and their contentious anti-communist leaders, and another version in workers' memories, passed down to younger generations, oftentimes their own children or family members. For Lety Elvir Lazo, a poet, literature scholar, and former student leader in the 1980s, the north coast and her father's experiences as a "survivor" of the 1954 strike were a source of grounding for her consciousness. She felt implicated as a child in her father's organizing work:

> I am the daughter of one of the survivors. My father is still alive; he is 87 years old, and he participated in the 1954 strike. Since I [was old enough to] reason, this topic was common; it was spoken . . . only with friends, and trusted people when they met up. This was in the 70s . . .

the topic was as present as the air we breathed. . . . I remember very clearly at four or five years old going with my father to visit other families in other banana regions, or his friends who still worked in the bananeras, and they would sit to talk. All I know is that this topic [of the strike] was as present as the air was present. People [banana workers] shared anecdotes. They would also make comparisons between the past struggles and those happening in their present moments, always taking guidance from experiences. That struggle was their school [training] . . . people would share their memories as anecdotes.[27]

But her most vivid memories were of going to land takeovers with her father, a member of the Communist Party at the time:

My father was a man who was very committed; he continues to be. By the time of the strike, he was already linked to the Communist Party of the time. After the strike he continues to be committed, and since I was four years old I would accompany him to land takeovers. He would ask me to go play near where the police were stationed and listen in and tell him what they were saying. I did that work; I would come and tell my dad what their plans were; using bad words, they [police] would say that he was the leader and instigator and that they were going to hurt him. This land they were recuperating was not for him; it was for landless campesinos.[28]

Elvir's parents separated, and she moved to Tegucigalpa. Her father continued to be the primary source of her radicalism when she entered the student movement in the capital. She explains that politics did not truly enter her consciousness until she was in junior high at age 15. Despite the clear connection to the strike stories and memories, she felt it was like "air," which is breathed almost without thinking—it was just there, present. Her real political awakening transpired through other students in high school and her teachers, much later than her childhood memories. Lety and many other students were organizing for Honduran sovereignty and part of solidarity campaigns to support Nicaragua, which at the time was facing a revolutionary war waged by the Contras with the backing of Ronald Reagan and the CIA.

Ventura Ramos Alvarado, one of the founders of PDRH and an organic intellectual, wrote a critique of the right-wing efforts to stomp out radical student organizing in solidarity with Nicaragua through covert war:

The pressure against the people and their organizations has intensified and has amplified so much that the participation of the "Contras" of Somoza is admitted. That repressive participation is manifested in the student struggles in the university and in secondary schools, a symbiosis between Nicaraguan Somocista youth, turned fascists by the CIA, and reactionary students in Honduras, without control by respective authorities of the excesses committed.[29]

Ramos critiques the omnipresent role of the United States in the affairs of the nation:

> In Honduras, nothing of political importance moves without the consent of the United States. Our foreign policy is an echo of the voice in Washington. Development policies and decision are made by AID [USAID]. In military questions and maintaining internal order, decisions are made in the Pentagon and at the CIA, and in financial matters, everything comes through the International Monetary Fund-IMF and the banking institutions of the same nationality.[30]

In 2018, the deposed president Manuel Zelaya, looking back on his presidency, echoed the same sentiment as Ramos did in the 1980s:

> Capital is permanent; politicians are temporary. When I came to power as President of the Republic, because that is not power, [I realized that] the power continues to be in the hand of those who control the economy, those who control the weapons, international interests, which is the US Embassy.[31]

These eerie connections, between Honduras as both a source of resistance and a hub for anti-communist activists prompted by the United States, still haunt the country. Lety and the thousands of other students who organized for the liberation of Nicaragua from the hands of the Somoza family did it because they thought that this would help the Honduran movement achieve the same thing—just as the young organizers of the 1940s and 1950s exiled in Guatemala had supported the October Revolution, thinking this would aid the Honduran movement of that era. The twentieth century was a fertile period for the US right-wing agenda of anti-communism and "scorched earth" policies, particularly during the presidency of Ronald Reagan, who condoned the murder and torture of many whose bodies have not yet been found.

Honduras is caught in a historical tension between the persistence of resistance (albeit sometimes disjointed) and the legacy of murder and death, on the one hand, and those who want to suppress memories, on the other. A campesino best explained it to me when he said, "We made life out of death." He refers to the more than 500 families who have made a home on the 5,000 hectares in the community of Guadalupe Carney, which once belonged to the Regional Center of Military Training (Centro Regional de Entrenamiento Militar).[32] The location was perceived to be a place not only where Contras were trained but also where many leftists from Honduras and the rest of Central America were tortured, killed, or disappeared throughout the 1980s. Though forensic investigations have not yet been done in this region, campesinos continue to fight for the land, to protect it, and to farm it for subsistence. The community is named after Father Guadalupe Carney, who fought and lost his life for campesinos' right to arable land.

The example of post–Dirty War Uruguay is pertinent here, where Gabriela Fried Amilivia notes:

> The processes manifested in public waves of memory include generational processes in families and political communities whereby the direct witnesses of and participants in the events transmit aspects of their experiences to the young through stories, symbols, and non-narrative processes that nourish the contemporary collective emotions, forms of language, and moral judgments; intersubjective and cultural processes from the personal and intimate sphere to the public realm; and the generation by communities of memory (including memory of professionals and historians) of alternative versions of the history of the contentious period bidding for political, symbolic, and moral recognition.[33]

Many of the workers laid off during the strike continued to organize, this time to settle land and fight for agrarian reform in the north coast areas, especially in Bajo Aguán.[34] Father Guadalupe Carney, who lived and organized with campesinos, was persecuted and disappeared during the Cold War. In his autobiography, he reflected on the 1954 strike and its Marxist origins:

> Many of these Marxist workers were fired after the strike and lived as campesinos in the villages near [El] Progreso. They started in 1959, the first campesino organization, the Central Committee of Campesino

Unity, which later became the National Federation of Campesinos of Honduras (FENACH). Its principal groups were in the villages of [El] Progreso and Tela.[35]

During his parish work, Father Lupe, as he was known to locals, got to know the area well and remembers:

> After the strike, the Tela reduced the number of workers from about twenty-five thousand to twenty thousand by mechanizing many of their jobs. Some years later the Panama disease attacked many of the farms of the Tela, and they were abandoned, leaving another ten thousand workers without jobs. A large number of these fifteen thousand former workers of the Tela lived in the villages I visited. Each year the Tela would rent some of the land of the abandoned farms so that each could plant a small milpa (cornfield).[36]

The emergence of the agrarian reform movement, and its historical antecedents, can be linked to the 1954 strike, for it allowed workers, many of whom became farmers after being laid off by the company, to challenge the nation, and foreign and domestic landowners, for land tenure. Organized campesinos, many of them formerly militants of the 1954 strike and migrants from other impoverished parts of Honduras or El Salvador, defined a strategy for a movement. By then, the PDRH was broken, and the Communist Party was emerging as the organizing force in the region. Though the Great Banana Strike efforts were truncated in the moment and the original strike committee and the PDRH did not get to assist in negotiating a contract, attempts to erase them were not successful, as new generations would unearth the workers' actions and create meanings in critical moments—and in subversive ways.

Many workers intended to come to the north coast in order to make enough money to return home and buy a plot of land. The hope that staying in the north coast could lead to successful land claims kept them there, as did their rootedness to the banana regions. They did not belong in the hometowns they might have left decades ago. In John Connolly's testimony, he eloquently describes rootedness, and why the campeños and campeñas of the early 1990s fought for Tacamiche banana camps after the Tela Railroad Company closed those fincas for production and attempted to evict them. On one occasion, a buyer came to look at the land and the barracón to buy it; John responded to him:

Listen, compa—if you really want this house, you will have to enter the lottery [get in line] to get us out of here, if you have the balls to do so, because for us, a barracón like this is not only made of rustic wood, full of roaches and moths. For us, without any doubt, a barracón means the life and death of our generations, inherited by our sons and grandsons, the dark secrets of its old structure. A barracón, sir, is something like a sacred symbol to our nature. It is part of our being and our own history, so please do not come at me with that bogus claim and go back to where you came from.[37]

Eventually workers were removed from the areas and given lands elsewhere. But this struggle brought about the collaboration of various organizations in the north coast and across the nation. Once again, banana workers were standing up to the big transnational corporation. To support their claim to the land meant defending the Honduran working class from Washington, DC.

The strike was a necessary and critical moment for other important social movements and demands in Honduras; it was a moment in which Hondurans saw that they could organize and that it would be effective. Those workers who remained in the union pushed for better wages and other union benefits. While leftist strike leaders were jailed and others exiled, most banana workers remained in the campos to work and build their union after the strike, even after the 1963 coup that Ramón Villeda Morales.[38] Well into the military dictatorship, a group of progressive workers, many of them Communist Party members, set out to take the union movement back from the ORIT and free labor. These leaders, though tired from dictatorship and military rule, managed to do this by the 1970s, bolstered by a new group of young workers. The rank and file, those who continued to labor in the banana plantations, were joined by women packers in 1962, and although women did transform the work and organizing, their voices were not heard in the union halls due to hostile gender dynamics.[39] The agricultural workers, generation after generation, did the work of everyday remembering, passing down memories of the strike to their kids and to younger workers in union meetings, commemorating May 1 not only as International Worker's Day but also as the day when in 1954 workers had the boldness to organize and stand up to US foreign power. For the average worker, the strike was powerful, regardless of the political outcome. The workers in the fields spoke of it in dramatic terms that denoted power, excitement, and accomplishment at pulling it off. These workers performed the work of remembering for the next generations—even when it was prohibited and dangerous, deemed a crime to national security. These memories were further carried by many of their children, who became educated teachers, health care workers, university students, and leaders in the same labor movement.

THE COUP AND THE COMMITTED NEW GENERATION

Numerous coups d'état in Honduras have robbed entire generations of their political dreams. Several major watershed moments haunt Honduras's past with eventual losses that foreclosed possibilities for working-class advancement. In 1944, the founding of the PDRH, and its later organizing of the 1954 strike with a leftist negotiating committee, portended the birth of a new, militant, working-class movement.[40] Potential coalitions formed with and within the Liberal Party and with then-president Ramón Villeda Morales against authoritarianism, along with the second founding of the Communist Party in 1954. These opportunities for progressive transformation were forestalled by authoritarian leaders, including a military coup in 1963. Most recently, President José Manuel Zelaya Rosales, elected democratically and with large popular support, embarked on progressive and democratic reforms but was deposed by the coup d'état of 2009. Ruptures—such as coups d'état, military juntas, and the rise of authoritarian rulers—destroyed multiple political dreams, for communists and leftists, Liberal Party members, and all workers across the country. These disruptions upset political alignments among parties and political constituencies, broke faith in democracy, and led to authoritarianism and persecution of those seeking change. The history of Honduras's aspirations as a liberal and working-class democracy can be viewed as a series of disruptions, but also as important working-class resistance that persists despite those ruptures. The strike was important to the history of all Hondurans and not just the labor movement. With their actions, striking workers paralyzed the country and undermined dominant US capitalist interests. The next time this happened was in 2009, when a resistance movement arose against the coup and the meddling of the United States and its capitalist interests. The new leaders, those who rose up in ten years of protest to the illegitimate coup, have learned a version of the history of the strike from family, other leftists, and committed radical teachers—not the state.

The official history of Honduras, primarily that of the official political electoral parties, omits Marxists (and other leftists and even leftist feminists) and their striving for a different vision of democracy and equitable society. Even less is known about how the fervor generated in 1954 spurred new civic and political participation and catalyzed grass-roots organizing throughout the nation. Silences have been imposed and remain. Repression during military rule (1963 to 1980s) suppressed much of the history of the left, which was deemed a threat to national security during Ronald Reagan's Cold War, and strangled citizens' political rights in the name of weeding out the *enemigo interno* (internal enemy). Much of the history of the 1954 strike and the valiant workers who stood up to UFCo, known as *el Pulpo* (the Octopus) because of its reach in the region, has been silenced and omitted from classroom curricula at all levels and taught only in union halls and in political formation workshops given clandestinely by organizers, activists, feminists, and teachers. It was not until after the 1994 amnesty law, when leftists and exiles were allowed to return to Honduras, that texts such as Ramón Amaya Amador's *Prisión Verde* resurfaced, but much work still needs to be done to rescue working-class history.

In the previous chapters, workers of the earlier period detailed the persecution they faced for being associated with the Liberal Party or for being communists, indeed for seeking change, in the banana camps at the midcentury. Many led clandestine lives full of silences, resulting in gaps in the historical record. An organizer from the 1980s, living in the United States, told me he would never let me record a formal interview with him; he said it was too dangerous for him and for me as a Honduran scholar. I was struck that he felt he needed to maintain utter silence on his past and his experience of the remarkable legacy of the Cold War and the Honduran government's hunting down of students, activist, organizers, and communists in the Reagan era, which often led to death or exile—the other face of death, for many. Much of what we know from on-the-ground organizers of this era has been filtered through the lens of repression, and emerging only just now are their own reflections on their collective and political losses, the melancholy of what could have been. Perhaps they are right to be fearful of breaking their silence wide open. Perhaps their knowledge and a full telling of their history could still be considered dangerous to share and would bring about another round of repression. Silences surround the history of Central Americans, a heritage of clandestine organizing life since 1954—almost all of working-class Honduras has been touched by this phenomena, a result of the Cold War and US-backed state persecution. Silences, or the omission of memories or stories, have not interfered in the transmission of memories within the movement and among family. Silences, as theorized by Michel Truillot, have an "active and transitive process: one 'silences' a fact or an individual as a silencer silences a gun. One engages in the practice of silencing. Mentions and silences are thus active, dialectical counterparts of which history is the synthesis."[41] The dialectical relationship between silence and mention of the past are the moments I have asked social movement leaders to reflect on, in an attempt to understand the legacy of the 1954 strike through their remembrances. Based on their accounts and remembrances, I confront the challenges of memory, myth, influence, and legacy. The strike is memorialized alternatively as a story of hope and success and of hardship and defeat. The progress workers fought for in 1954 is an ongoing battle; the legacy of the historic moment informs various generations of present organizers and leaders, who fight not only for material gains but as a moment of defiance to US capitalism.

Descendants of the strike movement in present-day Honduras also reflect on the persecution facing the resistance of today. In 2011, a sector of the movement driven by Manuel Zelaya would form the political party Libertad y Refundación (LIBRE), while others remained committed to a nonelectoral social movement strategy because they felt that FNRP was not ready to be a party, or that the social movement bases were not yet consolidated.[42] International statistics on violence and human rights reports cite Honduras after the 2009 coup d'état as the most dangerous country in the world.[43] While the government insistently promotes the notion that violence is due to gangs and drug traffickers operating in the region, there has been a remarkable spike in violence against organizers, human rights defenders, women activists, and Indigenous people in their fight to protect their right to land and livelihoods.[44] For new generations, strategies and tactics have shifted, but the original demands remain integral and important: self-determination for the Honduran people to be free of US capital dependence and military intervention; respect for the sovereignty of the Honduran constitution, its land and water, and its people and laws; and just and fair processes of checks and balances within their government that cannot be manipulated by the US Embassy and thereby the US State Department.

On June 28, 2009, President José Manuel Zelaya Rosales was forcefully taken out of his home and flown to Costa Rica in what hours later would become evident to the international community as a politico-military coup d'état orchestrated by his own party, the Liberal Party, with ample support from the US State Department.[45] His ouster came on the heels of a forcibly aborted campaign called the Cuarta Urna (Fourth Ballot Box, or as north-coast popular sectors renamed it, La Consulta Popular), an effort to advance a plebiscite on whether to add to the November 2009 general election ballot a question on an amendment to call a constitutional assembly.[46] Before the plebiscite could take place, Zelaya was ousted by a collusion of military strongmen, conservative and corrupt government officials, and neoliberal businessmen, under the aegis of the US Embassy. What followed was a massive response from Honduran working people who spilled into the streets and workplaces in daily protest for over six months. Demonstrations of 300,000 or more people in San Pedro Sula and Tegucigalpa were impressive and had never been seen before in Honduras; the 2009 protests were even larger than the 1954 general strike. In the early days, protestors called it La Resistencia (The Resistance) and later renamed it the FNRP.[47] Since the early days, a myriad of organizations, fronts, and coalitions have emerged; the strongest are led by Indigenous and Afro-Indigenous campesinos, who are fighting against land concessions and extractive industries, such as mining corporations, dams, and charter cities (ZEDES, *Zonas de empleo y desarrollo económico*, Zone for Employment and Economic Development)—employment and economic development zones with their own judicial and law enforcement system. Miriam Miranda, Garifuna leader of the Organización Fraternal Negra Hondureña (OFRANEH; Black Fraternal Organization of Honduras), considers how the coup in Honduras served as a kind of laboratory for testing capitalists to figure out how to gain an advantage in the region:

This country has come to be a laboratory for a coup d'état that will serve as a prescription for other countries in Latin America that want to make their own decisions and take the reins in their own hands. This coup comes about in a country where there were some decisions being made that would have benefited the poor, those who are dispossessed; transcendental decisions were made and the product of that is the coup. It is like saying, hold on a minute, you cannot make decisions for yourselves; you are tied to those [decisions] coming from the outside. What we lived in Honduras in 2009 can happen in any country of Latin America, and this is why we need to fight day to day to make decisions and take the reins for ourselves. Honduras is a country in which after the coup d'état the oligarchy has positioned itself [in power] and enriched itself. The coup d'état was promoted and backed by the [US] empire; it has left us a profound constitutional crisis within which the state has opened [the country] to foreign investors as if [selling the country] were the only salvation for Honduras. . . . The [new] invention created is that of charter cities; the worst that can happen is when a government not only grants the territory to an investor but grants the possibility to make decisions [on the land] that violate sovereignty.[48]

Control of the land has become so important that military police have led multiple attacks against Garifuna and Indigenous campesinos, who are perceived to be "in the way" of the model of development constructed in postcoup neoliberalism.[49] On March 6, 2016, protecting natural resources of the Gualcarque River cost Berta Cáceres, Lenca Indigenous leader and founder of COPINH, her life; she was killed by armed men working for Desarollos Energéticos SA (DESA). The coup has made Honduras an arena of murder and death as well.

The coup d'état changed Hondurans' lives, in all aspects. For contemporary social movement leaders, it was important not only to challenge and denounce the coup but also to provide leadership and structure to the protest that emerged. José Manuel Zelaya Rosales, the deposed president and now head of the LIBRE Party, links the legacy of the strike to the coup:

> The strike of 1954 happens when the world is in a bipolar state. That response of the people to capitalism in the bananeras, which exploited them, [forcing them to live] without rights, with excessive hours of work, without recognizing them—the reaction of the people is against the system. Don't look at it as [just] a strike; look at it as an emancipation of the people looking to live in this world. We all have the right to equality. . . . This is the same in 2009, an emancipation of a people against a system that oppressed [them].[50]

Politicians can always make something connect and sound good, and Zelaya is certainly a politician, but this linking of public memory, as he is doing here, is interesting—it speaks to the overall memory of the strike as transcendental for the nation, not just because of its outcome but also because it came from disenfranchised workers standing up to the giant, the banana companies, and US capitalist interests.

On the north coast, the banana unions and organizations, such as SITRATERCO and COSIBAH—now renamed Federación de Sindicatos de Trabajadores de la Agroindustria (FESTAGRO; Agro-Industry Federation of Workers)[51]—and other local organizations with a past in the banana industry, such as Radio Progreso (formerly owned by UFCo), were at the forefront of protest and mobilization. The strike of 1954 was being remembered in everyday ways. "We haven't seen so many people in the street since '54," was commonly expressed among people in La Lima, El Progreso, and La Ceiba, cities that were also sites of massive protests against the coup.[52] As the protests in the streets continue, and the resistance has evolved into other forms of opposition to the current regime originated by the coup, the north coast continues as a site of working-class protest and resistance today, with workers engaged both at the union level and in the larger movement. At the same time, US intervention has been a persistent force in recent Honduran history and has left an indelible mark in the region, which continues to haunt protest and resistance actors.

Social movements, and their actors, have memory. The memories social movement actors transmit from generation to generation of earlier forms of protest and resistance persist, even when every effort has been made to erase the memory of that resistance. "Memory" is the appropriate term here rather than "history," because the strike has been erased from the official record. It is not taught in school as a part of formal textbook curricula, and many books, newspapers, and pamphlets that describe its legacy, or anything to do with workers or organizing, were banned for most of the twentieth century, considered subversive literature. The memory of the 1954 strike has informed social actors in the subsequent decades in multiple ways. First, the strike left an important legacy for the labor movement and related movements by creating avenues for voicing and seeking redress on labor issues by establishing the right to organize. In addition to enabling the birth of the labor movement and cementing the Ministry of Labor, the strike also birthed the contemporary Communist Party, establishing an alternative project for the country during the period. The strike was influential to working-class women, campeñas who worked alongside banana workers in the trenches, as they participated in and benefited from the movement in the public sphere, unlike the middle-class and elite women's movement for suffrage. Contemporary generations of workers and union leaders have been passed down memories about victory in resistance to US capitalism, which offer hope and show the way for civil society to reignite demands against dictatorship and other national injustices. Remembrances of heroic valor among workers are laced consistently with memories of persecution, injustice, and violence.

Shortly after the strike, and once the union contract was signed, there was a coup d'état in 1963, ousting a democratically elected president and bringing about two decades of military dictatorship. The strike movement and the founding of the new Communist Party represented a moment of possibility couched between two dictatorship periods. The return to a liberal democracy was a process heavily influenced by the US State Department during the Cold War period. But Hondurans remember the strike and the year 1954 as a time of possibility. For the youth of today, it stands out as a legitimate revolutionary experiment in history—perhaps one that failed in its revolutionary mission, but one from which they could learn. Gerardo Torres reflects, "I never saw it through the eyes of an individual hero; I think I saw it as a process of organizing: I [wanted to know]: How did people organize and liberate themselves with their own hands? . . . But I also wanted to know about the PDRH: why had something so strong broken so easily, why had it fallen apart after the strike?"[53] As discussed in chapter 5, the original strike committee was thrown in jail, and another strike committee was chosen in a rushed election, sanctioned by the Honduran government in collusion with the ORIT and the US Embassy. Still, the first strike committee is remembered for their organizing success within UFCo. The younger generations I spoke with look to this David-and-Goliath story as a source of inspiration, as they themselves now craft radical political resistance to the present regime.[54]

The memory of the strike of 1954 has been transformed over time and taken up by younger generations. The term campeño/a today connotes not just people from the banana regions but in particular those who organized a strike that shook the nation and a powerful transnational company. The memory of their parents and grandparents surviving by eating boiled green bananas when staple foods ran out constitutes an important narrative, a narrative that memorializes not only the strike itself but also the everyday individual family's experience of the strike. This was a family history of hardship, a memory passed down among campeños, and indeed anywhere you go in the banana towns of Honduras, such as La Lima and El Progreso, and in the campos; people more or less can speak of the strike and tell common narratives. As the banana regions have been shrinking due to the companies' flight after closing fincas in the aftermath of Hurricane Mitch (1998) and Tropical Storm Gamma (2005), under the aegis of a new global capital order, and given workers' own migration to the United States, how is it that the 1954 banana strike got passed down to youth outside of the banana regions? How did the strike become important to emerging leftist and youth movements? To understand this I want to end with a focus on the "critical moments" that demonstrate what Gabriela Fried Amilivia calls "undercurrents" in the preservation of memory, where "layers of memory . . . [persist] and generate social space and subjectivity."[55] The layers of Honduran memory are best seen in the following critical moments: the student movement in the second half of the twentieth century, the roaring 1990s, and the 2009 coup.

A critical link between the strike and youth movements is the so-called *generación de los ochenta* (generation of the eighties), a diverse sector of civil society consisting of campesino, labor union, and student leaders who together form a cohort of radicals and revolutionaries, engaged in clandestine organization and sometimes even armed struggle. This cohort was critical to resurfacing the memories of the 1954 strike, yet their clandestine activities make their stories dangerous to document, a project that merits longer meditation and reflection in a scholarly analysis of its own. These actors, at the intersection of class and political sectors, formed the foundation of the movements we are seeing emerge in Honduras presently. The coalitional efforts that emerged in the second half of the twentieth century were complicated, sometimes tenuous and sometimes contentious; the forging of the left in Honduras is still a project under construction.

Bartolo Fuentes, a former student organizer in the 1980s and now a leader in the LIBRE party, says knowing the history of the 1954 strike has served as a lesson for organizing in the north coast:

> The 1954 strike and the resistance against the coup d'état, what is the big difference? The movement in 1954 was usurped by one party [Liberal Party], which has no major worker participation, and a movement arises that is controlled by the transnationals—the union movement comes out ideologically controlled by the transnationals. And the resistance [after 2009] is the opposite—there is resistance because a social movement exists; it's the other way around: without the social movement we had there would have never been a resistance to the coup d'état. We had been organizing actions for many years with the Coordinating Body of the Popular Resistance [Coordinadora de Resistencia Popular], which was formed in 2003. The lessons from the strike that helped us in those moments [when founding the resistance movement in 2009], at least for me, because I actually met the comrades who were leaders of the original strike committee and, after listening to their

testimonies, was seeing how they ended up—that their efforts were exploited by others, and not by the party they founded. So now we have a party founded by us—a party in construction, I am clear on that—but it is a party; it is an instrument.[56]

Bartolo's reflections remain hopeful, positive, and grounded in lessons for the future, even in the current context: since the 2017 elections, his party has been working in coalition with other opposition parties against authoritarian rule. One clear lesson from the strike was the importance of having a clearly demarcated leadership in the organization or party when working in coalitional settings, in order to prevent outside control. But this is tough in the era of social media, with the dispersion of organizations, competing interests, and severe repression against organizers.

A new generation of resistance actors, such as Bartolo, emerged after the 2009 coup d'état. There was clear break with bipartisan politics, and, more importantly, the protests and organizing ignited La Resistencia, later FNRP, and eventually LIBRE, a new political party. Above all it ignited a clearer proposal for Indigenous and Afro-Indigenous rights. The generation of 2009, the young organizers who were students during the 2009 coup d'état, present an even more exciting and dynamic repository of the memory of the strike; they have inherited knowledge about organizing from the past but do not feel tied to the anguish and loss of it.[57]

The FNRP social movement and its political party LIBRE fit into the long trajectory of a social movement that began with the 1954 strike, one in the process of formation, with many internal and external contradictions. New players, younger organizers, are constantly disrupting the old order and redefining ideological beliefs and practices. The days after the coup d'état brought together diverse sectors of the population in immediate response; people marched shoulder to shoulder, sharing the streets and standing up against repression. The fervor of the movement in those days, the impassioned meetings and the coalition work, demonstrated that coalitional work was possible. Once the process of social change began, it could not be turned back; the loss of fear could not be turned back, the knowledge of what was possible through collaboration could not be turned back; consciousness could not be turned back. The process must simply roll forward. Berta Cáceres, in a speech given 51 days after the coup, explains:

It is a reality that the Honduran people have built a resistance movement that surpassed and surpasses any leadership, all organizations, all spaces we once knew as powerful, both regionally and nationally. It surpassed all of that and demanded, concretized a clear and energetic struggle, a dignified struggle, and that is the lesson for us in social and political movements. We did not understand the dimensions of what would come; we did not have much space to consciously analyze the advances President Zelaya was promoting—for example, the pressure that he put on intermediaries, those who have benefited from thermal energy, the entering into the ALBA [Alianza Bolivariana para los Pueblos de Nuestra América (Bolivarian Alliance for the Americas)], the incorporation of PetroCaribe, the advances in agrarian reform, the veto of the congress-approved prohibition of the contraceptive pill, well, the many advances that we witness—but we did not see that in Honduras we have an aggressive oligarchy under the tutelage of the gringo and European transnational companies. . . . They are also responsible not only for the coup d'état but also for the murders, the torture, the imprisonment, the repression against the people of Honduras, all for that project of capitalism, that predator capitalism.[58]

Cáceres's words are reflective, if not in awe, of the resistance movement forming against the coup that year. But she is also circumspective, which now, ten years later, reads like an ominous prediction of the challenges the resistance movement would face over the years—the largest internal disagreement was the decision to go from the streets, where a social movement from below was growing, to the electoral ballot box, forming into a new political party.[59] Cáceres also courageously offered a vision at that moment of a new kind of social movement, one that would center the struggles of those on the margins:

We must dream of a constitution that unseats other systems of domination: patriarchy, not only capitalism. They are really afraid that we are not afraid to propose that the rights of women should be constitutional rights, that we also are clear that racism is a form of domination and that we need unseat it.[60]

These words, from a powerful woman leader, as Berta Cáceres was, resonated in every sector of society, but most importantly among students from secondary school to college, especially poor, disenfranchised students, many of whom make up the current resistance movement of today. Cáceres provides an acute analysis of the national moment and pushes listeners to think more comprehensively about the nation. This is an important characteristic of social movement organizers in Honduras—where local struggles reverberate at the national or international level. The nation was up in revolt over the kidnapping and exile of the democratically elected president, and even the most radical leftist sectors embraced the ousted liberal president as an opportunity to fight for broader change in the country, to refound it.

When disparate sectors of society, such as Garifuna communities, campesinos, feminists, and transgender women, came together to protest the coup d'état, they did not share the same strategies or tactics as the 1954 organizers, except perhaps that they were all also the targets of state violence or had a long history of exclusion. But the possibility of coalitional work surfaced again, brought on precisely by their own groups' intersectionality, which was easily transformed into action and organization against the backdrop of the extreme violence inherent in the neoliberal state.

Garifuna communities, who faced displacement and racial discrimination years before the 2009 coup, emerged as leaders of the resistance movement against the coup and of the Afro-Indigenous movement, and when asked to reflect on the 1954 strike movement, Dr. Luther Castillo Harry, whose grandparents lived through the strike, remembers that he learned about the strike at an early age from his grandparents:

The first we heard of the 1954 strike was what our elderly grandparents told us. They narrated that history when they talked among themselves, when they would talk about the process of organizing and the social struggles, their incorporation into the struggle. They told these stories at a level they understood but always with the consequence that they were always on the side of the cause, on the side of workers, of the protests, and coherently in support of dignified work. . . . Later I got more context about our history with Erasmo Zúñiga Sambula; I managed to talk with him when I went to La Ceiba to study my first years in high school, in 1992 or 1993. I was a kid, and I became really interested in the origins of the Black Fraternal Organization of Honduras (OFRANEH) that was founded by these pioneers, and one of them was Erasmo Zúñiga Zambula. He was an eloquent man in his discourse and was also a good poet. It was beautiful to hear him speak about poetry, and he would also speak about the strike of 1954, including the origin of the OFRANEH, which was organized by those men who worked on the pier of La Ceiba with the banana companies. The organization was a product of the humiliation and injustices that they lived there, people unloading and loading those bananas without shirts, without any protection, those abuses that occurred there, and a product of their involvement in the struggle, as a historical legacy of the strike of 1954, with that effervescence they had, what they learned from their ancestors. From the 1954 strike comes the creation in 1975 of the OFRANEH, the first organizations that united the entire Garifuna community. These men had such an organizing skill, a product of the 1954 strike, so for us it was like the genesis of everything, this is what we heard, and it was more than reading about it; it is passed from generation to generation.[61]

When asking younger organizers about the strike and whether or not they were influenced by it in their own organizing, many of them consider the campeños not just as inspiration but as superheroes. Gerardo Torres reflects:

My parents' generation did not have it easy when they were growing up. It was the Honduras of the sixties, seventies. To speak of *Prisión Verde*, it meant to speak of a legacy, of a history, and a bit to speak of hope. It was to see that things could be done, that it was possible, despite everything that was happening at that moment in their [his parents'] lives: the military dictatorship, the persecution of campesino organizations, the failure of the armed organizations. In those moments, and I am talking of the seventies and eighties, when they [his parents' generation] were surrounded by four armies: the US Army, the Honduran armed forces, the counterrevolutionaries from Nicaragua on the eastern front, and the Salvadoran army on the western front. So, to speak of the strike of 1954 was to speak of a dream of what had been in Honduras and the possibility of what Honduras was capable of if we organize again like they did in the 1950s. [An organized campeño] was someone I could relate to; he was like me—he was a Honduran who had had to live in a Honduras that was the property of the United States, where Hondurans felt like they were renting their little bit of land. But that campeño went through an organizing process, and that is the key for me about the 1954 strike. Because of our skin color, our hue . . . I imagined the campeño was like my father, or myself when I got older. What made the campeños different was their organization, and it got in my head, ever since I was a child, that it is possible to develop a process of popular organizing and organization. If people organized, they could always liberate themselves by their own hands. In 2009 people used to say, if we manage to organize we could have a strong political expression, as strong as what we had in 1954.[62]

The new generation is different, younger, and not only masculine but also composed of women and gender-nonconforming individuals. The diversity of La Resistencia gives it a dynamic position among the new social movements in the region. FNRP overall demonstrated its coalitional character, allowing for participation of multiple sectors with international dimensions. But more importantly, members of generations two or three times removed from the strike, like Gerardo, a journalist, are reconstructing its memory, studying its failures, and processing the divisions in leadership. They are looking back but also looking forward. The strike represented a moment of hope and an opportunity for workers, for leftists, and for civil society to reignite demands for participatory democracy and against US empire. This strike is a movement that they could see themselves reflected in and even look up to, as Gerardo explains:

> I grew up with the legends they told me about in the Bible, and the legends they told me about the strike of 1954, two points of hope. It felt like a mythical legend—the creation of revolutionary newspapers, the youths who organized with campeños in the fincas, the clandestine reading of newspapers in clandestine groups—to imagine an oppressed people that organized for their liberation. That was a heroic strike. They [campeños] were legendary figures, I imagined fantastic revolutionaries. Like my parents said, they were the greatest expression of a human being.[63]

Gerardo's reflections on the organizing demonstrates how early he entered the movement and became an organizer himself, recognizing the efforts of his predecessors to organize, and how they did it. For example, when he reflects on "the clandestine reading of newspapers in clandestine groups," he refers to the Marxist newspapers that were banned by the Carías Andino regime and heavily policed by local company-paid security. He also reflects on the workers' will to organize and what it took for them to prepare themselves. His keen admiration for the organizing process, despite the extreme oppression, is an important takeaway for him, as he is also in the process of organizing. Indyra Mendoza Aguilar, great-granddaughter of Zoroastro Montes de Oca, grew up with stories about him that seemed like great adventures:

When I was a child, my grandmother and grandfather would tell stories of their livelihoods or their family members; for me they were fantastical stories, stories that still float in my head and that I have had to share with new generations. But at the time I did not quite understand that those ordinary actions were extraordinary for many people.[64]

In reality, the workers and leftist organizers they both refer to were not mythical but rather part of an organized political project and something to aspire to be, to inspire the current context. This parallel vision of past and present is relevant today because there has not been a process of vindication for workers, neither for Gerardo's mom in the 1980s, nor for Indyra's grandfather in the first half of the twentieth century, nor in their own struggles against the coup d'état of 2009 and the stolen elections of the LIBRE party in 2017 or the extrajudicial murders facing lesbian, gay, and transgender people in the country.[65]

Although various generations have different stakes in the memory of the strike and connections to it, they all experienced it, though differently, as an important moment of possibility and audacious might for the working class. Gerardo's recounting of the strikers as superheroes and mythical figures also speaks to the transmission of memories of admiration for those who stood up to the foreign-owned US companies. To do the work of organizing at the time was an act of valor against a giant; it was almost impossible.

THE WORK OF MEMORY

Keeping the memory of the 1954 strike alive has been hard work, especially because members of the original strike committee were imprisoned or exiled as military rulers ushered in a period of anti-communism and a national security state at war with an internal enemy.[66] The losses of the left in the 1950s led social actors, the working class, to enter into a process of mourning that, as David Scott reminds us, works in two ways: as "remains—memory traces through which the mourner both lets go and internalizes the lost object," and as a practice of "reparative remembering."[67] Mourning, both as remains and practice, and memories of the past have led to a surfacing of new passions, new struggles, new movements, and new efforts made continuously by newer generations because, as David Scott reminds us, "in a somewhat paradoxical way . . . political ideas are founded on object loss."[68] Thus through this process, and despite repression and omission from the national narrative, the organizing strategies and tactics of the campeños and campeñas in the

1950s served as a lesson in organizing, passed down to current organizers, both in the union and in the social movement at large, and served as important inspiration for their own organizing goals and challenges.

When Iris Munguía was of school age, in the late 1960s and early 1970s, she attended the company schools, where they did not study the strike of 1954. While in school in the camps, she would hear that the banana workers were in session (meaning union meetings) and was curious to know what happened in meetings. She explains that they did not learn about the 1954 strike in the company schools because "the school teachers were paid for by the company, and not the union; if the union ran the schools, we would have gotten a totally different history."[69]

Labor leader Carlos H. Reyes, president of the Sindicato de Trabajadores de la Industria de la Bebida y Similares (STIBYS; Union of Beverage Industry and Allied Workers) and a leader of the FNRP, reflects on the strike of 1954, when in his youth he led a campaign to support the striking workers:

> In 1954, I was in secondary school at the Central Institute for Boys; I was the treasurer of the Red Cross Club in school, and I was in charge of collecting money for the [1954] strike. What did we collect? Small coins . . . I was 14 years old. The principal called me in one day and asked, "Who told you to collect money for the strike?" I told him I did not make the decision alone but that the group did because we had to help those poor people—they need food. The principal said that is not something that corresponds to the Red Cross. I told him we agreed to do this as a group. The principal then told me, "You know what? I think what you are is a communist." . . . I did not even know what a communist was. I did not say either yes or no . . . all I said was that the group decided and we would continue collecting money. We were not harming anyone. . . . We continued the collection, we gave it to someone they [the strikers] sent to pick it up, and we sent it. We did not raise great quantities—what we raised were cents, but those cents were worth something back in the day.[70]

Carlos Humberto Reyes was 14 years old at the time, and after graduating from school, he went to work for a bottling company, where he worked for over 40 years and where he became union president and leader of one of the union federations in 1959. In his union, they developed popular educational teaching materials for rank-and-file members:

> We develop a set of notebooks . . . precisely to train workers on class
> consciousness because if we do not have ideological training, we be-
> come economists or reformists. We have a series of notebooks where
> we teach the strike of 1954. We do workshops—just recently we had a
> training with 70 workers, and we also invited workers from all over the
> nation; we invited workers from the Standard Fruit union [Dole] and
> Sitrabarimasa union [Dole] from the banana camps. We engage the topic
> of what produces—the work and not capital.[71]

The training is comprehensive and comprises 15 notebooks of courses,
and it combines ideology with pragmatic workshops on how to run a
union and perform its various functions, as well as how to deal with
supervisors. For Carlos, this work is a continuity of the 1954 struggle;
it has always been present in his life. In 1965 he led two powerful and
massive strikes, for which he was politically persecuted and imprisoned
for 51 days for one and imprisoned 14 days for the other, accused of
being an enemy of the state. He says, "Undoubtedly when you are going through that [persecution], one relives, or imagines, what that strike
was like, though now in different contexts."[72]

Those who learned about the strike as adolescents did so through
committed community organizers, teachers, and professors who
brought this curriculum from the streets into the classroom. Lety Elvir Lazo, though raised in the banana fincas, came of age and into
her political consciousness in Tegucigalpa, where she was thrust into
organizing:

> I got to the Instituto Central Vicente Cáceres in 1979, and Central
> America was in the midst of a revolution, all of which stemmed from
> the Cold War. In my school there were posters of young women hold-
> ing guns—it impressed me and moved me. . . . I saw the war as tempo-
> rary. I was well aware that there was no option because we had to end
> the dictatorship of Somoza. The principal of the institute would give us
> permission to go to the popular protest. Thousands of students partici-
> pated in protests, 3,000 students at the time. . . . By age 15, I was clearly
> a self-possessed young woman; I was talking to teachers and adults
> about national politics. . . . I am sure it has to do with my childhood in
> the north coast [banana regions].

While school curricula lacked a history of the strike, committed teachers and older students passed on lessons and brief historical

anecdotes—"little bits," as Lety, who was about to become a teacher, right after high school, referred to them:

> I got to know the plans of study [curriculum] around 16 or 17 years old; I was about to graduate as a teacher of primary education, and we had to elaborate plans for teaching classes, but I do not remember these topics. I do not remember exactly. . . . But I do remember learning about it in texts in the university, where some professors taught the strike. The only thing is that it was little bits—a quick study, as fast as a bird passes—about the strike. We read the novel *Prisión Verde*. The novel taught us more, and maybe [there was] a little paragraph [about the strike] in high school.[73]

It was not until she co-founded the Movimiento Estudiantil Progresista (MEP; Progressive Student Movement) in her school, that the strike was studied historically and ideologically:

> For example, in the MEP, we had trainings where the students would come together and study the history of Honduras. Teachers would also participate in this program we did in the student movement in high school or in the university.[74]

Lety had multiple exposures outside of her home. Her dad was an activist, but she mostly attributes her knowledge of the strike to committed teachers who were involved in the union movement and would share many things about labor history with the class.

Gilberto "Grillo" Ríos, a LIBRE organizer, also comes from a family committed to the social movements, and while in the university he belonged to a group called *Los Necios*:

> In high school, the social studies teacher would include these topics in the lesson plan because she was an ally to social movements. The materials were not school textbooks; they were pamphlets and fliers from the popular movement that she would give us. There were always rumors of the strike of 1954 because of the massiveness of the organized workforce, but we did not give it the historical importance that it truly merited. In 1994, good work was done to bring together the survivors, the fighters, so they could give their testimony of how they had organized the strike, and forums were organized in the university that we as students could attend.[75]

Though Gilberto was lucky to have been in school during the 40-year anniversary of the strike and to have had progressive teachers and professors, in these spaces instances of celebration and recognition of the strike were few and far between, and definitely not part of the country's official history.

For Garifuna communities, disenfranchised historically from the education and welfare services of the state for years, getting to school was nearly impossible. Even in school, the subject of the strike was never taught, as Dr. Luther Castillo Harry, who worked in the Ministry of Foreign Relations during the Zelaya administration and was the founder of the first Garifuna hospital in Ciriboya, Colón, explains:

> We did not have classes on the [history] of the strike in school or in high school. But I lived in Tocamacho, which is next to La Mosquitia and very far away. It is a rural community without electricity or roads; the only way to leave there is by boat, small boats, and the journey took a full day or more than 24 hours to get to La Ceiba. These boats would go to La Ceiba to bring back merchandise to sell [in the town], and that was the only way to travel because there were no roads. . . . We'd sleep in the little boat, more than 24 hours to get there. Similarly, sometimes it took 36 hours or three or four days to get back to town from La Ceiba. . . . The other option was to walk 12 hours on the beach to get close to Limón, then to Limoncito, another 14–16 hours walking, to get to the bus stop to take the bus to the city. . . . But I do not remember that in school, or in any class where teachers talked about the strike of 1954. All that history for us was orally transmitted by the grandparents who worked there [in the banana plantations] and participated in the struggle [strike of 1954].[76]

The popular movement was heavily repressed beginning in 1963, due to military dictatorial rule. Essential texts such as *Prisión Verde* were banned from the country, alongside the key organizing newspaper *Vanguardia Revolucionaria*, both of which were published not in Honduras but in Mexico and Guatemala. Still, the lessons of the strike were passed on to younger generations, as organizers shared their experiences and recollections. New versions of the newspapers were reborn in student movements each decade. But state abandonment of working-class poor communities, like the Garifuna community, also served as a silent form of violence and stifled the opportunities for communities and their youth to learn about their past, their resilience, and leadership in formal ways. Indyra Mendoza Aguilar, lesbian leader and pioneer in the country, remembers how she learned about her great-grandfather, one of the founders of the first Communist Party in Honduras, Zoroastro Montes de Oca:

> [A] few decades ago, my grandmother María would always tell us stories of her father Zoroastro Montes de Oca, but all the people called him "camarada." She would tell us how he gave speeches that would make people cry, speeches based on labor rights that the company refused workers, and how the working class was exploited. Of the many times he was imprisoned [one stands out]—the time he was taken to the wall [execution wall], and the head of the guards let him live, and he went home unshaven because of the number of days he was in jail, and while walking on the street they asked him, "Where are you going, camarada?" He responded, "Headed to be shot again." . . . In early 1954 he was detained again, and as his release letter explains, he was accused of insults against the National Congress.[77]

The passing down of oral stories—and cultural meanings—happened in person from the elderly to the young—mostly boys, but some women too.

While the rescue of historical memory of the Honduran leftist and revolutionary social movement is still incomplete, memories of the strike's mobilization have been transmitted from worker to worker and to their offspring. Though seemingly individual moments of remembering, these are in actuality instances of collective recollection that have been useful to younger generations organizing now. They have also served to radicalize workers in the union movement; even if the memories are told in broad strokes, they are symbolic and important. These narratives, seemingly mundane to the outsider, are actually highly nuanced moments of transference of memories to younger generations of workers through everyday forms of communication, and sometimes through secrets and silences.[78] Dunia Montoya, a journalist and a campeña, recalls that it was her father who socialized her on the history of the 1954 strike: "In school they shared very little. My father influenced me [about the strike of 1954]; in high school I would also read *Prisión Verde*, but not in the Tela Company school. My father was very close to the SITRATERCO union and the teacher's union, and he dedicated his life to the party, he had a very strong role in the party [Communist Party]."[79]

Gerardo, who was exiled in the United States as child with his mother, a labor leader in the teacher's union movement, grew up understanding the symbolism of the strike as it was taught in his home:

I first read [Prisión Verde] when I was little. Once I learned to read, I read Prisión Verde on my own. I must have been seven or eight years old. The only books I had available to me in Spanish were Prisión Verde; Cuando las Tarántulas Atacan, by Longino Becerra; and the Bible. In my home they taught us to read when we were very little. My grandfather, an important figure in my life, would make us read between one and 15 pages a day. It just so happens that Prisión Verde is one of the first books I read.[80]

For Lety and Dunia, who grew up on the north coast, and Gerardo, who grew up in Tegucigalpa, they inherited memories from their parents who were involved in unions and leftist parties. They relied on knowledge passed down through the family unit and were taught to read Prisión Verde, not only as text, but as lived experience as it was identified with and embraced as the country's history of workers' lives and the transnational companies. The inheritors, Lety, Dunia, Gerardo's parents, and their offspring, have remolded and renewed, or even repeated, the well-known and accepted narratives about the strike, added their own twists, and have used the past to make sense of their own memories. Lety's and Dunia's fathers and Gerardo's grandfather loom large in their memories most associated with the strike, linking the strike with masculine, paternal figures and the leftist parties or the Communist Party. Though Gerardo's mom was the exiled labor leader, the masculinity associated with the strike remains stable in his memories. Union members, sons and daughters of banana workers, and those who still live in the campos continue to keep the memory open to remold it for newer generations, as they do the conventional narratives of masculinity and race reviewed in previous chapters.

To tell the past was important and served as a form of intentional organizing work among the rank and file, students organizing in high schools and universities, and other activists and organizers who were in solidarity with workers in the 1950s. Campeños proudly shared their firsthand knowledge with their children and fellow younger workers. These stories were also shared in wonderment, recalling their audacity in managing to pull it off, as Lety hints: "I remember my father laughing a lot with his friends, other workers. . . . I knew it was something special, that to talk about it [the strike] was a happy thing—it was optimistic."[81] In this way, memories of the 1954 strike in Honduras have encouraged younger generations to believe in organizing, and through this collective process, these memories have nurtured the belief in the possibility to create change, influencing visions of contemporary political and social movements.

The memories of social movement actors are germinated in previous struggles and foundational events, and they resurface when deemed necessary by the people and their demands. Memory, "the temporal site of mourning,"[82] is critical to the formation of new ideas about the past; memory allows for David Scott's theory of "reparative remembering," which is important to obtaining realistic outcomes,[83] where a collective or social actor incorporates lessons learned—and, more importantly, skills and assessments about the past—and learns from them to identify what is possible and realistic, and also when to keep pushing forward. The ongoing construction of a base of knowledge about movement organizing, over time and through generations, is an important factor in our understanding of contemporary dynamics in Honduras and our explanations of the persisting need and demand for justice in the face of authoritarianism and military rule.

There is a struggle in Honduras, not unlike other places that have seen civil strife, between those who want to remember and those who prefer to forget. The forms of authoritarian military governments throughout much of the twentieth century in Honduras have transitioned into neoliberal and neoconservative regimes, where elite leaders wield power—arguably as dictatorially as past military juntas. Despite their participation in the peace process marking the end of civil war in the region in 1987—namely, the Esquipulas II Peace Agreement—the Honduran state and its two main parties, the Liberales and Nacionalistas, have not done the work of transforming their actions to fully respect human rights or the will of the people in the nation. They have simply and easily transitioned from a war state to a neoliberal state, with new forms of everyday violence sanctioned by capitalists and global economic interests, such as femicide and *mano dura* policies (firm hand) against gangs and youth, both of which affected the working class.[84] Simply put, the right, thanks in large part to its ties to global capitalist interests in the United States and Canada, has thrived following the 1980s civil-war period in Honduras. The capitalist elite in Honduras operate from a collective amnesia about their own past, much less aware of opposition struggles, and in direct contradiction to the persistence of the memory of the working class.

The elite capitalist class, and the military that sustains it, has not done the work of memory and, in fact, has gotten in the way of those who attempt to do it—namely, the working class of the north coast and others who remember the years of repression against workers and the retrenchment of a military dictatorship, in spite of suppression and a narrative of silence enforced by the state. Imposed silence made remembering mandatory. Memory and the processing of what happened and why have not been beneficial to the emerging global capital system, which seeks rapid development policies that do not include benefits for or accommodate the aspirations of disenfranchised people, or they address them only nominally. The neoliberal state urges everyone to forget the past and start anew, but insisting that the same oligarchic and family structures of the past should remain in power.[85] The state does not honor the past strike or the campeños' history because corrupt leaders, including military leaders, cover up their actions, and with it, the history of the state. An example of this can be discerned in the incomplete records of UFCo on Honduras, or the incomplete and almost nonexistent records on the national railroad. When I arrived at the National Railroad building in San Pedro Sula, I realized that not only are there no records for 1954, there are no records at all. I was later told that whenever a president of the national railroad left, it was customary for the records to be burned inside one of the metal train carriages—a customary practice to cover up wrongdoing or corruption by the outgoing administration. Sometimes the incoming president would burn papers to get rid of all that paper and mess. In 2011, two years after the coup d'état, I was pulled out of the judicial archives in La Ceiba, Atlántida, and questioned by its local director, who looked more like a military operative than an attorney of the court. In the Municipal Archives of San Pedro Sula, I endured sexual harassment and was unable to consult the police records of the 1950s, or any record that would be useful to me; instead the archive director gave me photocopies of records given to him by other US historians. At one point he cornered me in a dusty corner, near old microfilm machines. Later, the secretary, who had been out to lunch at the time, warned me to use only the archive when she was there, for safety. I learned he does this to all the women of color who come seeking archival records for their research projects. The archive director would not let me consult any other records I wanted to see without a letter from the mayor approving it, a very different response than most of my male colleagues received. A deeply patriarchal society like Honduras, where abuse of power is built into these posts granted based on party affiliation, often has missing, or hidden, records and gatekeepers, making the memories of the working class even more valuable in a postcoup Honduras. Records are dangerous when a state is corrupt and authoritarian—they tell truths.

Memory requires an investment of labor to exist; either it is recognition of collective trauma (or individual trauma) due to the past, or it is "worked through" in the process of mourning, to become informative for the present.[86] If it is not worked through, it may suffer repetition, or as Elizabeth Jelin calls it, "acting out," where oppressive military regimes repeat actions and do not allow a grieving process for the people most affected, or any acknowledgment, and therefore little institutional change and true progress can occur.[87] For the working class, memory involves multiple forms of grieving losses, both collectively and individually. As Jelin asserts, "At the collective level, the big challenge is to overcome repetitions, to surmount silences and political abuses, to simultaneously be able to distance from and promote active debate and reflexivity about the past and its meaning for the present/future."[88]

The working class of the banana sectors, and the various leftist groups that saw their hopes flushed away with the first strike committee, those who radicalized the region in Honduras in 1954, hold space for remembering despite repression, hoping to achieve justice and also redirect politics.[89] The working class has also played an important role in the work of memory to seek justice, at critical moments, in what Gabriela Fried Amilivia calls "waves of memory."[90] During moments of repression, this allows for the "irruption of memories," in "undercurrents," at the intersection with public politics, as Fried Amilivia explains:

Maurice Halbwachs has defined a *current* of memory as a plurality of coexisting collective memories, thus conceptualizing the space in which individual freedom and agency can articulate a diversity of experiences and ideas in the intersection of a plurality of groups, emphasizing their heterogeneity. The notion of *undercurrents*, undeveloped in Halbwachs's work, accurately describes the invisible sources of nonpublic memory processing that takes place in the intersection with public politics. That intersection is not entirely controlled by the political process, thus allowing one to visualize other realms (or layers) of memory in society: the psychosocial, symbolic, and cultural processes being negotiated.[91]

In Fried Amilivia's undercurrent scenarios, memories are held perhaps in silences and secrets. Their resurgence is a product of key intersectional moments, where the demands to protest an authoritarian regime may allow for the remembrance of what happened. The demand for truth about what happened and the demand for justice may be transmitted to younger generations through these undercurrents, through gaps and silences, or through key moments of protest and organizing, or through secrets in the family.[92]

Drawing on Fried Amilivia's insights on the intergenerational transmission of memories, I apply this concept to the narrative of Honduras by looking at Carlos's, Lety's, Dunia's, Grillo's, and Gerardo's memories. The loci of this transmission are, first, the generation that lived through these events in their formative years and passed down their knowledge to younger generations from their own experiences, and, second, "the way the transmission is received, acknowledged, and transformed—metabolized or digested, so to speak—by the generation of their offspring who then remember the events in their own ways."[93] To this I would add a third locus: the grandchildren's generation and beyond, who have a completely imagined memory, through stories transmitted second-, third-, and fourth-hand by activists in various movements and in the current resistance period. This younger generation, multiple-times removed, has still learned to remember the past powerfully, to mourn in different ways, and at the same time to imagine a new possibility, without the trappings of the lived past.[94]

The working people of the banana fields have undertaken the collective and societal work of remembering, as reflected by the oral testimonies collected for this study. The working class has sustained their own collective memory of the strike, during repressive military dictatorships in invisible and nonpublic ways, as "undercurrents"[95] that form critical nodes of memory. They sustained a memory of past resistance to US capital and the miserly companies, as well as their audacity in challenging oppression. Specific narratives of suffering and sacrifice were passed down, but so were narratives of the power workers garnered through collective organizing in the union. Banana workers, for instance, have sustained a memory of the strike that has helped them not only to organize new union members but also to radicalize workers, often passing down stories in union meetings and at home, to their children. Even though the history of the strike has not been taught officially in school curricula, and all the occurrences and details have not been completely revealed or made transparent in retellings, the transmission of collective memories of resistance is critical to campeños/as' own identity and has been told by survivors, activists, and leftist organizers as an important motivator for newer generations.[96] These newer organizers have adopted, adapted, and improved on past strategies and tactics. The waves of memory have functioned as undercurrents surfacing in the Honduran political process, while actions taken from the grassroots by working-class actors culminate in the formation of various movements. The most recent of these in Honduras are the resistance movements formed in the north coast after the 2009 coup. The postcoup 2009 resistance movement was further amplified by the transmission of memories of those various past movements against capitalism and the legacy of authoritarian regimes. In 2009, the new generations came out of the closet as leftists and anti-regime. In forming their politics, they looked to the past for any radical politics they could adopt and constructed memories that resonated with their present conditions.

While the generation that lived through the strike feels the loss and grief of the "stolen" and unfinished process, the new generation sees them, and the strike, with fresh eyes and constructs memories of them and the first strike committee as legendary, victorious, and heroic. The younger generations did not live through the series of movements and *alzamientos* (uprisings), nor did they experience the failures of those movements. Still, they see these movements, beginning with the 1954 strike, as an inheritance that has informed their politics.[97] The most common narrative transmitted from workers to their offspring, and also repeated in the union, was a narrative of oppression and suffering that could only be changed through the strike and its organizing. For workers it was not easy; they suffered on strike, ate poorly, and feared for the uncertainty of their wages and livelihoods, but they were determined to bring about change.[98] A far less common narrative, but one with currency among contemporary leftist organizers and activists, is that of the radical first strike committee that was arrested and jailed in Tegucigalpa, which prevented them from negotiating a fair union contract and allowed the companies to control the negotiation process through the ORIT and US Embassy. Notably, new generations do not hold the same memories of what happened, or the grief and anger, as the generations that lived through it—even of the first strike committee they value. Among the new generations, almost everyone repeats the story of the strike as a victory for worker rights, and people commonly cite workers' ingenuity and might in standing up for their rights, in forming radical political groups that would lead to the formation of the union and other leftist movements. Later generations of leftists, activists, and organizers repeat the truncated history of the strike as a victory over capital and Washington, DC, and foreign power, when the campeños stood up for the country.

Contemporary organizing efforts, such as union building, have been influenced by the victorious memory. The legacy of organizing, now followed by younger generations, is perhaps the true historical merit of the strike, as Gilberto reflected on earlier. The undercurrents of the memories of the past, including the strike, and the movement against US empire have persisted as generations of organizers have evolved through the twentieth and twenty-first centuries. Roberto Sosa, one of Honduras's most famous poets, issued this lament of failed opportunity and broken efforts: "La Historia de Honduras se puede escribir en un fusil, sobre un balazo, o mejor, dentro de una gota de sangre" (Honduran history can be written on a shotgun, on a bullet, or rather, inside a drop of blood).[99] There were so many missed opportunities in the Honduran labor movement and leftist organizing, dreams and hopes broken by brutal repression and the heavy hand of US intervention. The new resistance movement may be a new opportunity for change and renewed hope. These new actors are looking to the past, learning from it and crafting a new path forward, a legacy of those banana workers who struck so long ago.

CONCLUSION

Lorenzo is a former banana worker and member of SITRATERCO, a former organizer who worked for FESTAGRO, now exiled in Los Angeles, California, making up one of the more than 11 million un-documented immigrants in the country. We met in Honduras in 2004 and then again in 2006, and every time I asked him for an interview or to interview his father, who participated in the 1954 strike, he skirted around and avoided the request. It was clear he did not want to be interviewed or for me to interview his father. In all those years we worked in solidarity, I never brought it up again in Honduras.

We reconnected back in Los Angeles, and I asked him once again. "The next time we meet," he yielded. Over the course of a meal, he shared so much about his own life, and I understood his hesitation about allowing me to interview his father about the 1954 strike: his father was nostalgic about the times when the United Fruit Company was in its heyday. He reflected on the fact that many people had nostalgia for the company—the company that was, and not the company he had come to know—through labor negotiations, skirmishes, and strikes—as an oppressive transnational giant. "Workers became too dependent on the company," he said with a sadness and longing for the militancy of the strike that was overshadowed by worker leaders he considered to have sold out and professionalized the labor movement.

The left's fight for control of the SITRATERCO took place on multiple occasions, during the 1954 strike and in the seventies, eighties, and nineties. When the left and more progressive workers took over the SITRATERCO in 1990, they had 12,000 worker members. Now, and with the excuse of damage and losses to the company after Hurricane

Mitch and Tropical Storm Gamma, they have less than 2,000 members total, a sliver of what there had been. This process of de-unionizing and demobilization is one of the effects of neoliberalism and its assault on worker protections and flexibilization of labor laws, subcontracting of the workforce, a new way to extract labor from workers without protections. Much that was won in 1954 seems to be eroding starting with the advent of the neoliberal economy in the 1990s and the hastening efforts to suppress resistance to complete transnational dominance of the country after 2009.

Lorenzo's labor militancy and involvement in La Resistencia fighting against the coup led to his political persecution and exile, first in Nicaragua and then the United States. While working on a labor campaign to organize melon workers, he received death threats for his radio show at Radio Progreso in El Progreso. He was followed by unmarked cars without license plates and suspicious drivers who looked like a cross between a military man and a narco. His wife and family also received death threats. To preserve his life, at a time when Honduras boasted the largest per capita murder rate of journalists (as it still does), he had to flee. Now Lorenzo is one of the immigrant workers who make Los Angeles run on a daily basis. As an immigrant worker in some of the most vulnerable sectors of the global economy (garment factories and service industries), he faces ever more callous assaults on his human dignity due to changing immigration policies, inadequate labor rights for immigrants, and the lack of organized labor power.

As for the Honduran labor movement, unions are facing a decline, as in most of Latin America, and while Honduras was for a time perceived to be the most "peaceful" of all the countries in Central America, this notion has been erased in the new era of free trade. *Maquiladora* towns (towns around processing zones) in what used to be banana campos and fincas now host a new sector of immigrants, those from the countryside, and a highly gendered workforce of mostly women. This is the point of departure to the United States for many, who after a few years of trying to survive on low wages decide to trek north for better opportunities. To the naked eye it may seem that banana production has declined, overall, but upon closer scrutiny we see that the company (probably after lawsuits around pesticide use and worker violations) sold the land back to national growers or the state of Honduras via their municipalities. The land that the company obtained through concessions 100 years ago is now being sold back to Hondurans. Honduran producers are actually producing fruit for export, as well as extinguishing access to resources previously available to workers through the union. Everyone in the north coast knows that domestic producers cannot afford to pay, or simply choose not to incentivize, workers in the way that the international corporations could. Workers actually feel that the local producers are the worst violators of their own labor laws.

Lorenzo's father, like so many other workers, remembers fondly the golden days of the company because they were able to benefit from the paternalistic policies in exchange for worker control and surveillance. The state was not able to do this for its citizens, so the company became a de facto state, a benevolent provider, in the first half of the twentieth century and well into the 1960s.

Labor unions today are losing power and their ability to negotiate for workers' rights and wages in the face of a brutal neoliberal policies and a globalized economy throughout the world. This could not be truer for Honduran banana unions and other labor unions. The flexibilization of labor in the region has weakened the labor code in the face of transnational companies, which get tax cuts and other incentives to do business in Honduras. The country is unable to sustain itself without agriculture or *maquilas* (sweatshop factories) exports, but one export most people do not talk about is workers, even as Hondurans migrate at exorbitant rates to the exterior—the United States, Spain, or other Central American nations. Internally, unions are also facing a new challenge: how to recognize, train, and allow for leadership from women, young workers, and even LGBTTI (Lesbian Gay Bisexual Transgender Transvestite Intersex) workers in their ranks. Externally, the challenge is to survive as opportunities for sustainable careers continue to stagnate and new members are often recruited and trained, only to see them migrate. What the twenty-first-century movement will look like or re-create remains to be seen.

As I finalized the manuscript for publication of this book, my heart was racing at the fact that there were stories left untold, for we have lost many of the labor and social movement leaders to tell them. Some people went to their graves with their lived experiences of the short period of democratic potential in Honduras from roughly 1944 to 1962. I also struggled with the desire to tell the story using US archives and narratives of the time, for I wanted to tell the story from the perspective of Hondurans living at that time—and though I was trained to read and analyze against the grain, using the US foreign policy documents felt complicitous.

As I did this, I asked myself time and again: Could Hondurans tell their own story from the bottom up? The chapters in this book have focused on that bottom-up story, prioritizing Honduran workers' words, actions, and aspirations, as seen by them and by the Honduran scholars who first heard about them. I hope this text can perhaps help us answer, from a Honduran perspective, what it was like for the workers who fought for their nation's future and forged their own national identity. This is a challenge for all future scholarly work on Honduras and Central America as a whole: to tell the story of the everyday worker, the everyday migrant, the everyday Honduran woman, in their own words, so that their history is not written solely by the "victors." Are the stories of Honduran workers sufficient to tell the larger collective story without the perspectives of foreign owners and operatives coloring the entire narrative? This is still a question to pose to scholars of the region.

US capitalist, ideological, and geopolitical interests have served as a tourniquet designed to stop communism, yet it was futile in stopping the social reproduction of progressive labor and social movements in the country. We did not, and do not, know the full story from those social actors' perspectives. The US State Department and foreign service apparatus, bolstered by military and financial power, could not stop the will of a people to love their country enough to want to change it. In fact, the surveillance leftist organizers encountered led to secrecy and silence in the general population, but their audacity to confront the company and the state was not forgotten.

The Honduran 1954 strike was the first time that Hondurans stood up to capitalism and the US State Department alike, with nothing but their machetes for work, their pans and *hornillas* (stoves) for everyday sustenance, tortillas, their weathered hands and backs, and a lot of hope for change to get out from under the boot of a complicit dictator. This demonstrated the will and possibility of the people to forever change the working class, and the nature of the political left in Honduras. As Honduras became a locus of the United States' ideological battle during the Cold War, these labor organizers and leftists were designated internal enemies and subjected to murder, death, and exile. "Es que ni siquiera somos país" (We're barely a country), says a contemporary young leftist on a WhatsApp communication referring to the still-heavy hand of US domination today. But I want to argue that the persistence in challenging this domination, despite repression, is what makes the 1954 strike a veritable school on resistance for the generations of today—workers and social movements alike. The story of the strike, the PDRH, the Communist Party, and other actors is still being recovered and told, and it still resonates, over 60 years later, with younger generations. There is still much to be told and much to be learned.

The ideological battles that emerged after the strike are the subject for an entirely different manuscript project, particularly from 1963 on. As the Cold War raged on across the entire continent, self-identified anti-communists, free-labor adherents, and the state under the tutelage of the US State Department joined together with the military juntas to subvert democratic processes and generate sordid campaigns against the nation's future, young campesinas and campesinos, students and labor organizers, who had not bought into the US foreign-policy notion of democracy and free labor and the myth of trickle-down corporate prosperity. In that period many were killed, and we will never know of their deaths or disappearances, not unless clandestine police records are opened and made searchable and amnesty laws are repealed. We know that between 1980 and 1993, 184 Hondurans were forcefully disappeared and presumably tortured and killed in extrajudicial executions.[1] The disappeared, perhaps, now lay in 26 hidden graves (*cemeterios clandestinos*) designated for "political opposition, members of popular organizations, or members of armed opposition" by the elite Batallion 3-16 led by Billy Joya, trained in the School of the Americas.[2] Since the 2009 coup, there have been over 2,000 murders of people defending their rights to a sovereign nation, like the one envisioned in the first part of the twentieth century, free of elites' greed and US intervention.

THE 2009 COUP AND THE PROBLEM WITH HISTORICITY

Several books have emerged analyzing the 2009 coup d'état—some were published before the ten-year anniversary and others since then. Almost all rush through a very sticky history that brought the country to the coup and the illegalities beyond then, namely drug trafficking and violations to the constitution. Many of these are written from a US perspective—the United States as the earth, Honduras as its moon, the United States as painter, Honduras as nude—continuing the western gaze on Central America. The complex web of stories that emerge almost weekly about Honduras, from drug trafficking at the highest echelons of the government to struggles for environmental justice, imprisonments under false pretenses, a disappearance, the extrajudicial murder of activists—all ugly symptoms of a neocolonial relationship to US empire and capitalism. But why can't Hondurans stop the illegalities and atrocities that happen daily? How do Hondurans allow for this to happen? Is the US State Department so omnipotent that Hondurans do not bother at all to organize and resist?

For me the key to answering these questions lies in the past: the persecution of the leftists, but also the deployment and protection of capitalism by local elites who pacified, expelled, or killed resisters. The times of Carías Andino are upon Honduras again with pseudo-dictator Juan Orlando Hernández—only this time with the viciousness and trappings of what capitalists call "modernity," another word for capitalism, in its new phase of neoliberalism and natural-resource extraction.

How will the story of the strike and its resonance with the current generation of leftist organizers and leaders manifest in today's movements? What innovations will emerge from what is learned from the 1954 strike organizers? We cannot know, but doing our best to learn the story and its lessons from those who made this history is a start. No book can be the last word on the strike, the coup, or Honduras, of course. This book is merely a conversation starter meant to unearth the interstices of race, gender, and ethnicity—from the bottom up.

To close, I return to the question that has been my preoccupation for at least the last decade: Can Hondurans tell their own story on their own terms (unencumbered by empire)? I believe—and this project has taught me—that the answer is yes.

LOS 30 PUNTOS

TELA RAILROAD COMPANY WORKER
DEMANDS[1]

Tela, May 11, 1954
Mr. J. F. Aycock,
General Manager
Tela Railroad Company
La Lima, Cortés, Honduras

Sir:
We, the undersigned, in representation of all workers of the different branches of the company, base ourselves on the Universal Declaration of the Rights of Men, adopted by the General Assembly of the United Nations, which proclaims that every person has the right to equitable and satisfactory conditions of work and the right to organize for the defense of material, social, cultural, and political rights, a right clearly expressed in the Inter-American Charter of Social Guarantees signed in Bogotá that was approved by our National Congress.
Whereas: In these times the cost of living has risen considerably.
Whereas: While the cost of living is rising, the salaries we earn not only remain frozen but are dropping, reducing our acquisition power. This is further aggravated by the devaluation of our currency.
Whereas: We are obligated to work under deplorable conditions.
Therefore: We have agreed to submit the following petitions to you:

1)
a) A substantial salary increase in the wages of the employees and workers taking into account the actual cost of living. See attached tables.

b) Abolish work by contract, with the exception of the agricultural workers from the Agricultural Department and other special jobs from the district of Guaymas, for which we attached special tables.

c) Direct payment from the company to the maids and service employees, and not via an intermediary, who are assigned to work for the employees; their salaries should be L.60.00 for cooks, L.50.00 for laundresses and L.100.00 to patio workers [yarderos], including their housing and meals.

d) Hourly employees: Piers/Docks
A 50% increase in salaries for the regular day of eight hours, double pay for overtime (time over the eight-hour day). 50% increase in pay for the regular workday of six hours at night, and double pay for overtime. For dock/pier workers, the workday will be recognized and counted from the beginning when the tickets [*boletos*] of identification are distributed.

2)

a) Improvement in hospitals and dispensaries (clinics) in every way; the latter [clinics] should be staffed by certified physicians [*graduados*]. Hospitals should have a doctor on call at night.

b) The employees will contribute 2% of their salaries to sustain the hospital, covering free service for them and their families, parents, spouses, and children.

c) In the event that the company and employees in its hospitals for any reason cannot cover the health needs of workers, the company should reimburse the workers for the cost of their medical expenses.

d) The service workers (maids, cooks, washerwomen, yarderos) assigned to the employees will receive health services in the same way that the rest of the workers and employees receive them.

e) Establish an emergency rail ambulance service fully equipped to respond to any first aid/emergency case, properly attended by both a doctor and a nurse.

3) Pay hourly workers their wages when sick and absent from work.

4) Implement weekly payroll.

5) Abolish unjust firing of workers. A worker can be fired only after receiving three warnings, appropriately justified, in a month.

6) The maximum daily work time should be eight hours long, and overtime should be remunerated with double pay for monthly contract workers and for hourly workers.

7) The daily maximum night work time will be six hours, and double pay for overtime work for monthly as well as hourly workers.

8) 15-day paid vacation with pay will be given every year to employees who earn less than L.200.00 a month and 30 days' vacation for those who earn more than L.200.00, regardless of their position as monthly or hourly employees, provided they have worked for the company for at least a year.

9) Provide free rail/train transportation for the workers, employees, and their families every time they request it.

10) The company will provide the necessary tools and materials to the workers to accomplish their work.

11) For equal work there should be equal pay for any person regardless of sex, race, credo, and nationality of the worker.

12) Fair treatment for all workers.

13) Provide bonuses for all workers without exceptions in June and December.

14)

a) Improve the food at the docks/piers; build clean and appropriate dining facilities for the distribution of food.

b) Concede a paid hour for lunch time.

c) Recognize any interruption or delays in the workplace not caused by the workers as part of the workday.

d) Recognize the half hour after five minutes worked and the hour after 35 minutes worked [to be paid for half an hour or hour even if they did not work the full half hour or hour].

e) Standardize salaries for watchmen [security guards], customs workers, and miscellaneous work that are paid out of the dock/pier payroll.

f) Retire all pier workers [stevedores] at 50 years of age who have worked at least five years, because it is an exhausting job, due to the demands of working nights, and due to hard conditions of work, particularly for the night shifts.

15) Hotel and hospital employees should be given a stipend of L.60.00 per person, the value of meal expenses, so that they may take meals outside the facilities.

16) Laundry workers should be considered monthly employees with wage increases that correspond to this position in the table of wages provided.

17) Guarantee permission [leave of absence] to any employee or worker when they request it with justification or for compelling reasons.

18) Recognize first-class food expenses for all the employees and workers who have to leave their home to execute their work. Place strict control over the food vouchers, because many vouchers are reduced. Give an extra voucher for night shift.

19) The workweek should be 45 hours of work and 48 paid hours for day workers, for monthly workers, and for workers per assignment [*por tarea*]. All workers will be paid the seventh day, Sunday.

20) The cooks and laundresses will be provided free food in the houses they work in. They will also not be charged for any lost or damaged dishes and other utensils.

21) Abolish the obligation to have meals at the foreman's home.

22) Abolish all discrimination by race and job category in hospitals, dispensaries, ambulances, and hotels.

23) The company should provide protective personal equipment to protect workers' health, such as masks, goggles, gloves, and raincoats.

24) Provide decent and hygienic housing for the workers who need it.

25) Provide secular and free elementary education (up to sixth grade) [primary school education] for all the children of the workers and employees. In the rural schools [the schools in the campos], each teacher should be able to teach two school grades maximum [not all grades]. School supplies and materials should be provided for free as they have been. The school curriculum must adhere to standards of the Ministry of Public Education.

26) Assign maids and house maintenance workers to employees who earn L.200.00 or more and who are married.

27) Guarantee that there will be no company retaliation against any worker in the strike leadership, workers, and people involved in the strike committee and strike activities. Return workers who

were fired for their role in the strike, before and during strike movement, to their positions.

28) Pay salaries in full to all workers from the beginning of the strike until the day they return to work.

29) Recognize and respect the workers' union, its sections and subsections, that exist at this time. Do not change or alter the organization leadership that already exist. Adhere to the same guarantees and rights granted by the law. The union will be independent of the state and municipal [patronal] governance. Workers will have the right to strike and organize (to meet according to Article 61 of the Constitution). This union will seek and oversee all the points demanded and listed in this petition document.

30) We will wait in El Progreso for the resolution to put an end to the protest.

Puerto Cortés Delegate:_____
Juan B. Canales

La Lima Delegate:_____
Cesar Augusto Coto

Progreso Delegate:_____
S. Lilio Pineda M.

Tela Delegate:_____
Luis B. Yanes

CENTRAL STRIKE COMMITTEE 7 DEMANDS OF THE COMPANY AND HONDURAN GOVERNMENT[1]

May 17, 1954

1. That the company make immediate payment of all the withheld salaries to all the workers, in the different locations where they may be located due to circumstances of the strike: La Lima, Puerto Cortés, Tela, El Progreso, and Bataán, notifying us of the day and time when those payments will be made.

2. That the government unconditionally release all those people who have been incarcerated for collaborating or participating in our struggle. Concrete cases: Efraín Garay and those companions of the La Ceiba and Olanchito sector; Martin Bonilla, Antonio Fajardo and other companions of Puerto Cortés; Gustavo Andara Bulnes, Emilio Sánchez Guevara, and other compañeros of Tegucigalpa.

3. That the authorities cease all the intimidation and persecution of participants and collaborators of our strike throughout the country.

4. That the government remove all the military forces assigned to guarding the company's property as soon as possible. The Central Strike Committee, the highest authority in the strike's movement, will take charge of its custody and protection while our movement is proceeding.

5. That the company provide transportation to facilitate the preparatory work for the negotiations taking place at the Central Strike Committee.

6. That the Minister of Government and Justice, General J. Antonio Inestroza, in his limited participation as mediator and government representative, abstain from using improper language to mediate and from making threats when participating in the negotiations.

7. That the negotiations occur between the Tela Railroad Company and the Central Strike Committee, in representation of all the workers, with both parties preserving all due respect during the discussions.

STANDARD FRUIT COMPANY WORKER STRIKE DEMANDS, MAY 7, 1954[1]

1. Immediate dismissal of the railroad superintendent, J. A. Girdner, of the hospital administrator, D'Antoni, Jaime Ramírez, and the assistant to the dock [*muelle*] superintendent, Ramón Cerril.

2. General increase in salary for urban and city employees and workers of 50 percent of their current accrued monthly pay or pay per work hour or task.

3. Obligatory commitment of the company to grant paid vacations to employees and workers in general, after a year of uninterrupted work, paying those workers who are due vacations, in advance, the salary that corresponds to the vacation time.

4. The right to benefit from the company's hospital services, and that this service not be limited solely to those who regard themselves as the family of the worker—that is, wife and children—but also all close family members.

SIGNED CONTRACT BETWEEN STANDARD FRUIT COMPANY, AGÚAN VALLEY, THE MEMBERS OF THE CENTRAL STRIKE FOR LABOR RELATIONS[1]

In the city of Puerto de La Ceiba, D. D. on the 19th day of the month of May of 1954, the representatives of the Strike Committee, the general manager of the Standard Fruit Co., and the manager of Aguán Valley Co. met with the objective of resolving the conflict that has motivated the current strike and, recognizing that the progressive improvement of living standards and work conditions for the working population depend on an extensive measure of development of the production, increase of productivity, and the cooperation of the workers and their managers, expressed in the harmony of their relations in reciprocal fulfillment of their duties and rights, to that end, they sign the agreement and detail ahead before the commission appointed by the government: Political Governor, the Commander of Arms, the Income and Customs Administrator, the attorneys representing the strike, and the members of the Chamber of Commerce and Industries.

First: The first [parties] will be called "employers and workers" [day laborers], and the second and third, the "company." The company commits to grant its employees who have worked for a full year and whose monthly pay is 150 lempiras more vacations paid in advance, consisting of two weeks of rest if the employee will enjoy them on this coast, and four weeks if the rest will be enjoyed outside of it. These vacations will be extended to the workers who carry out their work per day [day laborers] on consecutive days and their monthly salary exceeds the previously established base, 150 lempiras.

Second: a) Employees and workers will enjoy the privilege of the special rate already established for the payment of medical-hospital services provided at the D'Antoni Hospital and the dispensaries of the companies. To family members who depend on those who owe directly, the companies will publish these rates and make them available to the workers who enjoy these benefits and enroll family members who depend on them in person in the offices of the companies. b) The Companies will establish an ambulance service for employees and workers and for family members included in the letter [contract].

Third: The companies commit to establishing sanitary services [bathrooms] for the dockworkers of this port.

Fourth: To the monthly employees and the day laborers on consecutive days, they will be paid time and a half for the hours they work outside the legal eight-hour day or 48-hour week, without prejudice to the provisions of the law regarding holidays.

Fifth: The companies will pay monthly employees and day laborers who work on consecutive days the salary corresponding to the days of work stoppage resulting from the strike. The dockworkers will be recognized for eight days of salary at the rate of five lempiras with 60 cents a day; in order for employees and workers to enjoy this benefit, they must resume their work on the morning of the 20th or no later than 21st.

Sixth: The companies will increase the salary of the workers in the following proportion:

a) To the employees and workers who earn up to five lempiras per day, [an increase of] 10%; to the employees and workers who earn up to five lempiras with a penny to eight lempiras per day, [an increase of] 5%.

Seventh: The companies will not retaliate against any of the employees and workers because of [their participation in] the strike, understanding that the suspension or closure of any of the [company] dependencies, for economic reasons, will not be considered a [form of] retaliation.

Eighth: To resolve future conflicts between the companies and employees and workers, a Joint Committee [Comité Paritario] will be constituted, consisting of six members, three of them appointed by the companies and three by the employees and workers. The relationships that arise from the labor contract, in what was not provided for in this agreement and the laws of the country, will be governed by the provisions of the special regulations, which the committee will approve to settle the disagreements that arise within the committee as they are made known; [the parties] will defer to the resolution by the General Direction of Work and Social Security. The resolutions issued by said committee and, where appropriate, the General Directorate of Work and Social Security, will be mandatory for both parties.

Ninth: When any of the parties deems a revision of this agreement necessary, they will submit the case to the Joint Committee [Comité Paritario].

Tenth: For the duration of this agreement, the employees and workers agree not to resort to a work stoppage, to a strike, before they have exhausted the conciliatory procedures established in the regulations issued by the committee in accordance with clause no. 8 of this agreement.

In faith of the aforementioned, both parties ratify their content and are faithfully obliged to abide by it; signing it in triplicate, each one must keep their copy, and the original will be collected by the Government Commission to be deposited at the Ministry of Development and Labor.

For the Central Strike Committee
Roberto Zúniga, President; Alfredo Matute, General Secretary; Ramón Quintanilla Jácome, Héctor Romero, Nicolás Laffite, Darío Maxier, Eduardo Maldinof, Alejandro Bustillo, Jesús Villalta, Andrés Víctor Artiles, Lucas Peralta, Anael Hernández, Luis Chirinos, Enrique Alcántara, Loyd Sentine, Medardo Agurcia H., Francisco Quesada, and Max Villalobos.

For the Companies
Bertie R. Hogge, General Manager; Tomás A. Ledyard, Manager

For the Government Commission
Francisco J. Velásquez, Tomás Cálix Moncada, Carlos A. Matute, Ricardo Callejas

DEPARTMENTAL AUTHORITIES
Simón Reyes J., Political Governor; Tulio González, Commander of Arms; Aníbal Crespo A., Customs Administrator

LAWYERS REPRESENTING THE STRIKE
Álvaro Raúl for the Chamber of Commerce and Industries
Rafael H. Rodriguez, Ernesto Crespo Mejía, Juan Lafitte, and Raúl Pineda

PROGRAM OF THE HONDURAN REVOLUTIONARY DEMOCRATIC PARTY

PDRH [Spanish acronym]¹

Agreement
THE CENTRAL EXECUTIVE BOARD OF THE HONDURAN REVOLUTIONARY
DEMOCRATIC PARTY,

Whereas, the Honduran Revolutionary Democratic Party rises up from the union of the Honduran Democratic Party and the Revolutionary Democratic Party, which had their respective political platforms, and which remain effective after the union, and, therefore, it was necessary to unite them into just one political platform.

Whereas, due to the special circumstances in which these programs were developed, they could not be written in a complete and specific way.

Whereas, the first conference of Honduran democratic groups held in Guatemala recommended the elaboration of a political platform that incorporates the demands of the new groups affiliated with the party.

Whereas, for the previous reasons the PDRH has felt the need to elaborate a more complete political platform that covers all the national demands and [those] of the different social sectors of the country.

Whereas, this political platform has been developed, discussed and approved by all party committees and by this central executive board.

Agrees: To put this present political platform into effect, publish and advertise it, and sufficiently motivate all the members of the PDRH to respect, comply with, and fight for the current political platform.

San Pedro Sula, June second of nineteen forty-eight.
Executive Central Committee of the Honduran Revolutionary

Democratic Party
Antonio Madrid H.
Rodolfo Pastor Zelaya
Ramón Rosa Figueroa H.

Program of the Honduran Revolutionary Democratic Party

Honduras in the economic aspect is a backward country where the latifundio [a large state of unused land], where the industry is just beginning to manifest itself artificially, where transport offers the same rudimentary development, and where there is still no national banking. In the social aspect, Honduras does not have organized labor forces; it does not have the social security institution. It has not seriously faced the problems of health and culture of the people, and in regard to the political aspect, it continues to operate under an old state, without modern services, an army, or a good financial system.

Aside from the aforementioned underdevelopment of Honduras, which suffers from a strong intervention of powerful foreign corporations, which by meddling in our policy make the Honduran state subject to its large businesses, preventing the full development of the national economy.

Due to the realities noted, Honduras suffers a tremendous national deformation in its economy and in its politics that should be corrected with the healthy methods of democracy. In addition, it is understood that until Honduras has suffered this structural correction, until then will it be able to march along the straight path of its history.

In Honduras, there are backward classes and sectors attached to underdevelopment and to foreign interests. These classes and sectors prevent the full development of the independence, sovereignty, and progress of the nation. However, there are also classes and sectors struck by foreign interests that aspire and fight for a Honduras that is independent, sovereign, and progressive in all aspects. These classes and sectors that have concrete demands to UNITE the NATION are now being grouped together to achieve their just objectives and build a better homeland.

The internal condition of Honduras makes you think of its international situation. In reality, Honduras is a country without its own economy and without independent politics. Honduras, economically, is simply a small business market and a source of raw material, and politically, a smaller nation that subordinates its will to the convenience of the major nations.

This visible and unjust dependence of Honduras moves the sectors to gather under the NATION UNITED to fight democratically so that the country can improve economically, and politically, in its international political status and one day come to enjoy its rights as an independent and sovereign nation.

Briefly, considering the internal and external situation of Honduras, the Honduran Revolutionary Democratic Party offers the people the present political platform, in which the problems of the nation as a whole are formulated, as well as the particularities of each social sector.

II
National Demands

1. **Industrialization.** The PDRH fights for the mobilization and organization of the country's economic forces, under the guidance or direction of the state, in order to lay the foundations and develop the national industry. Create the industrial schools and the institutions necessary for agricultural industrial development.

   Special attention will be given to the promotion of the mining industry, with the right of preference for national investors. The mining corporations established in the country will retain those acquired rights that harmonize with the imprescriptible rights of the nation.

   The industrialization of Honduras, on the basis of inter–Central American treaties and financial agreements of a democratic character, will be achieved as much as possible.

2. **Agrarian Reform.** The PDRH fights for the broad plan of colonization of the public land and of those particular properties that, due to their extension or geographical location, deserve to be declared of public utility. The colonization of the aforementioned particular properties will carry out previous acquisition and fair payment by the state. Modernization of agriculture in its many aspects in order to increase production. Appropriate legislation that allows achieving the above objectives.

   Such legislation will limit the landowner. Foundation of agricultural schools of experimentation. Special economic organization of those isolated areas of the national territory for the civilization and for the strengthening of sovereignty.

3. **Means of communication.** Transportation. The PDRH strives for the creation of a road system that meets the most urgent needs for the country's agricultural and industrial development.

   Review of the management of the national railroad and its extension.

Creation of an air merchant fleet.

Creation of a national merchant fleet and nationalization of the docks and the necessary services for better functioning.

Improvement of the telegraph, telephone, and radio-telephone system.

Review of the concessions related to the communications system.

4. **National Banking.** Establishment of the Central Reserve Bank, the sole issuer and responsible for the stability of the national currency. Foundation of all those auxiliary credit institutions that propose agricultural development, industrialization, modernization of agriculture, and the stimulation of national trade.

5. **Public Health.** The PDRH fights for the state to be responsible for the health of the Honduran people, organizing the necessary medical assistance services and requiring all companies to organize medical health services. Effectiveness of the mandatory social service.

6. The PDRH fights for the state to ensure strict compliance with the right to culture that all Hondurans have. Extensive literacy campaign. Foundation of a publishing house that provides all teaching centers with their respective texts. Support of National Art as a means of bringing about the flourishing of Honduran artistic expression.

7. **Legislation.** The PDRH fights for the enactment of a new political constitution and the other constitutive and civil laws, so that they will faithfully interpret the new democratic phase in Honduras. Said constitution and said laws shall conform to the norms of modern law, also presuming that they interpret the universal conquests in matters of legislation.

8. **Treaty Review.** The PDRH, seeking the welfare of Honduras and other nations in accordance with justice and international law, struggles for the revision of all those agreements, conventions, and treaties that have been concluded previously. The review will be done taking into account the democratic development of Honduras in its national and international relations.

III
Demands Related to the State

1. The PDRH struggles for the state to make effective the democratic freedoms of association, transit, emission of thought, assembly, voting, organizing, and political activities; for respect of human life, property, and individual safety; for democratic institutions, political constitution, and laws of the country; and for the removal of autocratic leadership.

2. **The state and its national services.** The PDRH struggles so that the state ceases to be an organism at the service of the political, social, and economic interests of a class, caste or elite, to become an organism that serves the interests of the Honduran people.

   The powers of the state will be forgotten when enacting policy legislation, governing, or imparting injustice for the benefit of the few and in detriment to the many. In this regard, a law of accountability of the officers will be issued. The bureaucracy of the government, paid by the people, will have no other obligation than to serve the people.

   Therefore, it is appropriate to improve, complete, and establish government services in the different administrative branches, so that they can fulfill their missions faithfully. The administrative and judicial career will be created, as well as the public employee law.

   The state will engage in economic intervention in hydroelectric companies in order to reduce energy needs and make it accessible and affordable to most of the population, as a principle of the gradual nationalization of public services. State employees will have the right to organize in unions in accordance with the public employee law and obligations of the labor code and social security.

3. **Civil Guard.** The PDRH struggles for the formation of a Civil Guard in order to preserve the social order and defend the interests legally acquired by the inhabitants, whether native or foreign. The civil guard will be a guarantee and not an apparatus of repression of the people. The economic investigative police will be founded to judge crimes of this nature.

4. **Armed Forces.** The PDRH struggles for better organizing skills and the independence of the Armed Forces from political

partisanship. To guarantee the democratic development of the nation and to defend the state against any foreign aggression.

Better economic, social, hygienic, and cultural conditions will be introduced for the benefit of the soldiers, various ranks, and in general of all those who constitute the popular army.

Review and progressive effectiveness of the law of military service is required.

5. **Fiscal Taxes.** The PDRH fights for an adequate study that replaces the current tax system with another one that applies to everyone and not just the people. It is hoped that Honduras has a budget of income and expenses that fully satisfies all the services of the state—a technical study with a view to adequately solving the problem of domestic and foreign debts.

6. **The state and its international services.** The PDRH fights for the state to serve the interests of interdependence, peace, progress, and culture and will not serve interests that break the harmony and provoke international wars.

The Honduran state will be a faithful and firm adherent to the Declaration of the United Nations.

The Honduran state will adjust its policies to adapt to fair international conventions. The Honduran state will work firmly for the Union of Central America.

The diplomatic and consular career will be created.

Particular Demands of the Different National Sectors

1. **Workers.** The PDRH struggles for the rights of trade unions and cultural organization of the labor sector. Labor code, minimum wage, and social security.

2. **Farm workers.** The PDRH struggles for the organizational rights of the farm worker sector. Land reform and industrialization of the agriculture. Defense and state protection of agricultural/farm workers through product pricing control, credit, grants, and marketing of products. Construction of warehouses for storage, conservation, and handling of agricultural products.

Formation of agricultural schools of experimentation and testing of new crops.

3. **Craftsmen.** The PDRH struggles for the rights of trade union organization and production, cooperatives, and consumer rights of

the craftsman sector. Credit and market for their products. Arts and crafts schools.

4. **National Capitalists.**

a) **Landowners.** The PDRH struggles for the state to guarantee their property, accessible credit, technical help, insurance, reduction of taxes on the imports of machinery.

b) **Industrial.** The PDRH struggles for the guarantee of the state and society for their investments and its products; access to low-interest credit to expand their businesses; schools for industrial preparation; freedom of association for their defense of economic rights.

c) **Merchants.** The PDRH struggles for the protection of the state, which must give all the necessary laws that allow and guarantee the prosperity of its businesses.

d) **Bankers.** The PDRH struggles for revision of the bank law that includes the creation of the new credit institutions for productive purposes in the national territory.

5. **Women's Sector.** The PDRH struggles for the equality of women with men in access to work and equal remuneration; equality in the exercise of rights contained in workers' legislation; specific rights of a woman as a mother; complete and practical equality with men in civil matters, in the maintenance, contracting, succession, administration of assets, culture, and professional practice; complete and practical equality with men in the exercise of political rights.

6. **Childhood Sector.** The PDRH struggles for state protection of infants and children. Adaptation of educational centers to the needs of infants and children of popular sectors. Absolute respect for children. Issuance of a children's rights code. Guarantee of the physical and mental health of children.

7. **Student Sector.** The PDRH strives for the complete renovation of the teaching centers and their educational methods, in its three aspects: primary, secondary, and university [education]. In the education system, it must close the big gap that exists between teaching [curriculum] and the existing social reality. University autonomy with the purpose of the university becoming the governing institution of the culture of the nation.

8. **Popular Youth Sector.** The PDRH struggles for full freedom of organization for cultural and political purposes; a board of democratic education of youth both in its content and in its extension; extensive technical preparation of the youth to improve their conditions of work and production. Job opportunities. Creation of the popular university.

9. **Professional Sector.** The PDRH struggles for the rights of unions and cultural organization of rural and urban teachers, in accordance with the law of the state of the public employee; adequate remuneration that stimulates and dignifies them; creation of an institute as a branch of the university, to expand the technical culture of the teachers. Create the University of the People. For other professionals, defense of association rights for cultural, economic, and scientific purposes. Abolition of arbitrary professional privileges; sanction and suspension of professionals without ethics. Opportunity to expand the culture by the state.

10. **Intellectual and Artistic Sector.** The PDRH struggles for the rights of organization and full use of the rights of intellectuals. Strong protection by the state of intellectual and artistic productions.

End

Call to Action:
The Honduran Revolutionary Democratic Party summons all the social sectors of the nation to agree on the present political platform of national unity, so that together all the forces make possible the constitution of a modern nation, independent in the political and economic sectors, with international relations based on equality and justice.

The present political platform reflects the national reality in all its aspects and has nothing in common with the platforms that have been put forth to the Honduran people in previous times, those that have never intended to end the underdevelopment of Honduras or the dependence on foreigners.

In the fight for the objectives established in this platform, all citizens have a place after sincerely pondering the seriousness of our current situation, to decide to turn their backs on the past; it does not matter what their previous political point of view was.

Countrymen: The Honduran Revolutionary Democratic Party

invites you at this culminating hour to support this program of national unity, which is aimed at building the new Honduras.

Men and women who have never exercised the right to vote or enjoyed human liberties, the Honduran Revolutionary Democratic Party invites you to strengthen its ranks for the conquest of that right and those freedoms.

San Pedro Sula, June 2, 1948

Party Central Executive Committee
Honduran Revolutionary Democratic Party
Antonio Madrid H.
Rodolfo Pastor Zelaya
Ramón Rosa Figueroa H.

BRIEF SELECTED CHRONOLOGY OF LABOR AND POLITICAL EVENTS IN HONDURAS[1]

1880 Founding of Honduras and Rosario Mining Company.

1899 The Vaccaro brothers receive land concessions in the eastern part of the north coast and found the Standard Fruit and Steamship Company.

The Boston Fruit Company and Minor Keith found the United Fruit Company in the western part of the north coast.

1900 Strike in the mines of San Juancito, near the capital of Tegucigalpa, one of the first strikes in the history of the Honduran labor movement.

1902 The Department of Atlántida is founded and becomes the most important region for companies working on the export of bananas.

1910 Samuel Zemurray, a steamship businessman in New Orleans, helps Honduran Manuel Bonilla to overthrow President Miguel Rafael Dávila Cuellar. Noteworthy here is Samuel Zemurray's interest and meddling in national politics, as well as his being a businessman and owner of Cuyamel Fruit Company.

1916 First worker strikes in the north coast.

1912 The Honduran state makes generous land concessions to US banana companies to build a railway system, benefiting the United Fruit Company and Cuyamel Fruit Company (Samuel Zemurray).

1913 Standard Fruit Company founds the Bank of the Atlántida, one of the most important banks of Honduras.

1920 Allegedly, H. V. Rolston sends a letter to lawyer Luis Melara explaining that the fruit companies should take over the land and make it usable land for plantation. Rolston states, "Estos pueblos envilecidos por el alcohol son asimilable para lo que se necesite y destine."(These people succumb to alcohol and are assimilable for whatever is needed).This letter was published in its entirety in *Vanguardia Revolucionaria*, no. 182 (October 20, 1949). Its veracity is contested.

1921 The Federación Obrera Hondureña (FOH; Federation of Honduran Laborers) is composed of mutual aid societies and artisan unions.The result is the first Congreso Obrero Hondureño (First Honduran Worker's Congress).

1923 The National Party is founded in Honduras by Tiburcio Carías Andino and Paulino Valladares.

1923–1925 First indications of Communist Party in Central America.

1925 The founding of La Liga Sindical del Norte by Manuel Cálix Herrera, Juan Pablo Wainwright, and Graciela García of the FOH, who sought to challenge more directly the banana companies and fortify a working-class movement. Military forces repress the worker strike in the Cuyamel Fruit Company Sugar refinery.

1926 Sociedad Cultura Femenina (Society of Feminine Culture) by Visitación Padilla and Graciela García, one of the first organizing efforts by women that brought together the suffragist movement and the worker movement in the mines near Tegucigalpa.

1929 Founding of the Communist Party of Honduras by Juan Pablo Wainwright and Manuel Cálix Herrera.

1927–1929 The Federación Sindical Hondureña (FSH; Federation of Unions in Honduras) is founded at the first Worker-Peasant Congress in Tela (north coast).

1930 In response to massive firings by the banana companies, strikes are organized by workers in the north coast.

1931 The US economic crisis affects the banana companies in Honduras, leading to more firings.Workers organize strikes and work stoppages.

1932 The Worker-Peasant Congress nominates Manuel Cálix Herrera as candidate for president.

Tiburcio Carías Andino, Nationalist Party founder and candidate wins the presidency and stays in power for 16 years by reforming the constitution to remain in power. He is considered to have stopped the civil strife in the country through state terror and centralized power.

1935 Flooding in the north coast due to overflowing rivers caused by excessive rains.

1945 Partido Democrático Hondureño (PDH; Honduran Democratic Party) is founded.

1946 Partido Democrático Revolucionario (PDR; Democratic Revolutionary Party) is founded in Tegucigalpa.

1948 The Honduran Revolutionary Democratic Party (PDRH; Partido Democrático Revolucionario Hondureño) is formed by the uniting of the Partido Democrático Hondureño (PDH; Honduran Democratic Party) and Partido Democrático Revolucionario (PDR; Revolutionary Democratic Party).

Members produce the worker newspaper *Vanguardia Revolucionaria*, and organize in the north coast. Military forces open fire and massacre the Liberal Party rally crowd in San Pedro Sula on July 6.

1949 Formation of Comité Coordinador Obrero (CCO; Worker Coordinating Committee). Juan Manuel Gálvez, former lawyer for the United Fruit Company and Nationalist Party member, assumes the presidency after Carías Andino's dictatorship.

1950 The government promotes the production and export of coffee.

1950 The Comité Sampedrano de Mujeres (The San Pedro Women's Committee), is organized by Graciela Bográn, a local teacher and suffrage pioneer.

1951 The Federación de Asociaciones Femeninas Hondureñas (Federation of Honduran Feminist Associations) is organized, the first federation of women in the nation.

1954 From April 26 to May 3, United Fruit Company strike, which lasts 69 days; Standard Fruit Company strike lasts 11 days. General strike in solidarity spreads throughout the country. Founding of the Sindicato de Trabajadores de la Tela Railroad Company (SITRATERCO; Tela Railroad Company Workers Union), the union for the Tela Railroad Company, a subsidiary of the United Fruit Company.

In late April, the second Communist Party of Honduras is formed.

On May 11, workers organize a negotiating committee and make demands of the company known as the Pliego de Peticiones, or Los 30 Puntos, with the main demands including wage increases.

In late June and July, Castillo Armas and other Guatemalan exiles prepare an invasion into Guatemala from Copán and Ocotepeque, Honduras.

Guatemalan labor organizers land in the north coast and the company uses this to call the worker negotiating committee a fraud for receiving Communist support from Guatemala. The committee is thrown in jail, and a new worker committee is formed in the United Fruit Company regions.

Ramón Villeda Morales, Liberal Party candidate, wins elections. The National Congress does not grant the presidency, and Julio Lozano Díaz declares himself president.

A devastating hurricane in September destroys the banana plantations; many workers, union members, and strike coordinators are fired and not rehired. The losses of the strike movement are great.

Women gain suffrage but are not able to vote until 1957. The labor code is approved but not put in the books until 1957–1959, with the labor court.

1957 Ramón Villeda Morales is able to take power until a military coup d'état in 1963 by Álvaro López Arellano.

1958 Founding of La Sociedad Cultural Abraham Lincoln (Abraham Lincoln Cultural Society), an organization by north-coast Garifunas which sought to combat racism against Garifunas.

1961 In October El Comité Central de Unificación Campesina (CO-CEUCA; The Central Committee for Campesino Unification) is formed.

1962 In August Federación Nacional de Campesinos de Honduras (FENACH; National Federation of Campesinos of Honduras) is formed; COCEUCA is transformed into FENACH to broaden the campesino base across Honduras and fight for land reform.

In September Asociación Nacional de Campesinos de Honduras (ANACH; National Association of Honduran Farmworkers) is founded by anti-communist AFL-CIO, ORIT, and US-backed SITRATERCO and FESITRANH unions to challenge the rapidly mobilizing FENACH campesinos.

1972 Formation of Unión Nacional de Campesinos (UNC; National Campesino Union).

1977 Founding of OFRANEH by former members of La Sociedad Cultural Abraham Lincoln. Formed by Garifunas and other Afro-descendants from the north coast.

1980 Return to negotiated democracy with the elections that brought Roberto Suazo Córdova to power in the middle of the Cold War.

1993 Workers in the former banana camp Tacamiche refuse to abandon the barracones and have a showdown with authorities to preserve their livelihood. Founding of Consejo Cívico de Organizaciones Populares e Indígenas de Honduras (COPINH; Council of Popular and Indigenous Organizations in Honduras), originally, Comité Cívico de Organizaciones Populares de Intibucá.

2000 Founding of Red Lésbica Cattrachas, LGBTTI organization dedicated to combating human-rights violations against LGBTTI (Lesbian Gay Bisexual Transgender Transvestite Intersex) peoples by documenting and archiving instances of violence and death.

2001 Founding of Movimiento Unificado de Campesinos del Aguán (MUCA; Unified Farmworker Movement of Aguán). Formed by 28 campesino groups in response to land encroachment by business elites.

2009 US-backed coup d'état that deposed President José Manuel Zelaya Rosales. Formation of Frente Nacional de Resistencia Popular (FNRP; National Popular Resistance Front). Broad-based mobilization by civic sectors of Honduran society in response to the coup d'état against President Zelaya.

2011 FNRP convenes the National Assembly with constituents from various sectors and officially decides to form the Libertad y Refundación party (LIBRE; Liberty and Refoundation) to contend in electoral politics.

2013 LIBRE party runs a slate of candidates including Xiomara Castro de Zelaya.

2015 Protests against corruption erupt after the news of money stolen from the Social Security Administration by the Nationalist Party (under President Porfirio [Pepe] Lobo Sosa) to run their election with Juan Orlando Hernández. Community members from all walks of life come out to protest with torches at night and are known as Los Indignados (The Outraged).

2016 Berta Cáceres is murdered on March 2. Four men are accused of the murder. The owners of the DESA Corporation have not been charged.

2017 LIBRE unites with Partido Anti-Corrupción (PAC; Anti-Corruption Party) and Partido Innovación y Unidad (PINU; Innovation and Unity Party) to form La Alianza de Oposición Contra la Dictadura (Alliance of Opposition against the Dictatorship). They win the elections, but after a week-long wait and five computer failures, the Nationalist Party with Juan Orlando Hernández declare victory. National protests erupt all over the country which continue until 2019, including roadblocks and *cacerolazos* (banging pots and pans in protest). Youth give birth to the hashtag #FueraJOH, which resonates internationally. Convergencia Contra el Continuismo (Convergence Against Continuity) is formed to organize civil society nationally to respond to the continuing dictatorial rule of Juan Orlando Hernández.

2018 In April the first migrant caravan leaves Honduras and crosses Guatemala and Mexico, in October the largest migrant caravan leaves Honduras, and in December the third migrant caravan leaves Honduras.

Red Lésbica Cattrachas files a legal suit with the supreme court advocating for the legalization of gay marriage.

2019 On January 9 multiple movements come together to form a unified coalition against the dictatorship of Juan Orlando Hernández. LIBRE party is not included but does not oppose group actions.

In May Red Lésbica Cattrachas files a suit on behalf of trans woman Vicky Hernández, the first person killed after the coup d'état in 2009, to be heard in the Inter-American Court of Human Rights.

In June the Platform for Health and Education is formed to respond to executive orders issued by the president that would lead to layoffs and privatization of public-sector education and health care.

The #FueraJoh movement intensifies throughout the nation.

2020   During the COVID-19 pandemic the country is under an extreme lockdown. The president is not consulting with the health professionals who protested in 2019.

TABLE OF EARLY SIGNS OF WORKER ACTIONS AND STRIKES IN HONDURAS

Year	Company or Industry	Workers and Demands	Resolution
1869	British Rail	Jamaican workers threaten walkouts	Honduran troops are called in by the company
1909	Rosario Mining Company	Workers object to mining accidents and seek better wages and working conditions	
1916	Cuyamel Fruit Company	600 workers demand a better exchange rate at the company commissary	400 workers are arrested and imprisoned
1919	Cuyamel Fruit Company	British office employees organize over workplace issues	
1920	Vaccaro Brothers and Company	1,000–1,200 banana workers demand better wages	The company threatens violence (massacre or other military response, as well as violence against workers)
1925	Cuyamel Fruit Company	Sugar mill workers make a range of demands, including eliminating pay by *ordénes* (coupons)	Government mediation and some improvements
1932	Tela Railroad Company and Truxillo Railroad Company	Banana workers, joined by stevedores and *esquiroles* (strike breakers), demand better wages	Wages are lowered (economic downturn)

NOTES

Preface

1. "Hondurans should look for solutions to this crisis from within, not from outside the country." Father Ismael Moreno, SJ, director of Radio Progreso/ERIC, El Progreso, Yoro. Analysis during a discussion with a religious delegation on January 27, 2018. Author's fieldnotes.

2. Juan Orlando Hernández's fraudulent 2017 elections. Although there were 8,000 international election observers, Hondurans turned to three international bodies for help in getting Juan Orlando Hernández (known as JOH) out of office: the Organization of American States, the European Union, and the US Embassy. What the international community witnessed during and after the elections in Honduras was the unashamed reach of the US Embassy, which had the last word on the election results of 2017.

3. Portillo Villeda, "Coup That Awoke a People's Resistance."

4. "Queer" is a political identity that represents the rejection of binary concepts, such as man/woman, citizen/noncitizen, undocumented/documented, and immigrant/nonimmigrant. Fem represents my identification with femininity. In my queer-fem expression, my gender identity matches my biological sex.

5. The term "Central American–American" was first coined by poet Maya Chinchilla in the poem "Central American-American." Chinchilla, *Cha Cha Files*, 21–22.

Introduction

1. Barahona, *Honduras en el Siglo XX*, 170 (author's translation).

2. See also Mahoney, "Radical, Reformist and Aborted Liberalism," 244.

3. Grandin, *Last Colonial Massacre*, xiv.

4. The amnesty law was approved in 1993, after the signing of the Central American Peace Accords in 1992 for El Salvador and the region (except Guatemala, which signed its peace accords in 1996). Negotiations for peace began with the Esquipulas II Peace Agreement of 1987.

5. Posas, *Luchas del Movimiento Obrero Hondureño*; Barahona, *Silencio Quedó Atrás*; Euraque, *Reinterpreting the Banana Republic*; Argueta, *Gran Huelga Bananera*; Echeverrí-Gent, "Forgotten Workers"; Chambers, *Race, Nation, and West Indian Immigration*; Soluri, *Banana Cultures*; Meza, *Historia del Movimiento Obrero Hondureño*.

6. Viotti da Costa, "Experience versus Structures," 9.

7. Putnam, "Work, Sex, and Power," 134; Tong, *Feminist Thought*, 101–105.

8. Villars, *Para la Casa*; Rodríguez Sáenz, *Siglo de Luchas*; Oyuela, *Notas sobre la Evolución Histórica*.

9. Levenson-Estrada, *Trade Unionists against Terror*; Levenson-Estrada, "Loneliness of Working-Class Feminism"; Klubock, *Contested Communities*; Tinsman, *Partners in Conflict*; Farnsworth-Alvear, *Dulcinea in the Factory*; French and James, *Gendered Worlds*; Hutchinson, *Labors Appropriate to Their Sex*; Putnam, *Company They Kept*; Porter, *Working Women in Mexico City*.

10. Dore, "Holy Family," 103.

11. Emilia Viotti da Costa in "Experience versus Structures" proposes new directions in the study of labor history, suggesting that we look at labor movements "from below."

12. As Viotti da Costa notes, traditional scholars who write about the workplace and labor movements do not write about women, not even to note their absence. Ibid., 16–18.

13. Susie Porter's work, for example, shows that Mexican industrialization was itself a gendered process. Porter, "In the Shadows of Industrialization."

14. Scott, "Gender," 1055.

15. French and James, *Gendered Worlds*, 4.

16. Levenson-Estrada, "Loneliness of Working-Class Feminism," 224.

17. Barahona, *Silencio Quedó Atrás*, 326.

18. Author's translation. Ibid., 332–333.

19. Putnam, *Company They Kept*; Chomsky, *West Indian Workers and the United Fruit Company in Costa Rica, 1870–1940*.

20. *Manta* was a common cloth used in campesino clothes and has been associated with Indigenous, campesinos, and the poorest communities in Honduras and other parts of Central America.

21. Euraque, *Conversaciones Históricas*, 174–177; Barahona, *Evolución Histórica*, 114–117.

22. The practice of explicitly keeping out West Indian and other Black populations by the Honduran Foreign Ministry was heinous, brutal, and bloody. In 1910, a Honduran officer and men under his command killed three West Indians. In 1916 the British pursued the case, and the banana companies dissuaded them, out of concern that Honduras could not afford the high costs of these penalties. The Honduran government saw the West Indian laborers brought by the companies as a liability, generating more xenophobic sentiment. From 1916 on, Hondurans fought for an immigration law, which was finally enacted in 1929, barring West Indian and Palestinian migration. Echeverrí-Gent, "Forgotten Workers," 299–301.

23. "Observaciones del Comité Central de Huelga al Plan Propuesto por la Honorable Comisión Mediadora," in "Aspectos Fundamentales," APMP.

24. Barahona, *Silencio Quedó Atrás*.

25. The Liberal Party was founded in 1894, and for most of the twentieth century it has been the main opposition to the Nationalist Party. One of its most influential leaders, and a rival of Carías Andino, was José Ángel Zúñiga Huete. Euraque considers the PDRH a "wing of the Liberal Party." Ibid., n. 56, 65; Euraque, *Reinterpreting the Banana Republic*, 39, 47, 51.

26. Barahona, *Honduras en el Siglo XX*.

27. Euraque, *Reinterpreting the Banana Republic*, xix.

28. Euraque, *Conversaciones Históricas*; Euraque, Gould, and Hale, *Memorias del Mestizaje*.

29. The Garifuna people in Honduras are of Arauco-Caribbean (Arawak and Carib) origins. They trace their roots and traditions to both West Africa and northern South America. Garifuna communities settled in beachfront villages in close proximity to the ports of Tela, Puerto Cortés, and La Ceiba since their arrival in 1797 from the island of Saint Vincent. While the communities tend to remain local, the need for

survival led Garifuna males to seek work as seamen on fishing boats, and later on UFCo or Standard Fruit Company banana export ships. There are 47 Garifuna towns in Honduras and two major neighborhoods in Tela and La Ceiba. Gargallo, *Garífuna, Garínagu, Caribe*, 13.

30. Echeverrí-Gent, "Labor, Class and Political Representation"; Echeverrí-Gent, "Forgotten Workers"; Chambers, *Race, Nation, and West Indian Immigration*.

31. Soluri, *Banana Cultures*; Soluri, *A la Sombra del Bananal*.

32. Soluri, *Banana Cultures*, 8–9.

33. Marvin Barahona, Mario Posas, Iris Munguía, and Ingris Soriano spent significant amounts of time with me discussing the north coast, the labor movement, the railroad system, and life in the banana company towns and fincas.

34. I attempted to contact Dole and Chiquita Bananas in the United States and Honduras. Both efforts were futile.

35. Pieces of these newspapers and leaflets can occasionally be found at the US State Department records in the United Sates National Archives in College Park, MD (henceforth USNA).

36. Bourgois, "One Hundred Years," 138–140.

37. Hurricane Mitch struck Honduras in 1998, flooding most of the north-coast territory for days. The SITRATERCO union lost most of its files and archives because the entire first floor was flooded. People I consulted for their private papers also reported losing newspapers and other records to flooding in their homes.

38. I found archives in this condition in San Pedro Sula, Tegucigalpa, and Olanchito. The task of conservation and preservation in Honduras is gargantuan. The best efforts at the time were the work of both the CEDIJ and the Instituto Hondureño de Antropología e Historia (Honduran Institute of Anthropology and History).

39. Trouillot, *Silencing the Past*.

40. Oral history gathering is the process by which a historian uses the method of conducting in-depth interviews of people in order to record their personal history and memories. Armitage, Hart, and Weathermon, *Women's Oral History*, ix.

41. Portelli, *Death of Luigi Trastulli*, 1–2, 26, 31.

42. James, *Doña María's Story*, 123–124.

43. Ana Patricia Rodríguez notes that in El Salvador the prolific testimonial literature in the 1980s amplified Salvadoran voices during the civil war, so as to "speak strategically and critically about power, although often under the threat of punishment and the cloak of secrecy." Rodríguez, *Dividing the Isthmus*, 79.

44. Beverley, "Margin at the Center," 13.

45. Beverley and Zimmerman, *Literature and Politics*, 173.

46. Beverley, "Margin at the Center," 13–14; Schwarzstein, "Oral History," 420.

47. Beverley, "Margin at the Center," 13–14.

48. Influenced by US trends in oral history gathering, other Latin American countries such as Mexico, Brazil, Argentina, Costa Rica, and Ecuador undertook efforts in the 1970s to collect oral histories. Schwarzstein, "Oral History," 413.

49. Randall, *Testimonios*. This document was developed in workshops with Sandinistas and future *brigadistas* (literacy brigade workers) in literacy campaigns. It functions as a sort of primary document in that it was developed collectively and was used as a manual by many *brigadistas* who collected many oral histories as they worked

on literacy campaigns in the countryside. See Beverley and Zimmerman, *Literature and Politics*; Craft, *Novels of Testimony and Resistance*. See also the journal *Latin American Perspectives* dedicated two special issues to the topic "Testimony:Voice of the Voiceless in Testimonial Literature" and Randall, *Testimonios*.

50. Menchú Tum, *I, Rigoberta Menchú*; Randall, *Sandino's Daughters*; Benjamin, *Don't Be Afraid, Gringo*;Villars, *Porque Quiero Seguir Viviendo*.

51. Menchú Tum, *I, Rigoberta Menchú*; Stoll, *Rigoberta Menchú*.

52. Rodríguez, *Dividing the Isthmus*, 117; Arias, *Rigoberta Menchú Controversy*.

53. See the special issues "Testimony:Voice of the Voiceless." See also Arias, *Rigoberta Menchú Controversy*.

54. Rodríguez, *Dividing the Isthmus*, 117.

55. Examples are Amaya Amador, *Prisión Verde*; Fallas, *Mamita Yunai*. For an analysis of this genre, see Rodríguez, *Dividing the Isthmus*, 44–75.

56. Ibid., 54, 55.

57. Amaya Amador, *Prisión Verde*; Fallas, *Mamita Yunai*.

58. Rodríguez, *Dividing the Isthmus*, 46.

59. Asturias, *Men of Maize*.

60. Darío Euraque's research has revealed that the Rolston Letter may have been produced in 1940 and for a 1940s audience, not in the 1920s, and not reflective of the period of the 1920s. This piece may have been useful in mobilizing workers in the 1940s. Workers' own testimonies mention this letter as an example of company oppression. Because it was important in worker memories, I mention it here. On the letter's veracity, see Euraque, *Conversaciones Históricas*, 112–115. For a copy of the letter, see Painter and Lapper, *Honduras: State for Sale*, 23–24.

61. Robleda Castro, *Verdad de la Huelga*; Benitez, *Nicomedes en los Bananales*.

62. Portelli, *Death of Luigi Trastulli*, 1–2.

63. Ramírez, "Living Archive of Desire," 119; Forster, *Time of Freedom*; Gould, *To Lead as Equals*; James, *Doña María's Story*; Stern, *Remembering Pinochet's Chile*.

64. James, *Doña María's Story*, 126.

65. The Communist Party was officially founded in 1954, but it is believed that one had been founded in 1929 but did not survive the Carías dictatorship.

66. Portelli, *Death of Luigi Trastulli*.

67. Ibid., 52.

68. Ibid.

69. Ibid., 1.

70. Ibid., 2–7.

71. Ibid., 7–8.

72. Ibid., 15.

73. I take the notion of "emblematic history" from Steve Stern's discussion of postdictatorship Chile; it refers "not to a single remembrance of a specific content, not to a concrete or substantive 'thing,' but to a framework that organizes meaning, selectivity, and countermemory." Stern, *Remembering Pinochet's Chile*, 105.

74. The first central strike committee was persecuted and incarcerated, accused of being communists. The second strike committee was formed and negotiated for workers. Many workers did not know the internal details of this change, except for those close to the leadership or those who were organizers.

75. Portelli, *Death of Luigi Trastulli*, 26.

76. This is also the preoccupation of the narratives of oral histories collected by Marvin Barahona, also in Agapito Robleda Castro's autobiography. Barahona, *Silencio Quedó Atrás*; Robleda Castro, *Verdad de la Huelga*.

77. Portelli, *Death of Luigi Trastulli*, 26.

78. Gould, *To Lead as Equals*, 10.

79. Portelli, *Death of Luigi Trastulli*, 26.

80. Ramírez, "Living Archive of Desire," 112, 16.

81. Patai, "U.S. Academics and Third World Women," 138.

82. Ramírez, "Living Archive of Desire," 113.

83. Ibid., 120.

84. Ibid., 122.

85. María Antonia Perla, interview by author, La Lima, Cortés, March 5, 2006.

86. I take this reference from Gioconda Belli's *Country under My Skin*.

Chapter 1: Intersecting Projects

1. Pablo Neruda, *The United Fruit Company*, Canto General, 1950.

2. On US State Department support of banana companies' actions via the local US Embassy, see Argueta, *Bananos y Política*; McCameron, *Bananas, Labor, and Politics*; d'Ans, *Honduras*.

3. Barahona, *Honduras en el Siglo XX*, 27–47.

4. A. C. McLellan Letter to Luis Alberto Monge, February 1, 1957, p. 6, Serafino Romualdi Correspondence Box 5, Folder 5, Kheel Center for Labor-Management Documentation and Archives, M. P. Catherwood Library, Cornell University (henceforth KCLMDA).

5. "Report from Honduras," undated, Serafino Romualdi Correspondence, Box 5459, File 5–6, KCLMDA.

6. Soluri, *Banana Cultures*, 36.

7. Ibid.

8. Ibid., 35–36.

9. Rivas, *Pueblos Indígenas*.

10. Soluri, *Banana Cultures*, 25.

11. England, *Afro-Central Americans*, 42.

12. Ibid.

13. Portillo Villeda, *Campeños, Campeñas y Compañeros*, 2011.

14. Soluri, *Banana Cultures*, 263; Casson, *Growth of International Business*, 202–203.

15. Luther Castillo Harry, interview by author, El Progreso, Yoro, February 14, 2018.

16. England, *Afro-Central Americans*, 60.

17. Soluri, *A la Sombra del Bananal*, 11; Soluri, *Banana Cultures*, 30–31.

18. Soluri, *Banana Cultures*, 24–25.

19. Ibid., 26.

20. Ibid., 26.

21. Ibid., 24.

22. Ibid., 21–24.

23. Canelas Díaz, *Estrangulamiento Económico*, 94–98.

24. Meza, *Historia del Movimiento Obrero Hondureño*, 4–5 (author's translation).

25. Argueta, *Bananos y Política*, 93–94.

26. Kepner, *Social Aspects of the Banana Industry*; Crowther, *Romance and Rise*,

212–215.

27. Crowther, *Romance and Rise*, 212–213.

28. Archivo del Poder Judicial, CEDIJ, sin número, Nicomedes Fajardo vs. Samuel Zemurray.

29. Some of the named landowners and associates of Sam Zemurray included Carlos Rapalo Ciruit, Santiago Meza Cálix, Leonardo Romero, and the person who appears as the owner of Compañía Bananera de Santiago, Rafael López Padilla and his counsel Juan Manuel Gálvez. Ibid.; Euraque, *Reinterpreting the Banana Republic*, 25–26; Canelas Díaz, *Estrangulamiento Económico*.

30. Euraque, *Reinterpreting the Banana Republic*, 25–26.

31. Archivo del Poder Judicial, CEDIJ, sin número, Nicomedes Fajardo vs. Samuel Zemurray, fol. 30.

32. Ibid.

33. Rodríguez, *Dividing the Isthmus*, 49.

34. Ibid., 9–10.

35. May and Plaza, *United Fruit Company in Latin America*, 8; Kepner, *Social Aspects of the Banana Industry*, 53; Morrow Wilson, *Empire of Green and Gold*, 4; Crowther, *Romance and Rise*, 246–247.

36. The first foreign investors to come to Honduras were the British mahogany companies in the 1840s and 1850s. Argueta, *Bananos y Política,* 10–11, 84–85; McCameron, *Bananas, Labor, and Politics*, 8; d'Ans, *Honduras*, 105–107.

37. The interoceanic canal and ideas of crossing Central America have been around since the colonial period. In 1853 E. G. Squier gained concessions from the Honduran government to begin this route. Huntington Library and Archives, Squier, *Honduras Interoceanic Railway*; Argueta, *Bananos y Política*; d'Ans, *Honduras*, 105–107; Rodríguez, *Dividing the Isthmus*, 6, 9.

38. Squier, *Honduras Interoceanic Railway*.

39. Acker, *Honduras*, 18–19.

40. Ibid., 19–20.

41. Rodríguez, *Dividing the Isthmus*, 48.

42. UFCo operated the White Fleet, ships painted white for visibility and to be easily distinguished from other companies' ships. Cockrill, *United Fruit Company*; Upham Adams, *Conquest of the Tropics*.

43. Davis, *Three Gringos in Venezuela*.

44. Ibid., 143.

45. Ibid., 147–148.

46. The phrase comes from one of Aesop's fables titled "The Dog in the Manger." See read.gov/aesop/081.html.

47. Upham Adams, *Conquest of the Tropics*, 9.

48. Kepner, *Social Aspects of the Banana Industry*, 54.

49. Melville, *Great White Fleet*; Morrow Wilson, *Empire of Green and Gold*, 126–127.

50. Ginetta E. B. Candelario defines racial projects as "simultaneously an interpretation, representation, or explanation of racial dynamics, and an effort to reorganize and redistribute resources along particular racial lines." Candelario, *Black behind the Ears*, 36.

51. Ibid.

52. D'Ans, *Honduras*, 128–131, 144; Oyuela, *Ramón Rosa*, 33.

53. Squier's preliminary report included worker provisions in hiring local labor,

who would be paid either the equivalent of $15 US a month in rations such as flour, pork, and living quarters (in manaca huts) or $13 US in cash. Squier, *Honduras Interoceanic Railway*.

54.Volante, 1854, 32 (Santos Guardiola), E. G. Squier Papers, Huntington Library and Archives (author's translation).

55. Barahona, *Honduras en el Siglo XX*, 27–47.

56. Mahoney, "Radical, Reformist and Aborted Liberalism," 222; Oyuela, *Ramón Rosa*, 39–40.

57. Barahona, *Hegemonía*, 6.

58. Ibid., 30–31.

59. D'Ans, *Honduras*, 126; Barahona, *Honduras en el Siglo XX*, 27–47.

60. Oyuela, *Ramón Rosa*, 75–76.

61. Ibid., 39; Finney, "Rosario," 81–83.

62. McCameron, *Bananas, Labor, and Politics*, 7-8; see also; Finney, "Rosario," 81; Oyuela, *Ramón Rosa*, 39.

63. Barahona, *Honduras en el Siglo XX*, 27–47.

64. Mahoney, *Legacies of Liberalism*, 170.

65. Ibid.

66. Barahona, *Honduras en el Siglo XX*, 32–33.

67. Ibid. (author's translation).

68.The crux of the liberal reform rested on the big-government theory that the "state was the only legitimate source of power and authority." It was then the government's responsibility to create communication systems like the telegraph, postal service, and roads—all activities of a modern society and fundamental to the building of the nation.The development of a primary education system was also required to strengthen and build the state.To accomplish these reforms, the government looked to the development of trade, enticing foreign investors to do business in Honduras. Barahona, *Hegemonía*, 28–29 (author's translation).

69. D'Ans, *Honduras*, 105–115.

70. Grandin, *Last Colonial Massacre*, 43.

71. Karnes, *Tropical Enterprise*, 14.

72.Argueta, *Bananos y Política*, 36–37; Kepner, *Social Aspects of the Banana Industry*, 53.

73. Soluri, *A la Sombra del Bananal*, 11–12.

74. Ibid., 5–11; Crowther, *Romance and Rise,* 210.

75. Soluri, *A la Sombra del Bananal*, 11.

76. Ibid., 10.

77. Honduras, Junta Registradora, "Datos relativos a las fincas de bananos," July 1899, Archivo Nacional de Honduras. Cited in Soluri, *A la Sombra del Bananal*.

78. Canelas Díaz, *Estrangulamiento Económico*, 102–104.

79. Mintz, *Sweetness and Power*, 51.

80.The history of the Cuyamel Fruit Company and owner Sam Zemurray is subsumed in the overall company history of UFCo, but the merger between the two companies did not take place until 1929. Born in Kishinev, Bessarabia, Zemurray, a Jewish immigrant, arrived in the United States in 1892 and quickly became a banana reseller in New Orleans. Kepner, *Social Aspects of the Banana Industry*, 54; Whitfield, "Strange Fruit," 309, 318.

81. Karnes, *Tropical Enterprise*.

82. Barahona, *Hegemonía*, 6.

83. Karnes, *Tropical Enterprise*.

84. Ibid., 18.

85. While in New Orleans, Bonilla Chirinos befriended Zemurray. This friendship would prove useful to him in regaining power in Honduras. Zemurray provided $100,000 US, guns, and a ship for the insurrection in 1911. Argueta, *Bananos y Política*, 81–83. Soluri, *Banana Cultures*, 72–73; Barahona, *Honduras en el Siglo XX*, 51.

86. Argueta, *Bananos y Política*, 81–83. Soluri, *Banana Cultures*, 72–73; Barahona, *Honduras en el Siglo XX*, 51; Karnes, *Tropical Enterprise* 11–12, 15–16. Argueta, *Bananos y Política*, 36.

87. One of the first US investors to obtain a land grant from the Honduran government was the New York and Honduras Rosario Mining Company, owned by Washington Valentine of New York, which eventually broke ground for other North American companies. D'Ans, *Honduras*, 136–137; Meza, *Historia del Movimiento Obrero Hondureño*, xi; McCameron, *Bananas, Labor, and Politics*, 1, 11.

88. Kepner, *Social Aspects of the Banana Industry*, 25.

89. McCameron, *Bananas, Labor, and Politics*, 11.

90. Sagastume, *Carías*, 44.

91. Ellis, *Transnacionales del Banano*, 63.

92. The first set of land concession contracts was known as the "concesiones de la Standard" and the second set of contracts is known as "concesiones de la Truxillo y la Tela." Ellis, *Transnacionales del Banano*, 64.

93. Ibid., 65–66.

94. Wilson, *Empire of Green and Gold*; Argueta, *Bananos y Política*.

95. Crowther, *Romance and Rise*, 208.

Chapter 2: Revolutionary Antecedents to the 1954 Strike

1. This was probably related to his arrest for protesting the Sacco and Vanzetti trial. Manuel Cálix Herrera, "Carta enviada al diputado Santiago Meza Cálix," October 14, 1929, El Trabajador Hondureño, no. 9, November 1, 1929, p. 3. Cited in Villars, *Lealtad y Rebeldía*, 97.

2. In 1869, the British Rail builders recruited Jamaican workers and enlisted the Honduran troops to prevent workers from deserting the job, suggesting there was worker dissatisfaction and action. Acker, *Honduras*, 78.

3. The labor movement and strikes before 1916 are nonexistent in the US State Department consular records. See Posas, *Luchas del Movimiento Obrero Hondureño*, 67; Euraque, "Threat of Blackness."

4. There were strikes in 1916, 1920, 1925, 1930, and 1932. Posas, *Luchas del Movimiento Obrero Hondureño, 67*.

5. Ibid., 70–83.

6. Villars, *Lealtad y Rebeldía*, 117–120.

7. Euraque, *Reinterpreting the Banana Republic*, 36.

8. Ibid., 37.

9. Villars, *Porque Quiero Seguir Viviendo*, 71–72.

10. Ibid., 74.

11. The AFL created this organization in New York City in 1919. Toward the

end of the 1920s, Central American communists took over the COCA. It was then that the FOH worked closely with COCA. Meza, *Historia del Movimiento Obrero Hondureño*, 32.

12. Villars, *Porque Quiero Seguir Viviendo*, 35, 40.

13. Ibid., 73.

14. Ibid., 73–75.

15. CEDIJ, San Pedro Sula, expediente sin número, exhibición personal de Manuel Cálix Herrera, San Pedro Sula, October 2, 1929.

16. In the 1920s these companies were the Truxillo Railroad Company, the Tela Railroad Company, the Cuyamel Fruit Company, and the Vaccaro Brothers.

17. Villars, *Porque Quiero Seguir Viviendo*, 75.

18. The COCA Congress, which brought together labor organizations from all over Central America, took place in November of 1926, in Honduras. Ibid., 74.

19. This clearly demonstrated a move from the mutual aid model to the organizing model, which prioritized recruitment and participation of workers. Ibid., 76.

20. Ibid., 79.

21. Meza, *Historia del Movimiento Obrero Hondureño*, 42.

22. Villars, *Porque Quiero Seguir Viviendo*, 81–82.

23. Ibid., 87.

24. Ibid., 87.

25. Ibid., 86–92.

26. Argueta, *El Pincel y el Martillo*, 2017; Villars, *Lealtad y Rebeldía*.

27. Villars, *Lealtad y Rebeldía*, 123–124; see also 61.

28. Ibid., 60.

29. Argueta, *El Pincel y el Martillo*, 46.

30. "Estatutos del Partido Comunista Hondureño Aprobados el 26 de Diciembre de 1948," 1/15:171/1/1-13, Archivo Nacional de Cuba, La Habana, Cuba. Special thanks to Jennicer Carcamo for sharing these documents from her archival dig in Cuba in March 2020.

31. Barahona, *Memorias de un Comunista*, 121.

32. Villars, *Lealtad y Rebeldía*; Bourgois, "One Hundred Years."

33. Villars, *Lealtad y Rebeldía*, 123.

34. Ibid., 122.

35. "Bandits Kill 3 in Honduras, Throw Bomb into Auto—Outrages Linked with Communist Activity," *New York Times*, October 6, 1932.

36. Villars, *Lealtad y Rebeldía*, 123–124.

37. Ibid., 124.

38. Ibid.

39. Ibid.

40. Ibid., 110–116; Villars, *Porque Quiero Seguir Viviendo*, 125.

41. Villars, *Lealtad y Rebeldía*, 110.

42. Ibid.

43. Ibid.

44. Ibid.

45. Manuel Cálix Herrera and Juan Pablo Wainwright are credited with founding the Communist Party in the late 1920s.

46. CEDIJ, *El Martillo*, June 2, 1929, loose document (*hoja suelta*).

47. This trend continued until the 1950s. Daniel Madrid Guevara, interview by author, La Lima, Cortés, February 5, 2006; Leonardo Bautista, interview by author, Campo Limones, La Lima, Cortés, May 5, 2006; José Reyes Pineda, interview by author, Campo Limones, La Lima, Cortés, May 5, 2006; Edmundo Cabrera Williams, interview by author, Finca Indiana, La Lima, Cortés, July 25, 2004.

48. CEDIJ, San Pedro Sula, "Worker and Campesino Newspaper Organ of the 'Group for the Defense of the Proletariat,'" *El Martillo*, June 2, 1929, loose document (*hoja suelta*).

49. Ibid.

50. Evidence of literacy among workers is nonexistent; interviews, however, do reveal that workers did have ways of sharing information with other workers. Nohemy Yanez, whose father attended clandestine organizing meetings and brought her along as a child, explains that in the period of the 1940s and 1950s workers would get together in a group in the dead of night, in the middle of a banana grove, and the person that could read would read aloud to others articles and notes from radical newspapers that had been buried in that area. Workers buried the newspapers and organizing pamphlets because if the local cabos de comisariato (police paid by the company) found these materials in their barracks the workers could face jail time and even lose their jobs. Nohemy Yanez, interview by author, La Lima, Cortés, July 28, 2017. Up until the 1980s, literature deemed subversive was penalized heavily by the Honduran state. Iris Munguía, labor leader, remembers her brother being detained for carrying a copy of *Prisión Verde* while on the bus to the campos. Iris Munguía, interview by author, La Lima, Cortés, February 25, 2006.

51. Nohemy Yanez, interview by author, La Lima, Cortés, July 28, 2017; Daniel Madrid Guevara, interview by author, La Lima, Cortés, February 5, 2006; Leonardo Bautista, Campo Limones, La Lima, Cortés, May 5, 2006; José Reyes Pineda, interview by author, Campo Limones, La Lima, Cortés, May 5, 2006; Edmundo Cabrera Williams, interview by author, Finca Indiana, La Lima, Cortés, July 25, 2004.

52. CEDIJ, San Pedro Sula, expediente sin número, "Amparo a favor de Manuel Cálix Herrera interpuesto por Hemergildo Briceno R.," August 29, 1929.

53. Ibid.; Archivo del Poder Judicial, San Pedro Sula, expediente sin número, "Consulta sobre instancia Manuel Cálix Herrra et al.," October 22, 1929.

54. Bourgois, "One Hundred Years," 138.

55. Ibid., 140.

56. Ibid., 103.

57. Local historians and current-day organizers claim that these are the Communist Party organizers who were the first to organize workers in the banana fincas, and that their main organizing tactic was to distribute *El Martillo*, a worker newspaper that circulated in the fincas of the banana companies at the time.

58. Villars, *Lealtad y Rebeldía*, 242.

59. "El lider comunista Juan P. Wainwright intentó quitarse la vida en Guatemala cortándose las venas con una cuchilla Gillette." Reproduced in *El Cronista*, Tegucigalpa, February 25, 1932, 1–6. Cited in Villars, *Lealtad y Rebeldía*, 372–373.

60. Villars, *Lealtad y Rebeldía*, 372–373.

61. Sagastume, *Carías*, 93.

62. Ibid.

63. Ibid., 46.

64. Euraque, *Reinterpreting the Banana Republic,* 52–53; Barahona, *Silencio Quedó Atrás,* 23.

65. Euraque, *Reinterpreting the Banana Republic,* 41.

66. McCameron, *Bananas, Labor, and Politics,* 17.

67. Ibid., 49.

68. Barahona, *Silencio Quedó Atrás,* 55–57. The CCO was an organization that brought together various other craft unions and worker committees; its main avenue of communication was the newspaper *Voz Obrera.* Posas, *Luchas del Movimiento Obrero Hondureño,* 120–121.

69. Ambassador John D. Erwin to the US State Department, quoted in Euraque, *Reinterpreting the Banana Republic,* 36; Barahona, *Silencio Quedó Atrás.*

70. The CLO was a worker committee of the Communist Party, formally founded in April 1954. Posas, *Luchas del Movimiento Obrero Hondureño,* 142.

71. Argueta, *Desafío al Tradicionalismo Político,* 42; Barahona, *Silencio Quedó Atrás,* 136.

72. Ibid. (author's translation). The US Embassy's real concern was the development of Guatemala's October Revolution and the risk that these ideals would eventually seep into Honduras and other countries. US consular reports closely watched and tracked Guatemalans.

73. Barahona, *Silencio Quedó Atrás, 136.*

74. Ibid., 67–68.

75. Programa del PDRH, in Argueta, *Desafío al Tradicionalismo Político,* 201–202, 34–36.

76. Ibid., 45.

77. Ibid., 204.

78. Ibid., 137.

79. Programa del PDRH in ibid. 201–211. See appendix.

80. Programa del PDRH in ibid. 201–211.

81. Programa del PDRH in ibid. 201–211.

82. "Desigualdad Política de la Mujer," *Vanguardia Revolucionaria* 4, no. 243, April 1, 1950, pp. 1–4. Cited in Villars, *Para la Casa,* 344–345.

83. "Artículo 191. La jornada máxima obligatoria asalariada será de ocho horas diarias y por casa seis días de trabajo habrá uno de descanso." Letter from the Central Strike Committee to the Mediation Commission, June 17, 1954, p. 13, in "Aspectos Fundamentales," APMP.

84. Acta no. 226, Libro Copiador 1946, pp. 60–65, Archivo de Gobernación de Cortés, San Pedro Sula, Honduras.

85. Acta no. 226, Libro Copiador 1946, pp. 60–65, Archivo de Gobernación de Cortés, San Pedro Sula, Honduras, 62.

86. Acta no. 226, Libro Copiador 1946, pp. 60–65, Archivo de Gobernación de Cortés, San Pedro Sula, Honduras.

87. The original name of the newspaper, *Vanguardia,* was later changed to *Vanguardia Revolucionaria.* In the 1920s the worker parties also used this tactic.

88. Barahona, *Silencio Quedó Atrás,* 144–145.

89. Ibid., 144.

90. Ibid.

91. Ibid., 145.

92. "Robert H. Smith, Vice President Overseas, Standard Fruit," Labor Folder 1954–1955, Box 176(2), November 26, 1954, Record Group 84, USNA.

93. Julio C. Rivera, interview by author, San José, Costa Rica, July 2008.

94. Barahona, *Silencio Quedó Atrás*, 145.

95. "Estatutos del Partido Comunista Hondureño Aprobados el 26 de Diciembre de 1948," 1/15:171/1/1-13, Fondo Primer Partido Marxista-Leninista M-26-7 y otros, Legajo Instituciones Extranjeras, Instituto de Historia Del Movimiento Comunista y de la Revolución Socialista de Cuba Anexo al CC del PCC Archivo, La Habana, Cuba. (Special thanks to Jennifer Carcamo for providing this document).

96. "Estatutos del Partido Comunista Hondureño Aprobados el 26 de Diciembre de 1948," 1/15:171/1/1-13, Fondo Primer Partido Marxista-Leninista M-26-7 y otros, Legajo Instituciones Extranjeras, Instituto de Historia Del Movimiento Comunista y de la Revolución Socialista de Cuba Anexo al CC del PCC Archivo, La Habana, Cuba, p. 4 (author's translation).

97. "Estatutos del Partido Comunista Hondureño Aprobados el 26 de Diciembre de 1948," 1/15:171/1/1-13, Fondo Primer Partido Marxista-Leninista M-26-7 y otros, Legajo Instituciones Extranjeras, Instituto de Historia Del Movimiento Comunista y de la Revolución Socialista de Cuba Anexo al CC del PCC Archivo, La Habana, Cuba, p. 5 (author's translation).

98. Barahona, *Memorias de un Comunista*, 87.

99. Such is the case of Ventura Ramos Alvarado and Rigoberto Padilla Rush. Many also kept in touch via letters and messages with other party members.

100. Barahona, *Silencio Quedó Atrás*, 144. Workers' testimonies also reflect the danger Rivera speaks of here: belonging to the Liberal Party or any left-leaning party was extremely dangerous for them as well. Daniel Madrid Guevara, interview by author, La Lima, Cortés, February 5, 2006; Julio C. Rivera, interview by author, San José, Costa Rica, July, 2008; Leonardo Bautista, interview by author, Campo Limones, La Lima, Cortés, May 5, 2006.

101. Letter from Ramón Villeda Morales to Serafino Romualdi, Tegucigalpa, March 2, 1956, Box 5459, File 5–5, KCLMDA.

102. Ramón Villeda Morales had authored at least two articles in the PDH newspaper *Vanguardia*, which was led by a more progressive wing of the Liberal Party in 1946. Argueta, *Desafío al Tradicionalismo Político*, 44.

103. Letter from Ramón Villeda Morales to Serafino Romualdi, San Jose, Costa Rica, August 15, 1956, Box 5459, File 5–5, KCLMDA.

104. Ibid.

105. Letter from Serafino Romualdi to Ramón Villeda Morales, August 21, 1956, 5-5, KCLMDA.

106. Ibid.

107. A. C. McLellan, Consultant Representative of ORIT to Arturo Jáuregui H., Assistant Secretary of ORIT, "Report on Labor Situation in Honduras. Period Aug. 6th–25th, 56," September 4, 1956, Box 5459, File 5–5, KCLMDA.

108. Ramón Villeda Morales, "To the Workers of Honduras," Washington, DC, August 15, 1957.

109. Teresina Rossi Matamoros, interview by author, Tegucigalpa, December 21, 2006; Barahona, *Silencio Quedó Atrás*, 361–362.

110. The Tela Railroad Company attempted to discredit the strike leaders of the first committee by accusing them of being "outside agitators" and not even workers. Their position as workers gave them power and access with finca workers.

111. Undated Note, Serafino Romualdi, Venezuela Documents, Collection 5459 Box 7–folder 7–4 Room 515 Address 31-B-3-C KCLMDA. Special thanks to Miguel Tinker Salas for providing this document.

112. "To the Workers of Honduras," Ramón Villeda Morales, Washington, DC, August 15, 1957; see also "Labor Troubles along North Coast of Honduras," quoted in Euraque, *Reinterpreting the Banana Republic*, 37.

113. "U.S. Embassy Memo." November 24, 1953, Box 177 (Box 3) Labor Affairs Folder 1953, Record Group 84, 300–570.5, USNA.

114. "Letter from Wymberly Coerr to William P. Hudson," July 20, 1954, US Embassy, Tegucigalpa, Box 176 (Box 2) Labor Affairs 1954–1955, Record Group 84, 300–570.5, USNA.

115. Romualdi is referring to using the Point Four program launched by President Truman as foreign aid in 1949. Press release, George Meany, AFL President, August 10, 1954, File 5–6, KCLMDA.

116. Patilla Chinchilla (pseudonym), interview by author, Los Angeles, January 1, 2020.

117. Macekura, "Point Four Program."

118. Rodolfo López and Carlos Bernhard, the editor and administrator of the newspaper, and José Argueta, the secretary general of the CCO. "Aide-memoire" no. 96, Box 177 (3), Labor Affairs 1953 Folder, Record Group, 84, USNA.

119. "Annual Labor Report-Calendar year 1952," Box 177 (Old Box 3), Folder Labor Affairs, 1953, Record Group 84, USNA.

120. Ibid.

121. Ibid.

122. Ibid.

123. The same memo reports that various newspapers accused "local commerce and foreigners of exploiting workers" (which included Turcos and Gringos, an all-inclusive term). Ibid.

124. Ibid.

125. Euraque, *Reinterpreting the Banana Republic*, 46–47.

126. Ibid., 5.

127. Holden, "Constructing the Limits."

128. Ibid.

129. Dunkerley, *Power in the Isthmus*, 87, 90.

130. Holden, "Constructing the Limits," 2.

131. Romualdi, *Presidents and Peons*.

132. A. C. McLellan, ORIT Consultant Representative, to Arturo Jáuregui H., ORIT Assistant Secretary, "Report on Labor Situation in Honduras, Period Aug. 6th–25th, 56," Box 5459, File 5–5, KCLMDA.

133. A. C. McLellan, ORIT Consultant Representative, to Luis Albert Monge, ORIT Secretary General, "Report on Trade Union Situation in Honduras Period Ending Jan. 26/27, Box 5459, File 5–5, KCLMDA.

134. The "four commitments" refers to US President Franklin Delano Roosevelt's speech on the freedoms of speech, freedom of worship, freedom from want, and

freedom from fear, given on January 6, 1941. Dunkerly marks this as the end of the "good neighbor policy" and its replacement by modernist agenda of the Cold War. Dunkerley, *Power in the Isthmus*, 88.

135. Grandin, *Last Colonial Massacre*, 75.

136. Holden, "Securing Central America," 6.

137. Ibid., 5.

138. Dunkerly, *Power in the Isthmus*, 527.

139. Ibid., 1.

140. Holden notes that increased surveillance and coercion was needed as industrial capitalism took root in various societies, in order to control, observe, and discipline the workplace. However, in Central America, surveillance and coercion developed without industrial capital development. Holden, "Constructing the Limits," 1–2.

141. Holden, "Constructing the Limits," 3.

142. Rabe, *Killing Zone*.

Chapter 3: Life and Labor in the Banana Fincas

1. Many north-coast inhabitants used "campos" or "campos bananeros" to refer to the rural banana-growing areas, without distinguishing between the fincas, the planted fields where workers labored, and the residential camps. But for the most part, workers used terms more precisely to make a distinction between the two. "Finca" denoted the place of work and "campos" referred to the living areas. In this chapter and in keeping with workers' words, finca refers to the banana groves or fields and campos to the residential camps.

2. Bucheli, *Bananas and Business*, 54, 58–64.

3. The company wanted to sell the land to national producers as an investment in the production of sorghum. Posas, "Tacamiche Conflict."

4. Ibid.

5. For the Standard Fruit Company, based in Louisiana, the same hierarchical structure existed, but their reach was less expansive than UFCo and relied mostly on outside growers to supply their bananas in the initial years.

6. Bucheli, *Bananas and Business*, 49–50.

7. Ibid., 50–64.

8. Ibid., 64–65, 66–70.

9. María Ángela Cardona, interview by author, El Carríl, Olanchito, Yoro, August 13, 2006.

10. Karnes, *Tropical Enterprise*.

11. Barahona, *Hegemonía*, 59 (author's translation).

12. Ibid.

13. Daniel Madrid Guevara, interview by author, La Lima, Cortés, February, 5, 2006; María Ángela Cardona, interview by author, El Carríl, Olanchito, Yoro, August 13, 2006.

14. The Honduran Republic is composed of 18 departments with a capital city (the twin cities of Tegucigalpa and Comayagüela). These departments are regional state-like demarcations within the republic.

15. Roberts's discussion of Thompson's work and Thompson's chapter on community are helpful in thinking about the banana workers and their construction

of community; see Roberts, "Peasants and Proletarians," 357; Thompson, *Making of the English Working Class*, 401–447.

16. In Limón, Costa Rica, there were various types of contracts, but usually a team of three worked in cutting, and "the pay, calculated by the piece, was split among three," as distinct from the Honduran model described later. In the context of Limón, Costa Rica, according to Lara Putnam, a *conchero* is the man "who received the stem on his back and hauled it into a nearby hut." In Honduras this work position is referred to as a juntero and is not to be confused with a *conchero*, who took the *concha* (skin of banana or plantain) of the banana or the banana tree leaves to pad the train car *(rejilla)* so that the stems would not be damaged in transit. Putnam, *Company They Kept*, 122.

17. Marx, *Capital*, 142–145.

18. Roberts, "Peasants and Proletarians," 364–366.

19. Ibid., 357.

20. Ibid.

21. Amaya Amador, *Prisión Verde*.

22. Edmundo Cabrera Williams, interview by author, Finca Indiana, La Lima, Cortés, July 25, 2004; Juan B. Canales, interview by author, La Ceiba, Atlántida, August 8, 2004; Francisco Portillo, interview by author, La Lima, Cortés, February 6, 2006; Angel Martinez, interview by author, Colonia Nuevo San Juan, La Lima, Cortés, January 29, 2006.

23. Francisco Portillo, interview by author, La Lima, Cortés, February 6, 2006; Francisco Amerto Lagos, interview by author, La Lima, Cortés, Febraury 6, 2006.

24. Jesús Gómez, interview by author, La Lima, Cortés, March 7, 2006; Daniel Madrid Guevara, interview by author, La Lima, Cortés, February 5, 2006; Angel Martinez, interview by author, Colonial Nuevo San Juan, La Lima, Cortés, June, 2006; Oscar Rodriguez Pagoada, interview by author, American Zone, La Lima, Cortés, September 2, 2006; Edmundo Cabrera Williams, interview by author, Finca Indiana, La Lima, Cortés, July 25, 2004.

25. Angel Martinez, interview by author, Colonial Nuevo San Juan, La Lima, Cortés, January 29, 2006.

26. Angel Martinez, interview by author, Colonial Nuevo San Juan, La Lima, Cortés, January 29, 2006.

27. Eduardo Padilla, interview by author, La Lima, Cortés, March 30, 2006.

28. Edmundo Cabrera Williams, interview by author, Finca Indiana, La Lima, Cortés, July 25, 2004.

29. Oscar Rodriguez Pagoada, interview by author, American Zone, La Lima, Cortés, September 2, 2006.

30. Oscar Rodriguez Pagoada, interview by author, American Zone, La Lima, Cortés, September 2, 2006.

31. Yardero, derived from "yardworker" is one among many English-language words adapted to Spanish and used by workers in the north coast. English was the language of trade, an indicator of the dominance of the US companies. Other common terms of the industry were enmenes from "M&S," poisero from "poison worker," and cuque from "cook."

32. Jesús Gómez, interview by author, La Lima, Cortés, March 7, 2006. The employer, in this case the North American Mr. Keller, wanted to know he could

trust this worker around his daughters. As Gómez explains, he was an honest and honorable person (*persona honrada*), which meant he could be trusted in the cultural context of Honduras. Gómez, a young man himself, had to prove that he was a good, honest man, who would not steal from him and would certainly not enamor or abuse Mr. Keller's daughters. Mr. Keller would confirm his honorability daily. If Gómez took them to the movies, he would be quizzed about which movie they saw, making sure that he was next to them at all times, and also making sure they did not sneak off with their boyfriends. Gómez had recently arrived from the interior of the country and felt nervous about these tests because he had not been exposed to films and the company town's social activities before.

33. Jesús Gómez, interview by author, La Lima, Cortés, March 7, 2006.

34. Casta Figueroa Portillo, interview by author, El Carríl, Olanchito, Yoro, August 13, 2006.

35. Edmundo Cabrera Williams, interview by author, Finca Indiana, La Lima, Cortés, July 24, 2006.

36. Edmundo Cabrera Williams, interview by author, Finca Indiana, La Lima, Cortés, July 24, 2006.

37. Edmundo Cabrera Williams, interview by author, Finca Indiana, La Lima, Cortés, July 24, 2006.

38. Alejandro Ortega, interview by author, La Lima, Cortés, February 8, 2006; Francisco Amerto Lagos, interview by author, La Lima, Cortés, February 6, 2006.

39. Alejandro Ortega, interview by author, La Lima, Cortés, February 8, 2006.

40. Edmundo Cabrera Williams, interview by author, Finca Indiana, La Lima, Cortés, July 24, 2006.

41. Francisco Amerto Lagos, interview by author, La Lima, Cortés, February 6, 2006; Edmundo Cabrera Williams, interview by author, Finca Indiana, La Lima, Cortés, July 24, 2006; Jesús Gómez, interview by author, La Lima, Cortés, March 7, 2006; Daniel Madrid Guevara, interview by author, La Lima, Cortés, February 5, 2006; Angel Martinez, interview by author, Colonial Nuevo San Juan, La Lima, Cortés, June, 2006; Oscar Rodriguez Pagoada, interview by author, American Zone, La Lima, Cortés, September 2, 2006; Edmundo Cabrera Williams, interview by author, Finca Indiana, La Lima, Cortés, July 26, 2006; Leonardo Bautista, interview by author, Campo Limones, La Lima, Cortés, May 5, 2006; Angel Martinez, interview by author, Colonial Nuevo San Juan, La Lima, Cortés, January 29, 2006, Pablo Raul Carcamo, interview by author, La Lima, Cortés, May 5, 2006; Narciso Duarte Cruz, interview by author, Savá, Colo, June 10, 2006; Isabel Moreira, interview by author, San Pedro Sula, Cortés, November 27, 2006; Juan Nuñez Sierra, La Lima, Cortés, Neftalí Rogel, interview by author, La Lima, Cortés, March 7, 2006; Soluri, *Banana Cultures*, 142–148.

42. Eduardo Padilla, interview by author, La Lima, Cortés, March 30, 2006.

43. Workers were generally paid in US dollars and frequently had deductions taken from their pay for company store purchases and other costs. No currency exchanges were necessary.

44. Eduardo Padilla, interview by author, La Lima, Cortés, March 30, 2006.

45. *Unifruitco*, March 1954, Unifruitco Magazine Collection, Huntington Library Archives.

46. Workers refer to the captain of the finca as mandador (supervisor; later called *administrador* in the 1960s). This was usually the company employee assigned to oversee a region or finca.

47. Olimpia Edelmira Figueroa, interview by author, La Lima, Cortés, 2006; Efraín Hernández Maldonado, interview by author, La Lima, Cortés, 2006; Daniel Madrid Guevara, interview by author, La Lima, Cortés, 2006; Angel Martinez, interview by author, Colonia Nuevo San Juan, La Lima, Cortés, January 29, 2006; Eduardo Padilla, interview by author, La Lima, Cortés, 2006; Oscar Rodriguez Pagoada, interview by author, Zona Americana, La Lima, Cortés, 2006.

48. Edmundo Cabrera Williams, interview by author, Finca Indiana, La Lima, Cortés, July 25, 2004; Juan B. Canales, interview by author, La Ceiba, Atlántida, August 8, 2004. Francisco Amerto Lagos, interview by author, La Lima, Cortés, February 6, 2006.

49. Jesús Gómez, interview by author, La Lima, Cortés, March 7, 2006.

50. Company towns were known to finca workers as "terminals" because the major train terminals were located in the towns.

51. Juan B. Canales, interview by author, La Ceiba, Atlántida, August 8, 2004; Barahona, *Silencio Quedó Atrás*, 277–316.

52. Juan B. Canales, interview by author, La Ceiba, Atlántida, August 8, 2004.

53. Angel Martinez, interview by author, Colonial Nuevo San Juan, La Lima, Cortés, January 29, 2006. The enmenes, the Materials and Supplies department, was located in the terminals (or company town centers). This department supplied all the building needs of the campos and fincas, supplying all other departments with a variety of objects for building and repairs.

54. Juan B. Canales, interview by author, La Ceiba, Atlántida, August 8, 2004.

55. Edmundo Cabrera Williams, interview by author, Finca Indiana, La Lima, Cortés, July 25, 2004.

56. Jesús Gómez, interview by author, La Lima, Cortés, March 7, 2006; Francisco Amerto Lagos, interview by author, La Lima, Cortés, February 6, 2006. The company experimental centers known as the Chemical Department were donated to the Honduran government and now operate under the name Fundación Hondureña de Investigación Agrícola, located in La Lima, Cortés.

57. Oscar Rodriguez Pagoada, interview by author, American Zone, La Lima, Cortés, September 2, 2006; Francisco Amerto Lagos, interview by author, La Lima, Cortés, February 6, 2006. See also Soluri, *Banana Cultures*.

58. Oscar Rodriguez Pagoada, interview by author, American Zone, La Lima, Cortés, September 2, 2006.

59. The *machanguay* (dervied from English "merchandise") was the train that ran on certain days of the week for workers' transportation and vendors, usually on Sundays. They consisted of cars that workers called *rejillas*, which were typically used to carry the fruit and therefore had no seats, only slabs of wood on the sides. The *pasajero* was the regular passenger train. The *mixto*, or mixed train, transported fruit and people in separate boxcars.

60. Angel Martinez, interview by author, Colonial Nuevo San Juan, La Lima, Cortés, January 29, 2006.

61. Alejandro Ortega, interview by author, La Lima, Cortés, February 8, 2006.

62. Ortega worked in a campo near the region of San Manuel; later he worked

in San Manuel. Jesús Gómez worked in three fincas in his lifetime: Guaruma Dos, Naranjo Chino, and later in Birichiche. Alejandro Ortega, interview by author, La Lima, Cortés, February 8, 2006; Jesús Gómez, interview by author, La Lima, Cortés, March 7, 2006.

63. Jesús Gómez, interview by author, La Lima, Cortés, March 7, 2006.

64. For workers' compañerismo in Costa Rican UFCo lands, see the case of M. G. L. in Putnam, *Company They Kept*, 118–120.

65. Alejandro Ortega, interview by author, La Lima, Cortés, February 8, 2006.

66. Angel Martinez, interview by author, Colonial Nuevo San Juan, La Lima, Cortés, June, 2006.

67. Angel Martinez, interview by author, Colonial Nuevo San Juan, La Lima, Cortés, January 29, 2006.

68. Juan Nuñez Sierra, interview by author, La Lima, Cortés, March 7, 2006; Juan B. Canales, interview by author, La Ceiba, Atlántida, August, 8, 2004.

69. Alejandro Ortega, interview by author, La Lima, Cortés, February 8, 2006.

70. María Ángela Cardona, interview by author, El Carríl, Olanchito, Yoro, August 13, 2006; Casta Figueroa Portillo, interview by author, El Carríl, Olanchito, Yoro, August 13, 2006.

71. Klubock, *Contested Communities*.

72. Daniel Madrid Guevara, interview by author, La Lima, Cortés, February 5, 2006.

73. Alejandro Ortega, interview by author, La Lima, Cortés, February 8, 2006.

74. This did not mean that tensions ended; three to six families lived in a barracón, and although each had its own separate *cuarto*, there were shared areas that were the site of many disagreements among women. Madrid Guevara, interview by author, La Lima, Cortés, February 5, 2006.

75. Madrid Guevara, interview by author, La Lima, Cortés, February 5, 2006.

76. Edmundo Cabrera Williams, interview by author, Finca Indiana, La Lima, Cortés, July 25, 2004.

77. Edmundo Cabrera Williams, interview by author, Finca Indiana, La Lima, Cortés, July 25, 2004.

78. María Ángela Cardona, interview by author, El Carríl, Olanchito, Yoro, August 13, 2006.

79. Oscar Rodriguez Pagoada, interview by author, American Zone, La Lima, Cortés, September 2, 2006.

80. Oscar Rodriguez Pagoada, interview by author, American Zone, La Lima, Cortés, September 2, 2006.

81. Juana Marquez was also a president of the committee responsible for cooking food during the 1954 strike. Daniel Madrid Guevara, interview by author, La Lima, Cortés, February 5, 2006.

82. Alejandro Ortega, interview by author, La Lima, Cortés, February 8, 2006.

83. The term in Spanish was *robar* (to steal). Women were *robadas*, which meant that the woman was taken without permission from her parents, and their partnership did not exactly mean that she was properly married. In some cases it meant they had eloped. In the case of an already partnered woman, she could also be *robada* (stolen) from her male partner in the finca. In oral testimonies, men refer to women as property that served a utilitarian purpose. Alejandro Ortego, interview by author, La

Lima, Cortés, February 8, 2006; Jesús Gómez, interview by author, La Lima, Cortés, March 7, 2006; Francisco Portillo, interview by author, La Lima, Cortés, February 6, 2006.

84. Angel Martinez, interview by author, Campo Nuevo San Juan, La Lima, Cortés, January 29, 2006.

85. Olimpia Figueroa, interview by author, La Lima, Cortés, February 15, 2010.

86. Olimpia Figueroa, interview by author, La Lima, Cortés, February 15, 2010.

87. Olimpia Figueroa, interview by author, La Lima, Cortés, February 15, 2010.

88. Although there were Chinese vendors and merchants in Honduras during this period, the term usually does not refer to a person of Chinese ancestry.

89. Tinsman, *Partners in Conflict*, 48.

90. Klublock found that in the El Teniente mine in Chile women *empleadas* often exchanged services for material support. See Klubock, "Morality and Good Habits," 236.

91. Olimpia Edelmira Figueroa, interview by author, La Lima, Cortés, February 15, 2006; María Antonia Perla, interview by author, La Lima, Cortés, March 5, 2006.

92. Olimpia Edelmira Figueroa, interview by author, La Lima, Cortés, February 15, 2006.

93. Olimpia Edelmira Figueroa, interview by author, La Lima, Cortés, February 15, 2006; María Antonia Perla, interview by author, La Lima, Cortés, March 5, 2006.

94. Klubock, "Morality and Good Habits," 236–237.

95. Olimpia Edelmira Figueroa, interview by author, La Lima, Cortés, February 15, 2006; María Ángela Cardona, interview by author, El Carríl, Olanchito, Yoro, August 13, 2006; Adela Chávez, interview by author, La Lima Nueva, Cortés, February 6, 2006; Casta Figueroa Portillo, interview by author, El Carríl, Olanchito, Yoro, August 13, 2006; Lucila Goodlitt, interview by author, El Carríl, Olanchito, Yoro, August 10, 2006; María Antonia Perla, interview by author, La Lima, Cortés, March 5, 2010; Lidia Aurora Lezama, interview by author, Campo Mucula, El Progreso, Yoro, December 9, 2006.

96. Olimpia Edelmira Figueroa, interview by author, La Lima, Cortés, February 15, 2006.

97. Ley de Estupro. See Centro de Derechos de la Mujer, "Obstáculos y Desafíos que Enfrentan las Mujeres Víctimas de Violación Sexual para Acceder a la Justicia," derechosdelamujer.org.

98. Tinsman, *Partners in Conflict*, 72.

99. María Antonia Perla, interview by author, La Lima, Cortés, March 5, 2010.

100. María Antonia Perla, interview by author, La Lima, Cortés, March 5, 2010.

101. María Antonia Perla, interview by author, La Lima, Cortés, March 5, 2010.

102. In a case of rape in Chile, Klublock found the same situation: the violated woman was deemed at fault, in accordance with the community's social, gender, and sexuality codes. Klubock, "Morality and Good Habits," 245. Similarly, Heidi Tinsman found that in Chile between 1950 and 1964 most of the women raped were adolescent and prepubescent girls and most of the perpetrators were members of the same community. Tinsman, *Partners in Conflict*, 73. Lara Putnam's incisive study of legal records also found that young prepubescent women maids in the banana zone were subject to rape and coerced sex. Putnam, *Company They Kept*, 86.

103. I could only find evidence of these alimony and food stipend documents dated after the strike. See Demandas Alimenticias Varias, La Ceiba, Archivo del Poder

Judicial. Tinsman comes to this conclusion when looking at cases of parents filing charges against men for rape of their young daughters to deal with courting, which may have involved sex and, potentially, pregnancies. Tinsman, *Partners in Conflict*, 281.

104. Ibid., 289.

105. María Ángela Cardona, interview by author, El Carríl, Olanchito, Yoro, August 13, 2006.

106. María Ángela Cardona, interview by author, El Carríl, Olanchito, Yoro, August 13, 2006.

107. Workers understood them as law enforcement. They used comandantes or cabos de comisariato to refer to law enforcement agents with higher authority and auxiliares to refer to other representatives in the outskirts of town. "Cabos de comsariato" literally translates as "commissary corporal."

108. Juan Nuñez Sierra, interview by author, La Lima, Cortés, March 7, 2006.

109. Sylvia Robleda, interview by author, San Pedro Sula, Cortés, July 4, 2004; Agapito Robleda Castro, interview by author, San Pedro Sula, Cortés, August 2, 2006.

110. Francisco Portillo, interview by author, La Lima, Cortés, February 6, 2006; Daniel Madrid Guevara, interview by author, La Lima, Cortés, February 5, 2006.

111. Francisco Portillo, interview by author, La Lima, Cortés, February 6, 2006; Daniel Madrid Guevara, interview by author, La Lima, Cortés, February 5, 2006.

112. Daniel Madrid Guevara, interview by author, La Lima, Cortés, February 5, 2006.

113. José Sánchez, interview by author, La Lima, Cortés, November 5, 2006; Daniel Madrid Guevara, interview by author, La Lima, Cortés, February 5, 2006.

114. Absenteeism did not become a notable problem until much later, during the introduction of the packing warehouses. In 1962 the banana companies and United Brands (formerly United Fruit and Steamship Company) introduced the packinghouses, where bananas were packed into boxes. Workers lost their freedom to move from contract to contract and finca to finca. Absenteeism was also easily tracked. Carlos Amaya Yanez, interview by author, La Lima, Cortés, 2004, 2006.

115. Juan B. Canales, interview by author, La Ceiba, Atlántida, August, 8, 2004; Daniel Madrid Guevara, interview by author, La Lima, Cortés, February 5, 2006; Francisco Portillo, interview by author, La Lima, Cortés, February 6, 2006.

116. José Sánchez, interview by author, La Lima, Cortés, November 5, 2006.

117. CEDIJ, San Pedro Sula, Ligas de Fútbol, 1956, expediente sin número, hojas sueltas.

118. Mayorga, "'Campeón' y 'Chuna,' Pura Vida," 140.

119. Ibid. (translation by author).

120. Archetti, *Masculinities*, 71.

121. Leandro Bautista, interview by author, Finca Indiana, La Lima, Cortés, May 5, 2006.

122. Leandro Bautista, interview by author, Finca Indiana, La Lima, Cortés, May 5, 2006.

123. Leandro Bautista, interview by author, Finca Indiana, La Lima, Cortés, May 5, 2006.

Chapter 4: The Making of a Campeño and Campeña Culture

1. Angel Martinez, interview by author, Campo Nuevo San Juan, La Lima, Cortés, January 29, 2006.

2. I use "mestizo" consistent with current academic analysis of race and the racial understandings of Honduras. Workers consistently used the term "indio."

3. Francisco Portillo, interview by author, La Lima, Cortés, February 6, 2006.

4. Euraque, *Conversaciones Históricas*, 42.

5. Euraque, "Threat of Blackness."

6. Euraque, *Conversaciones Históricas*, 60.

7. Ibid., 80–81, 83.

8. Ibid., 42.

9. Ibid., 42, 60.

10. Chambers, *Race, Nation, and West Indian Immigration*, 31–32, 50–51. Chambers also notes the eventual deportation of Jamaicans as part of the movement to construct a mestizo nation by elites and intellectuals in Honduras, and he shows how West Indian communities struggled for survival in light of their loss of Honduran citizenship.

11. Chambers, *Race, Nation, and West Indian Immigration*, 51; Barahona, *Evolución Histórica*, 263–264; Euraque, *Conversaciones Históricas*, 98–99.

12. Chambers, *Race, Nation, and West Indian Immigration*, 69.

13. Euraque, "Threat of Blackness," 243; Barahona, *Evolución Histórica*, 267; Chambers, *Race, Nation, and West Indian Immigration*, 54–55.

14. Froylán Turcios, "Inmigrantes Innecesarios," *El Nuevo Tiempo*, Tegucigalpa, July 18, 1916, quoted in Euraque, *Conversaciones Históricas*, 163.

15. Ibid.

16. Chambers, *Race, Nation, and West Indian Immigration*, 55.

17. Euraque, *Conversaciones Históricas*, 83.

18. Euraque, "Threat of Blackness," 243–244.

19. Glenn A. Chambers has documented that mestizos and local Hondurans used to confuse the Black communities of West Indians and Garifunas. Many of the supervisors were mestizos and may not have made the ethnic distinctions among the Black populations in the north coast. Chambers, *Race, Nation, and West Indian Immigration*, 132.

20. Barahona, *Evolución Histórica*, 245.

21. Ibid., 173.

22. Euraque, *Conversaciones Históricas*, 224–225.

23. Candelario, *Black behind the Ears*, 19, 58, 240. Candelario found, in the context of the Dominican Republic, that the term "indio" was a "middle term" at the center of the racial continuum, the "native" alternative to foreign Blackness and whiteness alike. Researchers argue that, in the Dominican Republic, during its process of mestizaje, "indio" was "a neutral, 'un-marked' term that excludes blackness as it affirms Hispanicity of a different hue and (hair) texture." This identification with *indio/a* is still used by Dominicans on and off the island: "To the extent that mulata has been semantically erased in favor of the *India* (who is understood to be representative of Dominican 'in-betweenness'), the India operates as an iconographic stand-in for contemporary Dominican women." In the case of the Dominican Republic, the notion of indio had been evolving since the time of the Trujillato, during the regime of military strongman and dictator General Rafael Leónidas Trujillo from 1930 to 1961, but it was also an accepted, more contemporary identity that Dominicans constructed and prioritized, on and off the island.

24. Because Salvadorans and other migrants competed for jobs, Hondurans also

wanted to claim the term "indio" to mean "native to Honduras." Most workers interviewed concurred on the uses of indio to mean native to Honduras.

25. In Rocío Tábora's work on masculinity in Honduras she argues that the construction of masculinity in Honduras emerges through the relationship between the feminine and masculine, the moments of solidarity between men and women and friendship between men, the construction and deconstruction of the hero and political violence and war. Her work, however, does not extend to the working-class subjects and their construction of masculinity. Because her textual analysis is of men, and due to limits in historiography, we never hear about the common men, the workers, and how they constructed their masculinity and hierarchies in a racial and class hierarchy. Tábora, *Masculinidad y Violencia.*

26. Efraín Hernández Maldonado, interview by author, La Lima, Cortés, March 28, 2006.

27. Eduardo Padilla, interview by author, La Lima, Cortés, March 30, 2006.

28. Juan B. Canales, interview by author, La Ceiba, Atlántida, August, 8, 2004.

29. Euraque, *Conversaciones Históricas,* 98–99.

30. Barahona, *Evolución Histórica,* 263–264; Euraque, *Conversaciones Históricas,* 98–99; González, *Dollar, Dove, and Eagle,* 90.

31. Euraque, *Conversaciones Históricas,* 83, 186; Chambers, *Race, Nation, and West Indian Immigration,* 121–123.

32. Euraque deduces that Salvadoran workers were a larger group than Jamaican workers in 1916. Echeverrí-Gent claims the opposite, there was a large presence of British West Indian workers. Both agree that this period was perilous for Black workers. Euraque, "Threat of Blackness," 234–239; Echeverrí-Gent, "Forgotten Workers," 301.

33. Soluri, *Banana Cultures,* 132–133.

34. Gerardo Pery Laredo, interview by author, Tornabé, Tela, Atlántida, August 8, 2006.

35. Juan B. Canales, interview by author, La Ceiba, Atlántida, August 8, 2004; Isabel Moreira, interview by author, San Pedro Sula, Cortés, November 27, 2006; Marina Graugnard, interview by author, Tela, Atlántida, June 9, 2006; Juan Nuñez Sierra, interview by author, La Lima, Cortés, March 7, 2006; Juan Bennett Bustillo, interview by author, La Lima, Cortés, February 6, 2006.

36. Juan B. Canales, interview by author, La Ceiba, Atlántida, August 8, 2004; Isabel Moreira, interview by author, San Pedro Sula, Cortés, November 27, 2006; Marina Graugnard, interview by author, Tela, Atlántida, June 9, 2006; Juan Nuñez Sierra, interview by author, La Lima, Cortés, March 7, 2006; Juan Bennett Bustillo, interview by author, La Lima, Cortés, February 6, 2006.

37. Juan B. Canales, interview by author, La Ceiba, Atlántida, August 8, 2004.

38. Gargallo, *Garífuna, Garínagu, Caribe,* 80.

39. Juan B. Canales, interview by author, La Ceiba, Atlántida, August 8, 2004.

40. Gerardo Pery Laredo, interview by author, Tornabé, Tela, Atlántida, August 8, 2006.

41. Gerardo Pery Laredo, interview by author, Tornabé, Tela, Atlántida, August 8, 2006.

42. Gerardo Pery Laredo, interview by author, Tornabé, Tela, Atlántida, August 8, 2006.

43. Gerardo Pery Laredo, interview by author, Tornabé, Tela, Atlántida, August 8, 2006.

44. Gerardo Pery Laredo, interview by author, Tornabé, Tela, Atlántida, August 8, 2006.

45. Gerardo Pery Laredo, interview by author, Tornabé, Tela, Atlántida, August 8, 2006.

46. Gerardo Pery Laredo, interview by author, Tornabé, Tela, Atlántida, August 8, 2006.

47. Patrocinia Martinez, interview by author, San Juan de Tela, Tela, Atlántida, August 8, 2006; Pedro Gonzalo Martinez, interview by author, San Juan de Tela, Tela, Atlántida, August 8, 2006; Gerardo Pery Laredo, interview by author, Tornabé, Tela, Atlántida, August 8, 2006.

48. Putnam, *Company They Kept*, 185. Similarly in Limón, Costa Rica, Putnam found that women were victims of violence when they were scarce.

49. At the other end of the spectrum were the white trusted company employees identified as "banana cowboys," a term "shorn of its associations with reckless behavior. A banana cowboy was a tough, efficient herder of fruit. He was a white-collar employee, by the 1920s usually college-educated, who worked on the land, wore a Stetson, rode a horse or a mule, often carried a pistol, and manages nonwhite laborers." Martin, *Banana Cowboys*, 9. The interesting thing is that white men did not carry fruit, and based on oral histories of the 1940s and 1950s, white supervisors rode on horses or on mules because they feared the *campeños'* dexterity and fierceness with the machete; riding also protected them from snake bites and other exposure to the environment. Angel Martinez, interview by author, Campo Nuevo San Juan, La Lima, Cortés, January 29, 2006.

50. Jesús Gómez, interview by author, La Lima, Cortés, March 7, 2006; Daniel Madrid Guevara, interview by author, La Lima, Cortés, February 5, 2006; Angel Martinez, interview by author, Colonial Nuevo San Juan, La Lima, Cortés, June, 2006; Oscar Rodriguez Pagoada, interview by author, American Zone, La Lima, Cortés, September 2, 2006; Alejandro Ortega, interview by author, La Lima, Cortés, February 8, 2006.

51. Recent articles on clandestine alcohol ties cususa (*gato de monte*) to the Indigenous and rural tradition of *chicha*, fermented corn liquor consumed during town fairs and spiritual ceremonies throughout the rural areas of Honduras and Nicaragua. "El Cususero," *Revista Enlace*, no. 1; Orlando Ortega, "La cususa, ese deleite prohibido," Los hijos de septiembre, blog, December 19, 2009, ortegareyes.wordpress .com/2009/12/19/la-cususa-ese-deleite-prohibido.

52. CEDIJ, San Pedro Sula, expediente sin nombre, Lorenzo Cerna Martinez, Hacienda Pública, 1955.

53. Many workers drank cususa and preferred it to company liquor and beer, and there were many narratives about how it was made. It was the specific skill of a *cususero/a* (man or woman), who fermented the grains for six months or more. The *cususero/a* kept his or her knowledge a secret and made the liquor behind closed doors for fear of punishment by the law. This is a custom that continues today, and contemporary accounts help to fill in the blanks. See Ortega, "La cususa, ese deleite prohibido."

54. I used the testimony of María Ángela Cardona, 2006, and the online source to piece together the process of making cususa. It was considered low-grade liquor when compared to the national aguardiente. Cususa is still made in rural areas of Nicaragua, see "El Cususero," *Revista Enlace*, no. 1.

55. Henriquez et al., *Historia sobre las Bebidas*, 178.

56. Amaya Banegas, *El que Esté Libre de Pecado*, 89.

57. Henriquez et al., *Historia sobre las Bebidas*, 178.

58. Ibid.

59. Carey, "Drunks and Dictators," 139–141.

60. Ibid., 135.

61. Archivo del Poder Judicial, CEDIJ, San Pedro Sula, expediente sin número, Perez v. Inspector de Hacienda, 1939; expediente sin número, Calderon Ayala v. Administración de Rentas, 1941; expediente sin número, María Celea Ardón Torres, Hacienda Pública, 1930; expediente sin nombre, Lorenzo Cerna Martinez, Hacienda Pública, 1955.

62. Archivo del Poder Judicial, CEDIJ, San Pedro Sula, expediente sin número, Calderon Ayala v. Administración de Rentas, 1941.

63. Ibid., fol. 1.

64. Archivo del Poder Judicial, CEDIJ, San Pedro Sula, expediente sin número, María Celea Ardón Torres, Hacienda Pública, 1953; expediente sin nombre, Lorenzo Cerna Martinez, Hacienda Pública, 1955.

65. Archivo del Poder Judicial, CEDIJ, San Pedro Sula, expediente sin número, María Celea Ardón Torres, Hacienda Pública, 1953; expediente sin nombre, Lorenzo Cerna Martinez, Hacienda Pública, 1955.

66. Archivo del Poder Judicial, CEDIJ, San Pedro Sula, expediente sin número, María Celea Ardón Torres, Hacienda Pública, 1953; expediente sin nombre, Lorenzo Cerna Martinez, Hacienda Pública, 1955.

67. Juan Nuñez Sierra, interview by author, La Lima, Cortés, March 7, 2006; Jesús Gómez, interview by author, La Lima, Cortés, March 7, 2006.

68. Durrant and Thankker, *Substance Use and Abuse*, 178. As Bradburd and Jankowiak suggest, "In later periods of [colonial] contact, when control over labor power had been consolidated through other means, drugs were used to increase the amount of the intensity of labor drawn from laboring populations. . . . [L]ater still drugs used to intensify the amount and durations of labor shifted to alcohol, opium, and marijuana, which were used to overcome both the drudgery of long, hard, physical labor and the pain and discomfort that came with it, to caffeine-based stimulants, which provided a more sober and alert workforce." Bradburd and Jankowiak, "Drugs, Desire, and European Economic Expansion," 3–4.

69. "The Rolston Letter," July 20, 1920. Found in Painter and Lapper, *Honduras: State for Sale*, 23–24. Its veracity is contested; see Euraque, *Conversaciones Históricas*, 112–113. I use it because the workers cited it often.

70. In turn-of-the-century Guatemala, coffee plantation owners believed that supplying indigenous workers with alcohol would secure their labor. Carey, "Drunks and Dictators," 133.

71. Archivo del Poder Judicial, CEDIJ, expediente 10495, San Pedro Sula, Causa Instruida contra Benedicto Dubón Ayala, Juzgado de Letras de lo Criminal, San Pedro Sula, July 29, 1950.

72. This demonstrated that workers finca-hopped to seek improved situations or to run away from unfavorable situations at work and in the living quarters. Before the 1954 strike and labor contract in 1957, workers were able to hop between fincas for work without any problems. They often did this if they were having trouble with a supervisor, if there was little work, or if they were involved in a crime, like Dubón. Ibid.

73. Ibid.

74. Archivo del Poder Judicial, CEDIJ, San Pedro Sula, expediente sin número, Perez v. Inspector de Hacienda, 1939, fol. 6.

75. Ibid.

76. Klubock, *Contested Communities*, 164.

77. Ibid., 164.

78. Ibid., 162–163.

79. Daniel Madrid Guevara, interview by author, La Lima, Cortés, February 5, 2006; Gilberto Rios, interview by author, February 8, 2017.

80. Menjívar Ochoa, in his work on Afro-descendant men and masculinity in Costa Rican banana plantations, uses the term "violencia viril" (potent violence) to refer to "a mechanism of resistance deployed by workers to confront state violence and the UFCo—and in that sense contributing to their survival and not heroic." Menjívar Ochoa, "Trabajadores Afro-Descendientes," 80.

81. Klubock, *Contested Communities*, 164.

82. A version of this poem can be found in the prologue to Menjívar, *Fragmented Ties*.

83. Most regulation was conducted through the sanitation department and national police. Amaya Banegas, *El que Esté Libre de Pecado*, 98.

84. Ibid., 76–78.

85. Ibid., 90–92.

86. Ibid., 79–80.

87. Ibid., 90–91.

88. Ibid., 84–85.

89. Ibid., 97–99.

90. "Resultado de una Encuesta sobre prostitución" por Francisco Blanco, Tegucigalpa, Imprenta de la Policia Nacional/Departmento de Salud Sanitaria, 1954. Cited in Amaya Banegas Banegas, *El que Esté Libre de Pecado*, 104–109.

91. Although the banana companies would suffer a slow decline following the stock market crash in the United States, the decline would not be felt in the north coast for a long time.

92. Archivo del Poder Judicial, CEDIJ, San Pedro Sula, Corte de Apelaciones en la demanda de Exhibición Personal y Amparo interpuesto por Eduardo (Fernando) Yanes a favor de Victoria Ayala (Camacho) Yanes, La Cieba, Atlántida, Juzgado de Letras Primero, San Pedro Sula, expediente sin número, 13 March, 1929.

93. Archivo del Poder Judicial, CEDIJ, San Pedro Sula, Corte de Apelaciones en la demanda de Exhibicion Personal y Amparo a favor de Ester de Young en contra de Delegado de Sanidad de Atlántida Miguel A. Fiallos, La Cieba, Atlántida, Juzgado de Letras Primero, San Pedro Sula, expediente sin número, 15 January, 1929.

94. Ibid.

95. Guy, *Sex and Danger in Buenos Aires*, 52.

96. Ibid., 52.

97. Ibid., 45, 46.

98. Ibid., 51.

99. Ibid., 46, 50.

100. ADPJ CEDIJ, San Pedro Sula, Corte de Apelaciones en la demanda de Exhibicion Personal y Amparo a favor de Ester de Young en contra de Delegado de Sanidad de Atlántida Miguel A. Fiallos, La Cieba, Atlántida, Juzgado de Letras Primero, San Pedro Sula, expediente sin número, 15 January, 1929, fol. 10.

101. Ibid.

102. Ibid., fols. 9r, 10.

103. CEDIJ, San Pedro Sula, Corte de Apelaciones en la demanda de Exhibicion Personal y Amparo interpuesto por Eduardo (Fernando) Yanes a favor de Victoria

Ayala (Camacho) Yanes, La Cieba, Atlántida, Juzgado de Letras Primero, San Pedro Sula, expediente sin número, 13 March, 1929.

104. Ibid., fol. 14, back of page.

105. Portillo Villeda, "Campeñas, Campeños y Compañeros."

106. Other and perhaps larger centers of a thriving sex economy include Puerto Cortés, to the west of San Pedro Sula, the major port for the Tela Railroad Company.

107. Guy, *Sex and Danger in Buenos Aires*, 8.

108. Rosaura Garcia, interview by author, La Lima, Cortés, July 19, 2011.

109. Rosaura Garcia, interview by author, La Lima, Cortés, July 19, 2011.

110. Rosaura Garcia, interview by author, La Lima, Cortés, July 19, 2011.

111. The practice of enrolling sex workers in a police registry originated in France, was adopted in Mexico, and in the 1920s came to Honduras. The registry also served to categorize the women by race: those in first class were white or foreigners from European countries and served men in the upper classes, those in second class were mestizas who served a middle-class clientele, and the third class were mestizas or poor indigenous women who served the working class. Amaya Banegas, *El que Esté Libre de Pecado*, 52.

112. *Trigueña* in the context of the north coast literally translates into the color of wheat, used to mean brown or light brown. It does not necessarily mean Black, but it is associated with Black; a mestiza, however, could also be *trigueña*.

113. Rosaura Garcia, interview by author, La Lima, Cortés, July 19, 2011.

114. Rosaura Garcia, interview by author, La Lima, Cortés, July 19, 2011.

Chapter 5: "Mujeres que cuidaban hombres y vendedoras ambulantes"

1. The term "campeña" refers to a woman who lived and worked in campos bananeros and who may have been a wife, sister, or daughter of a campeño, or merely a worker in the kitchens. This was a term used by most out-of-towners to refer to these women workers, but it was also a term of self-identification used by the women themselves. The campeña identity was very important to women and men in the campos as a form of community and contributed to the construction of the national identity of workers.

2. Drinot, "Food, Race and Working-Class Identity," 245–270.

3. Weinstein, "Unskilled Worker, Skilled Housewife," 72–73, 91.

4. Ibid., 95; Veccia, "My Duty as a Woman," 101; Klubock, "Morality and Good Habits," 233.

5. Drinot "Food, Race and Working-Class Identity," 246–247.

6. Ibid.

7. Villars, *Para la Casa*.

8. Olimpia Edelmira Figueroa, interview by author, La Lima, Cortés, February 15, 2006.

9. Olimpia Edelmira Figueroa, interview by author, La Lima, Cortés, February 15, 2006.

10. Francisco Portillo, interview by author, La Lima, Cortés, February 6, 2006; Daniel Madrid Guevara, interview by author, La Lima, Cortés, February 5, 2006; José Sánchez, interview by author, La Lima, Cortés, November 5, 2006. See also Soluri, *Banana Cultures*.

11. Villars, *Para la Casa*, 165–170; Klubock, "Morality and Good Habits," 236; Veccia, "My Duty as a Woman," 110. Lara Putnam found that neither West Indian nor

Hispanic women did formal banana harvesting work in the plantation. See Putnam, *Company They Kept*, 9, 131.

12. Klubock, "Morality and Good Habits," 233.

13. Ibid.

14. It was not until 1962 that women entered into formal labor at the banana packinghouses. While some women did work in the *banania* factory in La Lima, for instance, or in the offices and hospitals of the company, for the most part, the finca work and production of bananas in the campos bananeros limited women from entering into the formal economy of banana production. Isolated examples of women working alongside their husbands or helping men fulfill a contract exist, and workers report seeing women work in the fields; for the most part, however, company policies favored the nearly exclusive hiring of men. According to SITRATERCO Union President Carlos Amaya Yanez, women began working in the *banania* factory in 1962. Carlos Amaya Yanez, interview by author, La Lima, Cortés, July 1, 2006, and August, 2004; Iris Munguía, interview by author, La Lima, Cortés, February 15, 2006; Scott-Jenkins, *Bananas*, 123.

15. Olimpia Edelmira Figueroa, interview by author, La Lima, Cortés, February 15, 2006.

16. *Cuidar gente* translates literally to "take care of people" and refers to women in the campos who cooked meals for finca workers—men—in weekly or monthly paid arrangements. María Antonia Perla, interview by author, La Lima, Cortés, March 5, 2006.

17. "Cuque" refers to a cook or a cook helper, a sous-chef of sorts. The name has resonance in the north coast even now, and it is a remnant of the English language imposed by the company that permeated workers' lives daily, from their work positions to the company installations and rosters. The code-switching and Spanglish, a hybrid language combining words and idioms from English into everyday Spanish, that workers employed mark a form of ingenious and creative linguistic resistance to company worker control. Workers often remark on these terms with mischievousness and humor as they recall their days working for the company.

18. Olimpia Edelmira Figueroa, interview by author, La Lima, Cortés, February 15, 2006.

19. María Ángela Cardona, interview by author, El Carríl, Olanchito, Yoro, August 13, 2006; Casta Figueroa Portillo, interview by author, El Carríl, Olanchito, Yoro, August 13, 2006.

20. Klubock, "Morality and Good Habits," 244. On the family-based labor system, see Veccia, "My Duty as a Woman," 113.

21. Casta Figueroa Portillo, interview by author, El Carríl, Olanchito, Yoro, August 13, 2006.

22. Many ambulant vendors sent their sons out to sell in the streets, and many cooks employed their daughters for cooking and as cook helpers.

23. Gerardo Pery Laredo, interview by author, Tornabé, Tela, Atlántida, August 8, 2006; Juan Nuñez Sierra, interview by author, La Lima, Cortés, March 7, 2006.

24. Sylvia Robleda, interview by author, San Pedro Sula, Cortés, July 4, 2004; María Antonia Perla, interview by author, La Lima, Cortés, March 5, 2006; Ricarda Fernández Sabillón, interview by author, Nuevo San Juan, La Lima, Cortés, May 5, 2006; Candida Garay, interview by author, La Lima, Cortés, March 6, 2006; Lidia Aurora Lezama, interview by author, Campo Mucula, El Progreso, Yoro, April 9, 2006;

María Ángela Cardona, interview by author, El Carríl, Olanchito, Yoro, August 13, 2006; Adela Chávez, interview by author, La Lima Nueva, Cortés, February 6, 2006.

25. Olimpia Edelmira Figueroa, interview by author, La Lima, Cortés, February 15, 2006.

26. Adela Chávez, interview by author, La Lima Nueva, Cortés, February 6, 2006.

27. María Antonia Perla, interview by author, La Lima, Cortés, March 5, 2006.

28. Ibid. See also "Campo Guaruma Dos, Municipio de Villanueva, Cortés," *Informe del Secretario de Fomento, Agricultura y Trabajo*, 1943–1944; Microfilm MF13544, Center for Research Libraries.

29. María Antonia Perla, interview by author, La Lima, Cortés, March 5, 2006.

30. María Antonia Perla, interview by author, La Lima, Cortés, March 5, 2006.

31. María Antonia Perla, interview by author, La Lima, Cortés, March 5, 2006. Another woman, a former ayudanta, who suffered a similar fate did not want to be recorded or talk about it, simply saying, "Why would I want to remember?" Author's personal communication.

32. María Antonia Perla, interview by author, La Lima, Cortés, March 5, 2006.

33. They did not officially marry until four years after the incident, perhaps because of her young age at the time; the worker would have been forced to serve jail time.

34. Despite her daughter's pleas for help, Perla's mom said, "This is your destiny; my mother knows what she is doing." María Antonia Perla, interview by author, La Lima, Cortés, March 5, 2006.

35. Putnam found evidence of the rape of prepubescent girls in Limón. Putnam, *Company They Kept*, 86, 245–246n37.

36. María Ángela Cardona, interview by author, El Carríl, Olanchito, Yoro, August 13, 2006; Adela Chávez, interview by author, La Lima, Cortés, February 6, 2006.

37. Ricarda Fernández Sabillón, interview by author, Nuevo San Juan, La Lima, Cortés, May 5, 2006.

38. Ricarda Fernández Sabillón, interview by author, Nuevo San Juan, La Lima, Cortés, May 5, 2006.

39. Ricarda Fernández Sabillón, interview by author, Nuevo San Juan, La Lima, Cortés, May 5, 2006.

40. Ricarda Fernández Sabillón, interview by author, Nuevo San Juan, La Lima, Cortés, May 5, 2006.

41. Ayudantas found employment in established comedores for as little as 12 lempiras per month.

42. Mestizo workers spoke of the cuque in gendered ways because kitchen labor was seen as women's work. Mestizo workers were prejudiced against Black workers because they considered them too physically weak to work in the fincas. Rocío Tábora reminds us, in her seminal work on masculinity in Honduras, that "sexuality is a privileged space where the permanent manifestation of the suspicion . . . in any case of friendship among men and the spontaneity of their relations is limited by the suspicion that the other is 'more of a man than me.'" Tábora, *Masculinidad y Violencia*, 28.

43. María Ángela Cardona, interview by author, El Carríl, Olanchito, Yoro, August 13, 2006.

44. Gerardo Pery Laredo, interview by author, Tornabé, Tela, Atlántida, August 8, 2006; Juan Nuñez Sierra, interview by author, La Lima, Cortés, March 7, 2006.

45. Klubock, "Morality and Good Habits," 233.

46. Olimpia Edelmira Figueroa, interview by author, La Lima, Cortés, February 15, 2006.

47. Workers often referred to the western side of the north coast, and also the region where the United Fruit had its fincas, as Costa Abajo and referred to the eastern part of the north coast, where Standard Fruit had its fincas, as Costa Arriba. This distinction between the two coasts represented a geographic and imaginary divide, and each is imbued with its own analysis in workers' historical memories (those interviewed by author): each coast is associated with its corresponding company, and Costa Arriba is considered as having more ethnic and racial mixing than the more "indio" (mestizo) Costa Abajo. Darío Euraque's writings on "indo-mestizaje" in the construction of the nation are useful for thinking about ethnicity and race in this region. See Euraque, *Conversaciones Históricas*, 17–35; Euraque, "Banana Enclave," 151–164; Euraque, "Threat of Blackness," 229–247; Euraque, "Free Pardos and Mulattoes Vanquish Indians," 81–101.

48. Lucilla Goodlitt, interview by author, El Carríl, Olanchito, Yoro, August 10, 2006.

49. María Ángela Cardona, interview by author, El Carríl, Olanchito, Yoro, August 13, 2006; Lucilla Goodlitt, interview by author, El Carríl, Olanchito, Yoro, August 10, 2006.

50. María Antonia Perla, interview by author, La Lima, Cortés, March 5, 2006.

51. Patrocinia Martinez, interview by author, San Juan de Tela, Atlántida, August 8, 2006.

52. Local flour producers complained to the government that the foreign competition made it impossible for them to remain in business. Informe del Secretario de Fomento, Agricultura y Trabajo, 1928–1929, Microfilm MF13544, Center for Research Libraries.

53. Olimpia Edelmira Figueroa, interview by author, La Lima, Cortés, February 15, 2006.

54. Yuca, or manioc, is a tuber that is the staple of Garifuna cuisine, used to make *cassave* or *kassave*, a tortilla-like flat bread made by pounding the yuca. This is different from the cassava tuber, known as malanga in this region. Patrocinia Martinez, interview by author, San Juan de Tela, Tela Atlántida, August 8, 2006; María Ángela Cardona, interview by author, El Carríl, Olanchito, Yoro, August 13, 2006.

55. Although there is no clear origin of the *baleada*, the meaning of the word—a "shootout" or a "shooting"—suggests a reference to life in the banana fields and campos, where a certain level of violence was common. The name could also reference the fact that it was a to-go item, a quick meal, just like a shooting was considered to be quick.

56. Lucilla Goodlitt, interview by author, El Carríl, Olanchito, Yoro, August 10, 2006; Patrocinia Martinez, San Juan de Tela, Atlántida, August 8, 2006; María Ángela Cardona, interview by author, El Carríl, Olanchito, Yoro, August 13, 2006.

57. Lucilla Goodlitt, interview by author, El Carríl, Olanchito, Yoro, August 10, 2006; Patrocinia Martinez, San Juan de Tela, Atlántida, August 8, 2006; María Ángela Cardona, interview by author, El Carríl, Olanchito, Yoro, August 13, 2006.

58. Olimpia Edelmira Figueroa, interview by author, La Lima, Cortés, February 15, 2006; María Ángela Cardona, interview by author, El Carríl, Olanchito, Yoro, August 13, 2006; Casta Figueroa Portillo, interview by author, El Carríl, Olanchito, Yoro, August 13, 2006.

59. Casta Figueroa Portillo, interview by author, El Carríl, Olanchito, Yoro, August 13, 2006.

60. The Standard Fruit Company had barracones in certain campos, such as Coyoles Central, Agua Buena, and Palo Verde, at the time. For the most part, workers in this region lived in what were called *champerías*, huts made of mud and thatched manaca palm roofs. The location of the current town of El Carríl was the site of a worker *champería* at the time of the 1954 strike. Casta Figueroa Portillo, interview by author, El Carríl, Olanchito, Yoro, August 13, 2006; María Ángela Cardona, interview by author, El Carríl, Olanchito, Yoro, August 13, 2006.

61. María Ángela Cardona, interview by author, El Carríl, Olanchito, Yoro, 2006; Casta Figueroa Portillo, interview by author, El Carríl, Olanchito, Yoro, August 13, 2006.

62. María Ángela Cardona, interview by author, El Carríl, Olanchito, Yoro, August 13, 2006.

63. María Ángela Cardona, interview by author, El Carríl, Olanchito, Yoro, August 13, 2006.

64. Company supervisors, for instance, tended to only hire men in the fincas, though whether this was an official policy or an unspoken one is unclear. There is no evidence of an official company policy that excluded women from the formal work in the fincas. Women in the company offices needed to be bilingual secretaries, thereby excluding working-class women with scant educational resources. Teresina Rossi Matamoros, interview by author, Tegucigalpa, December 21, 2006.

65. In some cases, there may only have been one patrona's establishment in the area, or the patrona may have been the wife of a supervisor, a contratista or mandador. These circumstances limited workers' and patronas' choices, and would become a subject of workers' strike demands later.

66. Olimpia Edelmira Figueroa, interview by author, La Lima, Cortés, February 15, 2006.

67. Olimpia Edelmira Figueroa, interview by author, La Lima, Cortés, February 15, 2006; Adela Chávez, interview by author, La Lima Nueva, Cortés, 2006. Some workers would ask for a reduced-price meal plan, which meant there was less meat and more beans and tortillas. María Ángela Cardona, interview by author, El Carríl, Olanchito, Yoro, August 13, 2006; Edmundo Cabrera Williams, interview by author, Campo Indiana, La Lima, Cortés, August 7, 2004; Francisco Portillo, interview by author, La Lima, Cortés, February 6, 2006; José Sánchez, interview by author, La Lima, Cortés, November 5, 2006.

68. Edmundo Cabrera Williams, interview by author, Campo Indiana, La Lima, Cortés, August 7, 2004.

69. Another name for a *venenero*, *poisero* comes from the English word "poison." The names reflect code-switching by workers, who translated to Spanish from company English.

70. For gender mixing in the streets as a result of industrialization, see Porter, *Working Women in Mexico City*, 15.

71. *Poiseros* and *veneneros* are also known as *pericos* in Costa Arriba. Men sprayed plants with the Bordeaux pesticide to prevent Sigatoka disease. The solutions were of a blue-green color. Workers would spray upward, and more often than not particles would land on their faces, chests, and clothing. They would come out from work doused in blue-green spray. Olimpia Edelmira Figueroa, interview by author, La Lima,

Cortés, February 15, 2006; Edmundo Cabrera Williams, interview by author, Campo Indiana, La Lima, Cortés, August 7, 2004; Juan Bautista Canales, interview by author, La Ceiba, Atlántida, July 25, 2004; Soluri, *Banana Cultures*, 197–200.

72. Sylvia Robleda, interview by author, San Pedro Sula, Cortés, July 4, 2004; Olimpia Edelmira Figueroa, interview by author, La Lima, Cortés, February 15, 2006; Adela Chávez, interview by author, La Lima Nueva, Cortés, February 6, 2006; María Antonia Perla, interview by author, La Lima, Cortés, March 5, 2006; Casta Figueroa Portillo, interview by author, El Carríl, Olanchito, Yoro, August 13, 2006; María Ángela Cardona, interview by author, El Carríl, Olanchito, Yoro, August 13, 2006.

73. María Ángela Cardona, interview by author, El Carríl, Olanchito, Yoro, August 13, 2006.

74. Although many patronas were the bosses' wives, as was common in the remotest regions, others were not related to the bosses. These women established their own kitchens outside of any kinship relationship. Patronas who were not married to the contratistas or finca captains or were simply hired by them had a more complicated hierarchical position in the finca—one that was not always predetermined by men—but had independence in their earnings and labor.

75. A mandador is an overseer; a capitán de finca is a boss for the entire planting area, ranking above the mandador. María Ángela Cardona, interview by author, El Carríl, Olanchito, Yoro, August 13, 2006.

76. Olimpia Edelmira Figueroa, interview by author, La Lima, Cortés, February 15, 2006.

77. It is important to note that most patronas held many positions before becoming heads of their own kitchens; many had worked as street vendors, washerwomen, or maids in nearby company towns before and sometimes even after becoming patronas of the kitchen. Olimpia Edelmira Figueroa, interview by author, La Lima, Cortés, February 15, 2006.

78. Klubock, *Contested Communities*, 6. See also Topik and Wells, introduction to *Second Conquest*.

79. Informe del Secretario de Fomento, Agricultura y Trabajo, 1944–1945 to 1954–1955, Microfilm MF13544, Center for Research Libraries.

80. Suffragist struggles were taking place in Tegucigalpa, San Pedro Sula, and in the north-coast cities of El Progreso and La Ceiba; they took place via public debates and newsletters as well as legislative debates to which working-class women were not privy. While women suffragists engaged with anti-imperialist causes around the mining towns near Tegucigalpa, very few engaged the patronas or campesina women. Villars, *Para la Casa*, 232–242, 305–414.

81. Casta Figueroa Portillo, interview by author, El Carríl, Olanchito, Yoro, August 13, 2006.

82. Daniel Madrid Guevara, interview by author, La Lima, Cortés, February 5, 2006.

83. Mohanty, "Feminist Encounters."

84. Villars, *Para la Casa*, 251–256; Olimpia Edelmira Figueroa, interview by author, La Lima, Cortés, February 15, 2006; María Ángela Cardona, interview by author, El Carríl, Olanchito, Yoro, August 13, 2006.

85. Olimpia Edelmira Figueroa, interview by author, La Lima, Cortés, February 15, 2006; María Ángela Cardona, interview by author, El Carríl, Olanchito, Yoro, August 13, 2006; Adela Chávez, interview by author, La Lima Nueva, Cortés, February 6,

2006; Casta Figueroa Portillo, interview by author, El Carríl, Olanchito, Yoro, August 13, 2006.

86. Olimpia Edelmira Figueroa, interview by author, La Lima, Cortés, February 15, 2006; María Ángela Cardona, interview by author, El Carríl, Olanchito, Yoro, August 13, 2006; Adela Chávez, interview by author, La Lima Nueva, Cortés, February 6, 2006; Casta Figueroa Portillo, interview by author, El Carríl, Olanchito, Yoro, August 13, 2006; Villars, *Para la Casa.*

87. Her preoccupation arises out of the Marxist leftist movements in Guatemala; while these movements pushed the analysis toward a more critical evaluation of class, gender was left on the back burner, as a later goal. She refuses a "pigeonholing of women's activism into maternal or womanist politics." Levenson-Estrada, "Loneliness of Working-Class Feminism," 220. This sort of "ghettoizing," in Joan Wallach Scott's words, is actually where the history of relations between women and men sits within the history of pre-agrarian-reform Honduras; see Scott, "Gender."

88. Casta Figueroa Portillo, interview by author, El Carríl, Olanchito, Yoro, August 13, 2006.

89. María Antonia Perla, interview by author, La Lima, Cortés, March 5, 2006.

90. Daniel Madrid Guevara, interview by author, La Lima, Cortés, February 5, 2006.

91. Similarly, Klubock found that women workers engaged in *ollas comunes,* communal kitchens, during the El Teniente mine strike in Chile. Klubock, "Morality and Good Habits," 255.

92. Adela Chávez, interview by author, La Lima Nueva, Cortés, February 6, 2006; Lucilla Goodlitt, interview by author, El Carríl, Olanchito, Yoro, August 10, 2006.

93. Adela Chávez, interview by author, La Lima Nueva, Cortés, February 6, 2006.

94. Adela Chávez, interview by author, La Lima Nueva, Cortés, February 6, 2006.

95. Argueta, *Gran Huelga Bananera,* 65–108; Barahona, *Silencio Quedó Atrás,* 55–88.

96. Adela Chávez, interview by author, La Lima Nueva, Cortés, February 6, 2006; Sylvia Robleda, interview by author, San Pedro Sula, Cortés, July 4, 2004.

97. Standard Fruit Company workers went on strike for 11 days, a shorter period than the United Fruit Strike; street vendors gave away food for a shorter period, making it more sustainable.

98. Lucilla Goodlitt, interview by author, El Carríl, Olanchito, Yoro, August 10, 2006.

99. Lucilla Goodlitt, interview by author, El Carríl, Olanchito, Yoro, August 10, 2006.

100. Juan B. Canales, interview by author, La Ceiba, Atlántida, July 25, 2004; Olimpia Edelmira Figueroa, interview by author, La Lima, Cortés, February 15, 2006; María Antonia Perla, interview by author, La Lima Cortés, March 5, 2006; Daniel Madrid Guevara, interview by author, La Lima, Cortés, February 5, 2006; Julio C. Rivera, interview by author, San José, Costa Rica, July 9, 2008.

101. Oscar Amaya Yanez, interview by author, La Lima, Cortés, August, 2004.

102. Enloe, *Bananas, Beaches and Bases*; Soluri, *Banana Cultures.*

103. See one of the most famous commercials: youtube.com/watch?v=RFDOI24 RRAE.

104. *Unifruitco, 1954,* Unifruitco Magazine Collection, Rare Book Collection, Huntington Library Archives.

105. Promotional cookbooks were sent to housewives who wrote to the Home Economics Department of UFCo. These cookbooks explained when the banana was ripe enough to peel and cook or eat, its nutritional value, and a series of unique ways to integrate the banana into American meals—for example, fried with bacon or ham and eggs or on the Waldorf salad. *Chiquita Banana Recipe Book*, Home Economics Department, United Fruit Company, 1954; *Banana Recipes for Institutional Service and Menus*, Home Economic Department, United Fruit Company, 1954; *Tempting Banana Recipes*, pamphlet, Home Economics Department, United Fruit Company, 1953; *Chiquita Banana Presents 18 Recepies from Her Minute Movies*, Home Economics Department, United Fruit Company, 1951 (cookbooks in author's collection).

106. Gordon, *Ghostly Matters*, 8.

107. Archival omissions of women are true for most of Latin America, and new studies are finding creative ways to write women and sexuality into the historical record. See Findlay Suarez, 144–145.

108. See Crenshaw, "From Private to Mass Incarceration"; Crenshaw, "Demarginalizing the Intersection of Race and Sex"; Crenshaw, "Mapping the Margins."

109. Viotti da Costa, "Experience versus Structures," 16–18.

110. Mendoza, *Sintiéndose Mujer*, 24–25.

111. Villars, *Para la Casa*, 281.

112. "Working-Class Feminism" is borrowed from critical feminists who have studied working-class women in the United States. See Levenson-Estrada, "Loneliness of Working-Class Feminism, 208–231"; Greenwald, "Working-Class Feminism"; Hutchinson, *Labors Appropriate to Their Sex*.

113. Weinstein, "Unskilled Worker, Skilled Housewife"; Veccia, "My Duty as a Woman."

114. González-Rivera, *Before the Revolution*.

115. Villars, *Para la Casa*.

116. Daniel Madrid Guevara, interview by author, La Lima, Cortés, February 5, 2006.

117. This does not mean that it was not an important gain. But it is notable that many of the women fighting for suffrage were elite, married to elected officials, businessmen, or educated teachers. Their struggles rarely filtered into the ambit of working-class women. Political parties, both the Nationalist Party and the Liberal Party, sought women's support, even if they could not vote. Women's suffrage was gained in 1954, after the strike, but its ratification did not occur until 1957. Villars, *Para la Casa*.

118. Ibid.

119. Ibid., 228–229.

120. Ibid., 264–265.

121. Ibid., 300.

122. Mohanty, "Feminist Encounters," 461.

Chapter 6: ¡La Gran Huelga del 1954!

1. Leonardo Bautista, interview by author, Campo Limones, La Lima, Cortés, May 5, 2006.

2. Argueta, *Gran Huelga Bananera*, 65.

3. Juan B. Canales, interview by author, La Ceiba, Atlántida, August 8, 2004; Edmundo Cabrera Williams, interview by author, Finca Indiana, La Lima, Cortés, July

24, 2004; Francisco Portillo, interview by author, La Lima, Cortés, February 6, 2006; Angel Martinez, interview by author, Colonial Nuevo San Juan, La Lima, Cortés, January 29, 2006; Daniel Madrid Guevara, interview by author, La Lima, Cortés, February 5, 2006; Agapito Robleda Castro, interview by author, San Pedro Sula, Cortés, August 2, 2006; Julio C. Rivera, interview by author, San José, Costa Rica, July 9, 2008.

4. Barahona, *Silencio Quedó Atrás*, 21.

5. Teresina Rossi Matamoros, interview by author, Tegucigalpa, December 21, 2006.

6. Workers were inspired by the popular reforms taking place in nearby Guatemala during the period of 1944 to 1954. The strike in 1954 took place on the eve of the US-led coup d'état that ousted President Árbenz Guzmán in that country.

7. Workers received news of these labor movements through worker newspapers such as *Vanguardia Revolucionaria* (PDRH newspaper) and *Voz Obrera* (CCO newspaper). During the strike, workers received letters of solidarity from the labor movements in these countries via communication with the CTAL. Archivo Lombardo Toledano, copies provided by Archivo Privado de Tomás Erazo Peña, San Pedro Sula, Honduras.

8. Barahona, *Silencio Quedó Atrás*, 206.

9. Juan B. Canales, interview by author, La Ceiba, Atlántida, August, 8, 2004; Teresina Rossi Matamoros, interview by author, Tegucigalpa, December 21, 2006; Julio C. Rivera, interview by author, San José, Costa Rica, July 9, 2008.

10. In Bataán, the company produced a type of banana plant that had a fibrous material that could be made into rope to assist the United States during World War II. UFCo previously produced this in the Philippines and actually had a contract with the US State Department. This production center no longer exists, and I was not able to locate workers who actually worked there. Organizers, however, did mention this work center as an important one during the strike.

11. Barahona, *Silencio Quedó Atrás*, 62–63.

12. The PDRH voted in 1953 to celebrate International Worker's Day on May 1, 1953. The actual strike could not be pulled off that year because communication had not reached all sectors; while some sectors did stop work and strike, others did not. The May Day action was then postponed for the next year, 1954. Ibid., 206; Julio C. Rivera, interview by author, San José, Costa Rica, July 9, 2008; Teresina Rossi Matamoros, interview by author, Tegucigalpa, December 21, 2006.

13. Previous attempts to organize International Workers' Day marches were unsuccessful due to police repression. Barahona, *Silencio Quedó Atrás*, 57.

14. Julio C. Rivera, interview by author, San José, Costa Rica, July, 2008; Teresina Rossi Matamoros, interview by author, Tegucigalpa, December 21, 2006; Juan B. Canales, interview by author, La Ceiba, Atlántida, August, 8, 2004.

15. The finca regions were in the vicinity of La Lima, El Progreso, Tela, and Bataán in the outskirts of Tela.

16. Barahona, *Silencio Quedó Atrás*, 65 (author's translation).

17. Edmundo Cabrera Williams, interview by author, Finca Indiana, La Lima, Cortés, July 24, 2004; Leonardo Bautista, interview by author, Campo Limones, La Lima, Cortés, May 5, 2006.

18. Daniel Madrid Guevara, interview by author, La Lima, Cortés, February 5, 2006.

19. Francisco Portillo, interview by author, La Lima, Cortés, February 6, 2006; Daniel Madrid Guevara, interview by author, La Lima, Cortés, February 5, 2006; Edmundo Cabrera Williams, interview by author, Finca Indiana, La Lima, Cortés, July 25, 2004.

20. Daniel Madrid Guevara, interview by author, La Lima, Cortés, February 5, 2006; Edmundo Cabrera Williams, interview by author, Finca Indiana, La Lima, Cortés, July 25, 2004.

21. Morales Pineda, *La Rápida*, 33–34.

22. Daniel Madrid Guevara, interview by author, La Lima, Cortés, February 5, 2006.

23. Francisco Portillo, interview by author, La Lima, Cortés, February 6, 2006; Daniel Madrid Guevara, interview by author, La Lima, Cortés, February 5, 2006; Sylvia Robleda, interview by author, San Pedro Sula, Cortés, July 4, 2006.

24. Julio Antonio Cuellar Mendoza, interview by author, Los Angeles, June 5, 2010.

25. Most of the confrontation was initiated by the troops the company hired to observe them. McCameron, *Bananas, Labor, and Politics*, 49.

26. The Construction Department included workers who labored in the workshops in El Progreso but also workers who were deployed on construction assignments in the various fincas and campos.

27. Robleda Castro, *Verdad de la Huelga*.

28. Ibid., 71.

29. Ibid.; Agapito Robleda Castro, interview by author, San Pedro Sula, Cortés, August 2, 2006; Julio C. Rivera, interview by author, San José, Costa Rica, July 9, 2008.

30. Agapito Robleda Castro, interview by author, San Pedro Sula, Cortés, August 2, 2006; Robleda Castro, *Verdad de la Huelga*, 33–36.

31. Agapito Robleda Castro, interview by author, San Pedro Sula, Cortés, August 2, 2006.

32. The contract system (referred to as *trabajo por destajo* by workers) was not advantageous to workers in many departments because the contractor would be paid monthly, and then he would pay the workers. Some construction workers earned less or were not paid until a particular project or a certain part of the project was concluded, which took days or weeks or longer than if they were paid by the company directly. Prior to the strike workers could hop between fincas to find work. Workers also knew about work conditions in the Standard Fruit Company through their networks and the various worker newspapers that circulated in that region. Robleda Castro, *Verdad de la Huelga*, 33–36.

33. Ibid.

34. As construction workers were organizing to address their issues, the mechanics in the Engineering Department in El Progreso also felt discontent with the company and asked for a company supervisor, L. O. Meyer, who was known for being especially cruel to workers, to be fired. Their specific work issue led them to support the construction workers and walk out with them. Agapito Robleda Castro, interview by author, San Pedro Sula, Cortés, August 2, 2006; Julio C. Rivera, interview by author, San José, Costa Rica, July 9, 2008; Barahona, *Silencio Quedó Atrás*, 90.

35. Robleda Castro, *Verdad de la Huelga*, 46–53.

36. Jesús Gómez, interview by author, La Lima, Cortés, March 7, 2006.

37. Leonardo Bautista, interview by author, Campo Limones, La Lima, Cortés, May 5, 2006; Francisco Portillo, interview by author, La Lima, Cortés, February 6, 2006.

38. Jesús Gómez, interview by author, La Lima, Cortés, March 7, 2006.

39. Jesús Gómez, interview by author, La Lima, Cortés, March 7, 2006.

40. Edmundo Cabrera Williams, interview by author, Finca Indiana, La Lima, Cortés, July 24, 2004; Juan B. Canales, interview by author, La Ceiba, Atlántida, August 8, 2004; Daniel Madrid Guevara, interview by author, La Lima, Cortés, February 5, 2006; Agapito Robleda Castro, interview by author, San Pedro Sula, Cortés, August 2, 2006; Julio C. Rivera, interview by author, San José, Costa Rica, July 9, 2008; Teresina Rossi Matamoros, interview by author, Tegucigalpa, December 21, 2006.

41. Juan B. Canales, interview by author, La Ceiba, Atlántida, August 8, 2004.

42. Juan B. Canales, interview by author, La Ceiba, Atlántida, August 8, 2004.

43. Juan B. Canales, interview by author, La Ceiba, Atlántida, August 8, 2004.

44. It is unclear whether workers asked for double time or time-and-a-half pay. During strike negotiations, the company rebuttal suggests that paying time-and-a-half was already a policy in practice. It is clear, however, that the stevedores sought better treatment, demanding an end to racial discrimination, better food, and an acknowledgment of the grueling labor schedule by reducing the number of hours in the night shift.

45. Juan B. Canales, interview by author, La Ceiba, Atlántida, August 8, 2004; Agapito Robleda Castro, interview by author, San Pedro Sula, Cortés, August 2, 2006; Robleda Castro, *Verdad de la Huelga*, 72.

46. Juan B. Canales, interview by author, La Ceiba, Atlántida, August 8, 2004.

47. Juan B. Canales, interview by author, La Ceiba, Atlántida, August 8, 2004.

48. Canales was arrested for the first time on the day of the first meeting in his own house because he was seen as a worker agitator.

49. Teresina Rossi Matamoros first came across this youth organization before being introduced to the PDRH. Barahona, *Silencio Quedó Atrás*, 327.

50. Rossi Matamoros was a bilingual secretary and a member of the first Central Strike Committee. Though her role in the Central Strike Committee was that of secretary, typing up most of the demands and letters sent to the Mediation Commission and the company, Rossi Matamoros was also influential in trying to organize her department and other positions in the company offices to walk out. Teresina Rossi Matamoros, interview by author, Tegucigalpa, December 21, 2006; Julio C, Rivera, interview by author, San José, Costa Rica, July 9, 2008.

51. May Day activities were seen as a onetime event that may have made public all the workers' committees and workers within the company. The work of committee building was done with the larger goal of organizing a strike and not just a rally.

52. Although Liberal Party activists wanted worker votes for their candidate, Ramón Villeda Morales, they did not trust the government and feared unfair elections. Villeda Morales was not able to take office until 1957, despite winning the elections.

53. The Tela worker committees were led by Francisco (Chico) Rios and Teresina Rossi Matamoros, among other members of the PDRH. Teresina Rossi Matamoros, interview by author, Tegucigalpa, December 21, 2006.

54. Teresina Rossi Matamoros, interview by author, Tegucigalpa, December 21, 2006.

55. McCameron, *Bananas, Labor, and Politics*, 37.

56. Teresina Rossi Matamoros, interview by author, Tegucigalpa, December 21, 2006.

57. "Aspectos Fundamentales," APMP.

58. During his presidency, Gálvez signed on to the Inter-American Charter of

Social Guarantees, but its objectives were never observed, and it was rescinded two months later with an accord that declared it null (Acuerdo 1724; Acuerdo 2255). The letter called for countries to observe minimum-wage standards. During the Gálvez presidency, there was no Ministry of Labor, but instead the Dirección General de Trabajo y Prevision Social, which did not serve workers. Posas, *Luchas del Movimiento Obrero Hondureño*, 126; McCameron, *Bananas, Labor, and Politics*, 30–31.

59. The Tela Railroad Company refused to negotiate despite the Standard Fruit Company's decision to negotiate and settle a contract with the workers 19 days after the strike began in that region. The Standard Fruit workers went on strike on May 7 and the company began negotiations with their strike committee 11 days later. The Tela Railroad Company responded to the worker strike committee a month later.

60. The ad hoc committee that elaborated the 30 demands consisted of Juan B. Canales (Puerto Cortés), Cesar Agusto Coto (La Lima), S. Lilio Pineda M. (El Progreso), and Luis B. Yanes (Tela). There was no official representation for Bataán. Although not reflected in the actual document, the secretary responsible for typing and elaborating the report was Teresina Rossi Matamoros. The Tela Railroad Company's response on June 13, 1954, considers this to be the second petition made. The first was presented by the workers in the Construction Department on May 3, right before going on strike. That petition was specific to the construction workers' issues and demands. This longer set of demands reflects unity among all workers, departments, and regions.

61. Letter to Mediation Commission, June 17, 1954, in "Aspectos Fundamentales," APMP.

62. The eight-hour workday was cemented into law in Honduras in 1925 as "Artículo 191. La jornada máxima obligatoria asalariada será de ocho horas diarias y por casa seis días de trabajo habrá uno de descanso." Letter from the Central Strike Committee to the Mediation Commission, June 17, 1954, p. 13, in "Aspectos Fundamentales," APMP.

63. "Tabla de Porcentajes de Aumentos" y "Tabla Especial Para el Aumento de Salarios de los trabajadores de Departamento de Agricultura (Inciso b. del Artículo 1)," May 11, 1954, pp. 9–7, in "Aspectos Fundamentales," APMP.

64. Francisco Portillo, interview by author, La Lima, Cortés, February 6, 2006.

65. Soluri, *Banana Cultures*, 144.

66. Francisco Portillo, interview by author, La Lima, Cortés, February 6, 2006.

67. Francisco Portillo, interview by author, La Lima, Cortés, February 6, 2006.

68. Soluri, *Banana Cultures*, 144–148.

69. Ibid., 146.

70. Francisco Napoleon Galo, interview by author, El Progreso, Yoro, July 1, 2004; Oscar Rodriguez Pagoada, interview by author, American Zone, La Lima, Cortés, September, 2, 2006.

71. No. 1, sections 1b, 1c, in "Aspectos Fundamentales," APMP; Olimpia Edelmira Figueroa, interview by author, La Lima, Cortés, February 15, 2006.

72. No. 1, section 1d, no. 6, no. 7, in "Aspectos Fundamentales," APMP.

73. No. 4, no. 7 in ibid.

74. No. 17 in ibid.

75. Special attention was given to obtaining protective gear from pesticides, rest time, and food for stevedores, and adequate, quality health care for these workers and their families. During floods, outbreaks of malaria and typhoid were common, and the

company hospitals looked down on workers and were often not ready with adequate personnel to treat them. Women giving birth in the company hospitals were victims of racial discrimination. No. 2, sections 2a, 2b, 2d, no. 3 in ibid.; Barahona, *Silencio Quedó Atrás* 321–322; Argueta, *Gran Huelga Bananera*, 125–129.

76. No. 9, no. 10, no. 17, no. 18, no. 23, in "Aspectos Fundamentales," APMP.

77. This figure fluctuates between 2% to 5% in the sources, 2% being the most common estimate.

78. Pieces of information on conditions at the time are available; the biggest concern the workers cited was wages. However, there were many problems resulting from pesticides and injuries on the job from workers having to carry heavy bunches of bananas (*racimos*) onto ships. Pesticides were also dangerous to workers at the time, though not well documented in the sources consulted.

79. Letter from the Central Strike Committee to the Mediation Commission, June 17, 1954, p. 11, in "Aspectos Fundamentales," APMP.

80. Letter to Company with demands, May 11, 1954, in "Aspectos Fundamentales," APMP.

81. Lucila Goodlitt, interview by author, El Carríl, Olanchito, Yoro, August 10, 2006; María Ángela Cardona, interview by author, El Carríl, Olanchito, Yoro, August 13, 2006; Candida Garya, interview by author, La Lima, Cortés, March 6, 2006.

82. Juan B. Canales, interview by author, La Ceiba, Atlántida, August, 8, 2004; José Sánchez, interview by author, La Lima, Cortés, November 5, 2006. For the Pliego de Peticiones, see Letter to Company, May 11, 1954, in "Aspectos Fundamentales," APMP.

83. Barahona, *Silencio Quedó Atrás*, 71–75; McCameron, *Bananas, Labor, and Politics*, 133–137.

84. No. 2, section 2d, in "Aspectos Fundamentales," APMP; Olimpia Edelmira Figueroa, interview by author, La Lima, Cortés, February 15, 2006; Letter from the Central Strike Committee to the Mediation Commission, June 17, 1954, p. 11, in "Aspectos Fundamentales," APMP.

85. Pérez Sáinz, *From the Finca to the Maquila*, 17–18.

86. The Pliego de Peticiones demand no. 11: "A trabajo igual debe corresponder igual remuneración, cualquiera que sea el sexo, raza, credo o nacionalidad del trabajador." "Aspectos Fundamentales," APMP.

87. Juan B. Canales, interview by author, La Ceiba, Atlántida, August 8, 2004.

88. Juan B. Canales, interview by author, La Ceiba, Atlántida, August 8, 2004.

89. Edmundo Cabrera Williams, interview by author, Finca Indiana, La Lima, Cortés, July 25, 2004.

90. No. 11, in "Aspectos Fundamentales," APMP.

91. Don José Sánchez recalls that he often found a guard at the door to enter and buy him a piece of bread. To this day he feels uncomfortable entering the American Zone in La Lima. Similarly the demand for clean homes "for all workers who need them" spoke to the fact that many Black workers were often left to sleep outside the singles' barracones. José Sánchez, interview by author, La Lima, Cortés, November 5, 2006.

92. Juan B. Canales, interview by author, La Ceiba, Atlántida, August 8, 2004.

93. The additions to the 30-point petition included: "11a.) Equal Pay for Equal Work. and 12a.) Equal Justice for all workers and 22a.) Employees not to be subjected to racial discrimination in company hospitals." Original "30 Puntos," *Pliego*

de Peticiones de los Trabajadores de la Tela RRCo. Posas, *Luchas del Movimiento Obrero Hondureño*, 234–241.

94. Barahona, *Silencio Quedó Atrás*, 324.

95. No. 22, in "Aspectos Fundamentales," APMP.

96. Marina Graugnard, interview by author, Tela, Atlántida, June 9, 2006.

97. Though the labor union movement prioritized a mestizo and male strike committee, which may have been a reflection of the company-imposed order, there are some exceptions that reflect the individual departments and regional understanding of demands. This is important because there was an understanding that the strike committee should represent the value of all and not just of their own particular needs.

98. No. 11, in "Aspectos Fundamentales," APMP.

99. Barahona, *Silencio Quedó Atrás*, 69.

100. Posas, *Luchas del Movimiento Obrero Hondureño*, 147–148; Barahona, *Silencio Quedó Atrás*, 69–75.

101. Posas, *Luchas del Movimiento Obrero Hondureño*, 147–148; Barahona, *Silencio Quedó Atrás*, 156.

102. Many of PDRH were also sympathizers and worked jointly with the CLO of the newly formed Communist Party (1954).

103. The list of workers incarcerated was not just limited to workers of the strike centers; it also included workers in Olanchito and La Ceiba, Standard Fruit Company areas, demonstrating that the organizing committees had been in touch with the Standard Fruit Company strike committee since May 7, 1954, when a Tela worker sent a letter to Standard Fruit Company workers to join in the strike. See the appendix for the list of additional demands. Barahona, *Silencio Quedó Atrás*, 70.

104. Point 6, ibid., 76.

105. Ibid., 76.

106. Ibid., 75–77.

107. Point 4, ibid., 76.

108. Letter Response Tela Railroad Company, June 13, 1954, in "Aspectos Fundamentales," APMP.

109. Once again, women faced the reality of the informal economy in which they lived and worked, in and around the banana fields. Clearly these workers supported the banana economy, but at the same time the company claimed they had no rights to benefits.

110. Blow-downs were high winds that hit the fincas and literally blew down the trees and large leaves. Even lower-speed winds would damage the leaves, slicing through them. Soluri, *Banana Cultures*, 142.

111. In Costa Rica UFCo refused to negotiate with workers and instigated a dispute between Costa Rica and Nicaragua to avoid negotiations. Putnam, *Company They Kept*, 64.

112. Striffler, *In the Shadows*, 32–33.

113. Ibid.

114. It is interesting to note that the company directed their communication to the Mediation Commission and not to the workers directly, giving the governmental mediation team more power to influence the process, despite knowing very little about workers' issues and lives.

115. The company claimed that this practice was already the norm. Workers'

demands demonstrate that it was poorly upheld. Letter from Tela Railroad Company to Mediation Commission, June 13, 1954, in "Aspectos Fundamentales," APMP.

116. Letter to Mediation Commission, June 17, 1954, in "Aspectos Fundamentales," APMP; Letter Response Tela Railroad Company, June 13, 1954, in "Aspectos Fundamentales," APMP.

117. Letter to Mediation Commission, June 17, 1954, in "Aspectos Fundamentales," APMP.

118. The strike began in Puerto Cortés with committees of workers in El Progreso also taking the lead in making demands. The Tela committee was also very influential in the leadership of the strike. All these committees had members who would eventually form the Comité Central de Huelga on May 17, 1954. Teresina Rossi Matamoros, interview by author, Tegucigalpa, December 21, 2006.

119. On May 17, the Central Strike Committee elaborated an additional seven points to the 30 demands, geared toward the Honduran government. Barahona, *Silencio Quedó Atrás*, 75–76.

120. Ibid., 179; Julio C. Rivera, interview by author, San José, Costa Rica, July 9, 2008.

121. Barahona, *Silencio Quedó Atrás*, 395; Teresina Rossi Matamoros, interview by author, Tegucigalpa, December 21, 2006.

122. Edmundo Cabrera Williams, interview by author, Finca Indiana, La Lima Cortés, July 25, 2004.

123. Barahona, *Silencio Quedó Atrás*, 186.

124. Julio C. Rivera, interview by author, San José, Costa Rica, July 9, 2008.

125. Julio C. Rivera still lives in exile in San José, Costa Rica. Julio C. Rivera, interview by author, San José, Costa Rica, July 9, 2008.

126. Barahona, *Silencio Quedó Atrás*, 247.

127. Teresina Rossi Matamoros, interview by author, Tegucigalpa, December 21, 2006.

128. Edmundo Cabrera Williams, interview by author, Finca Indiana, La Lima Cortés, July 25, 2004.

129. Edmundo Cabrera Williams, interview by author, Finca Indiana, La Lima Cortés, July 25, 2004.

130. Edmundo Cabrera Williams, interview by author, Finca Indiana, La Lima Cortés, July 25, 2004.

131. Much of the organizing of the Partido Liberal and the PDRH happened from abroad by networks of exiles or clandestinely within the country. Even though most of the founders were killed or exiled to Guatemala during the *Cariato*. The party, its youth affiliates, and its newspaper, *Vanguardia Revolucionaria*, among others, were crucial to the support of the strike and in some areas, like El Progreso and Tela, helped organize the walkouts. *Voz Obrera* emerged after the persecution of staff and disruption of distribution of *Vanguardia Revolucionaria* prevented the latter's normal distribution. Euraque, *Reinterpreting the Banana Republic*, 41–42; Barahona, *Silencio Quedó Atrás*, 58–59.

132. Teresina Rossi Matamoros, interview by author, Tegucigalpa, December 21, 2006.

133. Juan B. Canales, interview by author, La Ceiba, Atlántida, August 8, 2004.

134. Juan B. Canales, interview by author, La Ceiba, Atlántida, August 8, 2004.

135. It is important to note that the worker organization was not controlled by the

PDRH; workers also organized around their own conditions and needs. Later, many company school teachers were elected to the leadership without doing the organizing work. This is how Valencia rose to lead the second strike committee. Throughout the strike, company school teachers and "anti-communist" members of the strike committee formed separate committees parallel to the ones elected by workers. The masses, as Rossi Matamoros tells us, were always on the side of the original strike committee and the demands that committee made. Barahona, *Silencio Quedó Atrás*, 349–351.

136. "A Communist Objective," *Life Magazine*, June 14, 1954, 40.

137. Ibid.

138. A train with workers headed to Puerto Cortés was stopped by the Central Strike Committee, believing they were traveling to Puerto Cortés to instigate an internal movement against El Progreso and the Central Strike Committee.

139. Barahona, *Silencio Quedó Atrás*, 163.

140. Ibid., 70–74; Posas, *Luchas del Movimiento Obrero Hondureño*, 234–248.

141. Barahona, *Silencio Quedó Atrás*, 84–88.

142. Cesar Augusto Coto spent the rest of the strike in the penitentiary in Tegucigalpa and was released in September of that year. Many of these leaders, with the exception of a few, were arrested without charges on May 31, were thrown in jail, and remained there for the rest of the strike. Ibid., 87.

143. The Liberal Party activists and organizers were worried about the upcoming election that same year. While some worried that the strike would be blamed on them, others saw it as an opportunity to gain votes.

144. The first strike committee was composed of members of the PDRH. The second strike committee was engineered by ORIT. The ORIT was created by the CIOSL in January 1951. Unions perceived to be communists were excluded. Serafino Romualdi, the US representative for Latin America, was chosen as director. The ORIT ensured that the men chosen in the new strike committee were local school teachers and men who were confirmed to not have radical-left politics. They were Raul Edgardo Estrada, Antonio Radillo B., Manuel de Jesús Valencia, José Roberto Pachame, Rufino Sosa. Adjunct secretaries were Rafael Alberty, Santos Ochoa, Beningno Gonzales, S. Lilio Pineda M., José Cubas Gross, Celeo Gonzalez, Henry Sheran, Israel Orellana, José Arnulio Espinoza, Humberto Diaz Zelaya, Carlos Ramírez. Letter to Mediation Commission, June 17, 1954, in "Aspectos Fundamentales," APMP.

145. Letter to Company with demands, May 11, 1954, in "Aspectos Fundamentales," APMP.

146. Letter Response Tela Railroad Company, June 13, 1954, in "Aspectos Fundamentales," APMP.

147. "Observaciones del Comité Central de Huelga al Plan Propuesto por la Honorable Comisión Mediadora," in "Aspectos Fundamentales," APMP.

148. Ibid.

149. Adela Chavez, interview by author, La Lima Nueva, Cortés, February 6, 2006.

150. Barahona, *Silencio Quedó Atrás*, 88.

151. The seven factories were owned by Arab immigrants or sons of Arab immigrants to Honduras and were the following: "Bolivar factory owned by Elias Katan, Presidente Paz Factory owned by Jacobo Katan, La Selecta Factory owned by Francisco Abuffele, Charalco Factory owned by Constantino Larach, the Hamilton

Factory owned by Elias Canahuati, La Esperanza Factory owned by A. Handal and lastly a factory owned by José Miselen." Barahona, *Silencio Quedó Atrás*, 93.

152. Ibid., 90; see Standard Fruit Company demands in the appendix.

153. Ibid.

154. Ibid., 90–92.

155. Ibid., 92–93.

156. He remembers that the strike leader was captured and never returned after the strike. Narciso Duarte Cruz, interview by author, Savá, Colon, June 10, 2006.

157. Narciso Duarte Cruz, interview by author, Savá, Colon, June 10, 2006.

158. At the same time, new work rules and regulations set up by the contract were perceived by finca workers as a loss of autonomy.

159. "Propuesta de la Comisión Mediadora para la Solución del Conflicto," June 21, 1954, in "Aspectos Fundamentales," APMP.

160. Report from Honduras, August 30, 1954, Box 5459, File 5–6, KCLMDA.

161. Barahona, *Silencio Quedó Atrás*, 88–100.

162. Salvadoran workers were somehow included in this rhetoric in the banana campos and fincas; they were known for their hard work and solidarity as workers for the Marxist labor committees.

163. The Organization of American States (OAS) is a US-dominated organization that emerged from the Pan-American Conference held in Mexico City before World War II ended. The military component met in Rio de Janeiro in 1947. In 1954 Secretary of State John Foster Dulles and the US delegation argued for the Caracas Declaration to oppose communism, targeting the Guatemalan government. The Guatemalan delegation hoped for hemispheric solidarity from the Latin American countries. Gleijeses suggests that there was "severe arm twisting" to get nations to endorse the US delegation and Dulles. Gleijeses, *Shattered Hope*, 270–276.

164. Ibid.

165. Halperín Donghi, *Contemporary History*, 257.

166. The invasion by General Carlos Castillo Armas was a successful coup d'état. The coup was "easy," proving the unthreatening nature of Jacobo Árbenz Guzmán's government and the United States' ability to establish hegemony over the region. Ibid., 256–257.

167. Oseguera de Ochoa, *Honduras Hoy*, 207–215.

168. Workers gave the Tela Railroad Company their initial 30 demands on May 7, and the company replied via the Mediation Commission on June 13. Their negotiation position was strong and uncompromising. On June 16, 1954, Colonel Carlos Castillo Armas invaded Guatemala from Honduras and in two weeks ousted Árbenz Guzmán. Halperín Donghi, *Contemporary History*, 256.

169. Memo November 24, 1953, John D. Erwin to US State Department, Box 177 (Box 3), Labor Affairs, Record Group 84, USNA.

170. Ibid.

171. Ibid.

172. VII-Honduras, 1956, Box 5459, File 5–6, KCLMDA.

173. Report from Honduras, August 30, 1954, Box 5459, File 5–6, KCLMDA.

174. Ibid.

175. Ibid.

176. A. C. McLellan, Consultant Representative ORIT to Arturo Jáuregui H., Assistant Secretary ORIT, "Report on Labor Situation in Honduras. Period Aug.

6th–25th, 56," September 4, 1956, Box 5459, File 5-5, KCLMDA.

177. Teresina Rossi Matamoros, interview by author, Tegucigalpa, December 21, 2006.

178. A. C. McLellan, Consultant Representative ORIT to Arturo Jáuregui H., Assistant Secretary ORIT, "Report on Labor Situation in Honduras. Period Aug. 6th–25th, 56," September 4, 1956, Box 5459, File 5-5, KCLMDA.

179. Ibid.

180. A. C. McLellan, ORIT Representative Central America to Luis Alberto Monge, General Secretariat of the ORIT, "Report on Trade Union Situation in Honduras Period Ending Jan 26/27," Guatemala City, February 1, 1957, Box 5459, File 5-5, KCLMDA.

181. Ibid.

182. Ibid.

Chapter 7: Contemporary Movement Leaders Reflect on the Legacy of the 1954 Strike

1. Trouillot, *Silencing the Past*, 152.

2. A lot of time has passed,
   life has elapsed
   and if these people do not forget what it could have been.
   Today a chimera has assaulted me
   In the plan that benefits us, let's arm another great strike
   And let's reclaim our power.

   Campeño singer and song writer, Mario de Mezapa, sings about the 1954 strike to workers on May 1, 2018. Mario de Mezapa, "La Huelga," *De Sucias, Cadejos y Cucuruchos*, Costa Norte Records, youtube.com/watch?v=bRewNXXFK_c.

3. Soluri, *Banana Cultures*; Posas, *Luchas del Movimiento Obrero Hondureño*.

4. Nohemy Yanez, interview by author, La Lima, Cortés, July 28, 2017.

5. COSIBAH was a coordinating body of banana unions that aimed to train in negotiations and other union education and leadership to build power in negotiations for banana unions; it is now called FESTAGRO (Federation of Agro-Industry Unions) and represents other unions in the agricultural sector in union negotiations and training of leadership. It also engages in building international solidarity.

6. Martinez, "Huelga de 1954," Revista Vision Sindical, Coordinadora de Sindicatos Bananeros de Honduras, 10.

7. Ibid., 11.

8. Ibid.

9. Fieldnotes by author, La Lima, Cortés, 2018.

10. Revista Vision Sindical, Coordinadora de Sindicatos Bananeros de Honduras, 2002, 13.

11. Connolly, *Tacamiche*.

12. COLSIBA stands for Coordinadora Latinoamericana de Sindicatos Bananeros Y Agroindustriales (Coordinating Body of Latin American Banana and Agro-industrial Unions); its president rotates among banana-producing nations in Latin America.

13. Iris Munguía, interview by author, Choluteca, Choluteca, August 3, 2016.

14. Iris Munguía, interview by author, Choluteca, Choluteca, August 3, 2016.

15. Iris Munguía, interview by author, Choluteca, Choluteca, August 3, 2016.

16. Iris Munguía, interview by author, Choluteca, Choluteca, August 3, 2016.

17. Gloria Garcia, interview by author, Choluteca, Choluteca, August 6, 2016.

18. Bartolo Fuentes, interview by author, El Progreso, Yoro, August 6, 2016.

19. Bartolo Fuentes, interview by author, El Progreso, Yoro, August 6, 2016.

20. Posas, *Perfiles de Líderes Populares*, 35.

21. Ibid., 36.

22. President José Manuel Zelaya Rosales, interview by author, Tegucigalpa, August, 13, 2018.

23. Iris Munguía, interview by author, La Lima, Cortés, February 15, 2006.

24. Barahona, *Memorias de un Comunista*, 30.

25. The Bloque Popular was a coalition of student, worker, and popular organization alliances that came together in the 1990s in Tegucigalpa. They were under the banner of the Coordinadora de Resistencia Popular, a larger umbrella group that brought together all the popular groups throughout the country and sought to respond to neoliberalism and impede free trade agreements at the time. Bartolo Fuentes, interview by author, El Progreso, Yoro, August 6, 2016; Gilberto Rios, interview by author, February 8, 2017.

26. "Free Labor" refers to the noncommunist labor unions promoted by the US State Department against the CTAL-affiliated unions, perceived to be Marxists.

27. Lety Elvir Lazo, interview by author, June 18, 2019.

28. Lety Elvir Lazo, interview by author, June 18, 2019.

29. Ramos, "Guerra del Imperio Norteamericano," 35.

30. Ibid.

31. José Manuel Zelaya Rosales, interview by author, Tegucigalpa, August, 13, 2018.

32. Campesino D, interview by author, Comunidad Guadalupe Carney, Trujillo, Colón, August 13, 2011 (name omitted to protect safety of interviewee); Portillo Villeda, "Honduras," 138.

33. Amilivia, "'Sealing' and 'Unsealing,'" 118.

34. Lety Elvir Lazo, interview by author, June 18, 2019; Carney, *To Be a Revolutionary*; Dunkerley, *Power in the Isthmus*, 522, 538.

35. Carney, *To Be a Revolutionary*, 188.

36. Ibid., 187.

37. Connolly, *Tacamiche*, 42.

38. Argueta, *Ramón Villeda Morales*, 232–243.

39. Iris Munguía, interview by author, La Lima, Cortés, February 15, 2006; Iris Munguía, interview by author, Choluteca, Choluteca, August 3, 2016.

40. I will use the term "leftist" to describe the plurality of the organizers, which included those from the PDRH; others identified with the Communist Party, others considered themselves progressive liberals, and many other identities fit in between.

41. Trouillot, *Silencing the Past*, 48.

42. Portillo Villeda, "Rethinking Latin American Social Movements," 121–145.

43. Global Study on Homicide, United Nations Office of Drug and Crime, Vienna, 2013, see unodc.org/documents/gsh/pdfs/2014_GLOBAL_HOMICIDE _BOOK_web.pdf. See also "Human Rights Violations in the Context of the 2017 Elections in Honduras," Report of the United Nations High Commissioner for Human Rights, February 2018.

44. "Honduras: The Deadliest Place to Defend the Planet," Global Witness, January 31, 2017, globalwitness.org/en/campaigns/environmental-activists/honduras-deadliest -country-world-environmental-activism.

45. See wikileaks.org/wiki/Category:Honduras.

46. *La Consulta Popular* was no more than a poll, an inquiry to the general citizenry, to get their opinion about having a fourth ballot that would then allow them to vote on the possibility of a national Constitutional Assembly. The Honduran people would have had two opportunities to voice their opinion on the issue, first in an informal poll that would ask them if the actual vote on the Constitutional Assembly should take place later that year, and then the vote itself that November. See Portillo Villeda, "Rethinking Latin American Social Movements," 123–124.

47. Ibid., 121.

48. Miriam Miranda, Interview Alba TV, YouTube, October 28, 2018, youtube.com/watch?v=tmysxs8q3bQ.

49. Ibid.

50. José Manuel Zelaya Rosales, interview by author, Tegucigalpa, August, 13, 2018.

51. The union formed after the strike was the Tela Railroad Company Workers Union (Sindicato de Trabajadores de la Tela Railroad Company; SITRATERCO); the coordinating body of all banana unions formed in the 1990s was COSIBAH, now called FESTAGRO.

52. In the days right after the coup d'état, I was in direct contact with local labor leaders who would send images to the United States and the media because the coup leaders were blocking all forms of media reports. In fact, their electricity was turned off intermittently, and activists used their cell phones to transmit information about protests against the coup and police abuses.

53. Gerardo Torres Zelaya, interview by author, December 17, 2016.

54. Bartolo Fuentes, interview by author, August 6, 2016; Gerardo Torres Zelaya, interview by author, December 17, 2016; Gilberto Rios, interview by author, February 8, 2017.

55. Amilivia, "'Sealing' and 'Unsealing,'" 105.

56. Bartolo Fuentes, interview by author, August 6, 2016.

57. Scott, *Omens of Adversity*, 121–122.

58. Berta Cáceres, public speech, video by Indyra Mendoza Aguilar, Archivo de Red Lésbica Cattrachas, 2009, youtube.com/watch?v=9UWSgs_yBd0.

59. Portillo Villeda, "Honduras."

60. Berta Cáceres, public speech, video by Indyra Mendoza Aguilar, Archivo de Red Lésbica Cattrachas, 2009.

61. Luther Castillo Harry, interview by author, El Progreso, Yoro, February 14, 2018.

62. Gerardo Torres Zelaya, interview by author, December 17, 2016.

63. Gerardo Torres Zelaya, interview by author, December 17, 2016.

64. Indyra Mendoza Aguilar, cited in Argueta, *El Pincel y el Martillo*.

65. Indyra Mendoza is the founder of Red Lésbica Cattrachas, a lesbian led LGBTTI violence monitoring NGO. Gerardo Torres is the Secretary of the LIBRE Party.

66. Barahona, *Memorias de un Comunista*. For a treatment of this period in South America, see Amilivia, *State Terrorism*.

67. Scott, *Omens of Adversity*, 101.

68. Ibid., 100.

69. Iris Munguía, interview by author, Choluteca, Choluteca, August 3, 2017.

70. Carlos H. Reyes, interview by author, Tegucigalpa, March 6, 2018.

71. Carlos H. Reyes, interview by author, Tegucigalpa, March 6, 2018.

72. Carlos H. Reyes, interview by author, Tegucigalpa, March 6, 2018.

73. Lety Elvir Lazo, interview by author, June 18, 2019.

74. Lety Elvir Lazo, interview by author, June 18, 2019.

75. Gilberto Rios, interview by author, February 8, 2017.

76. Luther Castillo Harry, interview by author, El Progreso, Yoro, February 14, 2018.

77. Indyra Mendoza, interview by author, January 23, 2020; Indyra Mendoza, interview by author, New York City, May 19, 2019.

78. Amilivia, *State Terrorism*.

79. Bartolo Fuentes and Dunia Montoya, interview by author, El Progreso, Yoro. August 6, 2018.

80. Gerardo Torres Zelaya, interview by author, December 17, 2016.

81. Lety Elvir Lazo, interview by author, June 18, 2019.

82. Scott, *Omens of Adversity*, 100–101.

83. Ibid., 100.

84. "Status of Violence against Women in Honduras: Submitted to the Special Rapporteur on Violence against Women, Its Causes and Consequences, in Her Visit to Honduras," Centro de Derechos de la Mujer, Red Nacional de Defensoras de Derechos Humanos, Foro de Mujeres por la Vida, Centro de Estudios de la Mujer, 2014.

85. Mahoney, "Radical, Reformist and Aborted Liberalism," 221–256.

86. Jelin, *State Repression*, 5–6.

87. Ibid., 7.

88. Ibid.

89. Ibid.

90. Amilivia, *State Terrorism*, 7–8.

91. Ibid., 8.

92. Ibid., 135, 151, 183.

93. Ibid., 29.

94. Scott, *Omens of Adversity*, 120.

95. Amilivia, *State Terrorism*, 9.

96. Iris Munguía, interview by author, Choluteca, Choluteca, August 3, 2016; Gloria Garcia, interview by author, Choluteca, Choluteca, August 6, 2016; Bartolo Fuentes, interview by author, El Progreso, Yoro, August 6, 2016; Gerardo Torres Zelaya, interview by author, December 17, 2016; Gilberto Rios, interview by author, February 8, 2017.

97. Iris Munguía, interview by author, Choluteca, Choluteca, August 3, 2016; Gloria Garcia, interview by author, Choluteca, Choluteca, August 6, 2016; Bartolo Fuentes, interview by author, El Progreso, Yoro, August 6, 2016; Gerardo Torres Zelaya, interview by author, December 17, 2016; Gilberto Rios, interview by author, February 8, 2017.

98. Eating poorly—boiled green bananas and beans—as a form of sacrifice and suffering was a critical narrative workers passed on to their children, indicating the bare minimum of food but also the fears of not having enough money for survival. The inclusion of these narrative details is important in passing down memories to younger generations, so that they might be able to relate the stories to their experience.

99. Roberto Sosa, "Secreto Militar," 1985, Círculo de Poesía, posted on March 22,

2013, circulodepoesia.com/2013/03/foja-de-poesia-no-192-roberto-sosa-2 (author's translation).

Conclusion

1. Comisionado Nacional de Protección de los Derechos Humanos, "Los Hechos Hablan Por Sí Mismos."
2. Ibid.

Appendix A

1. Letter from the Central Strike Committee to the Mediation Commission, May 11, 1954 in "Aspectos Fundamentales de la Mediación en el Conflicto Obrero-Patronal entre la Tela Railroad Company y los Trabajadores de la Empresa, Reporte de la Comisión Mediadora, San Pedro Sula, June 25, 1954," Archivo Privado del Dr. Mario Posas (henceforth "Aspectos Fundamentales," APMP) (translation by Marlom J. Portillo).

Appendix B

1. Barahona, *Silencio Quedó Atrás*, 75–76 (translated by Araceli Cortés).

Appendix C

1. Barahona, *Silencio Quedó Atrás*, 90 (translated by Araceli Cortés).

Appendix D

1. Napoleón Acevedo Granados, *La Clase Obrera Hondureña: Su Papel Histórico*. Tegucigalpa: Editorial Guaymuras, 2017. 57–61 (translation by Priscilla Cobian).

Appendix E

1. Argueta, *Desafío al Tradicionalismo Político*, 201 (translation by Priscilla Cobian and Marlom Portillo).

Appendix F

1. Compiled from Portillo Villeda and Padilla, *Honduran Social Movements, Then and Now*; Barahona, *Honduras en el Siglo XX*; Posas, *Luchas del Movimiento Obrero Hondureño*; Robleda Castro, *Verdad de la Huelga*; Centeno Garcia, *Historia del Pueblo Negro Caribe*; Argueta, *Desafío al Tradicionalismo Político*.

BIBLIOGRAPHY

ORAL TESTIMONIES

Unless otherwise noted I conducted all interviews in the following periods: between June and August of 2004, between January and December of 2006, summers between 2008 and 2016, January 2017, and between 2018 and 2019.

Amaya Yanez, Carlos. Interview by author. La Lima, Cortés, July 1, 2004.

Amerto Lagos, Francisco. Interview by author. La Lima, Cortés, February 6, 2006.

Argueta, Maribel. Interview by author. La Lima, Cortés, December 16, 2006.

Argueta, Marina. Interview by author. Los Angeles, 2008.

Arias, Lorena. Interview by author. La Lima, Cortés, April 10, 2006.

Bautista, Leonardo. Interview by author. Campo Limones, La Lima, Cortés, May 5, 2006.

Bennett Bustillo, Juan. Interview by author. La Lima, Cortés, February 6, 2006.

Cabrera Williams, Edmundo. Interview by author. Finca Indiana, La Lima, Cortés, July 25, 2004.

Campesino D. (pseudonym) Interview by author. Comunidad Guadalupe Carney, Trujillo, Colón, August 13, 2011.

Canales, Luis. Interview by author. La Lima, Cortés, July 2, 2006.

Canales Pineda, Juan Bautista. Interview by author. La Ceiba, Atlántida, August 8, 2004.

Carcamo, Pablo Raul. Interview by author. La Lima, Cortés, May 5, 2006.

Cardona, Juan Blas. Interview by author. La Cieba, Atlántida, August 8, 2004.

Cardona, María Ángela. Interview by author. El Carríl, Olanchito, Yoro, August 13, 2006.

Castillo Harry, Luther. Interview by author. El Progreso, Yoro, February 14, 2018.

Chavez, Adela. Interview by author. La Lima, Cortés, February 6, 2006.

Chinchilla, Patilla (pseudonym). Interview by author. Los Angeles, January 1, 2020.

Cuellar Mendoza, Julio Antonio. Interview by author. Los Angeles, June 5, 2010.

Duarte Cruz, Narciso. Interview by author. Sava, Colón, June 10, 2006.

Elvir, Esteban. Interview by author. San Pedro Sula, Cortés, April 12, 2018.

Elvir Lazo, Lety. Interview by author. Via Whatsapp, June 18, 2019.

Fernandez Sabillón, Ricarda. Interview by author. Nuevo San Juan, La Lima, Cortés, May 5, 2006.

Figueroa, Olimpia Edelmira. Interview by author. La Lima, Cortés, February 15, 2006.

Figueroa Portillo, Casta. Interview by author. El Carríl, Olanchito, Yoro, August 13, 2006.

Fortín, Rosa de. Interview by author. San Pedro Sula, Cortés, May 11, 2006.

Fuentes, Bartolo, and Dunia Montoya. Interview by author. El Progreso, Yoro, August 6, 2018.

Galo, Francisco Napoleon. Interview by author. El Progreso, Yoro, July 1, 2004.

Garay, Candida. Interview by author. La Lima, Cortés, March 6, 2006.

Garcia, Gloria. Interview by author. La Lima, Cortés, April 10, 2006 and August 3, 2016.

Garcia Ramírez, José María. Interview by author. Nuevo San Juan, La Lima, Cortés, February 30, 2006.

Garrido Lobo, Gavino. Interview by author. El Progreso, Yoro, December 16, 2006.

Gómez, Jesús. Interview by author. La Lima, Cortés, March 7, 2006.

Gómez, Juan Adalberto. Interview by author. La Lima, Cortés, January 29, 2006.

———. Interview by author. Nuevo San Juan, La Lima, Cortés, June 2006.

Goodlitt, Lucila. Interview by author. El Carríl, Olanchito, Yoro, August 10, 2006.

Graugnard, Marina. Interview by author. Tela, Atlántida, June 9, 2006.

Graugnard, Raul. Interview by author. Tela, Atlántida, June 9, 2006.

Guerra, Paco. Interview by author. Coyoles Central, Olanchito, Yoro, August 10, 2006. No recording.

Guevara Villanueva, José María. Interview by author. La Lima, Cortés, August 6, 2006.

Hernández, Domitila. Interview by author. Savá, Colón, June 6, 2006.

Hernández Hernández, Manuel. Interview by author. La Ceiba, Atlántida, December 16, 2006.

Hernández Maldonado, Efraín. Interview by author. La Lima, Cortés, March 28, 2006.

Lezama, Lidia Aurora. Interview by author. Campo Urraco, El Progreso, Yoro, December 9, 2006.

Lorenzo (pseudonym). Interview by author. Los Angeles, September, 2017.

Madrid Guevara, Daniel. Interview by author. La Lima, Cortés, February 5, 2006.

Martinez, Angel (pseudonym). Interview by author. Colonia Nuevo San Juan, La Lima, Cortés, January 29, 2006.

Martinez, Patrocinia. Interview by author. San Juan de Tela, Tela, Atlántida, August 8, 2006.

Martinez, Pedro Gonzalo. Interview by author. San Juan de Tela, Tela, Atlántida, August 8, 2006.

Membreño, Ernesto. Interview by author. San Pedro Sula, Cortés, August 31, 2006.

Mendoza Aguilar, Indyra. Interview by author, New York City, May 19, 2019, and January 23, 2020.

Molina Fuentes, Leonardo. Interview by author. Nuevo San Juan, La Lima, Cortés, May 5, 2006.

Montoya, Dunia. Interview by author. Via Whatsapp, Los Angeles and El Progreso, September 3, 2019.

Moreira, Isabel Miguel. Interview by author. San Pedro Sula, Cortés, November 27, 2006.

Munguía, Iris. Interview by author. La Lima, Cortés, February 15, 2006 and August 3, 2016.

Nuñez Sierra, Juan. Interview by author. La Lima, Cortés, March 7, 2006.

Oliva, José Eulalio. Interview by author. El Carríl, Olanchito, Yoro, August 10, 2006.

Ortega, Alejandro. Interview by author. La Lima, Cortés, February 8, 2006.

Padilla, Eduardo. Interview by author. La Lima, Cortés, March 30, 2006.

Pagoada, Oscar Rodriguez. Interview by author. Zona Americana, La Lima, Cortés, September 2, 2006.

Pascual, Edmunda. Interview by author. San Pedro Sula, Cortés, May 11, 2006.

Perla, María Antonia. Interview by author. La Lima, Cortés, March 5, 2006.

Pery Laredo, Gerardo. Interview by author. Tornabé, Tela, Atlántida, August 8, 2006.

Portillo, Francisco. Interview by author. La Lima, Cortés, February 6, 2006.

Recarte, Jovita. Interview by author. Los Angeles, November 4, 2007.

Regalado, María Luisa. Interview by author. San Pedro Sula, Cortés, April 15, 2006.
Reyes Pineda, José. Interview by author. Campo Laurel/Campo Limones, La Lima, Cortés, May 5, 2006.
Rios, Gilberto. Interview by author. Via Skype, February 8, 2017.
Rivera, Gilda. Interview by author. Tegucigalpa, D.C., April 4, 2018.
Rivera, Julio C. Interview by author. San José, Costa Rica, July 9, 2008.
Rivera Rosales, Leandro. Interview by author. Campo Limones, La Lima, Cortés, May 5, 2006.
Robleda, Sylvia. Interview by author. San Pedro Sula, Cortés, July 4, 2004.
Robleda Castro, Agapito. Interview by author. San Pedro Sula, Cortés, August 2, 2006.
Rodas, Ethelvina. Interview by author. Tela, Atlántida, September 2, 2006.
Rodriguez Aguilar, Gilberto. Interview by author. El Progreso, Yoro, 2006.
Rodriguez Pagoada, Oscar. Interview by author. Zona Americana, La Lima Nueva, September 2, 2006.
Rogel, Neftalí. Interview by author. La Lima, Cortés, March 7, 2006.
Romero Madrid, Manuel. Interview by author. La Lima, Cortés, September 2, 2006.
Rossi Matamoros, Teresina. Interview by author. Tegucigalpa, Honduras, December 21, 2006.
Salazar, Oscar. Interview by author. San Pedro Sula, Cortés, August 3, 2004.
Sánchez, José. Interview by author. La Lima, Cortés, November 5, 2006.
Suazo, Ignacio. Interview by author. Choloma, Yoro, August 3, 2006.
T. E. P. (pseudonym) Interview by author. San Pedro Sula, Cortés, September 5, 2006. Not tape recorded per wishes of interviewee.
Torres, Mario. Interview by author. San Pedro Sula, Cortés, October 27, 2006.
Torres, Miguel Angel. Interview by author. La Ceiba, Atlántida, August 9, 2006.
Torres Zelaya, Gerardo. Interview by author via Whatsapp/Skype, December 17, 2016.
Z. L. (pseudonym) Interview by author. San Pedro Sula, Cortés, 2006.
Zelaya Rosales, Manuel. Interview by author. Tegucigalpa, Honduras, August 13, 2018.

ARCHIVAL SOURCES

Archives in Tegucigalpa, Honduras
Archivo Nacional de La Nación, Tegucigalpa, Honduras
Informe de Fomento, Agricultura y Trabajo, 1944–1945
Boletín de Congreso Nacional Legislativo Serie IV 1953–1954
Memoria Presentada al Congreso Nacional Relaciones Exteriores, 1929–1930

Telegrams
Tropical Radio and Telegraph, Robert V. Howley
Telegramas de Ministerio de Fomento, 1950

Newspapers
Acción Democrática, 1952, 1954
Basta!, 1956
Boletín de La Asociación Anti-Alcohólica, 1953
Diario Comercial, 1945
El Chilillo, 1954
El Chilío, 1954–1955

El Ciclón, 1955
El Comercial, 1953–1954
El Cronista, 1954
El Cronista, 1960s
El Día, 1948–1954
La Época, 1937, 1954
El Espectador, 1952–1954
El Intruso, 1956
Juventud, 1954
Labor, 1956
Lucha, 1954
El Luchador, 1952–1954
El Machete, 1953–1956
El Marino, 1954
Noticiero Escolar, 1952
Orientación 1953–1954
El Oriental, 1953
El País, 1955
Patria, 1950
Radio Libre, 1952
El Rebelde, 1954
Revolución, 1954
Rugidos, Trujillo, 1952
Semáforo, 1953–1955
Simientes Juveniles-Asociación Evangélica, 1952–1953
El Sol, 1929–1930
Renovación, 1955
La República, 1955
Vanguardia, 1945

Archivo Privado de Mario Posas, Tegucigalpa, Honduras (APMP)
Documentos Sobre la Huelga Bananera 1954

Archivo CEDOH (Centro de Documentación de Honduras), Tegucigalpa, Honduras
Victor Meza Documents on Labor Movement

Archivo Privado de Indyra Mendoza Aguilar
Fotografía/Videografía (Archivo de Red Lésbica Cattrachas)
Periódicos, Varios

Archives in San Pedro Sula, Honduras
Archivo del Poder Judicial de Honduras, Centro de Documentación e Información de Justicia (CEDIJ)
Expedientes Varios, hojas sueltas: 1895–1962*

Loose Periodicals
El Pueblo, 1954

---

* This archive is in the process of being organized. All the folios were identified in this process of organization. Some cases have numbers; others do not. I cataloged them by year.

Hojas Sueltas, 1954
Vanguardia, 1948
Vanguardia Revolucionaria, 1949

Archivo Municipal, San Pedro Sula
Libros Copiadores, varios
Documentos de Pompeyo Melara

Archivo de Gobernación de Cortés
Libros de Actas, 1953–1959
Libros de Registros de Planillas de los cuerpos dependientes de la Gobernación
  Política y demás gastos de Gobernación, 1955

Archivo Privado de Thomas Erazo Peña
Documentos del Archivo de Lombardo Toledano en México, D. F.

Comité Sampedrano de Mujeres
Hojas Sueltas
Libros Copiadores, 1950–1962
Libro de Entradas, 1950

Archives in Santa Rosa de Copán
Biblioteca y Hemeroteca Manuel J. Fajardo
Cultura Femenina, 1929
Orientación Obrera, 1929, 1930
Periódicos Varios/Sueltos

Archives in El Progreso, Yoro
Municipalidad, Libros Copiadores

Archives in La Lima, Cortés
COSIBAH/FESTAGRO
Revistas Sindicales
Revista *Visión Sindical*, Coordinadora de Sindicatos Bananeros y Agroindustriales de
  Honduras (COSIBAH)
FESITRANH Revista

Archives in the United States
Baker Library, Harvard Business School, Cambridge, MA
United Fruit Company Photograph Collection

Center for Research Libraries, Chicago, Illinois
Informes de Fomento, Agricultura y Trabajo, MF 13544 (Microfilmed), 1928–1955

Huntington Library and Archives, San Marino, CA
E. G. Squier Rare Books, Papers in Microfilm
Unitfruitco Magazine Collection

United States National Archives, College Park, MD

Microfilmed Sources
Confidential US State Department Central Files: Honduras Internal and Foreign
  Affairs, 1950–1954

Textual
Record Group 59
Bureau of Interamerican Affairs. Records of the Special Assistant on Communism 1956–1961. Lot Files 62D24—NDD959039 Box 5 Honduras;Tegucigalpa Embassy,Top Secret Records 1950–1954.
Confidential US State Department Central Files: Honduras Internal and Foreign Affairs, 1950–1954.
General Records of the Department of State. Records of the Assistant Secretary Henry F. Holland, Subject File Dec 2, 1953–Nov 11, 1956. Lot file 57D295 (Box 4) 1 Box NND 867215.
Honduras;Tegucigalpa Embassy,Top Secret Records 1954–1955.
Records of the Assistant Secretaries for Interamerican Affairs. Lot Files 57D598, 57D634, 57D691 (Box #3).
Records of the Office of Regional American Affairs "Records Relating to the Mutual Security Program 1951–1955." Box 1.
Records of the Office of Middle American Affairs *1947–1955*. Lot File 57D95 Box 1-Box 6(part) NND867218.
Records of the Office of Middle American Affairs *1947–1955*. Lot File 57D95 "Records of William T. Bennet" Box 6 (part).
Records of the Office of Middle American Affairs "Miscellaneous Records 1951–1956" Lot Files 57D618 Box 1.
Records of Assistant Secretary John M. Cabot. Country File, Jan. 1953-March 1954. Entry 1131 Lot File 56D13 (1 Box)—NDD867202-Box 1.
State Central Decimal File, 1950–1954 611.15 (Memos within the United States).
State Central Decimal File, 1950–1954 615 (US relations with the world).
State Central Decimal File, 1950–1954, 715 (Political internal information—within the country).
State Central Decimal File, 1950–1954, 815 (Economic, Industrial, Social).
State Central Decimal File, 1950–1954, 915 (Military).

Record Group 84
Confidential US State Department Central Files: Honduras Internal and Foreign Affairs, 1950–1954.
Foreign Office Posts of the Department of State Honduras Tegucigalpa, 1950–1954.
Honduras;Tegucigalpa Embassy,Top Secret Records 1950–1954.
Honduras;Tegucigalpa Embassy,Top Secret Records 1954–1955.
Records of the Foreign Service Post: Honduras: US Embassy (Box 175, 176, 177), 1953–1955.

Other
Life Magazine
Cookbooks, Home Economics Department, United Fruit Company

PUBLISHED SOURCES
Acevedo Granados, Napoleón. *La Clase Obrera Hondureña: Su Papel Histórico*. Tegucigalpa: Editorial Guaymuras, 2017.
Acker, Alison. *Honduras: The Making of a Banana Republic*. Boston: South End Press, 1988.

Alba, Victor. *Politics and the Labor Movement in Latin America.* Stanford: Stanford University Press, 1968.

Alberti, Verena. *Ouvir Contar: Textos em História Oral.* Rio de Janeiro: Editora FGV, 2004.

Amaya Banegas, Jorge Alberto. *Los Árabes Palestinos en Honduras (1900–1950).* Tegucigalpa: Editorial Guaymuras, 2006.

———. *El que Esté Libre de Pecado . . . : Prostitución Femenina y Control Social en Honduras Durante la Época Liberal (1876–1950).* Tegucigalpa: Editorial Guaymuras, 2013.

Amaya Amador, Ramon. *Prisión Verde.* Tegucigalpa: Editorial Universitaria de la Universidad Nacional Autónoma de Honduras, 1987.

Amaya Amador, Ramón, and Rigoberto Padilla Rush. *Memorias y Enseñanzas del Alzamiento Popular de 1954.* Tegucigalpa: Ediciones Juan Pablo Wainwright, 1989.

Amilivia, Gabriela Fried. "'Sealing' and 'Unsealing' Uruguay's Transitional Politics of Oblivion: Waves of Memory and the Winding Road to Memory and Justice (1985–2015)," in *The Politics of Memory Making in Latin America,* edited by Roberta Villalón, special issue, *Latin American Perspectives* 43, no. 6 (2016): 103–123.

———. *State Terrorism and the Politics of Memory in Latin America: Transmissions Across the Generations of Post-Dictatorship Uruguay, 1984–2004.* Amherst, NY: Cambria Press, 2016.

Anderson, Mark. *Black and Indigenous: Garifuna Activism and Consumer Culture in Honduras.* Minneapolis: University of Minnesota Press, 2009.

Andrade Coelho, Ruy Galvão de. *Los Negros Caribes de Honduras.* Tegucigalpa: Editorial Guaymuras, 1995.

Ans, André-Marcel d'. *Honduras: Emergencia Difícil de una Nación, de un Estado.* Paris: Karthala, 1997.

Aparicio, Frances, and Susana Chávez-Silverman, eds. *Tropicalizations: Transcultural Representations of Latinidad.* Hanover: University Press of New England, 1997.

Appadurai, Arjun, ed. *The Social Life of Things: Commodities in Cultural Perspective.* Cambridge: Cambridge University Press, 1986.

Archetti, Eduardo P. *Masculinities: Football, Polo and Tango in Argentina.* Oxford: Berg, 1999.

———. "Playing Styles and Masculine Virtues in Argentine Football." In *Machos, Mistresses, Madonnas: Contesting the Power of Latin American Gender Imagery,* edited by Marit Melhuus and Kristi Anne Stolen, 34–55. London: Verso, 1996.

Argueta, Mario R. *Bananos y Política: Samuel Zemurray y la Cuyamel Fruit Company en Honduras.* Tegucigalpa: Editorial Universitaria de la Universidad Nacional Autónoma de Honduras, UNAH, 1989.

———. *Un Desafío al Tradicionalismo Político: El PDRH (1946–1954).* Tegucigalpa: Editorial Guaymuras, 2016.

———. *La Gran Huelga Bananera: 69 Días que Estremecieron a Honduras.* Tegucigalpa: Editorial Universitaria de la Universidad Nacional Autónoma de Honduras, 1995.

———. *1954 en Nuestra Historia.* Honduras: Editorial Universitaria de la Universidad Nacional Autónoma de Honduras, 1987.

———. *El Pincel y el Martillo: Confucio y Zoroastro Montes de Oca.* Tegucigalpa: Familia Aguilar Montes de Oca y Descendientes, 2016.

———. *Ramón Villeda Morales: Luces y Sombras de una Primavera Política.* Tegucigalpa, Honduras: Editorial Guaymuras, 2009.

Arias, Arturo, ed. *The Rigoberta Menchú Controversy*. Minneapolis: University of Minnesota Press, 2001.

Armitage, Susan H., Patricia Hart, and Karen Weathermon, eds. *Women's Oral History: The Frontiers Reader*. Lincoln: University of Nebraska Press, 2002.

Asturias, Miguel Ángel. *Men of Maize*. Translated by Gerald Martin. Pittsburgh: University of Pittsburgh Press, 1993.

Ávila, Cuauhtémoc Velasco, ed. *Historia y Testimonios Orales*, Divulgación. Mexico City: Instituto Nacional de Antropología e Historia, 1996.

Barahona, Marvin. *Evolución Histórica de la Identidad Nacional*. Tegucigalpa: Editorial Guaymuras, 2002.

———. *La Hegemonía de los Estados Unidos en Honduras (1907–1932)*. Tegucigalpa: Centro de Documentación de Honduras, 1989.

———. *Honduras en el Siglo XX: Una Síntesis Histórica*. Tegucigalpa: Editorial Guaymuras, 2005.

———. *Memorias de un Comunista: Rigoberto Padilla Rush*. Talanquera. Tegucigalpa: Editorial Guaymuras, 2001.

———. *El Silencio Quedó Atrás: Testimonios de la Huelga Bananera de 1954*. Tegucigalpa: Editorial Guaymuras, 2004.

Barriteau, Eudine. *The Political Economy of Gender in the Twentieth-Century Caribbean*. New York: Palgrave, 2001.

Belli, Gioconda. *The Country under My Skin: A Memoir of Love and War*. London: Bloomsbury, 2003.

Beneria, Lourdes, and Catherine R. Stimpson. *Women, Households, and the Economy*. New Brunswick: Rutgers University Press, 1987.

Benítez, Mario. *Nicomedes en los Bananales y las Tierras del Tío Sam*. Tegucigalpa: Editorial Guaymuras, 1991.

Benjamin, Medea. *Don't Be Afraid, Gringo: A Honduran Woman Speaks from the Heart; The Story of Elvia Alvarado*. New York: Harper Perennial, 1987.

Benz, Stephen. "Through the Tropical Looking Glass: The Motif of Resistance in US Literature on Central America." In *Tropicalizations: Transcultural Representations of Latinidad*, edited by Frances R. Aparicio and Susana Chávez-Silverman, 51–66. Hanover: University Press of England, 1997.

Berger, Maurice, Brian Wallis, and Simon Watson, eds. *Constructing Masculinity*. New York: Routledge, 1995.

Beverley, John. "The Margin at the Center: On *Testimonio* (Testimonial Narrative)." *Modern Fiction Studies* 35, no. 1 (1989): 11–28.

Beverley, John, and Marc Zimmerman. *Literature and Politics in the Central American Revolutions*. Austin: University of Texas Press, 1990.

Binns, Jack R. *The United States in Honduras, 1980–1981: An Ambassador's Memoir*. Jefferson, NC: McFarland, 2000.

Bourgois, Philippe. "One Hundred Years of United Fruit Company Letters." In *Banana Wars: Power, Production, and History in the Americas*, edited by Steve Striffler and Mark Moberg, 103–144. Durham, NC: Duke University Press, 2003.

Boyer, Christopher R. *Becoming Campesinos: Politics, Identity, and Agrarian Struggle in Postrevolutionary Michoacán, 1920–1935*. Stanford: Stanford University Press, 2003.

Bravermen, Harry. *Labor and Monopoly Capital: The Degradation of Work in the Twentieth Century*. New York: Monthly Review Press, 1974.

Buchard, Ethel Garcia. *Poder Político, Interés Bananero e Identidad Nacional en Centro*

América: Un Estudio Comparativo; Costa Rica (1884–1938) y Honduras (1902–1958). Tegucigalpa: Editorial Universitaria de la Universidad Nacional Autónoma de Honduras, 1997.

Bucheli, Marcelo. *Bananas and Business: The United Fruit Company in Colombia, 1899–2000.* New York: New York University Press, 2005.

Bulmer-Thomas, Victor. "Honduras since 1930." In *Central America since Independence,* edited by Leslie Bethell, 191–225. Cambridge: Cambridge University Press, 1991.

Butler, Judith. *Gender Trouble: Feminism and the Subversion of Identity.* New York: Routledge, 1990.

Candelario, Ginetta E. B. *Black behind the Ears: Dominican Racial Identity from Museums to Beauty.* Durham: Duke University Press, 2007.

Canelas Díaz, Antonio. *El Departamento de Atlántida, 100 Años de Historia: 15 de Septiembre de 1902 al 15 de Septiembre del 2002.* [Honduras]: n.p., 2002.

———. *El Estrangulamiento Económico de La Ceiba, 1903–1965.* Tegucigalpa: Editorial Guaymuras, 2001.

Carey, David, Jr. "Drunks and Dictators: Inebriation's Gendered, Ethnic, and Class Components in Guatemala, 1898–1944." In *Alcohol in Latin America: A Social and Cultural History,* edited by Gretchen Pierce and Áurea Toxqui, 139–141. Tucson: University of Arizona Press, 2014.

Carney, Padre Guadalupe J. *To Be a Revolutionary: The Explosive Autobiography of an American Priest, Missing in Honduras.* San Francisco: Harper and Row, 1985.

Casson, Mark. *The Growth of International Business.* RLE International Business. New York: Routledge, 2013.

Centeno Garcia, Santos. *Adhesión Étnica.* Tegucigalpa: Editorial Universitaria de la Universidad Nacional Autónoma de Honduras, 2004.

———. *Historia del Pueblo Negro Caribe y su Llegada a Hibueras el 12 de Abril de 1797.* Tegucigalpa: Editorial Universitaria de la Universidad Nacional Autónoma de Honduras, 1996.

Chambers, Glenn A. *Race, Nation, and West Indian Immigration to Honduras, 1890–1940.* Baton Rouge: Louisiana State University Press, 2010.

Chant, Sylvia. *Women and Survival in Mexican Cities: Perspectives on Gender, Labour Markets, and Low-Income Households.* Manchester: Manchester University Press, 1991.

Chenut, Helen Harden. *The Fabric of Gender: Working-Class Culture in the Third Republic of France.* University Park: Pennsylvania State University Press, 2005.

Chinchilla, Maya. *The Cha Cha Files: A Chapina Poética; Poems.* San Francisco: Kórima Press, 2014.

Chomsky, Aviva. *West Indian Workers and the United Fruit Company in Costa Rica, 1870–1940.* Baton Rouge: Louisiana State University Press, 1996.

Chomsky, Aviva, and Aldo Lauria-Santiago, eds. *Identity and Struggle at the Margins of the Nation-State: The Laboring Peoples of Central America and the Hispanic Caribbean.* Durham: Duke University Press, 1998.

Cockrill, Phillip. *United Fruit Company: The History, Ships, and Cancellations of the Great White Fleet.* Series Booklet no. 28. Berkshire: Maritime Postmark Society, 1940.

Colby, Jason M. *The Business of Empire: United Fruit, Race, and U.S. Expansion in Central America.* Ithaca: Cornell University, 2011.

Coleman, Kevin. *A Camera in the Garden of Eden: The Self-Forging of a Banana Republic.* Austin: University of Texas Press, 2016.

Comisionado Nacional de Protección de los Derechos Humanos. "Los Hechos Hablan por Sí Mismos: Informe Preliminar sobre los Desaparecidos en Honduras, 1980–1993." Tegucigalpa, Honduras: COFADEH, 1994.

Connolly, John. *Tacamiche: Cruce Lejano*. El Progreso, Honduras: Editorial "Ramón Amaya Amador," 1999.

Conrad, Joseph. *Heart of Darkness*. London: Penguin Books, 2000.

Counihan, Carole, ed. *Food and Culture: A Reader*. New York: Routledge, 1997.

Craft, Linda J. *Novels of Testimony and Resistance from Central America*. Gainesville: University Press of Florida, 1997.

Crenshaw, Kimberlé W. Mapping the Margins: Intersectionality, Identity Politics, and Violence Against Women of Color." *Stanford Law Review* 43, no. 6 (1991): 1241–1299.

Crowther, Samuel. *The Romance and Rise of the American Tropics*. New York: Doubleday, Doran, 1929.

Cuddy, Thomas W. *Political Identity and Archaeology in Northeast Honduras*. Boulder: University of Colorado Press, 2007.

"El Cususero." *Revista Enlace*, no. 1. https://www.simas.org.ni/revistaenlace/articulo/13.

Davis, Charles Belmont. *Adventures and Letters of Richard Harding Davis*. New York: Charles Scribner's Sons, 1918.

Davis, Richard Harding. *Three Gringos in Venezuela and Central America*. New York: Harper & Brothers, 1896.

Deere, Carmen Diana. *Household and Class Relations: Peasants and Landlords in Northern Peru*. Berkeley: University of California Press, 1990.

Dodd, Thomas J. *Tiburcio Carías: Portrait of a Honduran Political Leader*. Baton Rouge: Louisiana State University Press, 2005.

Dore, Elizabeth. "The Holy Family: Imagined Households in Latin American History." In *Gender Politics in Latin America: Debates in Theory and Practice*, edited by Elizabeth Dore, 101–117. New York: Monthly Review Press, 1997.

Drinot, Paulo. "Food, Race and Working-Class Identity: Restaurantes Populares and Populism in 1930s Peru." *Americas* 62, no. 2 (2005): 245–270.

Dunaway, David K., and Willa K. Baum, eds. *Oral History: An Interdisciplinary Anthology*. Walnut Creek, CA: Altamira Press, 1996.

Dunkerley, James. *Power in the Isthmus: A Political History of Modern Central America*. New York: Verso, 1988.

Durón, Rómulo E. *Bosquejo Histórico de Honduras, 1502 a 1921*. San Pedro Sula, Honduras: Tipografía del Comercio, 1927.

Durrant, Russil, and Jo Thankker. *Substance Use and Abuse: Cultural and Historical Perspectives*. London: Sage, 2003.

Echeverrí-Gent, Elisavinda. "Forgotten Workers: British West Indians and the Early Days of the Banana Industry in Costa Rica and Honduras." *Journal of Latin American Studies* 24, no. 2 (May 1992): 275–308.

———. "Labor, Class and Political Representation: A Comparative Analysis of Honduras and Costa Rica." 2 vols. PhD dissertation, University of Chicago, 1988.

Ellis, Frank. *Las Transnacionales del Banano en Centroamérica*. Translated by Juan Mario Castellanos. San José, Costa Rica: Editorial Universitaria Centroamericana, 1983.

Ellner, Steve, ed. *Latin America's Radical Left: Challenges and Complexities of Political Power in the Twenty-First Century*. Lanham: Rowan & Littlefield, 2014.

Emerson, Robert M., Rachel I. Fretz, and Linda L. Shaw. *Writing Ethnographic Fieldnotes*. Chicago: University of Chicago Press, 1995.

England, Sarah Elizabeth. *Afro-Central Americans in New York City: Garifuna Tales of Transnational Movements in Racialized Space*. Gainesville: University Press of Florida, 2006.

Enloe, Cynthia H. *Bananas, Beaches and Bases: Making Feminist Sense of International Politics*. Berkeley: University of California Press, 1990.

Euraque, Darío A. "The Banana Enclave, Nationalism, and Mestizaje in Honduras, 1910s-1930s." In *Identity and Struggle at the Margins of the Nation-State: The Laboring Peoples of Central America and the Hispanic Caribbean*, edited by Aviva Chomsky and Aldo Lauria-Santiago, 169–195. Durham: Duke University Press, 1998.

———. *Conversaciones Históricas con el Mestizaje y su Identidad Nacional en Honduras*. San Pedro Sula, Honduras: Centro Editorial, 2004.

———. "Free Pardos and Mulattoes Vanquish Indians: Cultural Civility as Conquest and Modernity in Honduras." In *Beyond Slavery: The Multilayered Legacy of Africans in Latin America and the Caribbean*, edited by Darién J. Davies, 81–105. New York: Rowan & Littlefield, 2007.

———. *Reinterpreting the Banana Republic: Region and State in Honduras, 1870–1972*. Chapel Hill: University of North Carolina Press, 1996.

———. "San Pedro Sula, Actual Capital Industrial de Honduras: Su Trayectoria entre Villorio Colonial y Emporio Bananero, 1536–1936." *Mesoamerica*, no. 26 (1993): 217–252.

———. "The Threat of Blackness to the Mestizo Nation: Race and Ethnicity in the Honduran Banana Economy, 1920s-1930s." In *Banana Wars: Power, Production, and History in the Americas*, edited by Steve Striffler and Mark Moberg, 229–249. Durham: Duke University Press, 2003.

———. "Una Nueva Visión sobre el Caudillismo y la Violencia Política en Honduras: Resumen y Comentario." *Revista de Historia* (Costa Rica) 33 (January–June 1996): 187–200.

———. "Political Economy, Race, and National Identity in Central America, 1500–2000." In *Oxford Research Encyclopedia of Latin American History*. Oxford: Oxford University Press, 2018.

Euraque, Darío A., Jeffrey L. Gould, and Charles R. Hale, eds. *Memorias del Mestizaje: Cultura Política en Centroamérica de 1920 al Presente*. Antigua, Guatemala: CIRMA, 2005.

Fallas, Carlos Luis. *Mamita Yunai: El Infierno de las Bananeras*. Buenos Aires: Editorial Platina, 1956.

Fantasia, Rick. *Cultures of Solidarity: Consciousness, Action, and Contemporary American Workers*. Berkeley: University of California Press, 1988.

Farnsworth-Alvear, Ann. *Dulcinea in the Factory: Myths, Morals, Men, and Women in Colombia's Industrial Experiment, 1905–1960*. Durham: Duke University Press, 2000.

Finney, Kenneth V. "Rosario and the Election of 1887: The Political Economy of Mining in Honduras." *Hispanic American Historical Review* 59, no. 1 (1979): 81–107.

Flores Valeriano, Enrique. *La Explotación Bananera en Honduras.*Tegucigalpa: Editorial Universitaria de la Universidad Nacional Autónoma de Honduras, 1987.

Forgacs, David, ed. *The Antonio Gramsci Reader: Selected Writings, 1916–1935.* New York: New York University Press, 2000.

Forster, Cindy. *The Time of Freedom: Campesino Workers in Guatemala's October Revolution.* Pittsburgh: University of Pittsburgh Press, 2001.

Frank, Dana. *The Long Honduran Night: Resistance, Terror, and the United States in the Aftermath of the Coup.* Boston: Haymarket Square Books, 2018.

———. *Bananeras: Women Transforming the Banana Unions of Latin America.* Cambridge, MA: South End Press, 2005.

Freitas, Sônia María de. *História Oral: Possibilidades e Procedimentos.* São Paulo: Imprensa Oficial São Paulo, 2002.

French, John D., and Daniel James, eds. *The Gendered Worlds of Latin American Women Workers: From the Household and Factory to the Union Hall and Ballot Box.* Durham: Duke University Press, 1997.

Galloway, Patricia. *Practicing Ethnohistory: Mining Archives, Hearing Testimony, Constructing Narrative.* Lincoln: University of Nebraska Press, 2006.

Garcia, Graciela. *Páginas De Lucha.*Tegucigalpa: Editorial Guaymuras, 1981.

Garcia, Roberto, and Arturo Taracena Arriola, eds. *La Guerra Fría y el Anticomunismo en Centroamérica.* Guatemala City: FLACSO Guatemala, 2017.

Garcia, Yesenia. "La Seguridad Social en Honduras entre la Revolución Guatemalteca y el Contexto de la Guerra Fría, 1944–1956." In *La Guerra Fría y el Anticomunismo en Centroamérica,* edited by Roberto Garcia and Arturo Taracena Arriola, 129–148. Guatemala City: FLACSO Guatemala, 2017.

Gargallo, Francesca. *Garífuna, Garínagu, Caribe: Historia de una Nación Libertaria.* Mexico City: Siglo XXI Editores, 2002.

Gleijeses, Piero. *Shattered Hope: The Guatemalan Revolution and the United States, 1944–1954.* Princeton: Princeton University Press, 1991.

Gluck, Sherna Berger, and Daphne Patai, eds. *Women's Words: The Feminist Practice of Oral History.* New York: Routledge, 1991.

González, Nancie L. *Dollar, Dove, and Eagle: One Hundred Years of Palestinian Migration to Honduras.* Ann Arbor: University of Michigan Press, 1992.

González Casanova, Pablo, ed. *Historia del Movimiento Obrero en América Latina.* Vol. 2, *Guatemala, Honduras, El Salvador, Nicaragua, Costa Rica, Panamá.* Edited by Instituto de Investigaciones Sociales de la UNAM. Mexico City: Siglo XXI Editores, 1985.

Gordon, Avery F. *Ghostly Matters: Haunting and the Sociological Imagination.* Minneapolis: University of Minnesota Press, 2008.

Gould, Jeffrey L. *To Lead As Equals: Rural Protest and Political Consciousness in Chinandega, Nicaragua, 1912–1979.* Chapel Hill: University of North Carolina Press, 1990.

Gould, Jeffrey L., and Aldo A. Lauria-Santiago. *To Rise in Darkness: Revolution, Repression, and Memory in El Salvador, 1920–1932.* Durham: Duke University Press, 2008.

Grandin, Greg. *The Last Colonial Massacre: Latin America in the Cold War.* Chicago: University of Chicago Press, 2004.

Greenwald, Maurine Wiener. "Working-Class Feminism and the Family Wage Ideal: The Seattle Debate on Married Women's Right to Work, 1914–1920." *Journal of American History* 76, no. 1 (1989): 118–149.

Halperín Donghi, Tulio. *The Contemporary History of Latin America*. Durham: Duke University Press, 1993.

Hanagan, Michael P. *The Logic of Solidarity: Artisans and Industrial Workers in Three French Towns, 1871–1914*. Urbana: University of Illinois Press, 1980.

Henríquez, Pavel, Joel Barahona, Julio Sevilla, Moisés Mayorquin, Jorge Torres, and Wilfredo Rivera. *Historia sobre las Bebidas, la Embriaguez y el Alcoholismo en Honduras*. Tegucigalpa: Litografía Lopez, 2013.

Hernández, Héctor F. *Solidarismo y Sindicalismo en Honduras*. Tegucigalpa: Federación Unitaria de Trabajadores de Honduras, 1991.

Hobsbawm, Eric, and Terence Ranger. *The Invention of Tradition*. Cambridge: Cambridge University Press, 1983.

Holden, Robert H. *Armies without Nations: Public Violence and State Formation in Central America, 1821–1960*. New York: Oxford University Press 2004.

———. "Constructing the Limits of State Violence in Central America: Towards a New Research Agenda." *Journal of Latin American Studies* 28, no. 2 (1996): 435–459.

———. "Securing Central America against Communism: The United States and the Modernization of Surveillance in the Cold War." *Journal of Interamerican Studies and World Affairs* 41, no. 1 (Spring 1999): 1–30.

Holden, Robert H., and Eric Zolov, eds. *Latin America and the United States: A Documentary History*. New York: Oxford University Press, 2000.

Hopkins, J. A. H., and Melinda Alexander. *Machine-Gun Diplomacy*. New York: Lewis Copeland, 1928.

Hutchinson, Elizabeth Quay. *Labors Appropriate to Their Sex: Gender, Labor, and Politics in Urban Chile, 1900–1930*. Durham: Duke University Press, 2001.

Ignacio Klich, Jeffrey Lesser. "Introduction: 'Turco' Immigrants in Latin America." *Americas* 53, no. 1 (1996): 1–14.

Inestroza Manzanares, Jesús Evelio. *Documentos Clasificados de la Policía Secreta de Carías (1937–1944)*. Tegucigalpa: Instituto Hondureño de Antropología e Historia, 2009.

James, Daniel. *Doña María's Story: Life, History, Memory, and Political Identity*. Durham: Duke University Press, 2000.

Jankowiak, William R., and Daniel Bradburd. *Drugs, Labor, and Colonial Expansion*. Tucson: University of Arizona Press, 2003.

Jelin, Elizabeth. *State Repression and the Labors of Memory*. Translated by Judy Rein and Marcial Godoy-Anativia. Minneapolis: University of Minnesota Press, 2003.

Johnson, Paul Christopher. *Diaspora Conversions: Black Carib Religion and the Recovery of Africa*. Berkeley: University of California Press, 2007.

Jones, Chester Lloyd. "Bananas and Diplomacy." *North American Review*, no. 198 (1913): 188.

Karnes, Thomas L. *Tropical Enterprise: The Standard Fruit and Steamship Company in Latin America*. Baton Rouge: Louisiana State University Press, 1978.

Kepner, Charles David, Jr. *Social Aspects of the Banana Industry*. New York: Columbia University Press, 1936.

Klubock, Thomas Miller. *Contested Communities: Class, Gender, and Politics in Chile's El Teniente Mine, 1904–1951*. Durham: Duke University Press, 1998.

———. "Morality and Good Habits: The Construction of Gender and Class in the Chilean Copper Mines, 1904–1951." In *The Gendered Worlds of Latin American Women Workers: From Household and Factory to the Union Hall and Ballot Box*, edited by John D. French and Daniel James, 232–263. Durham: Duke University Press, 1997.

Korzeniewicz, Roberto Patricio, and William C. Smith, eds. *Latin America in the World Economy*. Westport, CT: Greenwood Press, 1996.

Lancaster, Roger N. *Life Is Hard: Machismo, Danger, and the Intimacy of Power in Nicaragua*. Berkeley: University of California Press, 1992.

Langley, Lester D., and Thomas Schoonover. *The Banana Men: American Mercenaries and Entrepreneurs in Central America, 1880–1930*. Lexington: University Press of Kentucky, 1995.

Lauria-Santiago, Aldo, and Leigh Binford, eds. *Landscapes of Struggle: Politics, Society, and Community in El Salvador*. Pittsburgh: University of Pittsburgh Press, 2004.

LeGrand, Catherine C., ed. *Living in Macondo: Economy and Culture in a United Fruit Company Banana Enclave in Colombia*. Durham: Duke University Press, 1998.

León Gómez, Alfredo. *El Escándalo de Ferrocarril: Ensayo Histórico*. Tegucigalpa: Editorial Universitaria de la Universidad Nacional Autónoma de Honduras, 2000.

Levenson-Estrada, Deborah. "The Loneliness of Working-Class Feminism: Women in the 'Male World' of Labor Unions, Guatemala City, 1970s." In *The Gendered Worlds of Latin American Women Workers: From the Household and Factory to the Union Hall and Ballot Box*, edited by John D. French and Daniel James, 208–231. Durham: Duke University Press, 1997.

———. *Trade Unionists against Terror: Guatemala City, 1954–1985*. Chapel Hill: University of North Carolina Press, 1994.

Liss, Sheldon B. *Radical Thought in Central America*. Boulder: Westview Press, 1991.

Macekura, Stephen. "The Point Four Program and U.S. International Development Policy." *Political Science Quarterly* 128, no. 1 (Spring 2013): 127–60.

Mahoney, James. *Legacies of Liberalism: Path Dependence and Political Regimes in Central America*. Baltimore: Johns Hopkins University Press, 2001.

———. "Radical, Reformist and Aborted Liberalism: Origins of National Regimes in Central America." *Journal of Latin American Studies* 33, no. 2 (2001): 221–256.

Marín-Guzmán, Roberto. *A Century of Palestinian Immigration into Central America: A Study of Their Economic and Cultural Contributions*. San José, Costa Rica: Editorial de la Universidad de Costa Rica, 2000.

Martin, James W. *Banana Cowboys: The United Fruit Company and the Culture of Corporate Colonialism*. Albuquerque: University of New Mexico Press, 2018.

———. "Becoming Banana Cowboys: White-Collar Masculinity, the United Fruit Company and Tropical Empire in Early Twentieth Century Latin America." *Gender and History* 25, no. 2 (2013): 317–338.

Marx, Karl. *El Capital*. Mexico City: Editores Mexicanos Unidos, 1994.

May, Stacy, and Galo Plaza, eds. *The United Fruit Company in Latin America*. Washington, DC: National Planning Association, Library of Congress, 1958.

Mayorga, Wilfredo. "'Campeón' y 'Chuna,' Pura Vida." In *La Garra Catracha: Literatura y Fútbol*, edited by Helen Umaña, 140–41. Guatemala: Editorial Ventana, 2010.

McBee, Randy D. *Dance Hall Days Intimacy and Leisure among Working-Class Immigrants in the United States*. New York: New York University Press, 2000.

McCameron, Robert. *Bananas, Labor, and Politics in Honduras, 1954–1963.* New York: Maxwell School of Citizenship, 1983.

McCann, Thomas, and Henry Scammell. *On the Inside: A Story of Intrigue and Adventure, on Wall Street, in Washington, and in the Jungles of Central America.* Boston: Quinlan Press, 1987.

Melhuus, Marit, and Kristi Anne Stolen, eds. *Machos, Mistresses, Madonnas: Contesting the Power of Latin American Gender Imagery.* London: Verso, 1996.

Melville, John H. *The Great White Fleet.* New York: Vintage Press, 1976.

Menchú Tum, Rigoberta. *I, Rigoberta Menchú: An Indian Woman in Guatemala.* Edited by Elisabeth Burgos-Debray. Translated by Ann Wright. London: Verso, 1984.

Mendoza, Breny. *Sintiéndose mujer, pensándose feminista: la construcción del movimiento feminista en Honduras.* Tegucigalpa: Editorial Guaymuras, 1996.

Menjívar, Cecilia. *Fragmented Ties: Salvadoran Immigrant Networks in America.* Berkeley: University of California Press, 2000.

Menjívar Ochoa, Mauricio. "Trabajadores Afro-Descendientes, Masculinidad, y Violencia en la Bananera en Caribe de Costa Rica, 1900–1930." *Revista Internacional de Ciencias Sociales y Humanidades, SOCIOTAM* 20, no. 1 (2010): 59–84.

Meyer, Eugenia. "Oral History in Mexico and the Caribbean." In *Oral History: An Interdisciplinary Anthology*, edited by David K. Dunaway and Willa K. Baum, 343–350. Walnut Creek, CA: Altamira Press, 1996.

Meza, Victor. *Historia del Movimiento Obrero Hondureño.* Tegucigalpa: Centro de Documentación de Honduras, 1991.

———. *Historia del Movimiento Obrero Hondureño.* Tegucigalpa: Editorial Guaymuras, 1981.

Milla, Karla. "Movimiento de Mujeres en Honduras en las Decádas de 1950 y 1960: Cambios Jurídicos y Tradiciones Culturales." *Mesoámerica* 22, no. 42 (2001): 223–255.

Mintz, Disney W. *Sweetness and Power: The Place of Sugar in Modern History.* New York: Penguin Books, 1985.

Moberg, Mark. *Myths of Ethnicity and Nation: Immigration, Work, and Identity in the Belize Banana Industry.* Knoxville: University of Tennessee Press, 1997.

Mohanty, Chandra Talpade. "Feminist Encounters: Locating the Politics of Experience." In *Destabilizing Theory: Contemporary Feminism Debates*, edited by Michele Barrett and Anne Phillips, 74–92. London: Polity Press, 1992.

Morales Pineda, José Ramón. *La Rápida.* San Pedro Sula: Editorial Nueva Vision, 2006.

Morris, James A. *Honduras: Caudillo Politics and Military Rulers.* Boulder, Colorado: Westview Press, 1984.

Morrow Wilson, Charles. *Empire of Green and Gold: The Story of the American Banana Trade.* New York: Henry Holt, 1947.

Munguía, Iris, and José María Martinez. *Aprendamos Junt@S: Conozcamos De Contratación Colectiva.* Honduras: COLSIBA, 2006.

Norsworthy, Kent, and Tom Barry. *Honduras.* Albuquerque, NM: The Inter-Hemispheric Education Resources Center, 1993.

O'Brien, Thomas F. *The Revolutionary Mission: American Enterprise in Latin America, 1900–1945.* Cambridge: Cambridge University Press, 1996.

Olson, Karen, and Linda Shopes. "Crossing Boundaries, Building Bridges: Doing Oral History among Working-Class Women and Men." In *Women's Words: The Feminist Practice of Oral History*, edited by Sherna Berger Gluck and Daphne Patai, 175–187. New York: Routledge, 1991.

Oseguera de Ochoa, Margarita. *Honduras Hoy: Sociedad y Crisis Política.* Coordinadora Regional de Investigaciones Económicas y Sociales. Tegucigalpa: Centro de Documentación de Honduras, 1987.

Oyuela, Leticia. *Notas sobre la Evolución Histórica de la Mujer en Honduras.* Tegucigalpa: Editorial Guaymuras, 1989.

———. *Ramón Rosa: Plenitudes y Desengaños.* Tegucigalpa: Editorial Guaymuras, 1994.

Painter, James, and Richard Lapper. *Honduras: State for Sale.* Edited by the Latin American Bureau. London: Latin American Bureau, 1985.

Palmer, Steven. "Central American Encounters with Rockefeller Public Health, 1914–1921." In *Close Encounters of Empire: Writing Cultural History of U.S.-Latin American Relations*, edited by Catherine Legrand, Gilbert Joseph, and Ricardo Salvatore, 311–332. Durham: Duke University Press, 1998.

Patai, Daphne. "U.S. Academics and Third World Women: Is Ethical Research Possible?" In *Women's Words: The Feminist Practice of Oral History*, edited by Sherna Berger Gluck and Daphne Patai, 137–153. New York: Routledge, 1991.

Pérez Sáinz, Juan Pablo. *From the Finca to the Maquila: Labor and Capitalist Development in Central America.* Boulder, Colorado: Westview Press, 1999.

Perez-Brignoli, Hector. *A Brief History of Central America.* Translated by Ricardo B. Sawrey. Berkeley: University of California Press, 1989.

Perrot, Michelle. *Workers on Strike France, 1871–1890.* New Haven: Yale University Press, 1987.

Perry, Elizabeth J. *Shanghai on Strike: The Politics of Chinese Labor.* Stanford: Stanford University Press, 1993.

Pessar, Patricia R. "Transnationalism and Racialization within Contemporary U.S. Immigration." In *Problematizing Blackness: Self-Ethnographies by Black Immigrants to the United States*, edited by Percy C. Hintzen and Jean Muteba Rahier, 21–33. New York: Routledge, 2003.

Pierce, Gretchen, and Áurea Toxqui, eds. *Alcohol in Latin America: A Social and Cultural History.* Tucson: University of Arizona Press, 2014.

Pine, Adrienne. *Working Hard, Drinking Hard: On Violence and Survival in Honduras.* Berkeley: Univeristy of California Press, 2008.

Portelli, Alessandro. *The Death of Luigi Trastulli and Other Stories: Form and Meaning in Oral History.* Albany: State University of New York Press, 1991.

Porter, Susie S. "In the Shadows of Industrialization: The Entrance of Women into the Mexican Industrial Work Force, 1880–1940." PhD dissertation, University of California, San Diego, 1997.

———. *Working Women in Mexico City: Public Discourses and Material Conditions, 1879–1931.* Tucson: University of Arizona Press, 2003.

Portillo Villeda, Suyapa. "Campeñas, Campeños y Compañeros: Life and Work in the Banana Fincas of the North Coast of Honduras, 1944–1957." PhD dissertation, Cornell University, 2011.

———. "The Coup That Awoke a People's Resistance." *NACLA Report on the Americas* 43, no. 2 (2010): 26–27.

———. "Honduras: Refounding the Nation, Building a New Kind of Social

Movement." In *Rethinking Latin American Social Movements: Radical Action from Below*, edited by Richard Stahler-Sholk, Harry E. Vanden, and Marc Becker, 121–46. Lanham, MD: Rowman & Littlefield, 2014.

Portillo Villeda, Suyapa, and Cristian Padilla. *Honduran Social Movements, Then and Now*. Oxford: Oxford Encyclopedia, forthcoming.

Posas, Mario. *Breve Historia de la Ciudad de Olanchito*. Yoro, Honduras: Editorial El Jamo, 1993.

———. *Lucha Ideológica y Organización Sindical en Honduras, 1954–65*. Tegucigalpa: Editorial Guaymuras, 1980.

———. *Luchas del Movimiento Obrero Hondureño*. San José, Costa Rica: Editorial Universitaria Centroamericana EDUCA, 1981.

———. *Perfiles de Líderes Populares*. Tegucigalpa: Fundación Friedrich Ebert Stiftung, 2003.

———. "El Surgimiento de la Clase Obrera en Hondureña." *Anuario de Estudios Centroamericanos* 9 (1983).

———. "The Tacamiche Conflict: A Good Test." *Envío*, no. 170 (September 1995).

Posas, Mario, and Remy Fontaine. "Honduras at the Crossroads." *Latin American Perspectives* 7, nos. 2/3 (1980): 45–56.

Preston-Werner, Theresa. "Gallo Pinto: Tradition, Memory, and Identity in Costa Rican Foodways." *Journal of American Folklore* 122, no. 483 (2009): 11–27.

Putnam, Lara. *The Company They Kept: Migrants and the Politics of Gender in Caribbean Costa Rica, 1870–1960*. Chapel Hill: University of North Carolina Press, 2002.

———. "Work, Sex, and Power in a Central American Export Economy at the Turn of the Twentieth Century." In *Gender, Sexuality, and Power in Latin America*, edited by Katherine Bliss and William French, 133–162. Lanham, MD: Rowman & Littlefield, 2006.

Quiroga, Nicolas. "A Camera in the Garden of Eden: Questions to Kevin Coleman." *Hispanic American Review*, April 19, 2017.

Rabe, Stephen G. *The Killing Zone: The United States Wages Cold War in Latin America*. Oxford: Oxford University Press, 2012.

Ramírez, Horacio N. Roque. "A Living Archive of Desire: Teresita la Campesina and the Embodiment of Queer Latino Community Histories." In *Archive Stories: Facts, Fictions, and the Writing of History*, edited by Antoinette Burton, 111–135. Durham: Duke University Press, 2005.

———. "My Community, My History, My Practice." *Oral History Review* 29, no. 2 (2002): 87–91.

———. "'That's My Place!' Negotiating Racial, Sexual, and Gender Politics in San Francisco's Gay Latino Alliance, 1975–1983." *Journal of the History of Sexuality* 12, no. 2 (2003): 224–258.

Ramos, Ventura. "La Guerra del Imperio Norteamericano." *Antología del pensamiento hondureño contemporáneo* (2019): 29–36.

Randall, Margaret. *Cuban Women Now: Interviews with Cuban Women*. Toronto: Women's Press, 1974.

———. *Sandino's Daughters: Testimonies of Nicaraguan Women in Struggle*. New Brunswick: Rutgers University Press, 1995.

———. *Testimonios: A Guide to Oral History*. Toronto: Participation Research Group, 1985.

Reysoo, Fenneke, ed. *Social Construction of Masculinity in Mexico*. Edited by Diana and Anita Hardon Gibson. Amsterdam: Het Spinhuis, 2005.

Rivas, Ramón D. *Pueblos Indígenas y Garífunas de Honduras.* Tegucigalpa: Editorial Guaymuras, 1993.

Roberts, B. R. "Peasants and Proletarians." *Annual Review of Sociology* 16 (1990): 353–377.

Robleda Castro, Agapito. *La Verdad de la Huelga de 1954 y de la Formación del SITRATERCO.* San Pedro Sula, Honduras: Tegucigalpa: Ediciones del Sedal, 1995.

Rodney, Walter. *A History of the Guyanese Working People, 1881–1905.* Baltimore: Johns Hopkins University Press, 1981.

Rodríguez, Ana Patricia. *Dividing the Isthmus: Central American Transnational Histories, Literatures, and Cultures.* Austin: University of Texas Press, 2009.

Rodríguez, Ileana. *Transatlantic Topographies: Islands, Highlands, Jungles.* Minneapolis: University of Minnesota Press, 2004.

Rodríguez Sáenz, Eugenia. *Un Siglo de Luchas Femeninas en América Latina.* San José, Costa Rica: Editorial de la Universidad de Costa Rica, 2002.

Rohter, Larry. "Honduras Journal: Where Banana Was King, Workers Fight Evictions." *New York Times,* July 22 1996.

Romualdi, Serafino. *Presidents and Peons: Recollections of a Labor Ambassador in Latin America.* New York: Funk & Wagnalls, 1967.

Rose, Fred. "Toward a Class-Cultural Theory of Social Movements: Reinterpreting New Social Movements." *Sociological Forum* 12 (1997): 3461–3494.

Safa, Helen I. *The Myth of the Male Breadwinner: Women and Industrialization in the Caribbean.* Boulder, Colorado: Westview Press, 1995.

Sagastume, Alejandro. *Carías: El Caudillo de Zambrano 1933–1948.* Tegucigalpa: Editores Graficentro, 1988.

Said, Edward W. *Orientalism.* 25th anniversary ed. New York: Vintage Books, 1994.

Schwarzstein, Dora. "Oral History in Latin America." In *Oral History: An Interdisciplinary Anthology,* edited by David K. Dunaway and Willa K. Baum, 417–424. Walnut Creek, CA: Altamira Press, 1996.

Scott, David. *Omens of Adversity: Tragedy, Time, Memory, Justice.* Durham: Duke University Press, 2014.

Scott, James. *Domination and the Arts of Resistance: Hidden Transcripts.* New Haven: Yale University Press, 1990.

Scott, Joan Wallach, ed. *Feminism and History.* Oxford: Oxford University Press, 1996.

———. "Gender: A Useful Category of Historical Analysis." *American Historical Review* 91, no. 5 (1986): 1053–1075.

Scott-Jenkins, Virgina. *Bananas: An American History.* Washington, DC: Smithsonian Institution Press, 2003.

Solien Gonzalez, Nancie L. *Black Carib Household Structure: A Study of Migration and Modernization.* Seattle: University of Washington Press, 1969.

Soluri, John. *Banana Cultures: Agriculture, Consumption, and Environmental Change in Honduras and the United States.* Austin: University of Texas Press, 2005.

———. *A la Sombra del Bananal: Poquiteros y Transformaciones Ecológicas en la Costa Norte de Honduras, 1870–1950.* Edited by Colección Cuadernos Universitarios. Tegucigalpa: Editorial Universitaria de la Universidad Nacional Autónoma de Honduras, 2002.

Squier, Ephraim G. "Honduras Interoceanic Railway Company, Limited Incorporated, March 26, 1857: For the Construction and Working of a Railway between the

Atlantic and Pacific Oceans, through the State of Honduras, Central America." Prospectus. London: M. S. Rikerby Printer, 1857. Rare Book Collection, Huntington Library and Archives.

———. *Honduras Interoceanic Railway: Preliminary Report.* New York: Tubbs, Nesmith & Teall, 1854.

Stern, Alexandra Minna. *Eugenic Nation: Faults and Frontiers of Better Breeding in Modern America.* Berkeley: University of California Press, 2005.

Stern, Steve J. *Remembering Pinochet's Chile: On the Eve of London, 1998.* Book 1 of *The Memory Box of Pinochet's Chile.* Durham: Duke University Press, 2004.

Stoler, Ann Laura. *Capitalism and Confrontation in Sumatra's Plantation Belt, 1870–1979.* New Haven: Yale University Press, 1985.

Stoll, David. *Rigoberta Menchú and the Story of All Poor Guatemalans.* Boulder, Colorado: Westview Press, 1997.

Striffler, Steve. *In the Shadows of State and Capital: The United Fruit Company, Popular Struggle, and Agrarian Restructuring in Ecuador, 1900–1995.* Durham: Duke University Press, 2002.

Striffler, Steve, and Mark Moberg. *Banana Wars: Power, Production, and History in the Americas.* American Encounters/Global Interactions. Durham: Duke University Press, 2003.

Suazo, E. Salvador. *Los Deportados de San Vicente.* Tegucigalpa: Editorial Guaymuras, 1997.

Surkis, Judith. *Sexing the Citizen Morality and Masculinity in France, 1870–1920.* Ithaca: Cornell University Press.

Swedberg, Richard. *The Honduran Trade Union Movement, 1920–1982.* Cambridge, MA: Central American Information Office, 1983.

Tábora, Rocio. *Masculinidad y Violencia en la Cultura Política Hondureña.* Tegucigalpa: CEDOH, 1995.

Talavera, Sosa. "'El Choco' Sabillón Gran Inventor del 'Coco-Loco.'" *Revista Nocturnal* (2004).

Taylor, Douglas MacRae. *The Black Carib of British Honduras.* New York: Wenner-Gren Foundation for Anthropological Research, 1951.

"Testimony: Voice of the Voiceless in Testimonial Literature." special issue, *Latin American Perspectives* 18, nos. 3–4 (1991).

Thompson, E. P. *The Making of the English Working Class.* New York: Vintage Books, 1966.

Tilley, Virgina Q. *Seeing Indians: A Study of Race, Nation and Power in El Salvador.* Albuquerque: University of New Mexico Press, 2005.

Tinajero, Araceli. *El Lector de Tabaquería: Historia de una Tradición Cubana.* Madrid: Editorial Verbum, 2007.

Tinker Salas, Miguel. *The Enduring Legacy: Oil, Culture, and Society in Venezuela.* Durham: Duke University Press, 2009.

Tinsman, Heidi. *Partners in Conflict: The Politics of Gender, Sexuality, and Labor in the Chilean Agrarian Reform, 1950–1973.* Durham: Duke University Press, 2002.

Tong, Rosemarie. *Feminist Thought: A Comprehensive Introduction.* Vancouver: Crane Resource Centre, 2004.

Tonkin, Elizabeth. *Narrating Our Pasts: The Social Construction of Oral History.* Cambridge: Cambridge University Press, 1992.

Topik, Steven C., and Allen Wells. Introduction to *Second Conquest of Latin America: Coffee, Henequen, and Oil during the Export Boom, 1850–1930.* Austin: University of Texas Press, 2010.

Trouillot, Michel-Rolph. *Peasants and Capital: Dominica in the World Economy.* Baltimore: Johns Hopkins University Press, 1988.

————. *Silencing the Past: Power and the Production of History.* Boston: Beacon Press, 1997.

Tyner, James A. "The Geopolitics of Eugenics and the Exclusion of Philippine Immigrants from the U.S." *Geographical Review* 89, no. 1 (1999): 54–73.

Upham Adams, Frederick. *Conquest of the Tropics: The Story of the Creative Enterprises Conducted by the United Fruit Company.* New York: Doubleday, Page, 1914.

Veccia, Theresa R. "My Duty as a Woman: Gender Ideology, Work, and Working-Class Women's Lives in São Paulo, Brazil, 1900–1950." In *The Gendered Worlds of Latin American Women Workers: From Household and Factory to the Union Hall and Ballot Box,* edited by John D. French and Daniel James, 100–146. Durham: Duke University Press, 1997.

Villars, Rina. *Lealtad y Rebeldía: La Vida de Juan Pablo Wainwright.* Tegucigalpa: Editorial Guaymuras, 2010.

————. *Para la Casa más que para el Mundo: Sufragismo y Feminismo en la Historia de Honduras.* Tegucigalpa: Editorial Guaymuras, 2001.

————. *Porque Quiero Seguir Viviendo . . . Habla Graciela García.* Tegucigalpa: Editorial Guaymuras, 1991.

Viotti da Costa, Emilia. "Experience versus Structures: New Tendencies in the History of Labor and the Working Class in Latin America: What Do We Gain? What Do We Lose?" *International Labor and Working-Class History,* no. 36 (1989): 3–24.

Wade, Peter. *Race and Ethnicity in Latin America.* London: Pluto Press, 1997.

Watt, Ian. *Joseph Conrad: Nostromo.* New York: Cambridge University Press, 1988.

Webber, Jeffery R., and Barry Carr. *The New Latin American Left.* Lanham: Rowman & Littlefield, 2013.

Weinstein, Barbara. "Unskilled Worker, Skilled Housewife: Constructing the Working-Class Woman in São Paulo, Brazil." In *The Gendered Worlds of Latin American Women Workers: From Household and Factory to the Union Hall and Ballot Box,* edited by John D. French and Daniel James, 72–99. Durham: Duke University Press, 1997.

Wells, William V. *Explorations and Adventures in Honduras, Comprising Sketches of Travel in the Gold Regions of Olancho, and a Review of the History and General Resources of Central America.* New York: Harper & Brothers, 1857.

Whitfield, Stephen J. "Strange Fruit: The Career of Samuel Zemurray." *American Jewish History* 73, no. 3 (1984): 307–323.

Whitten, Norman E., Jr., and Arlene Torres, eds. *Blackness in Latin America and the Caribbean.* 2 vols. Bloomington: Indiana University Press, 1998.

Williams, Robert G. *Export Agriculture and the Crisis in Central America.* Chapel Hill: University of Carolina Press, 1986.

Wolfe, Joel. *Working Men, Working Women: São Paulo and the Rise of Brazil's Industrial Working Class, 1900–1955.* Durham: Duke University Press, 1993.

Woodward, R. L., Jr. "The Aftermath of Independence, 1821–1870." In *Central America since Independence,* edited by Leslie Bethell, 1–36. Cambridge: Cambridge University Press, 1991.

Young, Thomas. *Narrative of a Residence on the Mosquito Shore, with an Account of Truxillo and Adjacent Islands of Bonacca and Roatan.* London: Smith, Elder, 1847. Repr., New York: Kraus Reprint, 1971.

Zavella, Patricia. "Feminist Insider Dilemmas: Constructing Ethnic Identity with Chicana Informants." In *Feminist Dilemmas in Fieldwork*, edited by Diane L. Wolf, 138–159. Boulder, Colorado: Westview Press, 1996.

INDEX

absenteeism, company policing of, 114–115, 319n114

Adams, Frederick Upham, 40

advancement opportunities and job hierarchies, 93–101, 101

Afro-Hispanic ethnicity, 11, 124

Agrarian Law of 1895, 37

agrarian reform: advocacy for, 64, 64–65, 80, 229; emergence of, 1960s, 235, 238–239; vs. labor reform focus, 1–2

Agricultural Department of Tela, 86

Agro-Industry Federation of Workers. See Federación de Sindicatos de Trabajadores de la Agroindustria (FESTAGRO)

Aguán Valley Company, 35

aguardiente (hard liquor), 135, 158

ajuntada (partnered without marriage), 108

alcohol consumption: company policing of, 113–115, 136–137; drunkenness, 102, 136, 138–140; illicit alcohol, 102, 134, 135–137, 139; morality campaigns against, 136, 174; used as a work-control method, 137–138

Alemán, Paulino, 139

Alianza de la Juventud Democrática Hondureña (Alianza de la Juventud Democrática Hondureña), 8, 195

almacenes (local stores, independent), 164

alzamientos (uprisings), 265

amachinadas (informal man/woman partnership), 108–113. See also china (racialized term for women of low caste/virtue)

Amaya Amador, Ramón, 20, 91–92, 138, 231, 234, 242

American Federation of Labor (AFL), 54, 72, 74

American Federation of Labor and Congress of Industrial Organizations (AFL-CIO), 70

American Zone (la Zona), 109, 162, 192–193, 197, 200, 202

Anariva, Francisco, 145, 147

anti-communist agendas: against Central Strike Committee (Junta Directiva del Comité Central de Huelga), 213–214, 220–221; Cold War politics, influence of, 32, 78–82, 235, 242–243, 270–271; US-endorsed interference, 67–68, 72–80, 219–225, 243–244. See also Cold War politics, influence of

Arab immigrants, 125, 215, 340–341n151

Árbenz Guzmán, Juan Jacobo, 98, 219–220

archival work, challenges of, 15–17, 25–27. See also historical record, suppression of; oral history

Ardón Torres, María Celea, 135, 137

Argueta, Mario R., 11, 12, 56

Argueta Urquía, José, 76

Aríga, Matías, 114

Armando Amaya, Felipe, 56

Artiles, Andres Victor, 232–233

Asamblea Obrera y Campesina (Assembly of Workers and Campesinos), 55–56

Asturias, Miguel, 20

auxiliares (volunteer police), 113

Ayala Yanes, Victoria, 145, 147–148

Ayestas, Santos Reyes, 79

ayudantas (assistants to patronas), 5, 153, 159–162

bajos de los barracones (the areas underneath the barracks' stilts), 228

baleadas (large flour tortillas with beans and sour cream), 164

"banana cowboys," 14, 322n49

Banana Cultures (Soluri), 14

banana growers, domestic small-scale, 35–38, 45–48, 268–269

bananeras (banana companies), 57

Lightning Source UK Ltd.
Milton Keynes UK
UKHW012129051022
409984UK00007B/642